Queueing Theory
for
Telecommunications

John N. Daigle
The MITRE Corporation
and
Virginia Polytechnic Institute and State University

▲
▼▼
Addison-Welsey Publishing Company
Reading, Massachusetts • Menlo Park, California • New York
Don Mills, Ontario • Wokingham, England • Amsterdam • Bonn
Sydney • Tokyo • Madrid • San Juan • Milan • Paris

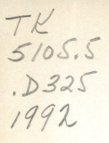

This book is in the
Addison-Wesley Series in Telecommunications

Many of the designations used by manufacturers and sellers to distinguish their products
are claimed as trademarks. Where those designations appear in this book, and Addison-
Wesley was aware of a trademark claim, the designations have been printed in initial caps
or all caps.

The programs and applications presented in this book have been included for their
instructional value. They have been tested with care, but are not guaranteed for any
particular purpose. The publisher does not offer any warranties or representations, nor
does it accept any liabilities with respect to the programs or applications.

Library of Congress Cataloging–in–Publication Data

Daigle, John N.
    Queueing theory for telecommunications / by John N. Daigle.
        p.   cm.
    Includes bibliographical references and indes.
    ISBN 0-201-06755-2
    1.   Computer networks.   2.   Queuing theory.   I.   Title.
TK5105.5.D325 1992
621.39'81–dc20   90-40889
                                                                   CIP

1 2 3 4 5 6 7 8 9 10 – MA – 9594939291

P R E F A C E

This text should be viewed as a tool for developing an intuitive understanding of how queueing systems work. It is an efficient introduction to the fundamental concepts and principles underlying the study of the queueing behavior of telecommunication systems and should provide the reader with the appropriate tools to model many interesting, nonstandard engineering problems associated with network design. The material provides the reader with a sufficient background to read the important queueing theory-based papers that have appeared in the literature in the area of computer communications and telecommunication networks and to understand their modeling assumptions and solution procedures and assess the quality of their results.

The presentation includes procedures for obtaining useful numerical results, and numerous exercises are incorporated within the text to reinforce understanding of the material on an ongoing basis. Supplementary problems are included at the close of each major chapter to provide an opportunity to integrate understanding of the material. An instructor's manual containing solutions to all exercises and supplementary problems is available to those adopting the text for classroom use.

The level of the text is appropriate for graduate and continuing education studies and was established by classroom testing over a period of ten years. In addition, the final manuscript was classroom-tested for one semester at three different universities. In its various draft forms, the manuscript has been used as the primary text for a one-semester course in computer communications in the Electrical and Computer Engineering Department at Clemson University since 1982 and for a one-semester course in queueing theory in the Industrial and Systems Engineering Department at Virginia Tech since 1988. It was also the primary text for the third quarter of a three-quarter course sequence in computer communications at Virginia Tech, a one-quarter course in applied queueing theory in the Graduate School of Business Administration at the University of Rochester, and a one-semester course in queueing theory in the Department of Industrial and Systems Engineering at Texas A & M University.

I have intentionally limited the coverage in the text to material that can reasonably be covered in a one-semester course and have provided pointers to reference materials for further study. While the book has more than ample content to provide lecture material for each class meeting, instructors may choose to cover some areas in less detail, reserving lecture periods at the end of the term for student presentation of papers. For example, I select approximately six papers from current literature, usually from *IEEE Transactions on Communications*, *IEEE Journal of Selected Areas in Communications*, and *Proceedings of the IEEE INFOCOM*. The students are organized into teams, and each team is responsible for examining the content of one paper, presenting a comprehensive overview of the paper to the class, and preparing a referee's report on the paper as though the paper had just been submitted for publication.

Placing the exercises within the text allows the instructor to vary the pace of the course according to the characteristics of individual classes. For example, the pace can be increased by assigning virtually every exercise as homework, testing often, and completing the semester with a larger selection of papers from the literature. The pace can be decreased to any desired level by discussing the solutions to selected exercises during the lecture periods.

I emphasize that I do not attempt to cover all aspects of queueing theory in this book. Rather, I cover topics that are very important from the standpoint of designing and analyzing practical systems. Some of these topics are very elementary; other are very complex. The text provides fundamentals that allow the reader to recognize the basic tools underlying analyses presented in the literature and formulate original problems rather than covering topics that are a direct application of particular results.

Although it is possible to approach the material in this book with minimal mathematical preparation, the results have been better when the students have had solid courses in both linear algebra and probability modeling, including at least some exposure to complex variables. The best results were obtained when students have also had an introductory level course in computer communications, but this is not a prerequisite. In fact, students have been inspired to take a course in computer communications after taking a course from this book and vice versa.

For their valuable contributions, I am indebted to many people. John Mahoney of Bell Laboratories guided my early study of communications. Sheldon Ross of the University of California at Berkeley introduced me to queueing theory and taught me how to think about queueing problems. Jim Meditch of the University of Washington, Ray Pickholtz of The George

Washington University, and Bill Tranter of the University of Missouri-Rolla initially encouraged me to get started writing this book. Tom Robbins of Addison-Wesley enthusiastically supported the project from the beginning. Marty Wortman of Texas A & M University has taught from the draft form and has provided encouragement and criticism for several years. Since 1982, John Spragins and (later) Dave Tipper of Clemson University have taught from the various draft forms and offered comments for improvement each time. Paul Schweitzer of the University of Rochester made several valuable suggestions after reading an early draft. Bob Cooper of Florida Atlantic University, Ralph Disney of Texas A & M University, and Jim Meditch have asked many penetrating questions and have made many valuable suggestions that have helped to bring the book to its present form. In addition, numerous students, most notably Nikhil Jain, John Kobza, Joe Langford, Naresh Rao, Stan Tang, and Steve Whitehead, have asked insightful questions that have resulted in many of the exercises and have suggested changes in the wording to improve clarity.

Finally, I thank my wife, Katherine, who has politely suffered through reading countless drafts and who finished her doctoral dissertation just in time to save herself from having to read the final draft.

Blacksburg, Virginia   *John N. Daigle*

C O N T E N T S

Preface   *iii*

Chapter 1
Introduction   *1*
    1.1   Queueing Theory: An Introduction   1
    1.2   Computer Communication Networks: An Introduction   2
            1.2.1   Early Communication Networks   4
            *1.2.2   Computer Communication
                     Network Architecture   9*
            1.2.3   Local Area Networks and Internets   15
            1.2.4   Some Additional Recent Developments   17
    1.3   Organization of the Text   20

Chapter 2
General Concepts and Preliminaries   *23*
    2.1   Introduction to Queueing Terminology   23
    2.2   Elementary Concepts and Preliminaries   30
            2.2.1   Exponential Distribution   30
            2.2.2   Poisson Process   37

Chapter 3
Continuous-Time Markov Chain Queueing Models   *47*
    3.1   M/M/1 Queueing System   49
            3.1.1   Time-Dependent M/M/1 Occupancy Distribution   49
            3.1.2   Stochastic Equilibrium M/M/1 Distributions   51
            3.1.3   Busy Period for M/M/1 Queueing System   70
    3.2   Dynamical Equations for A General Birth–Death Process   77
    3.3   Time-Dependent State Probabilities for Finite-State Systems   79
            3.3.1   Classical Approach   80
            3.3.2   Jensen's Method   84

3.4   *Balance-Equation Approach for Exponential
      Systems in Equilibrium   89*
3.5   *Networks of Single-Server Exponential Service Stations   96*
  *3.5.1   Feedforward Networks of Single
    Servers (Fixed Routing)   97*
  3.5.2   Arbitrary Interconnections (Random Routing)   99
  *3.5.3   Closed Networks of Single
    Servers (Random Routing)   101*
3.6   *Probability Generating Function Approach to
      Solving Balance Equations   114*
3.7   *Phase-Dependent Arrival and Service Rates   117*
  3.7.1   Probability Generating Function Approach   118
  3.7.2   Matrix Geometric Method   138
  3.7.3   Rate Matrix Computation via Eigenanalysis   143
3.8   *Service-Time Distributions of the Phase Type
      and Other Variations   147*
3.9   *Supplementary Problems   152*

Chapter 4
The M/G/1 Queueing System and Variants   *159*
4.1   *M/G/1 Queueing System Transform Equations   162*
  4.1.1   Sojourn Time for the M/G/1 System   167
  4.1.2   Waiting Time for the M/G/1 System   169
  4.1.3   Busy Period for the M/G/1 Queueing System   170
4.2   *Ergodic Occupancy Distribution for M/G/1   173*
  *4.2.1   Discrete Fourier Transform Approach to Ergodic
    Occupancy Computation   173*
  *4.2.2   Recursive Approach to Ergodic
    Occupancy Computation   185*
4.3   *Expected Values for M/G/1 via Renewal Theory   188*
  4.3.1   Expected Waiting Times and Renewal Theory   189
  4.3.2   Busy Periods and Alternating Renewal Theory   196
4.4   *M/G/1 Under Last-Come-First-Served,
      Preemptive-Resume Discipline   200*
4.5   *M/G/1 System with Exceptional First Service   204*
4.6   *M/G/1 with Head-of-the-Line Priority   213*
  4.6.1   Customers with Higher Priority   215
  4.6.2   Customers with Lower Priority   219

4.7   *Expected Waiting Times and Sojourn Times*
      for M/G/1 with HOL Priority   223
            4.7.1   *HOL Discipline*   226
            4.7.2   *HOL-PR Discipline*   227
4.8   *Supplementary Problems*   230

Chapter 5
Embedded Markov Chain Analysis:
The M/G/1 and G/M/1 Paradigms   235
      5.1   *The M/G/1 and G/M/1 Paradigms*   236
      5.2   *G/M/1 Solution Methodology*   243
      5.3   *M/G/1 Solution Methodology*   245
      5.4   *An Application to Statistical Multiplexing*   249
      5.5   *Concluding Remarks*   263
      5.6   *Supplementary Problems*   266

Chapter 6
Conclusions   *271*

Appendix A
PGF Inversion Program Listing   *275*

References   *295*

Index   *305*

C H A P T E R

$$\boxed{1}$$

Introduction

The analysis of computer communication networks is the driving force behind the development of this text. In this chapter, we first give a brief introduction to the topics of queueing theory and computer communication networks, and then we summarize the contents of the book. We intentionally limit our introductory remarks to those necessary for gaining a minimal appreciation of the connection between the two subjects.

1.1   QUEUEING THEORY: AN INTRODUCTION

Queueing theory is the study of the behavior of waiting lines. A typical queueing problem involves a system that services customers whose service requests occur according to some random process. The time required for the server(s) to service a request is typically random as well. In the general case, arrivals and service completions cannot be synchronized, so waiting time may result. For a typical queueing system, one is interested in answering questions such as the following: What is the distribution of the time a typical customer will have to wait? What is the distribution of the number of customers in the system at an arbitrary point in time? How large should the waiting room be to accommodate 99% of the potential customers? How many servers are needed to have less than a 1% chance that a customer experiences a waiting time greater than one minute? What is the distribution of the amount of time a server remains continuously busy serving customers between successive periods when no customers are present? What are the costs and benefits of introducing servicing priorities into the system?

Queueing theory has been under development for more than seven decades, and the literature surrounding the subject is voluminous. The interest in both theoretical and applied queueing theory can be explained, at least in part, by the following two observations. First, waiting times are a very visible fact of life, affecting virtually everyone. These waiting times are often costly in terms of lost production and personal discomfort, so there is great motivation to reduce waiting times and their accompanying costs as much as possible. Second, with constant technological development, new design issues that can be approached via queueing theory are generated at a very high rate, and these real-life situations often have special characteristics that seriously violate the conditions assumed in current theory, thus creating a need for new results. On the other hand, results from queueing theory have often been applied directly to obtain partial solutions to real-life problems. For an excellent summary covering many of the most important results in queueing theory, see the recent survey paper by Cooper [1990].

One of the real-life areas where queueing theory plays an important role is in the design of computer communication networks and systems. For the most part, simple models can be used to obtain useful results, and it is for this reason that we concentrate in this book on the analysis of simple queueing models applied to computer communications networks. Our goal is to provide a thorough introduction to the fundamental concepts in order to build a basis for understanding most of the performance evaluation literature and for developing new techniques to answer specific questions. In many cases, a vast amount of literature exists on the evaluation of queueing systems of a particular type; in these cases, we reference work that we perceive to be on the cutting edge at the time of this writing.

1.2   COMPUTER COMMUNICATION NETWORKS:
AN INTRODUCTION

In this section, we provide a brief introduction to computer communication networks and systems. Our objective is to provide just

enough of an introduction to allow the reader to gain an understanding of why queueing analysis plays a major role in the design
of computer communication networks. For a thorough introduction
to the subject, we refer the reader to several of the excellent texts
devoted to the topic, especially Schwartz [1987], Tanenbaum [1988],
Spragins [1991], and Stallings [1990a, 1990b, 1990c].

We begin our discussion with a brief statement of how computer
networking came about and a capsule description of the networks
that resulted from the early efforts. Networks of this generic class,
called wide area networks (WANs), are broadly deployed today and
there are still a large number of unanswered questions with respect to
their design. The issues involved in the design of those networks are
basic to the design of most networks, whether wide area or otherwise.

We next turn to a discussion of computer communication architecture, which describes the structure of communication-oriented
processing software within a communication processing system.
Our discussion is limited to the International Standards Organiza-
tion/Open Systems Interconnection (ISO/OSI) reference model because it provides a framework for discussion of some of the modern
developments in communications in general and communication networking in particular. This discussion is necessarily simplified in the
extreme—thorough coverage requiring on the order of several hundred pages—but we hope our brief description will enable the reader
to appreciate some of the issues. We encourage the reader to pursue
further study via some of the books mentioned earlier, particularly
Spragins [1991], and through the literature.

Having introduced the basic architectural structure of communication networks, we next turn to a discussion of an important variation on this architectural scheme: the local area network (LAN).
Discussion of this topic is important because it helps to illustrate
what the reference model is and what it is not. In particular, the
architecture of LANs illustrates how the ISO/OSI reference model
can be adapted for specialized purposes. Specifically, early network
architectures anticipate networks in which individual node pairs are
interconnected via a single link, and connections through the network
are formed by concatenating node-to-node connections.

LAN architectures, on the other hand, anticipate all nodes being
interconnected in some fashion over the same communication link
(or medium). This, then, introduces the concept of adaption layers

in a natural way. It also illustrates that if the services provided by an architectural layer are carefully defined, then the services can be used to implement virtually any service desired by the user, possibly at the price of some inefficiency.

After discussing local area networks, we turn to a discussion of two of the variants in packet switching transmission technology: fast packet switching and a recent development in basic transmission technology called the Asynchronous Transfer Mode (ATM), which is a part of the larger broadband integrated services digital network (BISDN) effort. Our intention is to give two examples that illustrate how some of the issues that arise in the design of computer communication networks come about and why queueing theory is important to the resolution of these issues. This discussion completes our brief introductory chapter.

1.2.1   Early Communication Networks

Data communication networks have existed since about 1950. The early networks existed primarily for the purpose of connecting users of a large computer to the computer itself, with additional capability to provide communications between computers of the same variety and having the same operating software. The lessons learned during the first 20 or so years of operation of these types of networks have been valuable in preparing the way for modern networks. For the purposes of our current discussion, however, we think of communication networks as being networks whose purpose is to interconnect a set of applications that are implemented on hosts manufactured by (possibly) different vendors and managed by a variety of operating systems. Networking capability is provided by software systems that implement standardized interfaces specifically designed for the exchange of information among heterogeneous computers.

During the late 1960s, many forward-looking thinkers began to recognize that significant computing resources (that is, supercomputers) would be expensive and unlikely to be affordable by many of the researchers needing this kind of computer power. In addition, they realized that significant computing resources would not be needed all the time by those having local access. If the computing resource could be shared by a number of research sites, then the cost of the resource could be shared by its users.

Many researchers at this time had computing resources available under the scenario described in the first paragraph of this section. The idea developed of interconnecting the computers to extend the reach of these researchers to other computers. In addition, the interconnection of the computers would provide for communication among the researchers themselves. In order to investigate the feasibility of providing the interconnectivity anticipated for the future using a new technology called packet switching, the Advanced Research Projects Agency (ARPA) of the Department of the Army sponsored a networking effort, which resulted in the computer communication network called the ARPANET.

The end results of the ARPA networking effort, its derivatives, and the early initiatives of many companies such as AT&T, DATA-POINT, DEC, IBM, and NCR have been far-reaching in the extreme. Any finitely delimited discussion of the accomplishments of those efforts would appear to underestimate their impact on our lives. We will concentrate on the most visible product of these efforts, which is a collection of programs that allows applications running in different computers or people and applications to intercommunicate. Before turning to our discussion of the software, however, we shall provide a brief description of a generic computer communication network.

Figure 1.1 shows a diagram of a generic computer communication network. The most visible components of the network are the terminals, the access lines, the trunks, and the switching nodes. Work is accomplished when the users of the network, the terminals, exchange messages over the network.

The terminals represent the set of communication-terminating equipment communicating over the network. Equipment in this class includes, but is not limited to, user terminals, general-purpose computers, and database systems. This equipment, either through software or through human interaction, provides the functions required for information exchange between pairs of application programs or between application programs and people. The functions include, but are not limited to, call set-up, session management, and message transmission control. Examples of applications include electronic mail transfer, terminal-to-computer connection for time sharing or other purposes, and terminal-to-database connections.

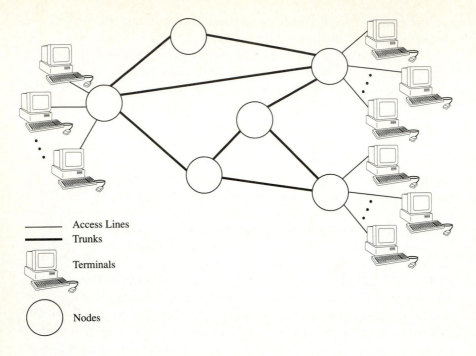

—————   Access Lines

————   Trunks

Terminals

Nodes

Figure 1.1 Generic computer communication network.

Access lines provide for data transmission between the terminals and the network switching nodes. These connections may be set up on a permanent basis or they may be switched connections, and there are numerous transmission schemes and protocols available to manage these connections. The essence of these connections, however, from our point of view, is a channel that provides data transmission at some number of bits per second (bps), called the channel capacity, C. The capacities of the access lines may range from a few hundred bps to in excess of millions of bps, and they are usually not the same for all terminating equipments of a given network. The actual information-carrying capacity of the link depends upon the protocols employed to effect the transfer; the interested reader is referred to Bertsekas and Gallager [1987], especially Chapter 2, for a general discussion of the issues involved in transmission of data over communication links.

Trunks, or internodal trunks, are the transmission facilities that provide for transmission of data between pairs of communication switches. Trunks are analogous to access lines, and from our point of view, they simply provide a communication path at some capacity, specified in bps.

Two basic types of transmission technologies are employed in networks: circuit switching and packet switching. In circuit switching, a call connection between two terminating equipments corresponds to the allocation of a prescribed set of physical facilities that provide a transmission path of a certain bandwidth or transmission capacity. These facilities are dedicated to the users for the duration of the call. The primary performance issues, other than those related to quality of transmission, are related to whether or not a transmission path is available at call set-up time and how calls are handled if facilities are not available.

In circuit switching, there is a one-to-one correspondence between the number of trunks between nodes and the number of simultaneous calls that can be carried. That is, a trunk is a facility between two switches that can service exactly one call, and it does not matter how this transmission facility is derived. Major design issues include the specification of the number of trunks between node pairs and the routing strategy used to determine the path through a network in order to achieve a given call blocking probability. When blocked calls are queued, the number of calls that may be queued is also a design question.

A packet-switched communication system exchanges messages among users by transmitting sequences of packets comprising the messages. That is, the sending terminal equipment partitions a message into a sequence of packets, the packets are transmitted across the network, and the receiving terminal equipment reassembles the packets into messages. The transmission facility interconnecting a given node pair is viewed as a single trunk, and the transmission capacity of this trunk is shared among all users whose packets traverse both nodes. Although the trunk capacity is specified in bps, the packet-handling capacity of a node pair depends on both the trunk capacity and the nodal processing power.

In most packet-switched networks, the path traversed by a packet through the network is established during a call set-up procedure, and the network is referred to as a virtual circuit packet-switching network. Some networks provide datagram service, a service that allows users to transmit individually addressed packets without the need for call set-up.

In either virtual circuit or datagram networks, packets from a large number of users may simultaneously need transmission services between nodes. Packets arrive at a given node at random times. The switching node determines the next node in the transmission path and then places the packet in a queue for transmission over a trunk facility to the next node. Packet arrival processes tend to be bursty; that is, the number of packet arrivals over fixed-length intervals of time has a large variance. Because of the burstiness of the arrival process, packets may experience significant delays at the trunks. Queues may also build due to the difference in transmission capacities of the various trunks and access lines. Combining of packets that arrive at random times from different users onto the same line, in this case a trunk, is called statistical multiplexing.

In addition to the delays experienced at the input to trunks, packets may also experience queueing delays within the switching nodes. In particular, the functions required for packet switching are effected by executing various software processes within the nodes, and packets must queue while awaiting execution of the various processes on their behalf.

Both transmission capacities and nodal-processing capabilities are available over a wide range of values. If the trunk capacities are relatively low compared to nodal-processing capability, then delays at switching nodes may be relatively small. But if line capacities are large compared to nodal-processing capabilities, then delays due to nodal processing may be significant. In the general case, all possible sources of delay should be examined to determine where bottlenecks, and consequently delay, occur.

Often a particular point in the communication network, either a processing node or a trunk, is the primary source of delay. In this case, this point is usually singled out for analysis, and a simple model is invoked to analyze the performance at that point. The results of this analysis, combined with results of other analyses, result in a profile of overall system performance. The key aspect of the analysis in this case is to choose an appropriate model for the isolated analysis. The material covered in this book provides sufficient background for choosing the appropriate model in most cases of interest.

1.2.2   Computer Communication Network Architecture

In this section, we begin with a brief, high-level definition ISO/OSI reference model. The reference model has seven layers, none of which can be bypassed conceptually. In general, a layer is defined by the types of services it provides to its users and the quality of those services. For each layer in the ISO/OSI architecture, the user of a layer is the next layer up in the hierarchy, except for the highest layer, for which the user is an application. Clearly, when a layered architecture is implemented under this philosophy, then the quality of service obtained by the end user, the application, is a function of the quality of service provided by all the layers. In order to clarify the communications strategy of the ISO/OSI architecture, we will provide a discussion of the layer 2 services in some detail.

Figure 1.2, adopted from Spragins [1991], shows the basic structure of the OSI architecture and how this architecture is envisaged to

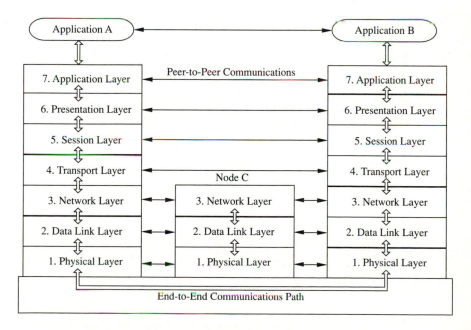

Figure 1.2 Layered architecture for ISO/OSI reference model.

provide for exchange of information between applications. As the figure shows, there are seven layers: application, presentation, session, transport, network, data link, and physical. Brief definitions of the layers are now given, but the reader should bear in mind that substantial further study will be required to develop an understanding of the practical implications of the definitions.

Physical layer: Provides electrical, functional, and procedural characteristics to activate, maintain, and deactivate physical data links that transparently pass the bit stream for communication between data-link entities.

Data-link layer: Provides functional and procedural means to transfer data between network entities; provides for activation, maintenance, and deactivation of data-link connections, character and frame synchronization, grouping of bits into characters and frames, error control, media-access control and flow control.

Network layer: Provides switching and routing functions to establish, maintain, and terminate network layer connections and to transfer data between transport layers.

Transport layer: Provides host-to-host, cost-effective, transparent transfer of data, end-to-end flow control, and end-to-end quality of service as required by applications.

Session layer: Provides mechanisms for organizing and structuring dialogues between application processes.

Presentation layer: Provides for independent data representation and syntax selection by each communicating application and conversion between selected contexts and the internal architecture standard.

Application layer: Provides applications with access to the ISO/OSI communication stack and certain distributed information services.

As we have mentioned previously, a layer is defined by the types of services it provides to its users. In the case of a request or a response, these services are provided via invocation of service primitives of the layer in question by the layer that wants the service performed. In the case of an indication or a confirm, these services are provided via invocation of service primitives of the layer in question by the same layer that wants the service performed.

This process is not unlike a user of a programming system calling a subroutine from a scientific subroutine package in order to obtain a service, say, matrix inversion or memory allocation. For example, a request is analogous to a CALL statement in a FORTRAN program, and a response is analogous to the RETURN statement in the subroutine that has been CALLed. The requests for services are generated asynchronously by all the users of all the services, and these join (typically prioritized) queues along with other requests and responses while awaiting servicing by the processor or other resource, such as a transmission line.

The service primitives fall into four basic types: request, indication, response, and confirm. These types are defined as follows:

Request: A primitive sent by layer $(N + 1)$ to layer N to request a service.

Indication: A primitive sent by layer N to layer $(N + 1)$ to indicate that a service has been requested of layer N by a different layer-$(N + 1)$ entity.

Response: A primitive sent by layer $(N+1)$ to layer N in response to an *indication* primitive.

Confirm: A primitive sent by layer N to layer $(N+1)$ to indicate that a response to an earlier *request* primitive has been received.

In order to be more specific about how communications take place, we now turn to a brief discussion of layer 2, the data-link layer. The primitives provided by the ISO data-link layer are as follows (Stallings [1990a]):

DL_CONNECT.request   DL_RESET.request
DL_CONNECT.indication   DL_RESET.indication
DL_CONNECT.response   DL_RESET.response

DL_CONNECT.confirm	DL_RESET.confirm
DL_DATA.request	DL_DISCONNECT.request
DL_DATA.indication	DL_DISCONNECT.indication
DL_DATA.response	DL_UNITDATA.request
DL_DATA.confirm	DL_UNITDATA.indication

Each primitive has a set of formal parameters, which are analogous to the formal parameters of a procedure in a programming language. For example, the parameters for the DL_CONNECT.request primitive are the called address, the calling address, and the quality-of-service parameter set. These four primitives are used in the establishment of data-link (DL) connections. The called address and the calling address are analogous to the telephone numbers of two parties of a telephone call; the quality-of-service parameter set allows for the negotiation of various agreements, such as throughput measured in bits per second.

All four DL_CONNECT primitives are used to establish a data link. An analogy to an ordinary phone call is now drawn so that the basic idea of the primitives can be better appreciated. The DL_CONNECT.request is equivalent to picking up the phone and dialing. The phone ringing at the called party's end is represented by the DL_CONNECT.indication. DL_CONNECT.response is equivalent to the called party lifting the receiver and answering, and DL_CONNECT.confirm is equivalent to the calling party hearing the response of the called party.

In general, communications take place between peer-layer protocols by the exchange of protocol data units (PDUs), which contain all the information required for the receiving protocol entity to provide the required service. In order to exchange PDUs, entities at a given layer use the services of the next lower layer. The data-link primitives listed above include both connection-mode primitives and connectionless-mode primitives. For connection-mode communications, a connection must be established between two peer entities before they can exchange PDUs.

For example, suppose a network-layer entity in host A wishes to be connected to a network-layer entity in host B, as shown in Figure 1.2. Then the connection would be accomplished by the concatenation of two data-link connections: one between A and C, and one between C and B. In order to establish the connection, the network-layer entity in host A would issue a DL_CONNECT.request to its associated data-link entity, providing the required parameters. This data-link entity would then transmit this request to a data-link entity in C, which would issue a DL_CONNECT.indication to a network entity in C. The network-layer entity in C would then analyze the parameters of the DL_CONNECT.indication and realize that the target destination is B. This network-layer entity would then reissue the DL_CONNECT.request to its data-link entity, which would transmit the request to a data-link entity in B. The data-link entity in B would send a DL_CONNECT.indication to a network-layer entity in B, and this entity would issue a DL_CONNECT.response back to the data-link entity in B. This DL_CONNECT.response would be relayed back to the data-link entity in A following the same sequence of events as in the forward path. Eventually, this DL_CONNECT.response would be converted to a DL_CONNECT.confirm by the data-link entity in A and passed to the network entity in A, thus completing the connection.

Once the connection is established, data exchange between the two network-layer entities can take place; that is, the entities can exchange PDUs. For example, if a network-layer entity in host A wishes to send a PDU to a network-layer entity in host B, the network-layer entity in host A would issue a DL_DATA.request to the appropriate data-link layer entity in host A. This entity would package the PDU together with appropriate control information into a data-link service data unit (DLSDU) and send it to its peer at C. The peer at C would deliver it to the network entity at C, which would forward it to the data-link entity in C providing the connection to host B. This entity would then send the DLSDU to its peer in host B, and this data-link entity would pass the PDU to the host B network entity via a DL_DATA.indication.

Now, network-layer PDUs are called packets, and DL-layer PDUs are called frames. But the data-link layer does not know that the information it is transmitting is a packet; to the DL-layer entity, the packet is simply user information. From the perspective of a data-link entity, it is not necessary to have a network layer. The network layer exists to add value for the user of the network layer to the services provided by the DL layer. In the example above, value was added by the network layer by providing a relaying capability since hosts A and C were not directly connected. Similarly, the DL layer functions on a hop-by-hop basis, each hop being completely unaware that there are any other hops involved in the communication. We will see later that the data link need not be limited to a single physical connection.

The philosophy of the ISO/OSI architecture is that in addition to the software being layered, implementations are not allowed to bypass entire layers; that is, every layer must appear in the implementation. This approach was developed after the approach defined for the ARPANET project, which is hierarchical, was fully developed. In the hierarchical approach, the layer interfaces are carefully designed, but any number of layers of software can be bypassed by any application (or other higher-layer protocol) that provides the appropriate functionality. These two approaches have been hotly debated for a number of years, but as the years pass, the approaches are actually beginning to look more and more alike for a variety of reasons that will not be discussed here.

The ISO/OSI layered architecture described above would appear to be very rigid, not allowing for any variations in underlying topology or in link reliability. However, as we shall see, this is not necessarily the case. As an example, ISO 8348, which developed as a result of the X.25 project, provides only connection-oriented service, and it was originally intended as the only network layer standard for ISO/OSI. However, ISO 8473, or ISO-IP, which is virtually identical to the DoD internet protocol developed in the ARPANET project, has since been added to the protocol suite to provide connectionless service as well as internet service.

The ISO/OSI protocol suite is in a constant state of revision as new experience reveals the need for additional capabilities and flexibility. Some of this additional flexibility and functionality is being provided through the use of so-called adaption sublayers, which enhance the capabilities of a given layer so that it can use the services of a lower layer with which it was not specifically designed for compatibility. We now turn to a discussion of LANs, which have inherent properties that make the use of sublayers particularly attractive. This discussion will introduce the reader to how performance issues may arise in formulating standards.

1.2.3   Local Area Networks and Internets

In this section, we discuss the organization of communications software for LANs. In addition, we introduce the idea of internets, which
were brought about to a large extent by the advent of LANs. We discuss the types of networks only briefly and refer the reader to the
many excellent texts on the subject. Layers 4 and above for local
area communications networks are identical to those of wide area
networks. However, because the hosts communicating over a LAN
share a single physical transmission facility, the routing functions
provided by the network layer, layer 3, are not necessary. Thus, the
functionality of a layer 3 in a LAN can be substantially simplified
without loss of utility. On the other hand, a DL-layer entity must
now manage many simultaneous DL-layer connections because all
connections entering and leaving a host on a single LAN do so over
a single physical link. Thus, in the case of connection-oriented communications, the software must manage several virtual connections
over a single physical link.

There are three basic types of transmission schemes in the early
local area network standards: the token ring, token bus, and carrier
sense multiple access (CSMA). In a token ring network, the stations
are configured on a physical ring around the medium. A token rotates
around this physical ring, visiting each host (or station) in turn. A
station wishing to transmit data must wait until the token is available to that station. In a token bus LAN, the situation is the same,
except that the stations share a common bus and the ring is logical
rather than physical. In a CSMA network, the stations are bus connected, and a station may transmit whenever other stations are not
currently transmitting. That is, a station wishing to transmit senses
the channel, and if there is no activity, the station may transmit. The
actual access protocol is significantly more complicated than this, of
course.

In the early 1980s, there was significant debate over which LAN
connection arrangement was superior to the others, a single choice
being viewed as necessary. This debate centered around such issues
as cost, network throughput, network delay, and growth potential.
Performance evaluation based on queueing theory played a major
role in putting these issues in perspective. For thorough descriptions

of LAN protocols and queueing models used to evaluate their performance, the interested reader is referred to Hammond and O'Reilly [1986].

All three of the access methods mentioned above became IEEE standards (IEEE 802) and eventually became ISO standards (ISO 8802 series) because all merited standardization. On the other hand, all existed for the express purposes of exchanging information among peers, and it was recognized at the outset that the upper end of the data-link layer could be shared by all three access techniques. On the other hand, the lower-level functions of the layer deal with interfacing to the physical media. Here, drastic differences in the way the protocol had to interface with the media were recognized. Thus, a different media access control sublayer was needed for each of the access techniques.

The decision to use a common logical link control (LLC) sublayer for all the LAN protocols apparently ushered in the idea of adaption sublayers. The reason for splitting the layer is simple: a user of the DLC layer need not know what kind of medium provides the communications; all that is necessary is that the user understand the interface to the DLC layer.

On the other hand, the media of the three types of access protocols provide transmission service in different ways, so software is needed to bridge the gap between what the user of the service needs, which is provided by the LLC, and how the LLC uses the media to provide the required service. Thus the media access control (MAC) sublayer was born.

This idea has proven to be valuable as new types of technologies have become available. For example, the new fiber distributed digital interface (FDDI) uses the LLC of all other LAN protocols, but its MAC is completely different from the token ring MAC even though FDDI is a token ring protocol. Reasons for needing a new MAC for LLC are provided in Stallings [1990b].

An interesting consequence of the advent of local area networking is that many traditional computer communication networks became internets overnight. LAN technology was used to connect stations to a host computer, and these host computers were already on a WAN. It was then a simple matter to provide a relaying, or bridging, service at the host in order to provide wide area interconnection of stations to LANs and to each other. In short, the previously established WANs became networks for interconnection of LANs; that is, they were interconnecting networks rather than stations. Internet performance suddenly became a primary concern in the design of networks.

More recently, FDDI is being thought of as a mechanism to provide LAN interconnection on a site basis, and a new type of network, the metropolitan area network (MAN) has been under study for the interconnection of LANs within a metropolitan area. The primary media configuration for MANs is a dual bus configuration; this configuration is implemented via the distributed queue, dual bus (DQDB) protocol (see Hahne, Choudhury, and Maxemchuk [1990]). The net effect of this protocol is to use the dual bus configuration to provide service approaching the FCFS service discipline to the traffic entering the FDDI network. This is remarkable considering that the LANs being interconnected are geographically dispersed. Again, performance evaluation can be accomplished to a large degree using simple queueing analysis.

1.2.4   Some Additional Recent Developments

In this subsection, we describe two recent developments of significant interest in communication networking from the point of view of performance: fast packet networks (FPNs) and transmission using the asynchronous transfer mode (ATM), which is a part of the larger broadband integrated services digital network (BISDN) effort.

As we have mentioned previously, there is really no requirement that the physical media between two adjacent data-link layers be composed of a single link. In fact, if a path through the network is initially established between two data-link entities, there is no reason for execution of DLC protocols at intermediate nodes. Figure 1.3, adapted from Bhargava and Hluchyj [1990], shows how the end-to-end connection might be implemented. A network implemented in the fashion indicated in Figure 1.3 is called a fast packet network.

From Figure 1.3, we can see that the DL layer is partitioned into three sublayers: the DL control sublayer (which parallels the LLC layer of LANs), the fast packet adaption (FPA) sublayer, and the fast packet relay (FPR) sublayer. The function of the fast packet adaption sublayer is to segment the layer 2 PDU, the frame, into

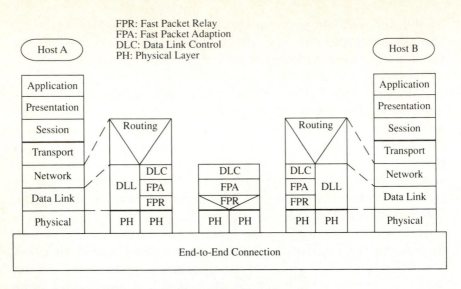

Figure 1.3 Fast packet switched layered architecture.

smaller units, called fast packets, for transmission over the FPN. These fast packets contain information that identifies the source and destination node names and the frame to which they belong so that they can be routed through the network and reassembled at the destination.

The fast packets are statistically multiplexed onto a common physical link by the FPR sublayer for transmission. At intermediate nodes, minor error checking, fast packet framing, fast packet switching, and queueing take place. If errors are found, then the fast packet is dropped. When the fast packets reach their destination, they are reassembled into a frame by the FPA sublayer and passed on to the DLC sublayer, where normal DLC functions are performed.

The motivation for FPNs is that since link transmission is becoming more reliable, extensive error checking and flow control is not needed across individual links; an end-to-end check should be sufficient. Significant issues are probability of fast packet loss and retransmission delay. Such factors will determine the retransmission strategy deployed in the network. Of course, the goal is to improve network efficiency, so a significant issue is whether FPNs are better than ordinary packet networks and, if so, by how much.

Another recent innovation is the ATM of BISDN (Sinha [1990]). The idea of ATM is to partition a user's data into many small segments, called cells, for transmission over the network. Independent of the data's origin, the cell size is 53 octets, of which 5 octets are for use by the network itself for routing and error control. Users of the ATM are responsible for segmentation and reassembly of their data. Any control information required for this purpose must be included in the 48 octets of user information in each cell. In the usual case, these cells would be transmitted over networks that would provide users with 135 Mb/s and above data transmission capacity (with user overhead included in the capacity).

Numerous options for use of ATM in the context of ISO/OSI exist, but the dominant one is the one shown in Figure 1.4. Below the data-link layer is the ATM adaption layer (AAL), which provides for call control across the ATM network and for segmentation and reassembly of frames from the data-link layer. The current estimate

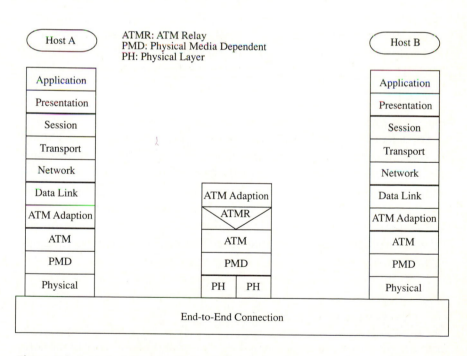

Figure 1.4 Asynchronous transfer mode layered architecture.

for the amount of overhead needed per cell for AAL purposes is 4 octets, leaving 44 octets for user information.

At the present time, end-to-end connections at the ATM level are expected to be connection oriented. As cells traverse the network, they are switched on a one-by-one basis, using information contained in the 5 ATM overhead octets to follow the virtual path established during the ATM call set-up. Cells outbound on a common link are statistically multiplexed, and if buffers are full, cells are dropped. In addition, if one or more errors are found in a cell, then the cell is dropped.

In the case of data transmission, a lost cell will result in an unusable frame unless the data are encoded to guard against cell loss prior to transmission. Coding might be provided by the AAL, for example. The tradeoffs involved in coding and retransmission and their impact upon network throughput, delay, and complexity are not well understood at the time of this writing. Part of the reason for this is that probability of cell loss is not thoroughly understood at this time, nor are the types of traffic that are likely to use the network. Activity surrounding these issues accounts for a significant portion of queueing system research in the area of computer communication networking at this time. Some examples of research in this area are Iliadis and Denzel [1990], Jiang and Meditch [1990], Kim and Leon-Garcia [1990], Lea [1990], Saha and Wagh [1990], and the references therein.

This concludes our brief introduction to computer communication networks. Our treatment has necessarily been abbreviated, but we trust that the brief description will provide the reader with some appreciation for the importance of queueing theory to the design of computer communication networks. Our intention now is to provide the reader with a thorough introduction to queueing theory in the hope that this background will be sufficient for the reader to be able to read and appreciate related research in the area of computer communications, and to be able to contribute in this area through additional research.

1.3   ORGANIZATION OF THE TEXT

This section presents an abbreviated summary of the technical content of this book. In Chapter 2, we introduce some general terminology from queueing systems and some elementary concepts and results from the general theory of stochastic processes, which will be useful in our study of queueing systems. The waiting-time process for a single-server, first-come-first-serve (FCFS) queueing system is discussed, and the exponential distribution and the Poisson process are introduced.

In Chapter 3, we study queueing systems that may be modeled using continuous-time Markov chains, that is, models for which the state intertransition times are exponentially distributed. We begin the chapter with a study of the simplest model in the class, the M/M/1 system. Stochastic equilibrium occupancy and waiting-time distributions are developed; the notion of busy period analysis is introduced; and, in addition, time-dependent occupancy distributions are discussed. We then examine both time-dependent and stochastic equilibrium solutions for general finite-state birth–death processes. The analysis of the former is addressed via both classical eigenanalysis and the more modern randomization, or uniformization, techniques.

After introducing the concept of balance equations, we present an introduction to open and closed queueing networks. We note that equilibrium analysis of most open networks can be carried out quite easily using elementary techniques already developed. For closed networks of single-server queues, we discuss a new technique, due to J. J. Gordon, for specifying the normalizing constant in closed form. Formulae for mean queue occupancy in terms of the normalizing constant are developed.

We then introduce probability-generating functions and show how they can be used to solve simple sets of balance equations. Next, we introduce more advanced queueing models and solve these via classical eigenanalysis and probability-generating-function techniques. We also introduce the matrix geometric techniques of Neuts [1981a] and use them to solve problems in the same class. The relationship between classical analysis and matrix geometric techniques is explained, and classical techniques are used to obtain matrix geometric solutions. Finally, distributions of the phase type are introduced and the equilibrium occupancy for the M/PH/1 queueing system is discussed.

In Chapter 4, we examine the behavior of the M/G/1 queueing system, the system having Poisson arrivals, a single server, a general service-time distribution, and an infinite waiting room. Our study includes a development of transform equations for the distribution of the number of customers in the system, the waiting time, and the length of the busy period. A numerical technique for obtaining the stochastic equilibrium occupancy distribution for the M/G/1 system is presented. Methods for obtaining average values for random variables of interest through renewal theory are introduced, and these methods are applied to the study of systems having prioritized service disciplines. Fuhrmann–Cooper decomposition is introduced and then applied to the analysis of several more advanced queueing systems including the M/G/1 with priority and the M/G/1 with exceptional first service, the M/G/1 system with set-up, and the M/G/1 system with vacations.

More advanced queueing models based on matrix versions of the M/G/1 and G/M/1 queueing systems are introduced in Chapter 5. These systems, which are modeled by embedding Markov chains at points in time just after customer departures and just prior to customer arrivals, are characterized by Markov chains of the M/G/1 and G/M/1 types, respectively. They are therefore said to be in the M/G/1 and G/M/1 paradigms, respectively. Solution methodologies are described, examples are presented, and references for further study are provided.

Finally, in Chapter 6, we summarize what we have studied and comment on areas for further study.

C H A P T E R

$$\boxed{2}$$

General Concepts and Preliminaries

In this chapter, we introduce the reader to the terminology of queueing theory and to some of the key results from the theory of stochastic processes that are needed in the study of queueing systems. In Section 2.1, we introduce the key random processes involved in queueing analysis, formally introduce the notion of an induced queueing process, and define some of the major quantities of interest. In Section 2.2, we introduce the exponential distribution and the Poisson process and develop some of their key properties.

2.1 INTRODUCTION TO QUEUEING TERMINOLOGY

In order to introduce notation and some of the dynamics of queueing systems, we consider the activities surrounding the use of a pay telephone, perhaps in an airport. Here, the telephone system itself is the server, and the customers who are waiting form the queue for the system. Figure 2.1 shows a schematic diagram of the queueing system.

Assume that at time zero the telephone is idle; that is, no one is using the phone. Now, suppose that at time $\tilde{\tau}_1$ the first customer, whom we shall call C_1, arrives at the telephone and places a call. The system is now in a busy state, and the amount of time required to satisfy the customer's needs is dependent upon how many calls

23

Arriving Customers   Waiting Line   Server   Departing Customers

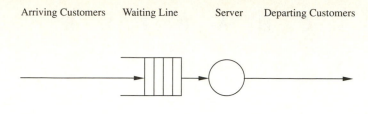

Figure 2.1 Schematic diagram for a single-server queueing
system.

the customer makes, how long it takes to set up each call, and how
long it takes the customer to conduct the business at hand. Define
the total amount of time the telephone system is occupied by this
customer as the *service time requirement,* or simply the *service time*
of C_1, and denote this quantity by $\tilde{x}_1$. Then, C_1 leaves the system
at time $\tilde{\tau}_1 + \tilde{x}_1$.

The waiting time, denoted by $\tilde{w}_1$, for C_1 is *zero,* and the total
time in the system for C_1 is $\tilde{x}_1$. We denote the total time in the
system, which is sometimes called the *sojourn time,* by $\tilde{s}_1$. Thus
$\tilde{w}_1 = 0$ and $\tilde{s}_1 = \tilde{x}_1$. Figure 2.2 shows the sequence of events in this
case.[1]

Now, suppose C_2 (the second customer) arrives at time $\tilde{\tau}_2$ and
has service time requirement $\tilde{x}_2$. Then C_2 will be ready to depart
the system at time $\tilde{\tau}_2 + \tilde{x}_2 + \tilde{w}_2$, where $\tilde{w}_2$ is the amount of time C_2
waits for C_1 to finish using the telephone system; that is, the time
between $\tilde{\tau}_2$ and $\tilde{\tau}_1 + \tilde{x}_1$, if any.

Clearly, if C_1 departs before $\tilde{\tau}_2$, then $\tilde{w}_2 = 0$; but if C_1
departs after $\tilde{\tau}_2$, then $\tilde{w}_2 = \tilde{\tau}_1 + \tilde{x}_1 - \tilde{\tau}_2$. Thus, we find $\tilde{w}_2 =$
max $\{0, \tilde{\tau}_1 + \tilde{x}_1 - \tilde{\tau}_2\}$. If we now define $(a)^+ =$ max $\{0, a\}$, then
we find

$$\tilde{w}_2 = (\tilde{\tau}_1 + \tilde{x}_1 - \tilde{\tau}_2)^+ .$$

In general, the waiting time of the $(n+1)$th customer, C_{n+1}, is
equal to the departure time of C_n minus the arrival time of C_{n+1}

---

[1] Note that random variables are designated by tildes and their values by the
same variables without tildes. For example, $\tilde{x}_1$ denotes a random variable, and
x_1 denotes its value.

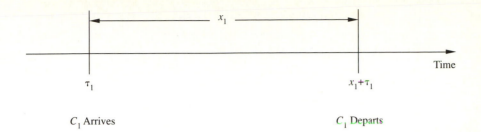

Figure 2.2 Sequence of events for customer 1.

provided that difference is greater than zero. But the departure time
of C_n is $\tilde{\tau}_n + \tilde{x}_n + \tilde{w}_n$, so

$$\tilde{w}_{n+1} = (\tilde{\tau}_n + \tilde{x}_n + \tilde{w}_n - \tilde{\tau}_{n+1})^+$$

or, equivalently,

$$\tilde{w}_{n+1} = (\tilde{w}_n + \tilde{x}_n - \tilde{t}_{n+1})^+, \tag{2.1}$$

where $\tilde{t}_{n+1} = \tilde{\tau}_{n+1} - \tilde{\tau}_n$ is called the *interarrival time* for C_{n+1}. Figure
2.3 gives a graphic description of the sequence of events experienced
by the general customer.

  We note in passing that $\{\tilde{w}_n, \; n = 1, \; 2, \; \ldots\}$, $\{\tilde{x}_n, \; n = 1, \; 2, \; \ldots\}$,
and $\{\tilde{t}_n, \; n = 1, \; 2, \; \ldots\}$ are all discrete-parameter stochastic processes. The random variables $\tilde{x}_n$ and $\tilde{t}_n$ may be discrete, continuous,
or mixed, depending upon the particular system under study. The
complexity of these distributions influences the difficulty of solving
a particular problem. For continuity, we remind the reader of the
following definition.

Definition 2.1   Stochastic Process (Ross [1983]).   A stochastic process (SP) $\{\tilde{x}(t), \; t \in T\}$ is a collection of random variables, $\tilde{x}(t)$,
indexed on t, $t \in T$. That is, for each $t \in T$, $\tilde{x}(t)$ is a random variable.   □

  We now turn to a more formal definition of a queueing process.
Before proceeding, we need the definitions for statistical independence and common distributions.

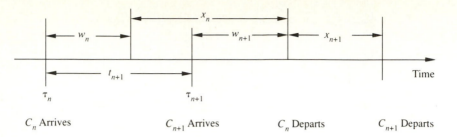

C_n Arrives C_{n+1} Arrives C_n Departs C_{n+1} Departs

Figure 2.3 Sequence of events for general customer.

Definition 2.2   **Common Distribution.**   A random variable $\tilde{x}$ having a distribution F means $F_{\tilde{x}}(x) \triangleq P\{\tilde{x} \leq x\}$. If $\tilde{x}_1$, $\tilde{x}_2$, ..., have common distribution F, then

$$P\{\tilde{x}_1 \leq x\} = P\{\tilde{x}_2 \leq x\} = \ldots P\{\tilde{x}_n \leq x\} \ldots = F_{\tilde{x}}(x). \qquad \square$$

Definition 2.3   **Statistical Independence.**   A set of random variables $\tilde{x}_1$, $\tilde{x}_2$, ..., $\tilde{x}_n$ are said to be statistically independent, or simply independent, if for all real x_1, x_2, ..., x_n,

$$P\{\tilde{x}_1 \leq x_1, \ldots, \tilde{x}_n \leq x_n\} = P\{\tilde{x}_1 \leq x_1\} \ldots P\{\tilde{x}_n \leq x_n\}.$$

A sequence of random variables $\{\tilde{x}_i, \; i = 1, \; 2, \; \ldots\}$ is said to be an independent sequence if every finite collection from the sequence is independent. In either case, the random variables are also said to be mutually independent. $\qquad \square$

Definition 2.4   **Induced Queueing Process** (Feller [1971], pp. 194–195).   Let $\tilde{u}_1$, $\tilde{u}_2$, ... be mutually independent random variables with common distribution F. Then the induced queueing process is the sequence of random variables $\tilde{w}_0$, $\tilde{w}_1$, ... defined recursively by $\tilde{w}_0 = 0, \tilde{u}_0 = 0$, and

$$\tilde{w}_{n+1} = (\tilde{w}_n + \tilde{u}_n)^+. \quad \square \qquad\qquad (2.2)$$

By analogy with the process defined by (2.1), we see that

$$\tilde{u}_n = \tilde{x}_n - \tilde{t}_{n+1}. \tag{2.3}$$

Intuitively, one might argue that the difference between the *service time* of the nth customer and the *interarrival time* of the $(n + 1)$th customer induces a delay for the customers that follow. If the difference is positive, the effect is to increase the waiting times of the customers that follow; if the difference is negative, the waiting times of the customers that follow tends to be decreased. Now, suppose that for every realization of the queueing process and for every n, $x_n < t_{n+1}$. Then there would never be any customers waiting because C_n would have completed service before C_{n+1} arrived for every n. On the other hand, if $x_n > t_{n+1}$ for every n, then the server would get further behind on every customer. Thus the waiting time would build to infinity as time increased beyond bound. But in the general case, for a given value of n, $\tilde{u}_n = \tilde{x}_n - \tilde{t}_{n+1}$ may be negative, zero, or positive, and $\tilde{u}_n$ is a measure of the "elbow room."

We note that it is sometimes, but not usually, convenient to work with (2.1) when solving a queueing problem for reasons that will be considered later. The reader is referred to Ackroyd [1980] for a description of a method for dealing directly with (2.1).

We now introduce the concept of unfinished work. This is a continuous-time, continuous-valued stochastic process that is sometimes extremely useful in the analysis of queueing systems operating under complicated service disciplines such as those employing service priority.

Definition 2.5   Unfinished Work. Let $U(t)$ denote the amount of time it would take the server to empty the system starting at time t if no new arrivals occur after time t. Then $U(t^-)$, which excludes any arrival that might occur at time t, is called the *unfinished work.* □

Sometimes $U(t)$ is called the *virtual waiting time* because $U(t)$ is the length of time a customer would have to wait in a first-come-first-serve (FCFS) queueing system if the customer arrived at time t. A typical realization for $U(t)$ is shown in Figure 2.4. Completing Exercise 2.1 will help the reader to understand the concept more

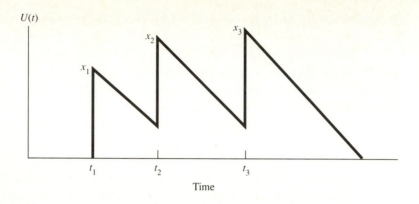

Figure 2.4 Typical realization for unfinished work.

fully and to see the relationship between waiting time and unfinished work.

In general, queueing systems are classified according to their properties. Some of these properties are now given.

General properties for classification of queueing systems:

1. The form of the interarrival distribution $F_{\tilde{t}}(t) \triangleq P\{\tilde{t} \leq t\}$, where $\tilde{t}$ represents a generic $\tilde{t}_j$;

2. The form of the service time distribution $F_{\tilde{x}}(x) \triangleq P\{\tilde{x} \leq x\}$, where $\tilde{x}$ represents a generic $\tilde{x}_j$;

3. The number of arrivals in a batch;

4. The number of servers;

5. The service discipline—the order in which service is rendered, the manner in which service is rendered (time shared, etc.), whether the system has priority;

6. The number of customers allowed to wait;

7. The number of customers in the population (usually denoted only if the population is finite).

A system is frequently described using a shorthand notation (due to D. G. Kendall) of the form G/G/s/K. In this notation, the first G denotes the form of the interarrival-time distribution, the second G denotes the form of the service-time distribution, the value of s denotes the number of servers, and the value of K denotes the number of customers allowed to wait. Sometimes the notation GI is used in place of G to emphasize independence, as, for example, in the notation GI/M/1/K to denote the queueing system having general and independent interarrivals, a single exponential server, and a finite waiting room.

Some of the quantities of interest in the study of queueing systems include the waiting-time distribution, the system-time distribution, the distribution of number of customers in the system, the probability that the server is busy (idle), the distribution of the length of a busy period, the distribution of the number of customers served during a busy period, averages for waiting time, time in system, number in system, and the number served in busy period.

Remark.   For a particular problem, all of these quantities are not necessarily of interest in themselves, but they are useful tools through which other more interesting quantities can be determined. For example, busy-period analysis is a useful tool in the study of priority queueing systems, as we shall see later.

Remark.   It's easy to state queueing problems that defy analysis, and it's easy to mistake one queueing problem for another. The reader is encouraged to think very carefully and rigorously before settling on assumptions and before using off-the-shelf results of questionable relevance. It is equally important to take special care not to define a queueing model that is overly complicated for a given application; the specific question being addressed should constantly be kept in mind when the analytical model is defined.

Exercise 2.1   Assume values of $\tilde{x}$ and $\tilde{t}$ are drawn from truncated geometric distributions. In particular, let $P\{\tilde{x} = n\} = 0$ and $P\{\tilde{t} = n\} = 0$ except for $1 \leq n \leq 10$, and let $P\{\tilde{x} = n\} = \alpha p_x (1 - p_x)^n$ and $P\{\tilde{t} = n\} = \beta p_t (1 - p_t)^n$ for $1 \leq n \leq 10$ with $p_x = 0.292578$ and $p_t = 0.14358$. Using your favorite programming language, generate a sequence of 20 random variates each for $\tilde{x}$ and $\tilde{t}$. Plot $U(t)$ as a function of t; compute u_n from (2.3) and w_n from (2.2) for $1 \leq n \leq 20$. Compute τ_n for $1 \leq n \leq 20$ and verify that w_n can be obtained from $U(t)$.

2.2   ELEMENTARY CONCEPTS AND PRELIMINARIES

Certain ideas and concepts from the theory of stochastic processes are basic in the study of elementary queueing systems. Perhaps the most important of these are the properties of the exponential distribution and the Poisson process. The purpose of this section is to discuss these and related concepts. We begin with a definition of the memoryless property of a random variable and then relate this to the exponential distribution. The idea of a counting process is then presented; this concept is used as a basis for discussing the Poisson process. We conclude the section with a summary of elementary properties of the Poisson process.

2.2.1   Exponential Distribution

Much of the literature and results in stochastic analysis is based upon the assumption that the times between events in the stochastic processes under study are drawn from exponential distributions. These assumptions are normally made for purposes of analytical tractability; the analyst chooses a simplified analysis in preference to no analytical results. In this section, we recognize the importance of making simplifying assumptions, but we introduce important concepts so that the implications of the assumptions are better understood.

Exponential distributions have the *memoryless property*, which is defined as follows:

Definition 2.6   Memoryless Property.   A random variable $\tilde{x}$ is said to be memoryless if and only if, for every $\alpha, \beta \geq 0$,

$$P\{\tilde{x} > \alpha + \beta | \tilde{x} > \beta\} = P\{\tilde{x} > \alpha\}. \qquad \square$$

The implication of the memoryless property is that the lifetime of the process in question begins all over again at every single point in time. Thus if, for example, $\tilde{x}$ represents the lifetime of a light bulb, and $\tilde{x}$ is memoryless, then at every single point in time, the light bulb is as good as new.

In general, from the definition of conditional probability, we know that

$$P\{\tilde{x} > \alpha + \beta | \tilde{x} > \beta\} = \frac{P\{\tilde{x} > \alpha + \beta,\ \tilde{x} > \beta\}}{P\{\tilde{x} > \beta\}}$$

$$= \frac{P\{\tilde{x} > \alpha + \beta\}}{P\{\tilde{x} > \beta\}}.$$

But if $\tilde{x}$ is memoryless, then

$$P\{\tilde{x} > \alpha + \beta \mid \tilde{x} > \beta\} = P\{\tilde{x} > \alpha\}.$$

Thus for $\tilde{x}$ memoryless, we have

$$P\{\tilde{x} > \alpha + \beta\} = P\{\tilde{x} > \alpha\}P\{\tilde{x} > \beta\}.$$

Definition 2.7   A random variable $\tilde{x}$ is said to be exponentially distributed if for some finite, positive λ, $P\{\tilde{x} > x\} = e^{-\lambda x}$ for $x \geq 0$. □

With regard to the memoryless property, we state the following two lemmas, the proofs of which are deferred to the exercises.

Lemma 2.1   If $\tilde{x}$ is exponentially distributed, then $\tilde{x}$ is memoryless. □

Exercise 2.2   Prove Lemma 2.1.

Lemma 2.2   Let g be a nonnegative right-continuous function with $g(t + s) = g(t)g(s)$ for all s, $t > 0$. Then either $g(t) = 0$ for $t > 0$ or $g(t) = e^{-\lambda t}$ for some positive $\lambda < \infty$.   □

Exercise 2.3   Prove Lemma 2.2. [*Hint*: Start with rational arguments. Extend to the real line using a continuity argument. The proof is given in Feller [1968], pp. 458–460, but it is strongly recommended that the exercise be attempted without first going to the reference.]

From Lemmas 2.1 and 2.2, we have the following theorem.

Theorem 2.1   A continuous random variable, $\tilde{x}$, is exponentially distributed if and only if $\tilde{x}$ is memoryless. That is, among continuous random variables, the memoryless property is unique to the exponential random variable.   □

Now, from Theorem 2.1 we find that for $\tilde{x}$ memoryless,

$$P\{\tilde{x} > x\} = e^{-\lambda x}, \qquad x \geq 0.$$

Thus

$$P\{\tilde{x} \leq x\} = 1 - e^{-\lambda x}, \qquad x \geq 0,$$

and the probability density function for $\tilde{x}$ is

$$\frac{d}{dx}P\{\tilde{x} \leq x\} = \lambda e^{-\lambda x}, \qquad \text{for } x \geq 0.$$

The parameter λ is sometimes called the rate, and we say "$\tilde{x}$ is exponentially distributed with rate λ." When there is no possibility of ambiguity, we sometimes write $\tilde{x} \sim E(\lambda)$.

Example 2.1   An office shared by a number of graduate students has two telephones. When Alice decides to use a telephone, she sees that Bob and Charlie are using them, but no one else is waiting. Alice knows she can use the phone as soon as either Bob or Charlie completes his call. Suppose the holding time of each call is drawn independently from an exponential distribution with parameter μ. What is the probability that Alice completes her call before Charlie?

Solution: Because service is exponential and therefore memoryless, when Alice enters, the remaining time for Bob's and Charlie's calls are independent exponential random variables with parameter μ. Thus Bob and Charlie are equally likely to finish last, and $P\{$Bob before Charlie$\} = 1/2$. If Bob completes his call before Charlie, then from the point when Bob finishes, Charlie and Alice will use the phones an amount of time drawn independently from an exponential distribution with rate μ. Hence $P\{$Alice before Charlie $\mid$ Bob before Charlie$\} = 1/2$. Thus, $P\{$Alice before Charlie$\} = 1/4$.   ■

If the holding times in the above example were deterministic

rather than exponential, then the result would have been quite different. Comparison between exponential and deterministic assumptions
are explored later in the text, but an initial comparison is encouraged
in the next exercise.

Exercise 2.4   Repeat Example 2.1, assuming all students have deterministic holding time of one unit. How do the results compare?
Would an exponential assumption on service time give an adequate
explanation of system performance if the service time is really deterministic?

Returning to the properties of the exponential distribution, it is
interesting to note that both the mean and the standard deviation
of the exponential random variable are equal to $1/\lambda$. The moments
of the exponential random variable as well as many other random
variables are readily determined via *Laplace transform* techniques.
Toward this end, we define the Laplace transform and state one of
its key properties as a theorem, leaving its proof to the exercises.

Definition 2.8   Laplace–Stieltjes Transform.   Let $\tilde{x}$ be a nonnegative
random variable with distribution $F_{\tilde{x}}(x)$. Then

$$F_{\tilde{x}}^*(s) = E[e^{-s\tilde{x}}]$$
$$= \int_0^\infty e^{-sx}\, dF_{\tilde{x}}(x)$$

is called the *Laplace–Stieltjes transform* of $\tilde{x}$ or the Laplace–Stieltjes
transform of $F_{\tilde{x}}(x)$. If $F_{\tilde{x}}(x)$ is differentiable, the same expression is
called the *Laplace transform* of $d/dx\ F_{\tilde{x}}(x)$.   □

Theorem 2.2   Let $\tilde{x}$ be a nonnegative random variable with distribution $F_{\tilde{x}}(x)$, and let $F_{\tilde{x}}^*(s)$ be the Laplace–Stieltjes transform of $\tilde{x}$.
Then

$$E[\tilde{x}^n] = (-1)^n \frac{d^n}{ds^n} F_{\tilde{x}}^*(s)\Big|_{s=0}.$$ □

Exercise 2.5   Prove Theorem 2.2. |

Theorem 2.3   Let $\tilde{x}$ and $\tilde{y}$ be independent, nonnegative, random variables having Laplace–Stieltjes transforms $F_{\tilde{x}}^*(s)$ and $F_{\tilde{y}}^*(s)$, respectively. Then the Laplace–Stieltjes transform for the random variable $\tilde{z} = \tilde{x} + \tilde{y}$ is given by the product of $F_{\tilde{x}}^*(s)$ and $F_{\tilde{y}}^*(s)$.   □

Exercise 2.6   Prove Theorem 2.3.

Exercise 2.7   Let $\tilde{x}$ be an exponentially distributed random variable with parameter λ. Find $F_{\tilde{x}}^*(s)$.

Exercise 2.8   Let $\tilde{x}$ be an exponentially distributed random variable with parameter λ. Derive expressions for $E[\tilde{x}]$, $E[\tilde{x}^2]$, and $\text{Var}(\tilde{x})$. [*Hint*: Use Laplace transforms.]

Exercise 2.9   Let $\tilde{x}$ and $\tilde{y}$ be independent exponentially distributed random variables with parameters α and β, respectively.

1. Find the distribution of $\tilde{z} = \min\{\tilde{x}, \tilde{y}\}$. [*Hint*: Note that $\tilde{z} = \min\{\tilde{x}, \tilde{y}\}$ and $\tilde{z} > z$ means $\tilde{x} > z$ and $\tilde{y} > z$.]

2. Find $P\{\tilde{x} < \tilde{y}\}$.

3. Show that the conditional distribution $F_{\tilde{z}|\tilde{x}<\tilde{y}}(z) = F_{\tilde{z}}(z)$.

Exercise 2.10   Suppose Albert and Betsy run a race repeatedly. The time required for Albert to complete the race, $\tilde{a}$, is exponentially distributed with parameter α, and the time required for Betsy to complete, $\tilde{b}$, is exponentially distributed with parameter β. Let $\tilde{n}_b$ denote the number of times Betsy wins before Albert wins his first race. Find $P\{\tilde{n}_b = n\}$ for $n \geq 0$.

Exercise 2.11   Let $\{\tilde{x}_i, \ i = 1, \ 2, \ \ldots\}$ be a sequence of mutually independent exponentially distributed random variables and let $\tilde{n}$ be a geometrically distributed random variable with parameter p, independent of $\tilde{x}_i, \ i = 1, \ 2, \ \ldots$; that is, $P\{\tilde{n} = n\} = p(1 - p)^{n-1}$ for $n = 1, \ 2, \ \ldots$. Let

$$\tilde{y} = \sum_{i=1}^{\tilde{n}} \tilde{x}_i.$$

Show that $\tilde{y}$ has the exponential distribution with parameter $p\alpha$.

Some interesting properties of the exponential random variables are now summarized together with a brief discussion of their implications. The proofs of these properties are deferred to the exercises. Relative to all of the properties, let $\tilde{x}$ and $\tilde{y}$ be independent exponentially distributed random variables with parameters α and β, respectively. Then we have the following properties.

Properties of exponential random variables:

1. The distribution of $\tilde{z} = \min\{\tilde{x}, \tilde{y}\}$ is exponential with parameter $\alpha + \beta$.

2. $F_{\tilde{z}|\tilde{x}<\tilde{y}}(z) = F_{\tilde{z}}(z)$.

3. $P\{\tilde{x} < \tilde{y}\} = \alpha/(\alpha + \beta)$.

4. Two numbers are drawn repeatedly from the distributions for $\tilde{x}$ and $\tilde{y}$. Let $\tilde{n}_x$ denote the number of trials required before the number drawn from $F_{\tilde{y}}(x)$ is smaller than that drawn from $F_{\tilde{x}}(x)$ for the first time. Then

$$P\{\tilde{n}_x = n\} = \left(\frac{\alpha}{\alpha + \beta}\right)^n \left(\frac{\beta}{\alpha + \beta}\right) \quad \text{for } n \geq 0.$$

5. Let $\{\tilde{x}_i, \ i = 1, \ 2, \ \ldots\}$ be a sequence of mutually independent exponentially distributed random variables, and let $\tilde{n}$ be a geometrically distributed random variable with parameter p, independent of $\{\tilde{x}_i, \ i = 1, \ 2, \ \ldots\}$. Let

$$\tilde{y} = \sum_{i=1}^{\tilde{n}} \tilde{x}_i.$$

Then $\tilde{y}$ has the exponential distribution with parameter $p\alpha$.

The implication of Property 1 is that if the state of a process changes whenever the first of two events occurs, and if the time to occurrence of the events are drawn independently from exponential distributions, then the time to change of state is exponentially distributed with parameter equal to the sum of the individual rates.

Since exponentiality implies memorylessness, the times to occurrence of the individual events start over again whenever either event occurs.

Property 2 says that even if one knows which event caused the change of state, the time to occurrence of the state change is still exponentially distributed with parameter equal to the sum of the rates. It is tempting to conclude that if one knows the state change was caused by the event having its interevent time drawn from the distribution $F_{\tilde{x}}(x)$, then the time to state change is exponentially distributed with parameter α, but this is false. These properties will be found to be very useful in studying queueing systems in which all interevent times are exponentially distributed.

Exercise 2.12   This exercise is intended to reinforce the meaning of Property 2 of exponential random variables. Let $\tilde{x}$ and $\tilde{y}$ denote two independent exponential random variables with rates 1 and 2, respectively, and define $\tilde{z} = \min\{\tilde{x}, \tilde{y}\}$. Using a spreadsheet (or a computer programming language), generate a sequence of 100 variates for each of the random variables. Denote the ith variate for $\tilde{x}$ and $\tilde{y}$ by x_i and y_i, respectively, and set $z_i = \min\{x_i, y_i\}$ for $i = 1, 2, \ldots, 100$.

Let n denote the number of values of i such that $x_i < y_i$, let i_j denote the jth such value, and define $w_j = z_{i_j}$ for $j = 1, 2, \ldots, n$. Compute sample averages for the variates; that is, compute $\bar{x} = (1/100)\sum_{i=1}^{100} x_i$, $\bar{y} = (1/100)\sum_{i=1}^{100} y_i$, $\bar{z} = (1/100)\sum_{i=1}^{100} z_i$, and $\bar{w} = (1/n)\sum_{j=1}^{n} w_j$. Compare the results. Is $\bar{w}$ closer to $\bar{x}$ or to $\bar{z}$?

Now, give an intuitive explanation for the statement, "It is tempting to conclude that if one knows the state change was caused by the event having its interevent time drawn from the distribution $F_{\tilde{x}}(x)$, then the time to state change is exponentially distributed with parameter α, but this is false."

Property 3 says that the probability that the state change was caused by completion of an $\tilde{x}$ event is simply the rate for $\tilde{x}$, α, divided by the sum of the rates, $\alpha + \beta$. Property 4 says that the number of state transitions due to $\tilde{x}$ completions before the first $\tilde{y}$ completion is geometrically distributed, the parameter being the rate for $\tilde{x}$ divided by the sum of the rates. By symmetry, the number of state transitions due to $\tilde{y}$ completions before the first $\tilde{x}$ completion is geometrically distributed, the parameter being β divided by the sum of the rates. The implication of Property 5 is that a geometric sum of exponential random variables is exponential. For example, if a message contains a geometric number of packets having independent and identically distributed exponential transmission times, then the total transmission time of the message is exponential.

The types of operations with exponential distributions described above yield exponential distributions, so the results are easily extended to the case of n, rather than 2, exponential random variables. This leads to a great deal of simplification in analyzing queueing systems in which all underlying distributions are exponential.

2.2.2   Poisson Process

The characterization of arrival processes for many queueing systems as Poisson has a solid physical basis, as was first discovered by A. K. Erlang during the 1910s. Although the Poisson characterization is often appropriate, there are many cases in which the Poisson assumption is simply not justifiable, and the distinction between the two cases is not necessarily obvious. The Poisson assumption can reduce the analytical complexity of a problem and lead to easily obtained and useful results, but the same assumption may also render the analysis useless. Thus an understanding of Poisson processes is enormously important in queueing analysis. Toward this goal, we will present three definitions of the Poisson process, each of which presents a different, but equivalent, view.

The Poisson process is perhaps the most important and well known member of a special class of stochastic processes called a *counting process*. Before proceeding to our discussion of the Poisson process, we introduce counting processes and some of their important properties.

Definition 2.9   Counting Process.   A stochastic process $\{\tilde{n}(t),\ t \geq 0\}$ is said to be a counting process (CP) if $\tilde{n}(t)$ expresses the number of events that have occurred by time t. Thus

1. $\tilde{n}(t)$ is integer valued,

2. $\tilde{n}(t)$ is nonnegative,

3. $\tilde{n}(t)$ is nondecreasing, and

4. for $s < t$, $\tilde{n}(t) - \tilde{n}(s)$ is the number of events that occur in the interval $(s, t]$. □

From the above definition, it is clear that a counting process is a process that evolves over time. Counting processes are characterized by the relationships between events that occur in nonoverlapping intervals of time, called increments. In particular, it is of interest to know how the occurrence of events in one interval of time affects the probability of occurrence of events in another, nonoverlapping interval of time. Counting processes are characterized on the basis of whether or not they satisfy the conditions of the following definitions.

Definition 2.10   Independent Increments.   If the numbers of events occurring in disjoint time intervals are independent, then the counting process is said to have independent increments. □

Definition 2.11   Stationary Increments.   If the distribution of the number of events that occur in a time interval depends only upon the length of the interval—that is, if $P\{\tilde{n}(t+s) - (t+s) = n\}$ is independent of t—then the counting process is said to have stationary increments. □

Exercise 2.13   Define counting processes that you think have the following properties:

1. independent but not stationary increments,

2. stationary but not independent increments,

3. neither stationary nor independent increments, and

4. both stationary and independent increments.

What do you think would be the properties of the process that counts the number of passengers who arrive at an airport by June 30 of a given year if time zero is defined to be midnight, December 31, of the previous year?

We are now ready to consider our first definition of the Poisson process, which is given in terms of the Poisson distribution.

Definition 2.12   Poisson Process (1).   The counting process $\{\tilde{n}(t), t \geq 0\}$ is said to be a Poisson process with rate λ, $\lambda > 0$, if

1. $\tilde{n}(0) = 0$,

2. $\{\tilde{n}(t), \ t \geq 0\}$ has independent increments, and

3. the number of events that occur in any interval of length t is Poisson distributed with parameter λt; that is,

$$P\{\tilde{n}(t+s) - \tilde{n}(s) = n\} = \frac{(\lambda t)^n e^{-\lambda t}}{n!} \qquad \text{for all s.} \qquad \square$$

Exercise 2.14   Show that $E[\tilde{n}(t+s) - \tilde{n}(s)] = \lambda t$ if $\{\tilde{n}(t), \ t > 0\}$ is a Poisson process with rate λ.

It is important to note that Property (3) of Definition 2.12 implies that the process has stationary increments; that is, the number of events that occur in an interval of length t is independent of the time at which the observation period begins. Also, note that it is not enough to verify that the distribution of the number of events in a fixed-length interval is Poisson distributed; the number of events counted in all nonoverlapping fixed-length intervals of every length must also be independent.

It is easy to define a process that results in a Poisson number of arrivals in a fixed-length interval but that is not itself Poisson. As an extreme example, suppose arrivals occur in groups every hour on the hour and the group sizes are drawn independently from a Poisson distribution. Then, if measurements of the number of arrivals that occur over intervals having length one hour are taken, then the number of arrivals over the measurement period will follow the Poisson distribution. In addition, the number of arrivals in nonoverlapping periods will be independent. The process is also stationary. But the arrival process is obviously not Poisson. The reason is that if the measurements were taken over intervals of a different fixed length, say 15 minutes, then the number of arrivals would not follow the Poisson distribution.

We could construct other examples, but suffice it to say at this point that there are many processes wearing Poisson clothing that are not Poisson. Thus extreme care must be taken in order to avoid making Poisson assumptions inappropriately. More will be said on this topic in Chapter 3; for now, we return to our alternate definitions of the Poisson process.

In order to state the second definition of the Poisson process, we need the notion of a special class of functions, $o(h)$. Functions belonging to this class diminish to zero "faster than linear functions" as their arguments are decreased. The second definition of the Poisson process basically says that over very short intervals, the probability of the occurrence of a single event is proportional to the length of the interval, and the probability of the occurrence of two or more events over the same interval is $o(h)$. Again, increments are stationary and independent. We now state these ideas more formally.

Definition 2.13   o(h) ("little-oh-of-h").   A function f is said to be $o(h)$ if f has the property

$$\lim_{h \to 0} \frac{f(h)}{h} = 0. \qquad\qquad \square$$

It is easy to show that sums and products of $o(h)$ functions are also $o(h)$. In addition, $o(h)$ functions themselves must tend to 0 as h tends to 0. Exercises are provided below to allow the reader to develop these and other properties of $o(h)$ functions and to gain a better understanding of the concept.

Exercise 2.15   For each of the following functions, determine whether the function is $o(h)$ or not. Your determination should be in the form of a formal proof.

1. $f(t) = t$
2. $f(t) = t^2$
3. $f(t) = t^{1/2}$

4. $f(t) = e^{-at}$ for a, $t > 0$

5. $f(t) = te^{-at}$ for a, $t > 0$

Exercise 2.16   Suppose that $f(t)$ and $g(t)$ are both $o(h)$. Determine whether each of the following functions is $o(h)$.

1. $s(t) = f(t) + g(t)$

2. $d(t) = f(t) - g(t)$

3. $p(t) = f(t)g(t)$

4. $q(t) = f(t)/g(t)$

5. $i(t) = \int_0^t f(x)\,dx$

We are now ready to introduce our second definition of the Poisson process.

Definition 2.14   Poisson Process (2).   The counting process $\{\tilde{n}(t),\ t > 0\}$ is said to be a Poisson process with rate λ, $\lambda > 0$, if

1. $\tilde{n}(0) = 0$,

2. $\{\tilde{n}(t),\ t > 0\}$ has stationary and independent increments,

3. $P\{\tilde{n}(h) = 1\} = \lambda h + o(h)$, and

4. $P\{\tilde{n}(h) \geq 2\} = o(h)$.   □

Exercise 2.17   Show that definition 1 of the Poisson process implies definition 2 of the Poisson process.

Exercise 2.18   Show that definition 2 of the Poisson process implies definition 1 of the Poisson process. [*Hint*: After satisfying the first two properties of definition 1, establish that $P_0(t) = \exp\{-\lambda t\}$, where $P_n(t) = P\{\tilde{n}(t) = n\}$, and then prove the validity of part (c) of definition 1 by induction.]

The Poisson process can also be characterized by its sequence of interarrival times, which is defined as follows.

Definition 2.15   **Sequence of Interarrival Times.**   Let $\tilde{t}_1$ be the time
of the first event from a counting process, and let $\tilde{t}_n$ be the time
between the $(n-1)$th event and the nth event. Then $\{\tilde{t}_1, \tilde{t}_2, \ldots\}$ is
called the sequence of interarrival times. Note that $\tilde{t}_1 > t \Rightarrow \tilde{n}(t) = 0$. $\qquad\qquad\square$

Exercise 2.19   Show that the sequence of interarrival times for a Poisson process with rate λ forms a set of mutually independent, identically distributed (iid) exponential random variables with parameter
λ.

We now turn to the third definition of the Poisson process. From
Property (3) of the first definition of the Poisson process, it is easy
to see that

$$P\{\tilde{n}(t+s) - \tilde{n}(s) = 0\} = e^{-\lambda t} \quad \text{for all s.}$$

Thus

$$P\{\tilde{n}(t) = 0\} = e^{-\lambda t}.$$

Now, the event that there are no events from the process by time t
is the same as the event that the first event from the process occurs
after time t. That is,

$$P\{\tilde{\tau}_1 > t\} = e^{-\lambda t}.$$

Since $\tilde{t}_1 = \tilde{\tau}_1$, we see that the first interarrival time from a Poisson
process is exponentially distributed. Now, because the second interarrival time begins at the end of the first interarrival time, and the
process has stationary and independent increments, the distribution
of $\tilde{t}_2$ is the same as the distribution of $\tilde{t}_1$, and in addition, these random variables are independent. Repeated use of these arguments will
reveal that the Poisson process yields a sequence of iid exponential
interarrival times.

Definition 2.16   **Poisson Process (3).**   Let $\tilde{t}_1, \tilde{t}_2, \ldots$ be iid exponential random variables with mean $1/\lambda$. Consider a counting process in

which the nth event occurs at time $\tilde{s}_n = \sum_{i=1}^{n} \tilde{t}_i$. Then the counting process is a Poisson process, and

$$\tilde{n}(t) = \max\{n : \tilde{s}_n \leq t\}. \qquad \Box$$

We have argued above that definition 1 of the Poisson process implies definition 3. It is left to the exercises to show that definitions 1 and 2 of the Poisson process stated above are equivalent, and that definition 3 implies definition 1. Thus all the definitions of the Poisson process given above are equivalent.

Exercise 2.20   Show

$$\frac{d}{dt} P\{\tilde{s}_n \leq t\} = \frac{\lambda(\lambda t)^{n-1} e^{-\lambda t}}{(n-1)!}.$$

[*Hint*: Start by noting $\tilde{s}_n \leq t \Longleftrightarrow \tilde{n}(t) \geq n$.]

Exercise 2.21   Show that definition 3 of the Poisson process implies definition 1 of the Poisson process.

From the three definitions of the Poisson process given above, it can be seen that the Poisson process is a time-homogeneous, continuous-time Markov chain on the nonnegative integers. For continuity of presentation, the definition of the continuous-time Markov chain and other closely related definitions follow.

Definition 2.17   Continuous-Time Markov Chain (Ross [1989]).   A stochastic process $\{\tilde{x}(t), t \geq 0\}$ is said to be a continuous-time Markov chain (CTMC) on the nonnegative integers if for all $s, t \geq 0$, and all nonnegative integers $i, j, x(u)$ for $0 \leq u \leq s$,

$$P\{\tilde{x}(t+s) = j \mid \tilde{x}(s) = i, \tilde{x}(u) = x(u)\} = P\{\tilde{x}(t+s) = j \mid \tilde{x}(s) = i\}.$$

The quantity $P\{\tilde{x}(t + s) = j \mid \tilde{x}(s) = i\}$ is called the transition probability from state i to state j in time s to time $s + t$. $\Box$

Definition 2.18   Time-Homogeneous CTMC (Ross [1989]).   A CTMC $\{\tilde{x}(t), t \geq 0\}$ is said to be a time-homogeneous CTMC on the nonnegative integers if $\{\tilde{x}(t), t \geq 0\}$ is a CTMC and for all $s, t \geq 0$,

$$P\{\tilde{x}(t + s) = j \mid \tilde{x}(s) = i\} = P\{\tilde{x}(t) = j \mid \tilde{x}(0) = i\}.$$

Again, the quantity $P\{\tilde{x}(t) = j \mid \tilde{x}(0) = i\}$ is called the transition probability from state i to state j over $(t, \ s + t]$.   □

Definition 2.19   Transition Probability Matrix for CTMC. For a time-homogeneous CTMC $\{\tilde{x}(t), \ t \geq 0\}$, the matrix $P(t) = (P\{\tilde{x}(t) = j \mid \tilde{x}(0) = i\})$ is called the transition probability matrix over $(t, \ s + t]$ (Ross [1989]).   □

Definition 2.20   Infinitesimal Generator for a CTMC (Cohen [1969]). For a time-homogeneous CTMC $\{\tilde{x}(t), \ t \geq 0\}$, the matrix $P(t)$ satisfies the following (possibly infinite dimensional) matrix differential equation:

$$\frac{d}{dt}P(t) = P(t)\mathcal{Q},$$

with $P(0) = I$. The (possibly infinite dimensional) matrix $\mathcal{Q}$ is called the infinitesimal generator, or simply the generator, for the CTMC $\{\tilde{x}(t), \ t \geq 0\}$.   □

The following additional properties of the Poisson process, stated without proof, are useful in studying queueing systems. They should be part of the working tools of every queueing theorist.

Properties of Poisson processes:

1. Let $\{\tilde{n}_1(t), \ t \geq 0\}$ and $\{\tilde{n}_2(t), \ t \geq 0\}$ be independent Poisson processes with rates α and β, respectively. Define $\tilde{n}(t) = \tilde{n}_1(t) + \tilde{n}_2(t)$. Then $\{\tilde{n}(t), \ t \geq 0\}$ is a Poisson process with rate $\alpha + \beta$.

2. Events occur according to a Poisson process with rate λ. Suppose each event, independent of anything else, is recorded with probability p. Let $\tilde{n}_1(t)$ be the number of events recorded by time t, and let $\tilde{n}_2(t)$ be the number of events not recorded by time t. Then the processes $\{\tilde{n}_1(t), \ t \geq 0\}$ and $\{\tilde{n}_2(t), \ t \geq 0\}$ are independent Poisson processes with rates $p\lambda$ and $(1 - p)\lambda$, respectively.

The implications of the above properties of Poisson processes are now discussed briefly. Suppose there are two independent arrival streams of customers converging on a service center. Property 1 says that if the arrival processes of the individual streams are Poisson, then so is the arrival process of the combined stream. This is a direct result of the facts that interarrival times from Poisson processes are exponentially distributed and that the minimum of two independent exponential random variables is also exponential.

The second property covers the following situation. Suppose potential customers arrive at a business establishment according to a Poisson process. Each customer upon approaching the establishment tosses a coin. If "heads" results, the potential customer enters the store; else the potential customer departs without entering. Property 2 says that the customers who actually enter the store do so according to a Poisson process, the process counting the potential customers who choose not to enter is a Poisson process, and furthermore (surprisingly), the two processes are independent.

The above properties, which also apply to more than two streams or choices, are extremely useful in the analysis of networks of exponential queues and in justifying simplified analysis of system bottlenecks. The first of these aspects will be explored in the next chapter. The reader is encouraged to complete the exercises to gain a mastery of these properties.

Exercise 2.22 Let $\tilde{n}_1$ and $\tilde{n}_2$ be independent Poisson random variables with rates α and β, respectively. Define $\tilde{n} = \tilde{n}_1 + \tilde{n}_2$. Show that $\tilde{n}$ has the Poisson distribution with rate $\alpha + \beta$. Using this result, prove Property 1 of the Poisson process.

Exercise 2.23 Suppose an urn contains $\tilde{n}$ balls, where $\tilde{n}$ is a Poisson random variable with parameter λ. Suppose the balls are either red or green, the proportion of red balls being p. Show that the distribution of the number of red balls, $\tilde{n}_r$, in the urn is Poisson with parameter $p\lambda$, the distribution of green balls, $\tilde{n}_g$ is Poisson with parameter $(1 - p)\lambda$, and that $\tilde{n}_r$ and $\tilde{n}_g$ are independent random variables. Use this result to prove Property 2 of the Poisson process. [*Hint*: Condition on the total number of balls in the urn and use the fact that the number of successes in a sequence of n repeated Bernoulli trials has the binomial distribution with parameters n and p.]

Exercise 2.24   Events occur at a Poisson rate λ. Suppose all odd numbered events and no even numbered events are recorded. Let $\tilde{n}_1(t)$ be the number of events recorded by time t and $\tilde{n}_2(t)$ be the number of events not recorded by time t. Do the processes $\{\tilde{n}_1(t), t \geq 0\}$ and $\{\tilde{n}_2(t), t \geq 0\}$ each have independent increments? Do they have stationary increments? Are they Poisson processes?

Exercise 2.25   Suppose $\{\tilde{x}(t), t \geq 0\}$ is a time-homogeneous CTMC having infintesimal generator Q defined as follows:

$$Q_{ij} = \begin{cases} -\lambda, & \text{if } j = i, \\ \lambda, & \text{if } j = i+1, \\ 0, & \text{otherwise.} \end{cases}$$

Show that $\{\tilde{x}(t), t \geq 0\}$ is a Poisson process. [*Hint*: Simply solve the infinite matrix differential equation term by term starting with $P_{00}(t)$ and completing each column in turn.]

C H A P T E R

$$\boxed{3}$$

Continuous-Time Markov Chain Queueing Models

In this chapter, we explore the analysis of several queueing models that are characterized as discrete-valued, continuous-time Markov chains. That is, the queueing systems examined in this chapter will have a countable state space, and the dwell times in each state will be drawn from exponential distributions whose parameters are possibly state-dependent.

The most elementary queueing systems in this class are characterized by one-dimensional birth and death models. The stochastic behavior of these systems at a particular point in time is completely described by a single number, which we shall think of as the "occupancy" of the system. The dwell times for each state are drawn from exponential distributions independently, but, in general, the parameter of the exponential distribution depends upon the current state of the system.

We begin by examining the well known M/M/1 queueing system, which has Poisson arrivals and exponentially distributed service times. For this model, we will consider both time-dependent and equilibrium behavior, with primary emphasis on the latter. In particular, we shall consider both the time-dependent and equilibrium occupancy distributions, the stochastic equilibrium sojourn and waiting time distributions, and the stochastic equilibrium distribution of the length of the busy period. Several related processes, including the departure process, are introduced, and these are used to obtain equilibrium occupancy distributions for simple networks of queues.

After discussing the M/M/1 system, we briefly discuss formulation of the dynamical equations for more general birth–death models in Section 3.2. The time-dependent behavior of finite-state general birth–death models is discussed in Section 3.3. A reasonably complete derivation based upon classical methods is presented herein, and the rate of convergence of the system to stochastic equilibrium is briefly discussed. Additionally, the notion of *randomization*, or equivalently, *uniformization*, is introduced. The basic idea is to study a finite-state, continuous-time Markov chain by embedding a finite-state, discrete-time Markov chain whose intertransition times are independent, identically distributed, exponential random variables. Randomization is described in general terms, and an example that illustrates its application is provided.

Section 3.4 presents the balance equation approach to formulating equilibrium state probability equations for birth–death processes and other more general processes. Elementary traffic engineering models are introduced, and blocking probabilities for these systems are discussed.

In Section 3.5, we discuss simple networks of exponential service stations of the feedforward, open, and closed varieties. We discuss the form of the joint state probability mass functions for such systems, which are of the so-called product form type. We discuss in detail a novel technique, due to Gordon [1990], for obtaining the normalizing constant for simple closed queueing networks in closed form.

The probability generating function technique for solving balance equations is introduced in Section 3.6. This technique is used in Section 3.7 to solve a more complicated two-dimensional queueing model in which both the arrival and service rates are determined by the state of a single independent continuous-time Markov chain. The matrix geometric technique is then introduced and used to solve the same model.

In Section 3.8, we introduce distributions of the phase (PH) type by modifying the class of models discussed in Section 3.7, and we provide the equilibrium occupancy distribution for the M/PH/1 system in matrix geometric form. We conclude the chapter with a set of supplementary exercises.

3.1   M/M/1 QUEUEING SYSTEM

This section comprises three subsections. In Sec. 3.1.1, we consider the time-dependent occupancy distribution. We then derive the stochastic equilibrium occupancy, sojourn, and waiting time distributions, together with their means, in the second subsection. Along the way, we introduce various related processes, including the occupancy processes as viewed by departing and arriving customers, respectively, which are needed to obtain these results. We also discuss the departure process and its role in obtaining occupancy distributions for simple feedforward networks of queues. In Sec. 3.1.3, we discuss the dynamics of busy-period processes and derive an expression for the expected length of the busy period in stochastic equilibrium. We also discuss other characteristics of the busy period and briefly discuss the role of busy-period analysis in examining more complicated systems.

3.1.1   Time-Dependent M/M/1 Occupancy Distribution

As mentioned in the introductory section, the M/M/1 queueing system has Poisson arrivals and exponentially distributed service. Because of the memoryless property of the Poisson process and the exponential distribution, the dynamics of the process that counts the total number of arrivals to and departures from the system over very short periods of time are exactly the same as those of the Poisson process. If there are customers in the system, then the rate for this process is the sum of the arrival and service rates. If there are no customers in service, the rate for the process is simply the arrival rate. Let $\tilde{n}(t)$ denote the system occupancy—the total number of customers in the system, including the one in service, if any—at time t. To simplify notation, let

$$P_n(t) \triangleq P\{\tilde{n}(t) = n\}, \qquad n \geq 0.$$

Clearly, the stochastic process $\{\tilde{n}(t),\ t \geq 0\}$ is a continuous-time Markov chain, and for $n > 0$ we find

$$P\{\tilde{n}(t + h) = n\} = P\{\tilde{n}(t) = n,$$
$$0 \text{ arrivals or departures in } (t,\ t + h]\}$$
$$+ P\{\tilde{n}(t) = n - 1,$$
$$1 \text{ arrival and no departures in } (t,\ t + h]\}$$
$$+ P\{\tilde{n}(t) = n + 1,$$
$$1 \text{ departure and no arrivals in}(t,\ t + h]\}$$
$$+ o(h).$$

Let λ and μ denote the arrival and service rates, respectively. Then, by applying definition 2 of the Poisson process, we find

$$\begin{aligned}
P\{\tilde{n}(t + h) = n\} &= P_n(t)[1 - \lambda h + o(h)][1 - \mu h + o(h)] \\
&\quad + P_{n-1}(t)[\lambda h + o(h)][1 - \mu h + o(h)] \\
&\quad + P_{n+1}(t)[\mu h + o(h)][1 - \lambda h + o(h)] + o(h) \\
&= P_n(t)[1 - (\lambda + \mu)h + o(h)] \\
&\quad + P_{n-1}(t)[\lambda h + o(h)] \\
&\quad + P_{n+1}(t)[\mu h + o(h)] + o(h).
\end{aligned}$$

Upon rearranging the terms of this equation, we find

$$\begin{aligned}
P_n(t + h) - P_n(t) &= -(\lambda + \mu)h P_n(t) + \lambda h P_{n-1}(t) \\
&\quad + \mu h P_{n+1}(t) + o(h).
\end{aligned} \tag{3.1}$$

Finally, division of both sides of (3.1) by h, taking limits, and applying the definition of $o(h)$ leads to the following dynamical equation relating the state probabilities to each other:

$$P'_n(t) = -(\lambda + \mu)P_n(t) + \lambda P_{n-1}(t) + \mu P_{n+1}(t) \quad \text{for } n > 0. \tag{3.2}$$

Similarly, we find for $n = 0$,

$$P'_0(t) = -\lambda P_0(t) + \mu P_1(t). \tag{3.3}$$

The solution to the system (3.2) and (3.3) depends upon the initial number of customers, i, in the system. Then, from Takács [1962], pp. 23–26, we find

$$P_n(t; i) = e^{-(\lambda+\mu)t}[(\lambda/\mu)^{n-i/2}I_{n-i}(2\sqrt{\lambda\mu}\,t)$$
$$+ (\lambda/\mu)^{(n-i+1)/2}I_{n+i+1}(2\sqrt{\lambda\mu}\,t)$$
$$+ (1 - \frac{\lambda}{\mu})(\frac{\lambda}{\mu})^n \sum_{\nu=i+n+2}^{\infty} (\frac{\lambda}{\mu})^{-\nu/2}I_\nu(2\sqrt{\lambda\mu}\,t)], \tag{3.4}$$

where $I_\nu(x)$ for $\nu = 0, \pm 1, \pm 2, \ldots$ is the modified Bessel function of order ν. For $\nu \geq 0$,

$$I_\nu(x) = \sum_{j=0}^{\infty} \frac{(x/2)^{\nu+2j}}{(j+\nu)!j!}$$

and

$$I_{-\nu}(x) = I_\nu(x). \tag{3.5}$$

For an application of (3.4) to a flow control problem in a computer communication network, see Stern [1979].

Evaluation of (3.4) would appear to be a formidable task. First of all, the results are given in the form of an infinite series of modified Bessel functions. Second, each of the modified Bessel functions is itself expressed as an infinite series. Fortunately, (3.4) and (3.5) are not the most efficient starting point for evaluating the time-dependent state probabilities (as indicated in many references). The most efficient starting point for numerical work appears to be an integral equation expression. For a discussion of numerical methods for computing these probabilities and other time-dependent quantities of interest, the reader is referred to two excellent papers: Abate and Whitt [1988] and Abate and Whitt [1989]. For a treatment of the time-dependent behavior of a more complicated version of the M/M/1 system, the reader is referred to Daigle and Magalhães [1991] and the references therein.

3.1.2   Stochastic Equilibrium M/M/1 Distributions

In the previous section, we obtained the time-dependent probability distribution for the system occupancy. In most cases of practical interest, the time-dependent probability distribution converges to a unique solution as time increases beyond bound. This solution is called the *stochastic equilibrium* solution, stochastic equilibrium meaning that the distribution is no longer changing as a function of time.

We note in passing that equilibrium is never actually reached, except in the sense of a limit, unless the initial distribution is chosen as the equilibrium distribution. On the other hand, for most applications, an understanding of the stochastic equilibrium behavior of the system is sufficient. In that case, we can solve (3.2) and (3.3) for the equilibrium probabilities and use those results to derive the stochastic equilibrium sojourn time and waiting time distributions.

Let $\tilde{n}$ denote the queue occupancy at an arbitrary point in time after the system has reached stochastic equilibrium. We define $P_n = P\{\tilde{n} = n\}$, or equivalently, $P_n = \lim_{t\to\infty} P_n(t)$. We then expect that $P_n'(t) \to 0$ (although this is not absolutely necessary from a mathematical point of view) and (3.3) and (3.2) become (3.6) and (3.7), respectively. That is,

$$\mu P_1 = \lambda P_0, \tag{3.6}$$

and

$$\mu P_{n+1} = (\lambda + \mu)P_n - \lambda P_{n-1}. \tag{3.7}$$

Upon substitution of (3.7) into (3.6) with $n = 1$, we find

$$P_2 = \frac{\lambda}{\mu}P_1,$$

and solving (3.6) for P_1 yields $P_1 = (\lambda/\mu)P_0$. Thus we find

$$P_2 = \left(\frac{\lambda}{\mu}\right)^2 P_0.$$

Repeating this procedure leads to the general expression

$$P_n = \left(\frac{\lambda}{\mu}\right)^n P_0 \qquad \text{for } n \geq 0.$$

Because the probabilities sum to unity, we find that if $\lambda/\mu < 1$,

$$P_0 = 1 - \frac{\lambda}{\mu}.$$

Thus, in general, the stochastic equilibrium occupancy probabilities are given by

$$P_n = \left(1 - \frac{\lambda}{\mu}\right) \left(\frac{\lambda}{\mu}\right)^n \qquad \text{for } n \geq 0. \qquad (3.8)$$

Note that $E[$number in system at time $t] \geq \lambda t - \mu t = (\lambda - \mu)t$ because $E[$ number of arrivals by time $t] = \lambda t$ and $E[$ number of service completions by time $t] \leq \mu t$. Thus, if $\lambda > \mu$, then $\lim_{t \to \infty} E$ [number in system at time t] grows beyond bound. So, in order to have an equilibrium solution, we cannot have $\lambda > \mu$; the arrival rate cannot exceed the service rate. In fact, for there to be an equilibrium solution, we actually need $\lambda < \mu$. To see why this is true intuitively, we can draw an analogy between the system occupancy and the position of a *random walker* on the nonnegative integers.

A random walker steps either to the left or right according to the following rules. If the walker is at position zero, one step to the right is taken with probability one. If the walker is not at position zero, then before taking a step, a coin is flipped. If the result is "heads," the walker steps one step to the right; else the walker takes one step to the left. Intuitively, it is clear that if the probability of "heads" exceeds one-half, then the walker tends to drift to the right. The longer the experiment continues, the further to the right we would expect the walker to be; no stochastic equilibrium distribution would be reached. On the other hand, if the probability of "heads" is less than one-half, then the walker tends to drift to the left. It would be possible for the walker to roam any distance to the right through a series of *heads* outcomes, but the positive tendency to move to the left would tend to return the walker to position zero occasionally. Thus one would expect a stochastic equilibrium solution to exist.

More formally, the position of the walker, measured in steps to the right from zero, is the state of an irreducible discrete-time Markov chain having a countable number of states. From the theory of Markov chains (see, for example, Wolff [1989]), it is well known that the states are *positive recurrent* if $P\{$heads$\} < 0.5$, *null recurrent* if $P\{$heads$\} = 0.5$, and *transient* if $P\{$heads$\} > 0.5$. An equilibrium solution exists if, and only if, all states are positive recurrent.

Exercise 3.1   Carefully pursue the analogy between the random walk and the occupancy of the M/M/1 queueing system. Determine the probability of an increase in the queue length, and show that this probability is less than 0.5 if and only if $\lambda < \mu$.

In the case of single-server queueing systems without state-dependent arrival and service rates, the quantity λ/μ is called the *traffic intensity*, and it is usually designated by ρ; that is, $\rho \equiv \lambda/\mu$. Since $\tilde{n}$ denotes the number of customers in the system at an arbitrary point in time after the system has reached stochastic equilibrium, and $P_n \equiv P\{\tilde{n} = n\}$, we have

$$P_n = \rho^n(1 - \rho). \tag{3.9}$$

The stability condition for the queueing system is then stated as $\rho < 1$.

From (3.9), we may find the probability that the total number in the system exceeds n. In particular,

$$P\{\tilde{n} > n\} = \sum_{j=n+1}^{\infty} \rho^j(1 - \rho) = \rho^{n+1}. \tag{3.10}$$

Graphs of the quantity $P\{\tilde{n} > n\}$, which is called the survivor function or complementary distribution for the number of customers in the system, are shown in Figure 3.1 for several values of traffic intensity. From these graphs we see that as traffic intensity nears unity, relatively small changes in traffic intensity result in large changes in the probability that the occupancy exceeds a given value. For example, at $\rho = 0.9$, $P\{\tilde{n} > 40\} \approx 0.01$, but at $\rho = 0.95$, $P\{\tilde{n} > 40\} > 0.1$. These probabilities are not to be confused with blocking probabilities, which are discussed in a later section.

We now turn to the computation of averages for the number in the system and the time spent in the system. In order to compute average values, we shall make use of the following theorem, the proof of which we leave to the exercises.

Theorem 3.1   Let $\tilde{x}$ be a nonnegative integer-valued random variable. Then

$$E[\tilde{x}] = \sum_{n=0}^{\infty} P\{\tilde{x} > n\}. \qquad \square$$

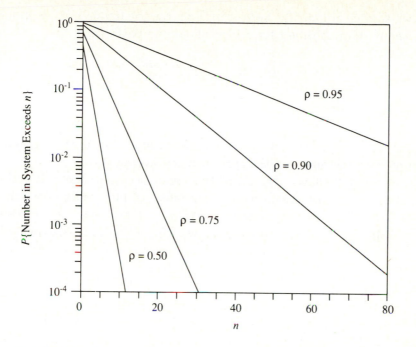

Figure 3.1 Survivor function for system occupancy for several values of ρ.

Exercise 3.2   Prove Theorem 3.1 and its continuous analog

$$E[\tilde{x}] = \int_0^\infty P\{\tilde{x} > x\} \, dx.$$

From Theorem 3.1, we find

$$E[\tilde{n}] = \sum_{n=0}^\infty P\{\tilde{n} > n\}.$$

Thus, upon substitution of (3.10) into this equation, we find

$$E[\tilde{n}] = \frac{\rho}{1-\rho}. \tag{3.11}$$

If we assume ergodicity[1] and let $n(t)$ denote the number of customers in the system at time t for a typical sample path, then

$$E[\tilde{n}] \triangleq \lim_{t \to \infty} \frac{\int_0^t n(s)ds}{t}$$

$$= \frac{\rho}{1 - \rho}.$$

That is, for a particular system under study, $E[\tilde{n}]$ is the expected number of customers in the system when averaged over time.

Figure 3.2 shows a graph of the mean occupancy as a function of traffic intensity. Again we see the effect of increasing occupancy due to increasing traffic intensity. As $\rho \to 1$ and the system nears instability, the mean occupancy grows without bound, as expected.

Another quantity of interest is the sojourn time, the total time customers spend in the system, including both waiting time and service time. Following our notation of Chapter 2, let $\tilde{s}$ denote the stochastic equilibrium value for this quantity, with $F_{\tilde{s}}$ being its distribution. The set of events $\{\tilde{n} = n, \ n = 0, \ 1 \ \ldots\}$ partitions the sample space, so we have

$$E[\tilde{s}] = \sum_{n=0}^{\infty} E[\tilde{s} \mid \tilde{n} = n]P\{\tilde{n} = n\}. \qquad (3.12)$$

Now, the sojourn time is measured from the time an *arbitrary arriving customer* enters the system, but $\tilde{n}$ represents the view of an *arbitrary observer*. The following exercise illustrates that these points of view are not necessarily the same.

Exercise 3.3   Suppose customers arrive to a system at the end of every even-numbered second and each customer requires exactly one second of service. Compute the stochastic equilibrium occupancy distribution, that is, the time-averaged distribution of the number of customers found in the system. Compute the occupancy distribution

---

[1] Ergodicity is a very technical concept, but basically it implies that time averages are equal to ensemble averages. That is, if we collect statistics at a single point in time from a large number of systems that are operating in stochastic equilibrium, then those measurements will be statistically the same as measurements taken from a single system over a long period of time.

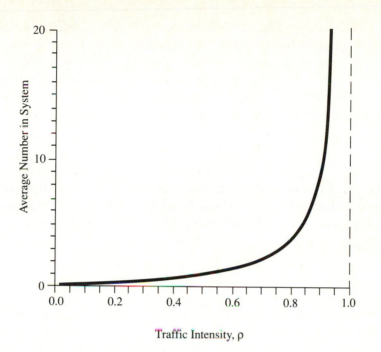

Figure 3.2 Average system occupancy as a function of ρ.

as seen by arriving customers. Compare the two distributions. Are they the same?

The following exercise shows that for the special case of the M/M/1 queueing system, the limiting distribution of the number of customers seen by a departing customer is equal to the limiting distribution of the number of customers found in the system by arriving customers, and these distributions are both equal to the stochastic equilibrium distribution. Thus, for the M/M/1 queueing system, the arrivals see the stochastic equilibrium occupancy distribution as given in (3.8). However, before presenting the exercise, we introduce some definitions and notation.

Define $\tilde{n}_d(k)$, for $k = 1, 2, \ldots$, to be the number of customers left in the system by the kth departing customer, and define

$$\pi_{dj} = \lim_{k \to \infty} P\{\tilde{n}_d(k) = j\}, \qquad \text{for } j = 0, 1, \ldots.$$

Then the process $\{\tilde{n}_d(k), \; k = 1, \; 2, \; \ldots\}$ is a discrete parameter Markov chain defined on the nonnegative integers and is called an embedded Markov chain. In particular, the process $\{\tilde{n}_d(k), \; k = 1, \; 2, \; \ldots\}$ is called the *occupancy process embedded at points immediately following customer departure*. For $\lambda < \mu$, the stationary probability vector, $\pi_d = [\pi_{d0} \quad \pi_{d1} \quad \cdots]$, exists and satisfies the system

$$\pi_d = \pi_d \mathcal{P}_d \quad \text{with} \quad \pi_d e = 1,$$

where $\mathcal{P}_d$ is the one-step transition probability matrix (Ross [1989]) for the embedded Markov chain $\{\tilde{n}_d(k), \; k = 1, \; 2, \; \ldots\}$ and e is the column vector in which each element is unity. For $i, \; j = 0, \; 1, \; \ldots$, the probability

$$\mathcal{P}_{d_{ij}} = P\{\tilde{n}_d(k+1) = j|\tilde{n}_d(k) = i\}$$

is called the one-step transition probability from state i to state j. We note that $P\{\tilde{n}_d(k+1) = j|\tilde{n}_d(k) = i\}$ is simply the probability of having exactly $j - (i-1)^+$ arrivals during the $(k+1)$th service time, where $(c)^+ = \max\{0, \; c\}$. Given the properties of the exponential distribution, we can readily determine the transition probabilities. For example, for $j = 0, \; 1, \; \ldots$,

$$\mathcal{P}_{d_{0j}} = \mathcal{P}_{d_{1j}} = \left(\frac{\lambda}{\lambda + \mu}\right)^j \left(\frac{\mu}{\lambda + \mu}\right).$$

Similarly, define $\tilde{n}_a(k)$, for $k = 1, \; 2, \; \ldots$, to be the number of customers found in the system by the kth arriving customer and

$$\pi_{aj} = \lim_{k \to \infty} P\{\tilde{n}_a(k) = j\} \quad \text{for} \quad j = 0, \; 1, \; \ldots.$$

Then the process $\{\tilde{n}_a(k), \; k = 1, \; 2, \; \ldots\}$ is called the *occupancy process embedded at points immediately prior to customer arrival*. Again, for $\lambda < \mu$, the vector $\pi_a = [\pi_{a0} \quad \pi_{a1} \quad \cdots]$ exists and satisfies the system

$$\pi_a = \pi_a \mathcal{P}_a \quad \text{with} \quad \pi_a e = 1,$$

where $\mathcal{P}_a$ is the one-step transition probability matrix for the embedded Markov chain $\{\tilde{n}_a(k), \; k = 1, \; 2, \; \ldots\}$. In this case, $P\{\tilde{n}_a(k+1) = j|\tilde{n}_d(k) = i\}$ is simply the probability of having exactly $i + 1 - j$ service completions during the $(k+1)$th interarrival time for $j = 0, 1, \ldots, i+1$; for $j > i + 1$, this probability is equal to zero.

Exercise 3.4   For the ordinary M/M/1 queueing system, determine the limiting distribution of the system occupancy

1. as seen by departing customers. [*Hint:* Form the system of equations $\pi_d = \pi_d \mathcal{P}_d$, and then solve the system as was done to obtain $P\{\tilde{n} = n\}$.]

2. as seen by arriving customers. [*Hint:* First form the system of equations $\pi_a = \pi_a \mathcal{P}_a$, and then try the solution $\pi_a = \pi_d$.]

3. at instants of time at which the occupancy changes. That is, embed a Markov chain at the instants at which the occupancy changes, defining the state to be the number of customers in the system immediately following the state change. Define $\pi = [\pi_0 \quad \pi_1 \quad \cdots]$ to be the stationary probability vector, and define P to be the one-step transition probability matrix for this embedded Markov chain. Determine π, and then compute the stochastic equilibrium distribution for the process $\{\tilde{n}(t), t \geq 0\}$ according to the following well known result from the theory of Markov chains (Wolff [1989]), pp. 215–216:

$$P_i = \frac{\pi_i E[\tilde{s}_i]}{\displaystyle\sum_{i=0}^{\infty} \pi_i E[\tilde{s}_i]},$$

where $\tilde{s}_i$ denotes the time the systems spend in state i on each visit.

Observe that the results of parts (1), (2), and (3) are identical, and that these are all equal to the stochastic equilibrium occupancy probabilities determined previously.

The results of the above exercise have several implications. First, the stationary departure and arrival distributions are equal. That is, for any n, the proportion of departing customers who leave n customers in the system must equal the proportion of arriving customers who find n customers in the system. A little thought will reveal that this must be the case for systems in which arrivals and departures occur one by one. Suppose, for example, an arriving customer finds n customers in the system. This represents a change in system occupancy from n to $n+1$. If there is ever to be another transition in system occupancy from n to $n+1$, then there must be a transition from $n+1$ to n in the interim. This means that the actual number of departures who find n in the system can never differ by more than one from the number of arrivals that find n in the system. In the limit as time goes to infinity, the two proportions must then be equal. For a formal proof, see Cooper [1981].

The second implication is that the stationary arrival and stochastic equilibrium distributions are equal in the case of the M/M/1 queue. This is a special case of the well known result in queueing theory: Poisson arrivals see time averages (PASTA) (see Wolff [1970,1982]), where time averages imply stochastic equilibrium distributions for ergodic systems. The PASTA property and a more general property, arrivals see time averages (ASTA), and its implications are discussed in detail in Melamed and Whitt [1990] and the references therein. For completeness, the reader is also referred to Green and Melamed [1990] and Wolff [1990] for discussions of Anti-PASTA, all arrivals do not see time averages. These articles are of only peripheral interest to our current discussion, except for the fact that the equivalence between stochastic equilibrium behavior and the behavior of the system as viewed by an arbitrary arrival is highly dependent on the nature of the arrival process and is, in general, not a system property.

Returning to our discussion of sojourn times, we find that because the service times are exponentially distributed with parameter μ, $E[\tilde{s} \mid \tilde{n} = n] = (n+1)/\mu$. By substituting this expression and (3.8) into (3.12), we find that

$$E[\tilde{s}] = \frac{1}{\mu - \lambda} = \frac{1/\mu}{1 - \rho}. \tag{3.13}$$

From (3.13) we see that the mean sojourn time displays the same kind of exponential increase as does the mean system occupancy as $\rho \to 1$.

Now, from (3.11) and (3.13), we see that

$$\frac{E[\tilde{n}]}{E[\tilde{s}]} = \frac{\rho}{1 - \rho} \bigg/ \left(\frac{1/\mu}{1 - \rho} \right) = \lambda$$

or, equivalently,

$$E[\tilde{n}] = \lambda E[\tilde{s}] \qquad (3.14)$$

The relationship (3.14) is usually written $L = \lambda W$ and is called *Little's result* (Little [1961]). Although we obtained this relationship for the M/M/1 queueing system, it is also true for most other complex queueing systems. The more general statement of Little's result is now stated as a theorem.

Theorem 3.2   Little's Result.   The expected number of customers in the *system* is equal to the product of the arrival rate of customers entering the system and the expected amount of time customers spend in the system.   □

The system need not be an entire service system; for example, the system can be defined as the server only or the waiting line only. In a network of queues, the system may include the entire network or all the servers of the network. For the purposes of this theorem, the arrival rate is defined as the average number of entities that enter the system per unit of time.

The primary constraint for the applicability of Little's result is that the notion of a time average for the quantities of interest must make sense in the system under consideration. This is always true if the stochastic processes of interest have a stochastic equilibrium distribution. Of course, in order to obtain correct results, a great deal of care must be taken to assure that L, λ, and W are all defined properly for exactly the same *system*.

As an example, let $\tilde{n}_q$ denote the number of customers in the queue (that is, the number of customers in the system not including the one in service, if any), let $\tilde{w}$ denote the waiting time of the customers in the queue, and let λ_q denote the arrival rate of the customers to the queue. Then, from Little's result, $E[\tilde{n}_q] = \lambda_q E[\tilde{w}]$.

By using Little's result, we can derive the mean waiting time in the system in a straightforward and intuitive manner as follows. It is left as an exercise to show that the probability that the server is busy is given by the quantity ρ. Now, a customer who has just arrived to the queue has to wait an average of $1/\mu$ for each customer in the queue and $1/\mu$ for the customer in service, if any.

Thus

$$E[\tilde{w}] = \frac{1}{\mu}E[\tilde{n}_q] + \frac{1}{\mu}\rho.$$

But $E[\tilde{n}_q] = \lambda E[\tilde{w}]$, so

$$E[\tilde{w}] = \frac{1}{\mu}\lambda E[\tilde{w}] + \frac{1}{\mu}\rho.$$

Solving for $E[\tilde{w}]$, we find

$$E[\tilde{w}] = \frac{1}{\mu}\frac{\rho}{1-\rho}. \qquad (3.15)$$

Exercise 3.5   Using Little's result, show that the probability that the server is busy at an arbitrary point in time is equal to the quantity (λ/μ).

   We now provide a proof of Little's result, which is not altogether rigorous, but which captures the basic elements of a rigorous proof. For more rigorous proofs, the reader is referred to the references following the current version.

Proof   Little's Result.   Customers accumulate system time linearly while they are in the system. Let $N(t)$ denote the number of customers in the system at time t for a typical sample path; the total amount of time in the system accumulated by all customers up to time τ is then given by

$$\int_0^\tau N(t)\,dt.$$

Also, let $T_i(\tau)$ denote the amount of time the ith customer spends in the system up to time τ, and let $M(\tau)$ denote the total number of customers who have arrived to the system by time τ. Then the total time spent in the system up to time τ by all customers is given by

$$\sum_{i=0}^{M(\tau)} T_i(\tau).$$

Thus, for any given sample path, it is always true that

$$\sum_{i=0}^{M(\tau)} T_i(\tau) = \int_0^{\tau} N(t)\,dt. \tag{3.16}$$

Now, so long as $\tau > 0$, we can divide both sides of (3.16) by τ. Also, so long as $M(\tau) > 0$, we may multiply the numerator and denominator of (3.16) by $M(\tau)$. It thus follows that

$$\frac{M(\tau)}{\tau}\,\frac{1}{M(\tau)}\sum_{i=0}^{M(\tau)} T_i(\tau) = \frac{1}{\tau}\int_0^{\tau} N(t)\,dt. \tag{3.17}$$

If the system has a stochastic equilibrium, then it is clear that

$$\lim_{\tau\to\infty}\frac{M(\tau)}{\tau},$$

$$\lim_{\tau\to\infty}\frac{1}{M(\tau)}\sum_{i=0}^{M(\tau)} T_i(\tau),$$

and

$$\lim_{\tau\to\infty}\frac{1}{\tau}\int_0^{\tau} N(t)\,dt$$

all exist individually. The first limit expression above defines λ, the second defines $E[\tilde{s}]$, and the third defines $E[\tilde{n}]$. Thus, Little's result follows by taking limits as $\tau\to\infty$ on both sides of (3.17).   □

Note that there is no assumption here about the form of the interarrival-time distribution or the service-time distribution. A somewhat different (heuristic) proof due to Paul Burke is given in Cooper [1972, 1981], and more formal proofs are given in Little [1961], Jewell [1967], and Stidham [1974].

We now turn to the derivation of the equilibrium system sojourn-time distribution $P\{\tilde{s} \leq x\}$, which we shall denote by $F_{\tilde{s}}(x)$. Consider the sojourn time of an arbitrary customer, the *tagged customer*, who arrives at the system at an arbitrary point in time, t_0, after the system has reached stochastic equilibrium. Now, the arrivals to the system, being Poisson, see the system in stochastic equilibrium. Hence the probability that the tagged customer finds n customers in the system is $P\{\tilde{n} = n\}$. Also, the service times are independently drawn from a memoryless distribution, and therefore the sojourn time of the tagged customer, given the tagged customer finds n customers in the system, can be expressed as the sum of $n + 1$ independent service times. In particular,

$$\tilde{s} \mid \{\tilde{n} = n\} = \sum_{i=1}^{n+1} \tilde{x}_i$$

where $\tilde{x}_i$ denotes the service time of the ith customer to receive service after time t_0, with the $(n + 1)$th service being that of the tagged customer.[2] Thus we have

$$
\begin{aligned}
E\left[e^{-s\tilde{s}}\right] &= \sum_{n=0}^{\infty} E\left[e^{-s\tilde{s}} \mid \tilde{n} = n\right] P\{\tilde{n} = n\} \\
&= \sum_{n=0}^{\infty} E\left[e^{-s\sum_{i=1}^{n+1}\tilde{x}_i}\right] P\{\tilde{n} = n\} \\
&= \sum_{n=0}^{\infty} E^{n+1}\left[e^{-s\tilde{x}_i}\right] (1 - \rho)\rho^n \\
&= (1 - \rho)E\left[e^{-s\tilde{x}_i}\right] \frac{1}{1 - \rho E\left[e^{-s\tilde{x}_i}\right]},
\end{aligned}
\tag{3.18}
$$

where the equality between the second and third steps results from the fact that $e^{-s\tilde{x}_i}$ and $e^{-s\tilde{x}_j}$ for $i \neq j$ are independent random variables, and the expectation of the product of independent random variables is the product of the expectations of the individual random variables.

We showed earlier that if $\tilde{x}$ is an exponentially distributed random variable with parameter α, then

$$E\left[e^{-s\tilde{x}}\right] = \frac{\alpha}{s + \alpha}.$$

---

[2]In general, the notation $\tilde{z} = \{\tilde{x}|E\}$, where $\tilde{x}$ and $\tilde{z}$ are random variables and E is an event, means that $P\{\tilde{z} \leq z\} = P\{\tilde{x} \leq z|E\}$.

Because the service times are drawn from exponential distributions with parameter μ, we find $E\left[e^{-s\tilde{x}_i}\right] = \mu/(s+\mu)$ so that

$$E\left[e^{-s\tilde{s}}\right] = \frac{(1-\rho)\mu}{s+\mu}\frac{1}{1-[\rho\mu/(s+\mu)]}$$
$$= \frac{(1-\rho)\mu}{s+(1-\rho)\mu}.$$

(3.19)

Thus we find that $\tilde{s}$ has the exponential distribution with parameter $(1-\rho)\mu$, and

$$F_{\tilde{s}}(x) = 1 - e^{-\mu(1-\rho)x}, \qquad \text{for } x \geq 0.$$

(3.20)

By following similar arguments, we can determine the distribution of the waiting time to be

$$F_{\tilde{w}}(x) = 1 - \rho e^{-\mu(1-\rho)x}, \qquad \text{for } x \geq 0.$$

(3.21)

This derivation is left as an exercise.

Exercise 3.6   Let $\tilde{w}$ and $\tilde{s}$ denote the length of time an arbitrary customer spends in the queue and in the system, respectively, in stochastic equilibrium. Let $F_{\tilde{s}}(x) \equiv P\{\tilde{s} \leq x\}$ and $F_{\tilde{w}}(x) \equiv P\{\tilde{w} \leq x\}$. Show that

$$F_{\tilde{s}}(x) = 1 - e^{-\mu(1-\rho)x}, \qquad \text{for } x \geq 0,$$

and

$$F_{\tilde{w}}(x) = 1 - \rho e^{-\mu(1-\rho)x}, \qquad \text{for } x \geq 0,$$

without resorting to the use of Laplace–Stieltjes transform techniques.

Another important stochastic process associated with the M/M/1 queueing system is its departure process. The characteristics of this process are now briefly addressed. For a much more detailed treatment, the reader is referred to Disney and Kiessler [1987]. This process is also discussed in many other books on probabilistic modeling, including Ross [1989] and Bertsekas and Gallager [1987]. We shall see that the departure process from the M/M/1 system in stochastic equilibrium is Poisson with the same parameter as the arrival process. After presenting a definition and the main result, we provide a brief discussion of the implications.

Definition 3.1   Departure Process.   Let $\tilde{d}_i$ denote the time between the ith and the $(i+1)$th departures from a queueing system. Then $\tilde{d}_i$ is called the ith interdeparture time for the system. The process $\{\tilde{d}_i, \; i = 0, \; 1, \; \ldots\}$ is called the departure process. A typical interdeparture time will be denoted by $\tilde{d}$, and the distribution of $\tilde{d}$ will be denoted by $F_{\tilde{d}}$.   □

Theorem 3.3   Burke's Theorem (Burke [1956]).   The sequence of interdeparture times for the M/M/1 system in stochastic equilibrium is a sequence of independent, identically distributed exponential random variables with parameter identical to that of the arrival process; that is, the departure process from the M/M/1 queueing system having arrival rate λ is a Poisson process with parameter λ.   □

Exercise 3.7   M/M/1 Departure Process.   Show that the distribution of an arbitrary interdeparture time for the M/M/1 system in stochastic equilibrium is exponential with the same parameter as the interarrival-time distribution. Argue that the interdeparture times are independent so that the departure process for this system is Poisson with the same rate as the arrival process (Burke [1956]). [*Hint:* Use the fact that the Poisson arrival sees the system in stochastic equilibrium. Then condition on whether or not the ith departing customer leaves the system empty.]

Proof of Burke's theorem can be accomplished very simply by using the concept of *reversibility*. We now briefly sketch the main ideas. Consider a general stochastic process $\{\tilde{x}(t), \; t \geq 0\}$ for which a stochastic equilibrium distribution exists. To assure that system is operating in stochastic equilibrium, assume that the distribution of $\tilde{x}(0)$ is the same as the stochastic equilibrium distribution so that the time derivatives of the occupancy probabilities are all equal to zero. Now observe the probability structure of the process at a very large point in time, say t_0. If the probability structure of the process looking forward in time from t_0 is identical to the probability structure of the process looking backward in time from t_0, then the process is said to be time-reversible.

Ross[1989], pp. 277–278, provides a simple proof that all *birth–death processes* (which are defined in Section 3.2) are time-reversible. The occupancy process for the M/M/m system is a special case of a birth–death process and is therefore time-reversible. This means that for the M/M/m system, the instants at which the occupancy increases when looking backward in time have exactly the same probability structure as the instants at which the occupancy increases when looking forward in time. Now, the instants at which the occupancy increases when looking backward in time are exactly the instants of customer departure. Because the instants at which the occupancy increases when looking forward in time are the instants of arrivals from a Poisson process, we see that the departure process is also Poisson with the same parameter as the arrival process.

Remark.   It is interesting to note that when a queueing process is reversible, then the Markov chain embedded just after points of departure is the reverse process for the Markov chain embedded just prior to points of arrival. The stationary probabilities of the two embedded chains are then equal, as has been shown in the specific case of the M/M/1 system. The interested reader is referred to Ross[1989], pp. 173–184, for an elementary treatment of time-reversibility of Markov chains and to Disney and Kiessler [1987] p. 99, for a proof of the result given in this remark.

Since all birth–death processes are time reversible, we see that Burke's theorem applies not only to single-server queueing systems but also to the M/M/m and M/M/∞ systems as well. The implications of this theorem in analyzing the occupancy process for systems having Poisson arrivals and exponential service are significant. For example, we showed in Chapter 2 that sums of Poisson processes are Poisson, and randomly split Poisson processes form two independent Poisson streams. Because the departure processes are also Poisson, complex systems of exponential servers can be analyzed by first determining the average arrival rates to each of the queues, and then analyzing the individual queues independently. The results of the independent analyses are then combined to analyze the system as a whole.

Poisson Arrivals　　　Exponential Service　　　Exponential Service　　　Exponential Service
　Rate λ　　　　　　　　Rate μ　　　　　　　　Rate α　　　　　　　　Rate ß

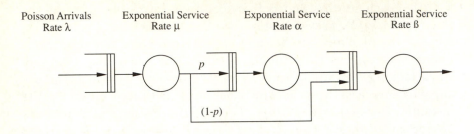

Figure 3.3 Block diagram for simple network of queues.

We now provide a simple example, leaving to a later section a more general treatment of networks of queues.

Example 3.1　Consider the system of Figure 3.3. Exogenous arrivals (that is, from outside the system) occur according to a Poisson process at rate λ to an exponential server having service rate μ. Following service, each customer decides with probability p, independently of everything, whether or not to enter the second service system, which has exponential service with rate α. Customers who decide not to enter the second service system proceed immediately to the third system, which has service rate β. There, they join the waiting line along with customers departing the second service system. We wish to determine the joint equilibrium state occupancy distribution for the three queues.

Solution:　Because the departure process from the first queue is Poisson with rate λ, arrivals to the second queue are Poisson with rate $p\lambda$. The departure process from the second queue is therefore Poisson with rate $p\lambda$, and this process is independent of the process due to customers who decide not to enter the second system. The stream of customers entering the third service system is the result of combining independent Poisson streams with rates $p\lambda$ and $(1-p)\lambda$, and is therefore Poisson with rate λ.

Stochastic equilibrium exists if $\lambda < \max\{\mu, \alpha, \beta\}$, and, in that case,

$$P\{\tilde{n}_1 = n_1\} = (1 - \lambda/\mu)(\lambda/\mu)^{n_1},$$
$$P\{\tilde{n}_2 = n_2\} = (1 - p\lambda/\alpha)(p\lambda/\alpha)^{n_2},$$

and

$$P\{\tilde{n}_3 = n_3\} = (1 - \lambda/\beta)(\lambda/\beta)^{n_3},$$

where $\tilde{n}_i$ denotes the occupancy at queue i. The joint queue length distribution is then the product of the individual occupancy distributions. ∎

It is worth pausing at this point to reflect on the implications of Burke's theorem. Although Burke's theorem does state that the interdeparture times are a sequence of *iid* exponential random variables, the theorem does not say that the departure process is independent of the state of the occupancy process.

In Example 3.1, the fact that the joint probability mass function for the occupancies of the three servers is given by the product of the marginal mass probabilities means that the server occupancies are independent random variables. On the other hand, the waiting times at the servers are not independent because the interdeparture times from a given server are not independent of the occupancy of that server, and the waiting time at the server is dependent upon the occupancy at that node. Finally, sojourn times of customers at each node are independent.

The result is that joint occupancies, the waiting-time distribution at individual servers, and average network delays can be computed via elementary analysis, but higher moments of network delay are more difficult to obtain. Thus we must exercise extreme care in drawing deep conclusions from elementary analysis of this form.

The following exercise emphasizes that a knowledge of the ergodic occupancy distribution for even a simple queueing system is insufficient information from which to compute the waiting-time distribution. The interested reader is referred to Disney and Kiessler [1987] for a more thorough discussion. We note that the aggregate arrival process (that is, including feedback) to the queue defined in this exercise is not a Poisson process (see Disney, McNickle, and Simon [1980] and Disney and Kiessler [1987], pp. 124–125).

Exercise 3.8 **M/M/1 with Instantaneous Feedback.** A queueing system has exogenous Poisson arrivals with rate λ and exponential service with rate μ. At the instant of service completion, each potentially departing customer rejoins the service queue, independent of system state, with probability p.

1. Determine the distribution of the total amount of service time rendered to an arbitrary customer by the server.

2. Compute the distribution of the number of customers in the system in stochastic equilibrium. How does your solution compare to that of the M/M/1 queueing system? What explains this behavior? [*Hint*: Consider the remaining service time required for each customer in the queue. Suppose customers that required additional increments of service returned immediately to service rather than joining the tail of the queue. What would be the effect on the queue occupancy?]

3. Argue that the departure process from the system is a Poisson process with rate λ.

4. Compute the average sojourn time for this system and comment on computation of the distribution of the sojourn time.

3.1.3   Busy Period for M/M/1 Queueing System

Recall that $\tilde{n}(t)$ is defined to be the number of customers in the system at time t. The system is said to be idle at time t if $\tilde{n}(t) = 0$ and busy at time t if $\tilde{n}(t) > 0$. A busy period begins at any instant in time at which the value of $\tilde{n}(t)$ increases from zero to one and ends at the first instant in time, following entry into a busy period, at which the value of $\tilde{n}(t)$ again reaches zero. An idle period begins when a given busy period ends and ends when the next busy period begins. From the perspective of the server, the M/M/1 queueing system alternates between two distinct types of periods: *idle periods* and *busy periods*, as illustrated in Figure 3.4. These types are descriptive; the busy periods are periods during which the server is busy servicing customers, and the idle periods are those during which the server is not servicing customers. For the ordinary M/M/1 queueing system, the server is never idle when there is at least one customer in the system.

Because of the memoryless property of the exponential distribution and the Poisson process, the length of an idle period is the same as the length of time between two successive arrivals from a Poisson process with parameter λ. The length of a busy period, on the other hand is dependent upon both the arrival and service processes. The busy period begins upon the arrival of its first customer, say customer 1, whom we shall denote by C_1. During the service time of C_1, the length of which we shall denote by $\tilde{x}_1$, K_1 additional customers arrive. If $K_1 > 0$, we call the K_1 customers "second-generation customers" and denote them by C_{11}, C_{12}, $\ldots$, C_{1K_1}. The service times of these customers follow that of C_1 in their order of arrival. During the service time of C_{11}, additional customers may arrive. They are denoted by C_{111}, C_{112}, $\ldots$, $C_{11K_{11}}$.

Additional arrivals that occur during the service times of the ith second-generation customer are denoted by C_{1i1}, C_{1i2}, $\ldots$, $C_{1iK_{1i}}$, and the collection of all these customers constitutes the third generation. Service for third-generation customers follows completion of service of second-generation customers. Arrivals occurring while the nth-generation customers are receiving service are classed $(n+1)$th-generation customers, and their service begins following completion of nth-generation servicing. The service and arrival processes continue until there are no longer any remaining customers, and at that point in time the system returns to an idle period. Thus, the length of a busy period is the total amount of time required to service all of the customers of all of the generations of the first customer of the busy period. Consequently, we can think of the busy period as being *generated* by its first customer. Alternatively, we can view the server

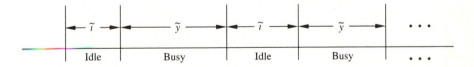

Figure 3.4 Sequence of idle and busy periods.

as having to work until all of the first customer's descendants die out.

We shall denote the length of a generic busy period by $\tilde{y}$, the length of a generic idle period by $\tilde{i}$, and the number of customers served during a generic busy period by $\tilde{h}$. The service time of the ith customer served in a generic busy period will be denoted by $\tilde{x}_i$. The length of the busy period is then the sum of the service times, or

$$\tilde{y} = \sum_{i=1}^{\tilde{h}} \tilde{x}_i. \tag{3.22}$$

The diagram of Figure 3.5 illustrates servicing during the busy period.

The distribution of the length of a busy period is of interest in its own right, but an understanding of the behavior of busy-period processes is also extremely helpful in understanding waiting time and queue length behavior in both ordinary and priority queueing systems. An alternative and instructive way to view the busy-period process is to separate the busy period into two parts: the part occurring before the first customer arrival after the busy period has started, and the part occurring after the first customer arrival after the busy period has started, if such an arrival occurs.

Let $\tilde{t}_1$ denote the length of the first interarrival time after the busy period has begun, and let $\mathcal{D}$ denote the event that the first customer completes service before the first arrival after the busy period begins; that is, let $\mathcal{D}$ denote the event that $\tilde{x}_1 < \tilde{t}_1$. Further, let $\tilde{z}_1 = \min\{\tilde{x}_1,\ \tilde{t}_1\}$.

We have shown previously that if $\tilde{x}_1$ and $\tilde{t}_1$ are exponentially distributed random variables with parameters μ and λ, respectively,

Figure 3.5 Sequence of service times during a generic busy period.

then $\tilde{z}_1$ is an exponentially distributed random variable with parameter $\mu + \lambda$. We also showed in an earlier exercise that the random variables $\tilde{z}_1 | \{\tilde{x}_1 < \tilde{t}_1\}$ and $\tilde{z}_1 | \{\tilde{x}_1 > \tilde{t}_1\}$ are also exponentially distributed random variables with parameter $\mu + \lambda$; that is, the distribution of the length of $\tilde{z}_1$ is independent of whether $\tilde{x}_1 < \tilde{t}_1$ or $\tilde{x}_1 > \tilde{t}_1$. Additionally, if $\tilde{x}_1 < \tilde{t}_1$, then the busy period ends after the initial interval, so that

$$\tilde{y} | \{\tilde{x}_1 < \tilde{t}_1\} = \tilde{z}_1. \tag{3.23}$$

On the other hand, if $\tilde{x}_1 > \tilde{t}_1$, then a period of length $\tilde{z}_1$ will have expired, but due to the memoryless property of the exponential distribution, the remaining service time of the first customer will be the same as it was initially. Thus, for all practical purposes, the service time starts over. The remaining time in the busy period is therefore equivalent to the length of a busy period in which there are initially two customers present rather than one. We denote the length of such a period by $\tilde{y}_2$. Thus we find that

$$\tilde{y} | \{\tilde{x}_1 > \tilde{t}_1\} = \tilde{z}_1 + \tilde{y}_2. \tag{3.24}$$

Now, the length of a busy period is independent of the order in which the customers of the busy period are served. The length of the busy period is simply the sum of the lengths of the service times of the customers that are served, as shown in (3.22) and Figure 3.5. A little thought will reveal that the length of the busy period generated by two customers is simply the sum of the lengths of the *sub-busy periods* generated by the first and second customers, respectively. That is,

$$\tilde{y}_2 = \tilde{y}_{21} + \tilde{y}_{22}, \tag{3.25}$$

where $\tilde{y}_{21}$ and $\tilde{y}_{22}$ denote the lengths of the sub-busy periods generated by the first and second customers, respectively. Additionally, $\tilde{y}_{21}$ and $\tilde{y}_{22}$ are independent, and their distributions are the same as that of an ordinary busy period, $\tilde{y}$. Figure 3.6 illustrates the decomposition of the busy period from this point of view.

We now turn our attention to the determination of $E[\tilde{y}]$. We define $\mathcal{A}$ as the complement of $\mathcal{D}$. Then, upon conditioning on the occurrence or nonoccurrence of $\mathcal{D}$, we find

$$E[\tilde{y}] = E[\tilde{y} | \mathcal{D}] P\{\mathcal{D}\} + E[\tilde{y} | \mathcal{A}] P\{\mathcal{A}\}. \tag{3.26}$$

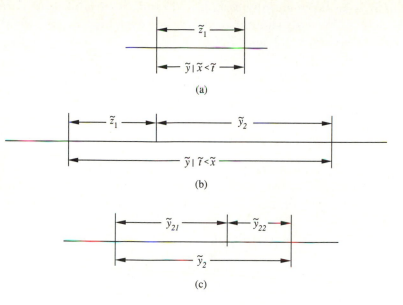

(a)

(b)

(c)

Figure 3.6 Busy-period decompositions depending upon interarrival versus service times: (a) service before arrival, (b) arrival before service, (c) decomposition of remaining busy period.

Upon substituting (3.23), (3.24), and (3.25) into (3.26), we find that

$$E[\tilde{y}] = E[\tilde{z}_1]P\{\mathcal{D}\} + E[\tilde{z}_1 + \tilde{y}_{21} + \tilde{y}_{22}]P\{\mathcal{A}\}. \qquad (3.27)$$

Using the fact that $\tilde{y}_{21}$ and $\tilde{y}_{22}$ each have the same distribution as $\tilde{y}$ in (3.27), we get

$$E[\tilde{y}] = E[\tilde{z}_1] + 2E[\tilde{y}]P\{\mathcal{A}\}$$
$$= \frac{E[\tilde{z}_1]}{1 - 2P\{\mathcal{A}\}}. \qquad (3.28)$$

Also, we showed earlier that $P\{\mathcal{A}\} = \lambda/(\mu+\lambda)$ and $E[\tilde{z}_1] = 1/(\mu+\lambda)$. Substituting these values into (3.28) leads to

$$E[\tilde{y}] = \frac{1}{\mu}\frac{1}{1 - \lambda/\mu} \qquad (3.29)$$

or, equivalently,

$$E[\tilde{y}] = \frac{1/\mu}{1-\rho}. \qquad (3.30)$$

The techniques leading to (3.27) are extremely useful in busy-period analysis, and they can be applied to determine $E[\tilde{h}]$ and $E\left[e^{-s\tilde{y}}\right]$. The arguments are also useful in studying the behavior of other queueing disciplines, such as last-come-first-serve (LCFS). Examination of these aspects of busy-period analysis is left to the exercises.

Exercise 3.9   For the M/M/1 queueing system,

1. find $E[\tilde{h}]$, the expected number of customers served in a busy period.

2. find $E[e^{-s\tilde{y}}]$, the Laplace–Stieltjes transform of the distribution of the length of a busy period. Show that $(d/dy)F_{\tilde{y}}(y) = 1/(y\sqrt{\rho})e^{-(\lambda+\mu)y}I_1(2y\sqrt{\lambda\mu})$. A Laplace transform pair,

$$\frac{\sqrt{s+2a}-\sqrt{s}}{\sqrt{s+2a}+\sqrt{s}} \Longleftrightarrow \frac{1}{t}e^{-at}I_1(at),$$

taken from *Mathematical Tables from Handbook of Chemistry and Physics*, will be useful in accomplishing this exercise.

We have previously stated that

$$\tilde{y} = \sum_{i=1}^{\tilde{h}} \tilde{x}_i. \qquad (3.31)$$

Given the formula for the expected length of the busy period, we can readily determine the expected number of customers served during a busy period through the application of *Wald's equation* (Ross[1989]), which states that the expected value of the sum of a random number, $\tilde{n}$, of identically distributed random variables, $\tilde{x}_i$, $0 \leq i \leq \tilde{n}$, is given by the product of the expected values of $\tilde{n}$ and $\tilde{x}_i$ provided that $\tilde{n}$ is a *stopping time* for the sequence of random variables $\{\tilde{x}_i,\ i =$

1, 2, ...}. For $\tilde{n}$ to be a stopping time for the sequence $\{\tilde{x}_i, \ i = 1, 2, \ldots\}$, it is sufficient to show that $\tilde{n}$ is independent of $\tilde{x}_{N+1}$.[3]

Exercise 3.10   For the M/M/1 queueing system, argue that $\tilde{h}$ is a stopping time for the sequence $\{\tilde{x}_i, \ i = 1, 2, \ldots\}$ illustrated in Figure 3.5. Find $E[\tilde{h}]$ by using the results given above for $E[\tilde{y}]$ in combination with Wald's equation.

Exercise 3.11   For the M/M/1 queueing system, argue that $E[\tilde{s}]$, the expected amount of time a customer spends in the system, and the expected length of a busy period are equal. [*Hint*: Consider the expected waiting time of an arbitrary customer in the M/M/1 queueing system under a nonpreemptive LCFS and then use Little's result.]

Exercise 3.12   Let $\tilde{s}_{LCFS}$ denote the total amount of time an arbitrary customer spends in the M/M/1 queueing system under a nonpreemptive LCFS discipline. Determine the Laplace–Stieltjes transform for the distribution of $\tilde{s}_{LCFS}$.

Exercise 3.13   Determine the Laplace–Stieltjes transform for the length of the busy period for the M/M/2 queueing system, the system having Poisson arrivals, exponential service, two parallel servers, and an infinite waiting room capacity. [*Hint*: Condition on whether or not an arrival occurs prior to the completion of the first service of a busy period. Then note that there is a very close relationship between the time required to reduce the occupancy from two customers to one customer in the M/M/2 and the length of the busy period in the ordinary M/M/1 system.]

Exercise 3.14   We have shown that the number of arrivals from a Poisson process with parameter λ, that occur during an exponen-

---

[3]It is interesting to note that the last service time of a busy period is stochastically shorter than the other service times because the last service time contains no arrivals with probability one. However, the $\tilde{x}_i$ are still drawn independently from a common distribution in exactly the same way as a gambler's winnings on the *i*th game. The gambler always loses on the last game, but the winnings on the *i*th game are drawn before the game is played. Similarly, the *i*th service time is drawn from the common distribution before it is decided whether or not it is the last service time of the busy period.

tially distributed service time with parameter μ, is geometrically distributed with parameter $\mu/(\mu + \lambda)$; that is, the probability of n arrivals during a service time is given by $[\lambda/(\lambda + \mu)]^n[\mu/(\lambda + \mu)]$. Determine the mean length of the busy period by conditioning on the number of arrivals that occur during the first service time of the busy period. For example, let $\tilde{n}_1$ denote the number of arrivals that occur during the first service time, and start your solution with the statement

$$E[\tilde{y}] = \sum_{n=0}^{\infty} E[\tilde{y}|\tilde{n}_1 = n]P\{\tilde{n}_1 = n\}.$$

[*Hint*: The arrivals segment the service period into a sequence of intervals.]

3.2 DYNAMICAL EQUATIONS FOR A GENERAL BIRTH–DEATH PROCESS

A variation on the M/M/1 queueing system is a system with exponentially distributed interarrival times and service times, but having state-dependent arrival and service rates. The arrival rate when there are n customers in the system is λ_n, and the service rate when there are n customers in the system is μ_n. The occupancy for such a system is modeled by a general *birth–death*, or *birth-and-death*, *process*.

Examples of queueing systems for which the occupancy can be modeled by a birth–death process are numerous. For example, the M/M/s queueing system is the system having s servers, Poisson arrivals at rate λ, and exponential service at rate μ. In this system, the arrival rate λ is independent of the current occupancy, but the service rate is $n\mu$ if the occupancy is less than s and $s\mu$ if the occupancy equals or exceeds s; that is, $\lambda_i = \lambda$ for $i \geq 0$, but

$$\begin{cases} \mu_n = n\mu, & \text{for } n < s; \\ \mu_n = s\mu, & \text{for } n \geq s. \end{cases}$$

This model is useful in modeling a circuit switching system for a system in which a large population of users share a relatively small number of lines and the customers are allowed to join a queue while waiting for a line to become available. A variation of this system, the *Erlang loss system*, is considered in a later section.

Another example is the M/M/1//K queueing system. There is a finite population, K, of customers, each operating in a constant *think–wait–service* cycle. The length of time the customer remains in the *think* state is drawn from an exponential distribution with rate λ, independent of everything; a customer may generate a request for service only while in the *think* state. Upon departure from the think state, the customer joins the queue to await service. Upon reaching the head of the queue, the customer receives service, the length of which is drawn from an exponential distribution with rate μ. For this model, we find $\mu_n = \mu$, independent of occupancy, but $\lambda_n = (K-n)\lambda$ for $0 \leq n \leq K$.

The dynamical equations for the general birth–death process are the same as those for the M/M/1 queueing system except that the arrival and service rates are replaced by state-dependent arrival and service rates. The resulting dynamical equations, the development of which are left as an exercise, are as follows:

$$P_n'(t) = \begin{cases} -(\lambda_n + \mu_n)P_n(t) + \lambda_{n-1}P_{n-1}(t) + \\ \quad \mu_{n+1}P_{n+1}(t), & \text{for } n > 0; \\ \\ -\lambda_0 P_0(t) + \mu_1 P_1(t), & \text{for } n = 0. \end{cases} \qquad (3.32)$$

We shall consider special cases of birth–death processes when we study the balance-equation approach to solving elementary queueing systems.

Exercise 3.15   Suppose that the arrival and service time distributions are memoryless, but that their rates depend upon the number of customers in the system. Let the arrival rate when there are k customers in the system be λ_k, and let the service rate when there are k customers in the system be μ_k. Show that the dynamical equations are as follows:

$$P_n'(t) = \begin{cases} -(\lambda_n + \mu_n)P_n(t) + \lambda_{n-1}P_{n-1}(t) \\ \quad +\mu_{n+1}P_{n+1}(t), & \text{for } n > 0; \\ \\ -\lambda_0 P_0(t) + \mu_1 P_1(t), & \text{for } n = 0. \end{cases}$$

3.3   TIME-DEPENDENT STATE PROBABILITIES
FOR FINITE-STATE SYSTEMS

In this section, we discuss approaches for obtaining the time-dependent probabilities for the special case in which the queueing system can be modeled as a continuous-time, finite-state, Markov chain. Our discussion focuses on the finite-state birth–death process, but extensions to the more general case are obvious.

Two methods of analysis are discussed: classical eigensystem analysis, and *randomization*. The latter is also often referred to in the literature as *uniformization* for reasons stated at the end of this section. Following Grassmann [1990], we adopt the name *Jensen's method*, which Grassmann argues is more appropriate.

We limit the maximum queue occupancy to K. For this special case, we find that $\lambda_n = 0$ for $n \geq K$ and μ_n has an arbitrary value for $n > K$. Under these conditions, the system (3.32) leads to the following system of $(K+1)$ linear differential equations:

$$\frac{d}{dt}P(t) = P(t)Q, \qquad (3.33)$$

where $P(t)$ is the row vector of state probabilities,

$$P(t) = [\, P_0(t) \quad P_1(t) \quad \cdots \quad P_K(t)\,],$$

and

$$Q = \begin{bmatrix} -\lambda_0 & \lambda_0 & 0 & \cdots & 0 & 0 \\ \mu_1 & -(\lambda_1 + \mu_1) & \lambda_1 & \cdots & 0 & 0 \\ \vdots & \vdots & \vdots & \cdots & \vdots & \vdots \\ 0 & 0 & 0 & \cdots & -(\lambda_{K-1} + \mu_{K-1}) & \lambda_{K-1} \\ 0 & 0 & 0 & \cdots & \mu_K & -\mu_K \end{bmatrix}$$

is the infinitesimal generator matrix for the (finite) Markov chain $\{\tilde{n}(t),\ t \geq 0\}$ (Cohen [1969]).

It is well known and easily shown that the above equation has the general solution

$$P(t) = P(0)e^{Qt}, \qquad (3.34)$$

where $P(0)$ denotes the vector of initial state probabilities. Thus, at least in principle, we can easily determine the time-dependent state probabilities for particular values of t.

Remark. The form (3.34) of the solution to the vector first order differential equation (3.33) has inspired the development of numerous ways to evaluate the required matrix exponential. A summary of the most prominent of these is given in Moler and van Loan [1978]. Matrix exponentiation is not, however, necessarily the best way to solve for the time-dependent solution to (3.33). In fact, it may be faster, computationally, simply to solve (3.33) directly using a standard ordinary differential equations solution package. The reader is referred to Giffin [1978] for a pedagogical presentation of this subject matter. Grassmann [1990] provides a perspective on computational complexity issues and on the pros and cons of the various computational approaches. The expression (3.34) is, nonetheless, very useful in discussing the behavior of the solution.

3.3.1   Classical Approach

Observation of (3.33) reveals that Q is a tridiagonal matrix, and the off-diagonal terms have the same sign. Thus, the matrix Q is similar to the symmetric matrix $\hat{Q}$ in which the diagonal terms are the same as those of Q, and the off-diagonal elements are given by

$$\hat{q}_{i,i+1} = \sqrt{q_{i,i+1}q_{i+1,i}} \quad \text{for } i = 0, 1, \ldots, K-1 . \tag{3.35}$$

That is,

$$\hat{Q} = R^{-1}QR, \tag{3.36}$$

where

$$R = \text{diag}\left(1, \sqrt{\frac{q_{1,0}}{q_{0,1}}}, \sqrt{\frac{q_{1,0}}{q_{0,1}}\frac{q_{2,1}}{q_{1,2}}}, \ldots, \right.$$
$$\left.\sqrt{\frac{q_{1,0}}{q_{0,1}}\frac{q_{2,1}}{q_{1,2}} \cdots \frac{q_{K,K-1}}{q_{K-1,K}}}\right). \tag{3.37}$$

It is readily verified that the matrix $\hat{Q}$ is negative semidefinite (Noble and Daniel [1977]), so the eigenvalues of $\hat{Q}$, and therefore of Q, are nonpositive. In addition, the columns of Q sum to a null column vector, so one of the eigenvalues of Q is equal to zero. This means that $\lim_{t\to\infty} P(t)$ exists, and the maximum negative eigenvalue of Q determines the rate at which $P(t)$ converges to its limiting value. The inverse of this maximum negative eigenvalue is sometimes referred to as the *relaxation time* of the system (Keilson [1979]).

If the eigenvalues of Q are distinct, then Q is similar to a diagonal matrix with the eigenvalues as the diagonal elements. That is, we can write diag $(\sigma_0, \sigma_1, \ldots, \sigma_K) = \mathcal{M}^{-1} Q \mathcal{M}$ or, equivalently,

$$Q = \mathcal{M} \text{ diag } (\sigma_0, \sigma_1, \ldots, \sigma_K) \mathcal{M}^{-1}, \tag{3.38}$$

where $\mathcal{M}$ is a nonsingular matrix spanning the $(K+1)$-dimensional space, σ_i denotes the ith eigenvalue of Q, and $0 = \sigma_0 > \sigma_1 > \cdots > \sigma_K$. Indeed, the ith column of $\mathcal{M}$ is (proportional to) the eigenvector corresponding to σ_i. Thus we can rewrite (3.34) as

$$P(t) = P(0) \mathcal{M} \text{ diag } (e^{\sigma_0 t}, e^{\sigma_1 t}, \cdots, e^{\sigma_K t}) \mathcal{M}^{-1}. \tag{3.39}$$

Because the eigenvalues are all nonpositive and we have labeled them in decreasing order, we find that σ_1 determines the rate at which $P(t)$ converges to its equilibrium value P.

For example, suppose $K = 1$, $\lambda_0 = \lambda$, and $\mu_1 = \mu$. Then we have

$$\frac{d}{dt}[P_0(t) \quad P_1(t)] = [P_0(t) \quad P_1(t)] \begin{bmatrix} -\lambda & \lambda \\ \mu & -\mu \end{bmatrix}. \tag{3.40}$$

The eigenvalues of Q are found to be 0 and $-(\lambda + \mu)$, and their corresponding eigenvectors are proportional to $[1 \quad 1]^T$ and $[-\lambda \quad \mu]^T$, respectively. Thus we find

$$P(t) = [P_0(0) \quad P_1(0)] \begin{bmatrix} 1 & -\lambda \\ 1 & \mu \end{bmatrix} \begin{bmatrix} 1 & 0 \\ 0 & e^{-(\lambda+\mu)t} \end{bmatrix}$$

$$\begin{bmatrix} \mu/\mu+\lambda & \lambda/\mu+\lambda \\ -1/\mu+\lambda & 1/\mu+\lambda \end{bmatrix}. \tag{3.41}$$

The time-dependent state probabilities can be computed from (3.41).

In case the equilibrium probabilities are needed, we find

$$\lim_{t \to \infty} P(t) = [P_0(0) \quad P_1(0)] \begin{bmatrix} 1 & -\lambda \\ 1 & \mu \end{bmatrix} \begin{bmatrix} 1 & 0 \\ 0 & 0 \end{bmatrix}$$

$$\begin{bmatrix} \mu/\mu+\lambda & \lambda/\mu+\lambda \\ -1/\mu+\lambda & 1/\mu+\lambda \end{bmatrix} \tag{3.42}$$

$$= [\mu/\lambda+\mu \quad \lambda/\lambda+\mu],$$

which is as expected from direct evaluation of the equilibrium probabilities.

Example 3.2 Suppose $\mu = 1$, $\lambda = 0.6$, and $P(0) = [1 \quad 0]$. Then (3.41) and (3.42) reduce to

$$P(t) = [1 - 0.375e^{-1.6t} \quad 0.375(1 - e^{-1.6t})],$$

and

$$\lim_{t \to \infty} P(t) = [0.625 \quad 0.375].$$

Figure 3.7 shows graphs of $P_0(t)$ and $P_1(t)$ as a function of time. Note that the limiting values of $P_0(t)$ and $P_1(t)$ are reached to a very high degree of accuracy by the time $t = 4$, which is between six and seven times the quantity $1/(\mu + \lambda)$. ∎

In the above case, we note that the equilibrium probabilities are proportional to the left eigenvector of Q corresponding to the eigenvalue $\sigma_0 = 0$. To see that this is always the case, we consider

$$\lim_{t \to \infty} P'(t) = 0 = P Q.$$

That is,

$$P Q = 0.$$

By definition, if M_0 is a left eigenvector of Q corresponding to the eigenvalue σ_0, then

$$M_0 Q = \sigma_0 M_0.$$

But with $\sigma_0 = 0$,

$$M_0 Q = 0.$$

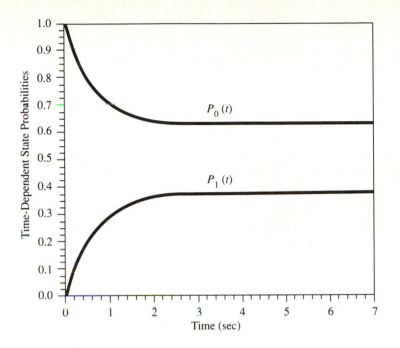

Figure 3.7 Time-dependent state probabilities for Example 3.2.

Thus P is proportional to M_0. The implication is that the equilibrium probabilities can always be determined by normalizing the left eigenvector of Q corresponding to the eigenvalue zero. Thus we find

$$P = \frac{1}{M_0 e} M_0, \tag{3.43}$$

where e is the column vector in which each element is unity.[4]

It is sometimes desirable to obtain the left eigenvectors of Q via hand calculation. With regard to this possibility, we state the following theorem.

Theorem 3.4   Let Q be a $(K+1)$-dimensional square matrix having

---

[4]We will use this definition for e in the remainder of the text.

distinct eigenvalues σ_0, σ_1, $\ldots$, σ_K and corresponding left eigenvectors M_0, M_1, $\ldots$, M_K, respectively. Then M_i is proportional to the rows of the adjoint of the matrix $(\sigma_i I - Q)$. That is,

$$\mathrm{adj}\,(\sigma_i I - Q) = \begin{bmatrix} c_0 M_i \\ c_1 M_i \\ \vdots \\ c_K M_i \end{bmatrix},$$

where c_0, c_1, $\ldots$, c_K are nonzero constants. $\square$

Theorem 3.5   Let Q be a $(K+1)$-dimensional square matrix having distinct eigenvalues σ_0, σ_1, $\ldots$, σ_K. Then the rows of $\mathrm{adj}\,(\sigma_i I - Q)$ are proportional to each other, and the columns of $\mathrm{adj}\,(\sigma_i I - Q)$ are proportional to each other. $\square$

The proofs of these theorems are left as exercises.

Exercise 3.16   Prove Theorem 3.4.

Exercise 3.17   Prove Theorem 3.5.

Exercise 3.18   Let $K = 1$. Use definition 2 of the Poisson process to write an equation of the form

$$\frac{d}{dt} [P_0(t) \quad P_1(t)] = [P_0(t) \quad P_1(t)] Q.$$

Show that the eigenvalues of the matrix Q are real and nonnegative. Solve the equation for $P_0(t)$ and $P_1(t)$ and show that they converge to the solution given in Example 3.2 regardless of the values $P_0(0)$, $P_1(0)$. [*Hint*: First, do a similarity transformation on the matrix Q, which converts the matrix to a symmetric matrix $\hat{Q}$. Then show that the matrix $\hat{Q}$ is negative semi-definite.]

3.3.2   Jensen's Method

An alternative method of computing the time-dependent probabilities can be formulated via the introduction of some additional state transitions into the dynamics of the system in such a way as to *uniformize* the amount of time the system spends in each state.

That is, we introduce self transitions into each state so that the amount of time spent in each state, on each visit, is exponentially distributed with identical parameter, say ν. This will allow us to study the system as though it were a discrete-time Markov chain with the transition epochs occurring according to a Poisson process with parameter ν. The latter is referred to as *randomization of time*.

Mathematically, we proceed as follows. First, we rewrite (3.34) as

$$P(t) = P(0) \; e^{(-\nu I + \nu I + Q)t}. \tag{3.44}$$

Then, because $\nu I t$ commutes with $(\nu I + Q)t$, then so do $e^{\nu I t}$ and $e^{\{\nu I + Q\}t}$. Thus the right-hand side of (3.44) can be rewritten as the product of two matrices:

$$P(t) = P(0) \; e^{-\nu I t} e^{(\nu I + Q)t}. \tag{3.45}$$

But, because $e^{\nu I t} = e^{\nu t} I$, we find that

$$P(t) = P(0) e^{-\nu t} e^{\nu [I + (1/\nu)Q]t}. \tag{3.46}$$

Expanding the matrix exponential on the right-hand side of (3.46) in a Maclaurin series, we obtain

$$P(t) = P(0) e^{-\nu t} \sum_{n=0}^{\infty} \frac{1}{n!} \left[\nu \{ I + \frac{1}{\nu} Q \} t \right]^n. \tag{3.47}$$

Upon regrouping the terms of (3.47), we find

$$P(t) = P(0) \sum_{n=0}^{\infty} \frac{(\nu t)^n}{n!} e^{-\nu t} \left(I + \frac{1}{\nu} Q \right)^n. \tag{3.48}$$

In terms of our former description, we can view (3.48) as describing the dynamics of a discrete-time Markov chain having state transition probability matrix $[I + (1/\nu)Q]$ and whose transition epochs are generated according to a Poisson process with rate ν. That is, the probability of n transitions in a period of length t is given by $(\nu t)^n e^{-\nu t}/n!$, the n-step transition matrix is $[I + (1/\nu)Q]^n$, and the initial state probabilities are given by $P(0)$.

For the above interpretation to be valid, we must have ν at least as large as the magnitude of the maximal term on the diagonal of Q because the diagonal terms of the matrix $[I + (1/\nu)Q]$ must be nonnegative. These terms are simply $1 + q_{ii}/\nu$, where q_{ij} represents the (i, j)th term of the Q matrix. The term q_{ii} represents the (exponential) rate at which the system departs state i, whenever it is in state i, and the term $1 + q_{ii}/\nu$ represents the probability that the system will return immediately to state i upon its departure. The terms q_{ij}/ν represent the probability of entering state j given a departure from state i, and q_{ij} denotes the rate at which the system enters state j from state i.

To illustrate what is happening here, consider the M/M/1 queueing system with a maximum occupancy of 1, as before. Then, from (3.40), we find

$$Q = \begin{bmatrix} -\lambda & \lambda \\ \mu & -\mu \end{bmatrix}, \tag{3.49}$$

and

$$\left(I + \frac{1}{\nu}Q\right) = \begin{bmatrix} 1 - \lambda/\nu & \lambda/\nu \\ \mu/\nu & 1 - \mu/\nu \end{bmatrix}. \tag{3.50}$$

Assuming $\lambda < \mu$, which is not required in this case, let us choose $\nu = \mu$. Then we find

$$\left(I + \frac{1}{\nu}Q\right) = \begin{bmatrix} 1 - \rho & \rho \\ 1 & 0 \end{bmatrix}. \tag{3.51}$$

Figure 3.8 illustrates the randomization process. The original state diagram for the M/M/1 system with finite waiting room of capacity 1 is shown in Figure 3.8(a). In Figure 3.8(b), additional self transitions have been added to each state such that the total departure rate from each state is ν. In Figure 3.8(c), time is scaled so that the mean occupancy time in each state on each visit is unity. Finally, in Figure 3.8(d), ν is chosen to be μ so that the resulting diagram corresponds to the above example.

Thus, in the randomized system, the system always returns to state 0 whenever it leaves state 1, just as it does in the real system; but the system also returns immediately to state 0 whenever it departs state 0 with probability $1 - \rho$, unlike in the real system.

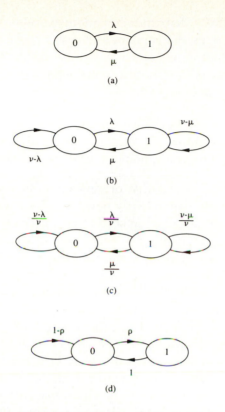

(a)

(b)

(c)

(d)

Figure 3.8 (a) State diagram for the original system; (b) addition of self transitions to
the original state diagram; (c) time
scaling of the modified state diagram;
(d) choosing $\nu = \mu$ in the modified
state diagram.

The system therefore returns to state 0 a geometric number of times,
with the probability of departure equal to ρ, before entering state 1.

The rate at which the system departs state 0 is μ, so that the
sojourn time in state 0 is exponential with rate μ. Thus the total
amount of time spent in state 0 before returning to state 1 is the
geometric, parameter ρ, sum of exponentials at rate μ. We have
shown that the latter quantity of time is exponentially distributed
with rate $\rho\mu = \lambda$, where we have used the fact that the geometric

sum of exponentially distributed random variables is exponentially distributed. Thus, in the randomized system, the sojourn time on each visit to each state is exponential, rate μ, but the total amount of time that the system spends in a state before it enters a different state is the same as that of the original system.

Exercise 3.19 For the specific example given here, show that the equilibrium probabilities for the embedded Markov chain are the same as those for the continuous-time Markov chain.

Randomization apparently originated with Jensen [1953] but seems to have been independently developed by Keilson and Wishart [1965]. It has been described in several recent books, including Keilson [1979] and Ross [1989]. The technique has been applied to the study of numerous systems in areas ranging from software reliability (Sumita and Shanthikumar [1986]) to local area networks (Beuerman and Coyle [1987]). Recently, Grassmann [1990], who provides an historical perspective on randomization, has advocated that this concept should be referred to as *Jensen's method.*

In this section, we presented the basics of Jensen's method and illustrated its use in the context of the finite-capacity M/M/1 queueing system. Note that uniformization techniques can be applied to obtain state-dependent probability distributions for any finite-state, continuous-time Markov chain. Readers seriously interested in using Jensen's method are urged to study Grassmann [1990] carefully. Serious issues such as computational complexity and difficulty of use are addressed in depth.

Exercise 3.20 Show that the equilibrium probabilities for the embedded Markov chain underlying the continuous-time Markov chain are equal to the equilibrium probabilities for the continuous-time Markov chain.

Exercise 3.21 For the special case of the finite-capacity M/M/1 queueing system with $K = 2$, $\lambda_0 = \lambda_1 = 0.8$, and $\mu_1 = \mu_2 = 1$, determine the time-dependent state probabilities first by solving the differential equation (3.33) directly and then by using uniformization for $t = 0.0, 0.2, 0.4, \ldots, 1.8, 2.0$ with $P_0(0) = 1$, plotting the results for $P_0(t)$, $P_1(t)$, and $P_2(t)$. Compare the quality of the results and the relative difficulty of obtaining the numbers.

3.4   BALANCE-EQUATION APPROACH FOR EXPONENTIAL SYSTEMS IN EQUILIBRIUM

Suppose all interarrival and service-time distributions are exponential. Then from any point in time, the amount of time until the state changes is exponentially distributed. Previously, we wrote differential equations for $P_n(t)$ and then let $P'_n(t) \to 0$. Instead, we could write the equations directly.

In equilibrium, the rate of entry into a state must equal the rate of departure from the same state; that is, the entrance and departure rates must *balance*. For example, Figure 3.9 shows a state diagram for the M/M/1 system, and the following table expresses the concept of balance.

state	rate leaves		rate enters	
0	λP_0	$=$	μP_1	(3.52)
1	$(\lambda + \mu)P_1$	$=$	$\lambda P_0 + \mu P_2$	(3.53)
2	$(\lambda + \mu)P_2$	$=$	$\lambda P_1 + \mu P_3$	(3.54)
n	$(\lambda + \mu)P_n$	$=$	$\lambda P_{n-1} + \mu P_{n+1}$	(3.55)

In the above, (3.52), (3.53), (3.54), and (3.55) are called "balance equations." More generally, we have a similar notion of balance in the case of state-dependent arrival and service rates, or equivalently, for general birth–death processes. That is, we might have

$$\lambda_n = \text{arrival rate when } n \text{ are in system}$$

and

$$\mu_n = \text{service rate when } n \text{ are in system.}$$

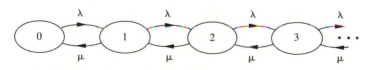

Figure 3.9 State diagram for the M/M/1 system.

Figure 3.10 shows the state diagram for the general birth–death process, and the following table expresses the concept of balance.

state	rate leaves		rate enters
0	$\lambda_0 P_0$	$=$	$\mu_1 P_1$
1	$(\lambda_1 + \mu_1)P_1$	$=$	$\lambda_0 P_0 + \mu_2 P_2$
2	$(\lambda_2 + \mu_2)P_2$	$=$	$\lambda_1 P_1 + \mu_3 P_3$
	$\cdots$	$\cdots$	
n	$(\lambda_n + \mu_n)P_n$	$=$	$\lambda_{n-1}P_{n-1} + \mu_{n+1}P_{n+1}$

In that case, we find that

$$P_1 = \frac{\lambda_0}{\mu_1}P_0,$$

$$P_2 = \frac{\lambda_1}{\mu_2}P_1 = \frac{\lambda_1}{\mu_2}\frac{\lambda_0}{\mu_1}P_0,$$

$$\vdots$$

$$P_n = \left[\frac{\prod\limits_{i=0}^{n-1} \lambda_i}{\prod\limits_{i=1}^{n} \mu_i}\right] P_0,$$

(3.56)

with

$$\sum_{i=0}^{\infty} P_i = 1.$$

(3.57)

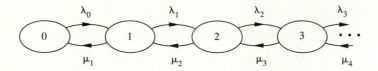

Figure 3.10 State diagram for general birth–death process.

Then

$$1 = P_0 + \sum_{n=1}^{\infty} \left[\frac{\prod_{i=0}^{n-1} \lambda_i}{\prod_{i=1}^{n} \mu_i} \right] P_0$$

or

$$P_0 = \frac{1}{1 + \sum_{n=1}^{\infty} \left[\left(\prod_{i=0}^{n-1} \lambda_i \right) / \left(\prod_{i=1}^{n} \mu_i \right) \right]}. \tag{3.58}$$

So for an equilibrium solution to exist, we must have

$$\sum_{i=1}^{\infty} \left[\left(\prod_{i=0}^{n-1} \lambda_i \right) / \left(\prod_{i=1}^{n} \mu_i \right) \right] < \infty.$$

Otherwise, $P_0 = 0 \Rightarrow P_1 = 0 \Rightarrow P_2 = 0$, and so on.

Example 3.3   Suppose that we have $\mu_i = \mu$ for all i, $\lambda_i = \lambda$ for $0 \le i \le K$, and $\lambda_i = 0$ for all $i > K$. That is, we have an M/M/1 queueing system with finite waiting room of size K including the customer in service. Then (3.58) becomes

$$P_0 = \frac{1}{1 + \sum_{n=1}^{K} (\lambda^n / \mu^n)} \tag{3.59}$$

$$= \frac{1 - \lambda/\mu}{1 - (\lambda/\mu)^{K+1}}.$$

Using this result in (3.56) leads to

$$P_n = \left[\frac{1 - \lambda/\mu}{1 - (\lambda/\mu)^{K+1}} \right] (\lambda/\mu)^n. \quad \blacksquare \tag{3.60}$$

When the waiting room's capacity is finite, customers attempting to enter the queue may be blocked, and it is of interest to specify the blocking probability. The blocking probability is defined as the proportion of the customers seeking admission to the queueing system who are denied. We can readily compute the blocking probability from the state probabilities.

Assuming a finite waiting room of capacity K, the average number of customers seeking admission to the system over a long period of time of length τ, once the system has reached stochastic equilibrium, is given by $\sum_{n=0}^{K} \lambda_n P_n \tau$. Note that λ_K does not play a role in determining the equilibrium probabilities because customers arriving while the system is in state K are blocked. On the other hand, the average number of customers blocked under the same condition is simply $\lambda_K P_K \tau$. Thus the probability that an arbitrary customer is blocked, which we shall denote by $P_B(K)$, is simply

$$P_B(K) = \frac{\lambda_K P_K}{\sum_{n=0}^{K} \lambda_n P_n}. \tag{3.61}$$

In the case of the finite-capacity M/M/1 system, the right-hand side of (3.61) reduces to P_K.

Figure 3.11 shows a graph showing $P_B(K)$ as a function of K. From this figure, we can readily compare $P_B(K)$ to $P\{\tilde{n} > K\}$ as obtained for the ordinary M/M/1 system. For example, at $\rho = 0.95$ and $K = 77$, $P_B(K) = 0.001$ and $P\{\tilde{n} > 77\} = (0.95)^{77} = 0.0193$; that is, the probability of exceeding the given occupancy level in the ordinary M/M/1 system is over 19 times as large as the probability of blocking for the capacity-limited system.

Exercise 3.22 For the special case of the finite-capacity M/M/1 system, show that for $K = 1,\ 2,\ \ldots$,

$$P_B(K) = \frac{\rho P_B(K-1)}{1 + \rho P_B(K-1)},$$

where $P_B(0) = 1$.

Exercise 3.23 For the finite-state general birth–death process, show that for $K = 1,\ 2,\ \ldots$,

$$P_B(K) = \frac{(\lambda_K/\mu_K) P_B(K-1)}{1 + (\lambda_K/\mu_K) P_B(K-1)},$$

where $P_B(0) = 1$.

An important special case of the birth–death process that finds broad application in traffic engineering is the *Erlang loss system*. This system has Poisson arrivals and s exponential[5] servers, each serving at rate μ. Customers who arrive to the system when all servers are busy are *cleared* from the system; that is, they are blocked from entry. Thus an important measure of system performance is the proportion of customers that are lost. Because arrivals are Poisson, the proportion of customers that are lost is simply P_K.

For the Erlang loss system, we find

$$\mu_i = i\mu \quad \text{for } i \leq s.$$

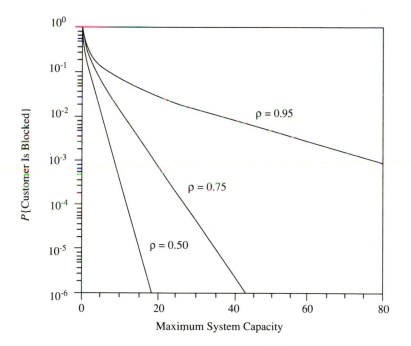

Figure 3.11 Blocking probability as a function of maximum system capacity for several values of ρ.

---

[5] Exponentiality is not required in order that the result hold for this case; that is, in this case, the results are *insensitive* to the form of the service-time distribution. There are many cases in which insensitivity holds in queueing systems; see Kelly [1979].

Also

$$\lambda_i = \begin{cases} \lambda, & \text{for } i < s; \\ 0, & \text{otherwise.} \end{cases}$$

Then, from (3.59) and (3.56), we find

$$P_n = \frac{(\lambda/\mu)^n/n!}{\sum_{i=0}^{s}(\lambda/\mu)^i/i!} \qquad \text{for } 0 \le n \le s. \tag{3.62}$$

Because potential customers arrive to the system according to a (state-independent) Poisson process, the blocking probability is given by P_s. Thus, for the Erlang loss system, we have

$$P\{\text{customer is blocked}\} = \frac{(\lambda/\mu)^s/s!}{\sum_{i=0}^{s}(\lambda/\mu)^i/i!}. \tag{3.63}$$

It is customary to express the blocking probability in terms of the *offered load*, a, which is defined as the ratio of the total arrival rate to the service rate of a single server; that is, the offered load is defined as

$$a = \lambda/\mu. \tag{3.64}$$

The blocking probability is then obtained from (3.63) and (3.64) and in the standard notation of traffic engineering is found to be

$$B(s,\ a) = a^s/s! \Big/ \sum_{i=0}^{s} a^i/i!. \tag{3.65}$$

This equation is called the *Erlang loss formula*. Another important term is the *carried load*, a', which is defined as the average number of busy servers for the system. It is easy to see that

$$a' = a[1 - B(s,\ a)]. \tag{3.66}$$

A typical application of the Erlang loss formula is to specify the number of lines needed to satisfy a certain level of blocking. For example, suppose a local division of a company knows the rate at which long-distance calls are generated and the average call holding time. Suppose further that the company wants these long-distance calls to be blocked less than 1% of the time. The company can use the

Erlang loss formula to determine the minimum number of lines that need to be available for making long-distance calls, provided that the assumption of Poisson arrivals for the calls is justified. Tables are provided in traffic engineering books (and some queueing books) for this purpose. We include at the end of this chapter a supplementary exercise that examines the difference between finite-population and infinite-population models of blocking. For a more thorough discussion and an historical perspective, the reader is referred to Cooper [1981].

Returning to the balance-equation approach, we note in passing that we can also write the differential equations by inspection by noting that the rate of change in the probabilities is given by the difference between the rate entering the state at time t and the rate departing the state at time t.

Exercise 3.24   Let K be arbitrary. Use the balance equation approach to write an equation of the form

$$\frac{d}{dt}P(t) = P(t)Q$$

where $P(t) = [\, P_0(t) \quad P_1(t) \quad \cdots \quad P_K(t)\,]$. Show that the eigenvalues of the matrix Q are real and nonpositive.

The above discussion presents the concept of *detailed* or *global* balance. It is sometimes easier to solve balance equations if they are initially written in terms of boundaries separating sets of states. For example, in Figure 3.12, we can consider everything to the left of

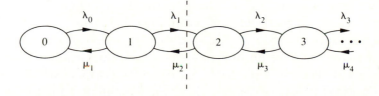

Figure 3.12 State diagram illustrating local balance.

the vertical line as one set of states and everything to the right as another set. Then, the rate of flow out of the set of states to the left must equal the rate of flow into the set of states to the right; the concept underlying this solution technique is called *local balance*. This concept, which has broad application in the analysis of networks of queues, will be mentioned again later in the text.

Exercise 3.25   Using the concept of local balance, write and solve the balance equations for the general birth–death process shown in Figure 3.12.

3.5   NETWORKS OF SINGLE-SERVER EXPONENTIAL
SERVICE STATIONS

In the previous sections, we have shown that the superposition and decomposition of Poisson processes form other Poisson processes. In addition, we have presented a theorem, the proof of which was left as an exercise, stating that the output process from the M/M/1 queueing system is a Poisson process. It is then apparent that a feedforward network of exponential servers with exogenous Poisson arrivals behaves as though it were a collection of independently operating M/M/1 queueing systems provided the service times of the entities are chosen independently at the various servers in the network.

Even in cases when the network has feedback, so that the arrival process to each node is not Poisson, the marginal occupancy distribution at each node can be computed as though the arrival process were Poisson, and the joint occupancy distribution for the system is simply the product of the marginal distributions. This property also carries through to the case of closed networks of exponential servers under a certain broad class of assumptions. In the case of closed networks, however, the solution contains an unknown constant that must be computed by normalizing the joint distribution so that the joint probabilities sum to unity. An interesting aspect of our coverage is that we include a recently developed technique, due to Gordon [1990], for specifying the normalizing constant of closed networks of single-server queues in closed form.

Simple networks of exponential queues have been used success-fully in a broad variety of modeling environments. Performance eval-uation of computing systems is discussed extensively in Lazowska, Zahorjan, Graham and Sevcik [1984], Chandy and Sauer [1981], Trivedi [1982], and to a lesser extent in Kobayashi [1978]. Klein-rock [1976] and Schwartz [1987] address the application of queueing networks to design problems in computer communications. All of these books provide significant coverage on the theory underlying networks of exponential servers and provide references for further study.

Single-server networks of this nature will be described in the fol-lowing sections. Many of the results presented herein can be modified so that they apply to networks of multiserver exponential queues as well as queues having other than exponential service under other ser-vice disciplines such as LCFS. The reader interested in applying the methodology to large problems may also wish to consult Schwartz [1987] and Gelenbe and Pujolle [1987] and, particularly, the refer-ences given there. For an excellent, highly readable discussion on the merits of applying queueing network methodology to practical problems and a discussion of why usable results can be obtained with minimal effort, the reader is referred to Lazowska, Zahorjan, Graham, and Sevcik [1986]. The reader seriously interested in traf-fic processes in networks of queues is strongly encouraged to consult Disney and Kiessler [1987]. Other significant books of interest in this area include Kelly [1979] and Walrand [1988].

3.5.1   Feedforward Networks of Single Servers
(Fixed Routing)

Consider an arbitrarily connected network of N sources and des-tinations, M exponential servers, and Poisson exogenous arrivals. Assume that routing in the network is fixed; that is, there is a spe-cific path that all customers having a particular source/destination pair must follow. Assume further that once a customer has received service from a particular server, the customer can never return to the same server; that is, the system allows no feedback.

Define $\delta_{jk}(i) = 1$ if units going from source j to destination k traverse server i and $\delta_{jk}(i) = 0$ otherwise; γ_{ij} as the rate units destined for destination j arrive to source i, μ_i as the service rate for server i, and λ_i as the aggregate unit arrival rate to server i. For each of the M servers, we have

$$\lambda_i = \sum_{j=1}^{N} \sum_{k=1}^{N} \gamma_{jk} \delta_{jk}(i).$$

As in the case of the M/M/1 system, the marginal occupancy density for server i is given by

$$P_i(n) = P\{\tilde{n}_i = n\} = (1 - \rho_i)\rho_i^n, \qquad (3.67)$$

where $\rho_i = \lambda_i/\mu_i$; and the joint occupancy density is given by

$$P\{n_1, n_2, \ldots, n_M\} = P\{\tilde{n}_1 = n_1, \ \tilde{n}_2 = n_2,$$
$$\ldots, \ \tilde{n}_M = n_M\}$$
$$= \prod_{i=1}^{M}(1 - \rho_i)\rho_i^{n_i}. \qquad (3.68)$$

Thus the expected delay at node i is

$$E[\tilde{s}_i] = \frac{1/\mu_i}{1 - \rho_i}. \qquad (3.69)$$

The average network delay for traffic entering node j destined for node k is therefore given by

$$E[\tilde{s}_{jk}] = \sum_{i=1}^{M} \delta_{jk}(i) E[\tilde{s}_i]. \qquad (3.70)$$

Note that the logic leading to (3.70) does not apply to any moment of waiting time other than the first.

We now turn to the computation of the average delay through the network. From Little's result, we know that the average number of customers present at server i is $E[\tilde{n}_i] = \lambda_i E[\tilde{s}_i]$. Thus the expected number of customers in the system is

$$E[\tilde{n}] = \sum_{i=1}^{M} \lambda_i E[\tilde{s}_i] \qquad (3.71)$$

or equivalently,

$$E[\tilde{n}] = \sum_{i=1}^{M} \frac{\rho_i}{1 - \rho_i}. \tag{3.72}$$

We also know that the total number of customers entering the system is

$$\gamma = \sum_{k=1}^{N}\sum_{j=1}^{N} \gamma_{jk}. \tag{3.73}$$

Because we know from Little's result that $E[\tilde{n}] = \gamma E[\tilde{s}]$, it follows that the total average time spent in the system is given by

$$E[\tilde{s}] = \frac{1}{\gamma} \sum_{i=1}^{M} \frac{\rho_i}{1 - \rho_i} \tag{3.74}$$

where γ is given by (3.73).

From (3.74), we see that the network delay may be dominated by a single server if the capacities of the servers are chosen arbitrarily. In the design of systems, sometimes capacities are assigned to minimize $E[\tilde{s}]$ for a given traffic pattern; this problem is called the capacity assignment problem (Kleinrock [1976]). Two recent examples in which (3.74) was used as a major factor in a network design algorithm are Gavish and Neuman [1986] and Gavish and Altinkemer [1990].

3.5.2   Arbitrary Interconnections (Random Routing)

We now turn our attention to the analysis of a network with arbitrary random routing among M single exponential servers. That is, a customer enters a particular service station, say station i, obtains service at station i, and then with probability r_{ij} proceeds next to station j independent of his past history. Customers depart the system from node i with probability r_{id}; that is,

$$\sum_{j=1}^{M} r_{ij} \leq 1,$$

with equality if and only if customers cannot depart the system from node i. Routing among the stations of the network is thus governed by a first-order Markov chain with $M \times M$ routing matrix $R = (r_{ij})$. We assume exogenous arrivals to server i to be Poisson with parameter γ_i and that the service rate for server i is μ_i for $i = 1, 2, \ldots, M$.

The arrival rate at a particular node is the sum of the exogenous arrival rate and the arrival rate due to customers entering from neighboring service stations. Thus the total arrival rate at node j is given by

$$\lambda_j = \gamma_j + \sum_{i=1}^{M} r_{ij} \lambda_i \qquad \text{for } j = 1, 2, \ldots, M \qquad (3.75)$$

or, in matrix form,

$$\lambda = \gamma + \lambda R, \qquad (3.76)$$

where $\lambda = [\lambda_1, \lambda_2, \ldots, \lambda_m]$ and $\gamma = [\gamma_1, \gamma_2, \ldots, \gamma_M]$. Thus we find that

$$\lambda = \gamma[I - R]^{-1}. \qquad (3.77)$$

Although the composite arrival processes at the service stations are not Poisson, the marginal occupancy density for server i is given by

$$P_i(n) = P\{\tilde{n}_i = n\} = (1 - \rho_i)\rho_i^n, \qquad (3.78)$$

where $\rho_i = \lambda_i/\mu_i$, and the joint occupancy density is given by

$$P(n_1, n_2, \ldots, n_M) = \prod_{i=1}^{M}(1 - \rho_i)\rho_i^{n_i}. \qquad (3.79)$$

Equivalently,

$$P(n_1, n_2, \ldots, n_M) = \frac{1}{G(M)} \prod_{i=1}^{M} \rho_i^{n_i}, \qquad (3.80)$$

where

$$G(M) = \prod_{i=1}^{M}(1 - \rho_i)^{-1}. \qquad (3.81)$$

This system is said to have a *product-form* solution, and the above
result is called Jackson's theorem (Jackson [1963]).

Exercise 3.26   Using Little's result, determine the average time spent
in the system for an arbitrary customer when the system is in
stochastic equilibrium.

Results similar to those above are available for many networks,
including those with finite population and state-dependent servers.
For an excellent summary of the results, refer to Chapter 3 of
Kobayashi [1978].

3.5.3   Closed Networks of Single Servers
             (Random Routing)

In a closed network, there is no exogenous traffic arriving to the
system, nor is there traffic leaving the system. Instead, we view the
network as representing a system in which a fixed number of jobs
continually circulates. Such networks have a surprising array of applications. For example, they are sometimes used to analyze flow control behavior in communication networks that limit the total number
of messages present in the system at any given time.

Closed queueing networks also have product form solutions of the
type described above (Gordon and Newell [1967]). That is, the joint
occupancy probabilities for the network have the form of a product
of marginal probabilities. That is,

$$P(n_1,\ n_2,\ \ldots,\ n_M) = P\{\tilde{n}_1 = n_1,\ \tilde{n}_2 = n_2,$$
$$\ldots,\ \tilde{n}_M = n_M\}$$
$$= P\{\tilde{n}_1 = 0,\ \tilde{n}_2 = 0,$$
$$\ldots,\ \tilde{n}_m = 0\} \qquad (3.82)$$
$$\prod_{i=1}^{M}\left(\frac{\lambda_i}{\mu_i}\right)^{n_i}$$

In the case of closed networks, however, $P\{\tilde{n}_1 = 0,\ \tilde{n}_2 = 0,\ \ldots,\ \tilde{n}_m = 0\}$ is not determined as simply as it was for the previous two network
types. In fact, in closed networks, the total occupancy of the system

is limited to N, so that we always have $\sum_{i=1}^{M} n_i = N$. Thus, to emphasize the dependence upon N and M, (3.82) is usually written as:

$$P(n_1,\ n_2,\ \ldots,\ n_M) = \frac{1}{g(N,\ M)} \prod_{i=1}^{M} \left(\frac{\lambda_i}{\mu_i}\right)^{n_i},\tag{3.83}$$

and $g(N,\ M)$ is thought of as the normalizing constant.

A peculiarity of closed queueing networks is that the flow balance equation analogous to (3.76) has the form

$$\lambda\,[I - R] = 0,\tag{3.84}$$

so that the vector λ is the left eigenvector of the matrix $[I - R]$ corresponding to its zero eigenvalue. Thus the vector of traffic intensities can be determined only to within a multiplicative constant. Obviously, the choice of λ influences the computation of the normalizing constant but not the occupancy probabilities.

Exercise 3.27   Argue that the matrix R is stochastic and that, therefore, the vector λ is proportional to the equilibrium probabilities of the Markov chain for which R is the one-step transition probability matrix.

If the state space of a closed queueing network is large, the determination of the normalizing constant via brute force would require the addition of $\binom{N+M-1}{N-1}$ scaled probabilities. Numerous algorithms have been developed to avoid summing this large number of terms, the major results being summarized in Kobayashi [1978]. Although very efficient algorithms have been developed, none seems to have resulted in closed-form expression for $g(N,\ M)$.

However, Harrison [1985] has recently found a closed-form expression for $g(N,\ M)$ for the special case of single-server systems under discussion here. Gordon [1990], apparently encouraged by Harrison's work, reformulated the problem in an elegant way and derived Harrison's result, in addition to many other results that will be mentioned below, via a more direct approach.

We now turn to our discussion of Gordon's approach to specifying the normalizing constant for closed queueing networks. Recall that there are always a total of N customers in the system, so

$$\sum_{i=1}^{M} n_i = N, \tag{3.85}$$

where n_i is the number of customers at node i. Define $\mathcal{S}_{N,M}$ to be the set of all admissible states, that is,

$$\mathcal{S}_{N,M} = \left\{ (n_1, \ n_2, \ \ldots, \ n_M) | \sum_{i=1}^{M} n_i = N \right\}. \tag{3.86}$$

We therefore have from the law of total probability that

$$\sum_{(n_1, n_2, \ldots, n_M) \in \mathcal{S}_{N,M}} P\{\tilde{n}_1 = n_1, \ \tilde{n}_2 = n_2, \ \ldots, \ \tilde{n}_M = n_M\} = 1. \tag{3.87}$$

From (3.83) and (3.87), we then have

$$g(N, \ M) = \sum_{(n_1, n_2, \ldots, n_M) \in \mathcal{S}_{N,M}} \prod_{i=1}^{M} \left(\frac{\lambda_i}{\mu_i} \right)^{n_i}. \tag{3.88}$$

The key to Gordon's success is replacement of the finite sum of the right-hand side of (3.88) by an infinite sum. Gordon [1990] does this by introducing an appropriate *delta* function into the summation. The delta function, a function of n, is defined as follows:

$$\delta(n - n_0) = \begin{cases} 1, & \text{if } n = n_0, \\ 0, & \text{otherwise,} \end{cases} \tag{3.89}$$

where n_0 is usually referred to as the *location of the delta function*. This function has the following representation as a contour integral on the complex plane:

$$\delta(n - n_0) = \frac{1}{j2\pi} \oint_C \phi^{(n-n_0)} \frac{d\phi}{\phi}, \tag{3.90}$$

where $j = \sqrt{-1}$ and $\oint_C$ indicates the integral around the unit circle, a closed contour, of the complex plane. It is readily verified, by performing the indicated integration using the residue theorem (see Churchill [1960]), that (3.89) and (3.90) are equivalent.

Exercise 3.28 Let x denote any integer. Show that

$$\frac{1}{j2\pi} \oint_C \phi^x d\phi = \begin{cases} 1, & \text{for } x = -1, \\ 0, & \text{otherwise}, \end{cases}$$

by direct integration.

From (3.89) and (3.90), we see that

$$\delta\left(\sum_{i=1}^{M} n_i - N\right) = \begin{cases} 1, & \text{if } \sum_{i=1}^{M} n_i = N, \\ 0, & \text{otherwise}, \end{cases}$$

and

$$
\begin{aligned}
\delta\left(\sum_{i=1}^{M} n_i - N\right) &= \frac{1}{j2\pi} \oint_C \phi^{(\sum_{i=1}^{M} n_i - N)} \frac{d\phi}{\phi} \\
&= \frac{1}{j2\pi} \oint_C \phi^{(\sum_{i=1}^{M} n_i)} \frac{d\phi}{\phi^{N+1}} \qquad (3.91) \\
&= \frac{1}{j2\pi} \oint_C \prod_{i=1}^{M} \phi_i^n \frac{d\phi}{\phi^{N+1}}.
\end{aligned}
$$

Now, if we multiply $\prod_{i=1}^{M} (\lambda_i/\mu_i)^{n_i}$ by $\delta\left(\sum_{i=1}^{M} n_i - N\right)$, then this product will be zero if $(n_1, n_2, \ldots, n_M) \ni S_{N,M}$, where $\ni$ stands for the relationship *not in*. Therefore, if we perform the above multiplication in (3.88), we find

$$g(N, M) = \sum_{n_1=0}^{\infty} \sum_{n_2=0}^{\infty} \cdots \sum_{n_M=0}^{\infty} \prod_{i=1}^{M} \left(\frac{\lambda_i}{\mu_i}\right)^{n_i} \delta\left(\sum_{i=1}^{M} n_i - N\right),$$

which is alternatively represented in contour integral form by

$$g(N,\ M) = \frac{1}{j2\pi} \oint_C \sum_{n_1=0}^{\infty} \sum_{n_2=0}^{\infty}$$

$$\cdots \sum_{n_M=0}^{\infty} \prod_{i=1}^{M} \phi^{n_i} \prod_{i=1}^{M} (\lambda_i/\mu_i)^{n_i} \frac{d\phi}{\phi^{N+1}}$$

$$= \frac{1}{j2\pi} \oint_C \sum_{n_1=0}^{\infty} (\rho_i\phi)^{n_1} \sum_{n_2=0}^{\infty} (\rho_i\phi)^{n_2}$$

$$\cdots \sum_{n_M=0}^{\infty} (\rho_i\phi)^{n_M} \frac{d\phi}{\phi^{N+1}},$$

(3.92)

where, as usual, $\rho_i = \lambda_i/\mu_i$. Upon performing the indicated infinite summations, which converge for $|\rho_i\phi| < 1$, we find

$$g(N,\ M) = \frac{1}{j2\pi} \oint_C g(N,\ M,\ \phi) \frac{d\phi}{\phi^{N+1}}, \tag{3.93}$$

where we have defined

$$g(N,\ M,\ \phi) = \prod_{i=1}^{M} \frac{1}{1 - \rho_i\phi}. \tag{3.94}$$

Now, $g(N,\ M,\ \phi)$ has been obtained from a finite product of infinite polynomials of the form $\sum_{j=0}^{\infty}(\rho_i\phi)^j$. Therefore, it is clear that $g(N,\ M,\ \phi)$ itself can be written in the form

$$g(N,\ M,\ \phi) = \sum_{j=0}^{\infty} g_j\phi^j. \tag{3.95}$$

In fact, the expression $\sum_{j=0}^{\infty}(\rho_i\phi)^j$ is the generating function (Hunter [1983]) for a sequence $\{a(i)\} = \{a_j(i),\ j = 0,\ 1,\ \ldots\}$ in which $a_j(i) = \rho_i{}^j$. Because $g(N,\ M,\ \phi)$ is the product of the generating functions for the M sequences $\{a(1)\}, \{a(2)\}, \ldots, \{a(M)\}$, it follows from the properties of sequences (Hunter [1983]) that the sequence $\{g_i\}$ is just the (m-fold) convolution of the sequences $\{a(1),\ a(2),\ \ldots,\ a(M)\}$.

Upon substitution of (3.95) into (3.93), we find

$$g(N, M) = \frac{1}{j2\pi} \oint_C \sum_{j=0}^{\infty} g_j \phi^j \frac{d\phi}{\phi^{N+1}}$$

$$= \frac{1}{j2\pi} \oint_C \sum_{j=0}^{\infty} g_j \phi^{(j-N)} \frac{d\phi}{\phi}.$$

(3.96)

From the residue theorem, it readily follows that

$$g(N, M) = g_N,$$

the coefficient of ϕ^N in the expression for $g(N, M, \phi)$. Note that when $g(N, M, \phi)$ is viewed as the generating function for the convolution of M sequences, (3.96) is not very surprising; this is exactly the (unpleasant) message conveyed by (3.88). The determination of the coefficient via convolution requires the addition of $\binom{N+M-1}{M-1}$ scaled state probabilities.

However, the form of (3.94) suggests that the determination of this coefficient can be carried out much more efficiently. In particular, $g(N, M, \phi)$ can be rewritten using partial fraction expansions (Hunter [1983]), and once this is done, the coefficient of ϕ^N will be obvious. For example, for the special case in which the ρ_i are distinct, we can rewrite $g(N, M, \phi)$ in the following form:

$$g(N, M, \phi) = \sum_{i=1}^{M} \frac{c_i}{1 - \rho_i \phi}.$$

(3.97)

We then find by expanding $1/(1 - \rho_i \phi)$ in geometric series form that the coefficient of ϕ^n for the ith partial fraction is simply $c_i \rho_i^N$. Thus, upon summing these values due to the respective partial fractions, we find

$$g(N, M) = \sum_{i=1}^{M} c_i \rho_i^N.$$

(3.98)

Using the procedures presented in elementary calculus courses, we can readily determine that

$$c_i = \frac{\rho_i^{M-1}}{\prod_{\substack{1 \le j \le M \\ j \ne i}} (\rho_i - \rho_j)}. \tag{3.99}$$

Upon substitution of (3.99) into (3.98), we find

$$g(N, M) = \sum_{i=1}^{M} \frac{\rho_i^{N+M-1}}{\prod_{\substack{1 \le j \le M \\ j \ne i}} (\rho_i - \rho_j)}, \tag{3.100}$$

which is the result given by Harrison [1985] and Gordon [1990].

Exercise 3.29   Suppose that the expression for $g(N, M, \phi)$ can be written as

$$g(N, M, \phi) = \prod_{i=1}^{r} \frac{1}{(1 - \sigma_i \phi)^{\nu_i}}, \tag{3.101}$$

where $\sum_{i=1}^{r} \nu_i = M$. That is, there are exactly r distinct singular values of $g(N, M, \phi)$—these are called $\sigma_1, \sigma_2, \ldots, \sigma_r$—and the multiplicity of σ_i is ν_i. We can rewrite (3.101) as

$$g(N, M, \phi) = \sum_{i=1}^{r} \sum_{j=1}^{\nu_j} \frac{c_{ij}}{(1 - \sigma_i \phi)^j}. \tag{3.102}$$

Show that

$$c_{ij} = \frac{1}{(\nu_i - j)!} \left(-\frac{1}{\sigma_i} \right)^{(\nu_i - j)} \\ \left. \frac{d^{(\nu_i - j)}}{d\phi^{(\nu_i - j)}} \left[(1 - \sigma_i \phi)^{\nu_i} g(N, M, \phi) \right] \right|_{\phi = 1/\sigma_i}. \tag{3.103}$$

Exercise 3.30   Define b_{nN} to be the coefficient of ϕ^N in the expansion of $(1 - \sigma_i \phi)^{-n}$. Show that

$$b_{nN} = \binom{N + n - 1}{N} \sigma_i^N. \tag{3.104}$$

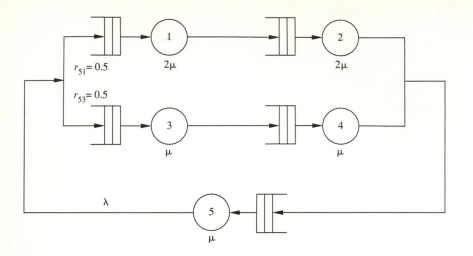

Figure 3.13 Block diagram for window flow controlled network.

Example 3.4   To illustrate the application of Gordon's ideas to a problem not specifically solved in Gordon [1990], we consider a window flow control technique in a communications network as in Figure 3-36 of Schwartz [1987]. Figure 3.13 shows the diagram for the system. We wish to determine the state probabilities for the network, which has five queues, a maximum occupancy of four, and a simple routing matrix.

Solution: From the diagram, we readily see that $\lambda_1 = \lambda_2 = \lambda_3 = \lambda_4 = 0.5\lambda_5$. Because $\mu = [2 \quad 2 \quad 1 \quad 1 \quad 1]$, we can choose $\rho_5 = \lambda_5 = \rho$, $\rho_1 = \rho_2 = \rho/4$, and $\rho_3 = \rho_4 = \rho/2$. We thus find from (3.83) that

$$P\{n_1, \, n_2, \, \ldots, \, n_5\} = \frac{1}{g(4, \, 5)}\rho_1^{n_1}\rho_2^{n_2}\rho_3^{n_3}\rho_4^{n_4}\rho_5^{n_5}$$

$$= \frac{1}{g(4, \, 5)}\left(\frac{\rho}{4}\right)^{n_1+n_2}\left(\frac{\rho}{2}\right)^{n_3+n_4}\rho^{n_5},$$

and from (3.94) that

$$g(N, 5, \phi) = \frac{1}{1 - \rho_1\phi}\frac{1}{1 - \rho_2\phi}\frac{1}{1 - \rho_3\phi}\frac{1}{1 - \rho_4\phi}\frac{1}{1 - \rho_5\phi}$$

$$= \frac{1}{[1 - (\rho/4)\phi]^2}\frac{1}{[1 - (\rho/2)\phi]^2}\frac{1}{1 - \rho\phi}.$$

On the basis of the results of Exercises 3.29 and 3.30, we first find that

$$g(N, 5, \phi) = \frac{-16/9}{[1 - (\rho/4)\phi]} + \frac{-1/3}{[1 - (\rho/4)\phi]^2} + \frac{-4}{[1 - (\rho/2)\phi]^2} + \frac{64/9}{(1 - \rho\phi)},$$

and then we find

$$g(N, 5) = -\frac{16}{9}\left(\frac{\rho}{4}\right)^N - \frac{1}{3}(N + 1)\left(\frac{\rho}{4}\right)^N - 4(N + 1)\left(\frac{\rho}{2}\right)^N + \frac{64}{9}\rho^N.$$

Now, in order to assure convergence of the infinite summation required to obtain $g(N, M, \phi)$ in closed form, we required that each $|\rho_i\phi|$ be less than unity. Thus the choice of the λ_i, and hence ρ_i, affects only the range of ϕ over which the summation converges. For consistency with Schwartz [1987], we choose $\rho = 4$. We then find that $g(4, 5) = 1497$ as given in Table 5-5 of Schwartz [1987]. We then find the joint queue occupancy probabilities to be

$$P\{n_1, n_2, \ldots, n_5\} = \frac{1}{1497}2^{(n_3+n_4)}4^{n_5}. \tag{3.105}$$

The reader should verify that there are a total of 70 possible states and that the probabilities obtained sum to unity.   ∎

Exercise 3.31   Verify that the probabilities as specified by (3.105) sum to unity.

Now that we have specified a procedure to obtain a closed-form expression for $g(N, M)$, it seems natural to ask whether or not it is possible to specify (marginal) node occupancy probabilities and moments of the node occupancy distribution in simple closed forms as well. As we shall see, the answer is "yes." In what follows, we shall first obtain simple expressions for the node occupancy probabilities and then use these results to obtain a simple expression for the expected node occupancy.

Recall from (3.83) that

$$P\{n_1,\ n_2,\ \ldots,\ n_M\} = \frac{1}{g(N,\ M)} \prod_{i=1}^{M} \rho_i^{n_i}. \tag{3.106}$$

To obtain the marginal occupancy probability for node i, we simply sum over all possible joint occupancy probabilities with $\tilde{n}_i = n$. Without loss of generality, we can reorder the nodes so that $i = M$ and consider node M to be arbitrary. Then, because the set of values over which $n_M = n$ is given by the set

$$\mathcal{S}_{N-n,M-1} = \left\{ (n_1,\ n_2,\ \ldots,\ n_{M-1}) \Big| \sum_{i=1}^{M-1} n_i = N - n \right\},$$

we readily find that

$$P\{\tilde{n}_m = n\} = \sum_{(n_1, n_2, \ldots, n_{M-1}) \in \mathcal{S}_{N-n, M-1}}$$

$$P\{\tilde{n}_1,\ \ldots, \tilde{n}_{M-1}\}$$

$$= \sum_{(n_1, n_2, \ldots, n_{M-1}) \in \mathcal{S}_{N-n, M-1}}$$

$$\frac{1}{g(N,\ M)} \prod_{i=1}^{M-1} \rho_i^{n_i} \rho_M{}^n \tag{3.107}$$

$$= \frac{1}{g(N,\ M)} \sum_{(n_1, n_2, \ldots, n_{M-1}) \in \mathcal{S}_{N-n, M-1}}$$

$$\frac{g(N-n,\ M-1)}{g(N-n,\ M-1)} \prod_{i=1}^{M-1} \rho_i^{n_i}$$

$$= \frac{\rho_M{}^n}{g(N,\ M)} g(N-n,\ M-1).$$

Now, (3.107) is in a reasonably simple form, but it involves terms of the form $g(\cdot,\ M-1)$, and it would be nicer to have all constants in the form $g(\cdot,\ M)$ because our normalizing constants are specified in closed forms for each M with N as a variable. From (3.107) and the law of total probability, we find

$$1 = \sum_{n=0}^{N} P\{\tilde{n}_m = n\} = \frac{1}{g(N,\ M)} \sum_{n=0}^{N} \rho_M{}^n g(N - n,\ M - 1),$$

so that

$$g(N,\ M) = \sum_{n=0}^{N} \rho_M{}^n g(N - n,\ M - 1), \qquad (3.108)$$

where we define $g(0,\ M) = 1$ for $M \geq 1$, $g(N,\ 0) = 0$ for all $N \geq 0$, and $g(N,\ M) = 0$ for all $N < 0$. Expanding (3.108), we find for $N,\ M \geq 1$,

$$g(N,\ M) = g(N,\ M - 1) + \sum_{n=1}^{N} \rho_M{}^n g(N - n,\ M - 1)$$

$$= g(N,\ M - 1) + \rho_M \sum_{n=0}^{N-1} \rho_M{}^n g(N - 1 - n,\ M - 1).$$

But, from (3.108), we recognize the summation of the right-hand side of the previous equation to be $g(N - 1,\ M)$. Thus we have

$$g(N,\ M) = g(N,\ M - 1) + \rho_M g(N - 1,\ M), \qquad (3.109)$$

with $g(0,\ M) = 1$ for $M \geq 1$ and $g(N,\ 0) = 0$ for all $N \geq 0$, as previously stated.

We note in passing that the recurrence equation (3.109) provides a handy way of generating the normalizing constants recursively for an arbitrary closed network of single-server queues. Kobayashi [1978] presents the same recursion for the special case described here.

The complexity of obtaining $g(N,\ M)$ for this special case via (3.100) is not substantially different from that of using (3.109). However, the power in Gordon's approach is that it makes it possible to obtain closed-form results for a variety of more complicated systems. In particular, Gordon easily derives closed-form expressions for single-server queues in the following special cases: $\rho_{M-1} = \rho_M$; $\rho_i = \rho$ for all i. Extensions to other special cases of the single-server class of networks are simply a matter of applying partial fraction expansion rules to obtain the coefficient of ϕ^N in (3.95).

In addition, Gordon derives a closed-form expression for the case in which each of the service stations may have a finite number, s_i, of servers, and the fractions ρ_i/s_i are distinct, and he indicates how this method can be extended to the case in which the fractions ρ_i/s_i are not distinct. These closed-form expressions and the extensions to more general cases do not seem to have appeared previously in the literature.

It is interesting to observe that the methods discussed by Kobayashi [1978] in explaining the recursive expressions also depend upon infinite summations and generating functions of exactly the same form as those used by Gordon. However, the relationship of the results to contour integration and the resulting utility of partial fraction expansions in obtaining closed-form results appear to have originated with Gordon.

Returning to our specification of the marginal occupancy probabilities, we note that the specification of N in (3.109) is arbitrary. We therefore can substitute $N - n$ for N, and after rearranging, we have

$$g(N - n,\ M - 1) = g(N - n,\ M) - \rho_M g(N - n - 1,\ M). \quad (3.110)$$

Upon substitution of (3.110) into (3.107), we obtain

$$P\{\tilde{n}_M = n\} = \frac{\rho_M{}^n}{g(N,\ M)} \qquad (3.111)$$
$$[g(N - n,\ M) - \rho_M g(N - n - 1,\ M)]\,.$$

We have seen earlier that expectations can be computed by summing complementary distributions; for example,

$$E[\tilde{n}] = \sum_{n=0}^{\infty} P\{\tilde{n} > n\}.$$

Clearly, $P\{\tilde{n}_M > N\} = 0$ because N is the population size. Thus we find from (3.111) that

$$P\{\tilde{n}_M > N - 1\} = P\{\tilde{n}_M = N\} = \frac{\rho_M{}^N}{g(N,\ M)}.$$

By successive substitutions into (3.111), we find

$$P\{\tilde{n}_M > n\} = \begin{cases} \rho_M{}^{n+1}/g(N, M) \\ \quad g(N - n - 1, M), & \text{for } 0 \leq n \leq N - 1; \\ 0, & \text{otherwise.} \end{cases} \quad (3.112)$$

Thus we have

$$E[\tilde{n}_M] = \sum_{n=0}^{\infty} P\{\tilde{n}_M > n\}$$

$$= \sum_{n=0}^{N-1} \frac{\rho_M{}^{n+1}}{g(N, M)} g(N - n - 1, M) \quad (3.113)$$

$$= \frac{1}{g(N, M)} \sum_{n=1}^{N} \rho_M{}^n g(N - n - 1, M).$$

Expressions for higher moments of the occupancy distribution at an arbitrary node can be derived in a similar fashion.

Given (3.113), the throughput at a given node can be specified exactly via Little's result. That is, (3.113) provides us with the average nodal occupancy, and we already know the average sojourn time at a node; therefore, Little's result can be used to solve for the average arrival rate to the node, which is the throughput.

Exercise 3.32   Carefully develop the argument leading from (3.109) to (3.110).

Exercise 3.33   Using the recursion of (3.109) together with the initial conditions, verify the expression for $g(N, 5)$ for the special case $N = 6$ numerically for the example presented in this section.

Exercise 3.34   Develop an expression for throughput at node M using Little's result and (3.113).

Before closing our discussion of queueing networks, we note that when only mean occupancies (or mean sojourn times) are desired, it is possible to compute the mean values directly through an iterative technique known as *mean-value analysis*. We emphasize that mean-value analysis is an iterative technique that should not be confused with other approaches that actually yield closed-form expressions for averages. The technique is described thoroughly in Schwartz [1987],

Galenbe and Pujolle [1987], Leon-Garcia [1989] and numerous other texts and papers. Although this technique has found broad application, we will not discuss it further in this volume.

3.6 PROBABILITY GENERATING FUNCTION APPROACH TO SOLVING BALANCE EQUATIONS

The solution of balance equations is not always straightforward. In some instances in which the solutions are not obvious, it is helpful to transform the system of equations, solve the transform equations, and then invert the transform to obtain the equilibrium probabilities. A useful transform is the *probability generating function* (PGF).

Definition 3.2   Probability Generating Function.   Let $\tilde{x}$ be a non-negative, integer-valued random variable. Then $\mathcal{F}_{\tilde{x}}(z) \triangleq E[z^{\tilde{x}}] = \sum_{i=0}^{\infty} z^i P\{\tilde{x} = i\}$ is called the probability generating function for $\tilde{x}$. $\square$

A thorough treatment of probability generating functions is presented in Hunter [1983]. Among the properties of the PGF which we shall find useful are the following:

$$E[\tilde{x}(\tilde{x} - 1) \cdots (\tilde{x} - n + 1)] = \frac{d^n}{dz^n} \mathcal{F}_{\tilde{x}}(z) \bigg|_{z=1} \tag{3.114}$$

and

$$P\{\tilde{x} = n\} = \frac{1}{n!} \frac{d^n}{dz^n} \mathcal{F}_{\tilde{x}}(z) \bigg|_{z=0}. \tag{3.115}$$

We note in passing that the latter property follows directly from the uniqueness of the Maclaurin series expansion of the function $\mathcal{F}_{\tilde{x}}(z)$, which is

$$\mathcal{F}_{\tilde{x}}(z) = \sum_{n=0}^{\infty} \left[\frac{1}{n!} \frac{d^n}{dz^n} \mathcal{F}_{\tilde{x}}(z) \bigg|_{z=0} \right] z^n,$$

and its comparison to the definition of the PGF.

Exercise 3.35   Prove (3.114).

Exercise 3.36   Prove (3.115).

Recall that for M/M/1, we found from detailed balance that

$$\lambda P_0 = \mu P_1, \tag{3.116}$$

$$(\lambda + \mu)P_n = \lambda P_{n-1} + \mu P_{n+1} \qquad \text{for } n \geq 1, \tag{3.117}$$

and from local balance (described at the close of Section 3.4) that

$$\lambda P_n = \mu P_{n+1} \quad \forall \quad n. \tag{3.118}$$

In order to illustrate the use of the probability generating function approach to the solution of balance equations, we solve the system of equations (3.118).

For the specific case in which the random variable of interest is the M/M/1 occupancy, we find

$$\mathcal{F}_{\tilde{n}}(z) = \sum_{n=0}^{\infty} z^n P\{\tilde{n} = n\}$$

$$= \sum_{n=0}^{\infty} z^n P_n.$$

After multiplying both sides of (3.118) by z^n, we find

$$\lambda z^n P_n = \mu z^n P_{n+1}.$$

Thus

$$\lambda \sum_{n=0}^{\infty} z^n P_n = \mu \sum_{n=0}^{\infty} z^n P_{n+1}.$$

After applying the definition of $\mathcal{F}_{\tilde{n}}(z)$ to the above equation, we find

$$\lambda \mathcal{F}_{\tilde{n}}(z) = \frac{\mu}{z} \sum_{n=0}^{\infty} z^{n+1} P_{n+1}$$

$$= \frac{\mu}{z}[\mathcal{F}_{\tilde{n}}(z) - P_0].$$

Thus

$$\mathcal{F}_{\tilde{n}}(z) = \frac{\mu P_0}{\mu - \lambda z}$$

$$= \frac{P_0}{1 - \rho z}.$$

But, from the properties of probability generating functions, $\mathcal{F}_{\tilde{n}}(1) = 1$, so $P_0 = 1 - \rho$. Finally, we obtain

$$\mathcal{F}_{\tilde{n}}(z) = \frac{1 - \rho}{1 - \rho z}. \tag{3.119}$$

We note

$$\frac{1 - \rho}{1 - \rho z} = (1 - \rho) \sum_{n=0}^{\infty} (\rho z)^n.$$

Thus

$$\mathcal{F}_{\tilde{n}}(z) = \sum_{n=0}^{\infty} [(1 - \rho)\rho^n] z^n.$$

But, by definition,

$$\mathcal{F}_{\tilde{n}}(z) = \sum_{n=0}^{\infty} P_n z^n.$$

So, by matching coefficients, we find $P_n = (1 - \rho)\rho^n$ as expected.

We will now work with (3.116) and (3.117) to illustrate how to handle slightly more complicated problems. To begin, multiply both sides of (3.117) by z^n to obtain

$$z^n(\lambda + \mu)P_n = \lambda z^n P_{n-1} + \mu z^n P_{n+1}. \tag{3.120}$$

Now sum both sides of (3.120) from $n = 1$ to $n = \infty$ to obtain

$$\sum_{n=1}^{\infty} z^n(\lambda + \mu)P_n = \lambda \sum_{n=1}^{\infty} z^n P_{n-1} + \mu \sum_{n=1}^{\infty} z^n P_{n+1}.$$

After using the definition of $\mathcal{F}_{\tilde{n}}(z)$ in the above equation, we find

$$(\lambda + \mu) \left[\sum_{n=0}^{\infty} z^n P_n - P_0 \right] = \lambda z \sum_{n=0}^{\infty} z^n P_n$$

$$+ \frac{\mu}{z} \left[\sum_{n=0}^{\infty} z^n P_n - z P_1 - P_0 \right],$$

$$(\lambda + \mu) \left[\mathcal{F}_{\tilde{n}}(z) - P_0 \right] = \lambda z \mathcal{F}_{\tilde{n}}(z) + \frac{\mu}{z} \left[\mathcal{F}_{\tilde{n}}(z) - z P_1 - P_0 \right].$$

But, from (3.116), we know that $\lambda P_0 - \mu P_1 = 0$. Substituting this fact into the previous equation and solving for $\mathcal{F}(z)$, we get

$$\mathcal{F}_{\tilde{n}}(z) = \frac{\mu(1 - z)P_0}{\lambda z^2 - (\lambda + \mu)z + \mu}.$$

Finally, upon dividing the numerator and denominator of the last equation by $\mu(1 - z)$, we obtain the same result as before for the probability generating function. That is, we get

$$\mathcal{F}_{\tilde{n}}(z) = \frac{P_0}{1 - \rho z}.$$

The remainder of the solution is as before.

Exercise 3.37   Use (3.114) to find $E[\tilde{n}]$ and $E[\tilde{n}^2]$. |

3.7   PHASE-DEPENDENT ARRIVAL AND SERVICE RATES

So far, we have discussed analyses of systems in which arrival and service rates may be state-dependent. In this section, we consider analysis of systems in which the rate at which units arrive to the server and the rate at which the units are serviced are dependent on the state of a so-called phase process. In particular, we assume that the phase (see Stern [1983]) of a system, $\{\wp(t), \ t \geq 0\}$, is a discrete-valued, continuous-time finite Markov chain with infinitesimal generator, Q (Cohen [1969], Chapter 3). We define $\{\wp(t), \ t \geq 0\}$ to be a continuous-time Markov chain that takes on integer values between 0 and K. Thus the dimension of the Q-matrix is $K + 1$, and

$$\frac{d}{dt}[P\{\wp(t) = 0\} \quad P\{\wp(t) = 1\} \quad \cdots \quad P\{\wp(t) = K\}]$$
$$= [P\{\wp(t) = 0\} \quad P\{\wp(t) = 1\}$$
$$\cdots \quad P\{\wp(t) = K\}]Q. \qquad (3.121)$$

The state diagram for the phase process is shown in Figure 3.14. As you can see from this diagram, the birth rate while the phase process is in state i, $i = 0$, 1, $\ldots$, K is equal to β_i, and the rate at which the process transitions from state i to state $i - 1$ is given by δ_i.

When $\{\wp(t), \; t \geq 0\}$ is in phase i, $0 \leq i \leq K$, the arrival rate of units to the server is λ_i and the service rate is μ_i. We first discuss solution of the equilibrium balance equations based on probability generating functions; then we discuss solution of the same equations using the matrix geometric technique of Neuts [1981a]; and finally, we discuss computation of the rate matrix needed in the matrix geometric approach via classical eigenanalysis. A numerical example is presented.

3.7.1   Probability Generating Function Approach

Figure 3.15 shows a partial state diagram for a queueing system having phase-dependent arrival and service rates. A typical state for this system is designated by $(i, \; j)$, where i specifies the current occupancy and j specifies the current phase. This process is a Markov process on the state space $\{(n, \; i), \; n \geq 0, \; 0 \leq i \leq K\}$, and it is called a quasi-birth–death (QBD) process (Neuts [1981a]). Let

$$P_{ni} = \lim_{t \to \infty} P\{\tilde{n}(t) = n, \; \wp(t) = i\}.$$

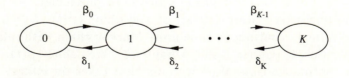

Figure 3.14 State diagram for phase process.

From the state diagram, it is straightforward to write the balance equations for the system. For a typical state on the interior of the diagram—that is, with $n \geq 1$ and $0 < i < K$—we find

$$(\lambda_i + \mu_i + \beta_i + \delta_i)P_{ni} = \lambda_i P_{n-1,i} + \beta_{i-1}P_{n,i-1}$$
$$+ \delta_{i+1}P_{n,i+1} + \mu_i P_{n+1,i}. \tag{3.122}$$

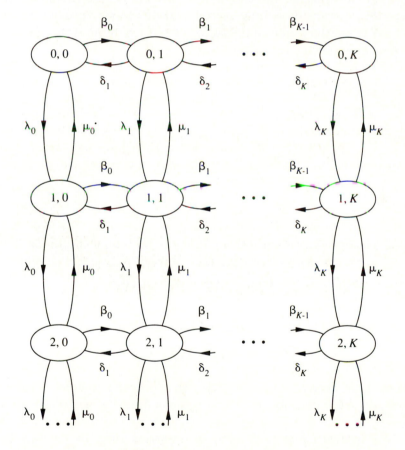

Figure 3.15 State diagram for system having phase-dependent arrival and service rates.

From this balance equation, the balance equations for those states not interior to the state diagram are readily determined. We simply specialize the above equation to account for the changes due to the quasi-birth–death boundary conditions. First, we consider the case $n = 0$ and $i = 0$ for which there are no transitions from state $(0, 0)$ due to "deaths," no transitions into state $(0, 0)$ due to "births," and no transitions into state $(0, 0)$ due to new arrivals. Thus we find that the balance equation for state $(0, 0)$ is

$$(\lambda_0 + \beta_0)P_{00} = \delta_1 P_{01} + \mu_0 P_{10}. \qquad (3.123)$$

Next, we consider the case $n = 0$, $0 < i < K$. On this boundary, there are no transitions from state $(0, i)$ due to service completions, and no transitions into state $(0, i)$ due to new arrivals. Thus we obtain the following set of equations:

$$(\lambda_i + \beta_i + \delta_i)P_{0i} = \beta_{i-1}P_{0,i-1} + \delta_{i+1}P_{0,i+1} + \mu_i P_{1,i}. \qquad (3.124)$$

Finally, we consider the case $n = 0$ and $i = K$. On this boundary, there are no transitions from state $(0, K)$ due to service completions or "births," and no transitions into state $(0, K)$ due to either new arrivals or "deaths." Thus the appropriate equation for this boundary is

$$(\lambda_K + \delta_K)P_{0K} = \beta_{K-1}P_{0,K-1} + \mu_K P_{1K}. \qquad (3.125)$$

Equations (3.123) through (3.125) can be rewritten in more compact form by using matrix notation. Toward this end, we define

$$P_n = [\,P_{n0} \quad P_{n1} \quad \cdots \quad P_{nK}\,].$$

Then, upon rearranging (3.123)-(3.125), we find

$$P_0(\Lambda - \mathcal{Q}) - P_1\mathcal{M} = 0, \qquad (3.126)$$

where $\Lambda = \mathrm{diag}(\lambda_0, \lambda_1, \ldots, \lambda_K)$ is a diagonal matrix of arrival rates and $\mathcal{M} = \mathrm{diag}(\mu_0, \mu_1, \ldots, \mu_K)$ is a diagonal matrix of service rates.

The matrix equation (3.126) summarizes all of the required information for the states in which $n = 0$. A similar set of equations is required for the states in which $n > 0$. These equations can also be obtained from (3.122). For $i = 0$, we find

$$(\lambda_0 + \mu_0 + \beta_0)P_{n0} = \lambda_0 P_{n-1,0} + \delta_1 P_{n1} + \mu_0 P_{n+1,0}. \qquad (3.127)$$

Finally, for $i = K$ with $n > 0$, by setting $P_{n,K+1} = 0$ in (3.122) and noting that the birth rate while in state $(n,\ K)$ is equal to 0, we find

$$(\lambda_K + \mu_K + \delta_K)P_{nK} = \lambda_K P_{n-1,K} + \beta_{K-1} P_{n,K-1} + \mu_K P_{n+1,K}. \quad (3.128)$$

Upon rewriting (3.122), (3.127), and (3.128) in matrix form, we can readily see that

$$P_{n-1}\Lambda - P_n(\Lambda - Q + M) + P_{n+1}M = 0, \qquad (3.129)$$

where all of the terms have been defined previously.

The matrix equations (3.126) and (3.128) are analogous to the scalar balance equations derived for the M/M/1 queueing system. Formulating the probability generating function is analogous to the scalar case as well. However, the generating functions so derived will be marginal probability generating functions rather than total probability generating functions; that is, the generating functions obtained by multiplying both sides of (3.129) by z^n and summing will generate marginal distributions. These marginal distributions can then be summed to yield probability generating functions if desired.

Define

$$\mathcal{G}(z) = \sum_{n=0}^{\infty} z^n P_n \qquad (3.130)$$

or, equivalently,

$$\mathcal{G}(z) = [G_0(z) \quad G_1(z) \quad \cdots \quad G_K(z)], \qquad (3.131)$$

where

$$G_i(z) = \sum_{n=0}^{\infty} z^n P_{n,i},$$

for $0 \le i \le K$. Then, upon multiplying both sides of (3.129) by z^n and summing, we find

$$\mathcal{G}(z)\Lambda z - [\mathcal{G}(z) - P_0]\,(\Lambda - \mathcal{Q} + \mathcal{M})$$
$$+ [\mathcal{G}(z) - P_1 z - P_0]\,\mathcal{M}\frac{1}{z} = 0. \tag{3.132}$$

After rearranging terms, we get

$$\mathcal{G}(z)\,\Lambda z - \mathcal{G}(z)\,(\Lambda - \mathcal{Q} + \mathcal{M}) + \mathcal{G}(z)\,\mathcal{M}\frac{1}{z} =$$
$$P_0\,\mathcal{M}\left(\frac{1}{z} - 1\right) - [P_0(-\mathcal{Q} + \Lambda) - P_1\mathcal{M}]. \tag{3.133}$$

Upon comparison of the last term on the right-hand side of (3.133) to (3.126), we see that this bracketed term is equal to zero. Thus, (3.133) reduces to

$$\mathcal{G}(z)\,\Lambda z - \mathcal{G}(z)\,(\Lambda - \mathcal{Q} + \mathcal{M}) + \mathcal{G}(z)\,\mathcal{M}\frac{1}{z} = P_0\,\mathcal{M}\left(\frac{1}{z} - 1\right) \tag{3.134}$$

or, equivalently,

$$\mathcal{G}(z)\left(\Lambda z^2 - (\Lambda - \mathcal{Q} + \mathcal{M})z + \mathcal{M}\right) = (1 - z)P_0\,\mathcal{M}. \tag{3.135}$$

To simplify the notation, define

$$\mathcal{A}(z) = \Lambda z^2 - (\Lambda - \mathcal{Q} + \mathcal{M})z + \mathcal{M}. \tag{3.136}$$

Then, we can rewrite (3.135) as

$$\mathcal{G}(z)\mathcal{A}(z) = (1 - z)P_0\,\mathcal{M}. \tag{3.137}$$

Upon solving (3.137), we find

$$\mathcal{G}(z) = \frac{1 - z}{\det \mathcal{A}(z)}P_0\mathcal{M}\ \text{adj}\ \mathcal{A}(z). \tag{3.138}$$

Analogous to the M/M/1 case, in which the probability generating function approach resulted in having to resolve an unknown constant, (3.138) contains an unknown vector of coefficients. This unknown vector can be determined using exactly the same principle as that used in the scalar case. We simply observe that the vector function $\mathcal{G}(z)$ is a vector of marginal probability generating functions and is therefore bounded at least for $|z| \leq 1$ (Hunter [1983]). This means that if there are zeros in the denominator of the right-hand side of (3.138) at z_i such that $|z_i| \leq 1$, then there is also a zero of the numerator of the right-hand side of (3.138) at z_i.

Because the rows of $\mathcal{A}(1)$ sum to a zero vector, det $\mathcal{A}(1) = 0$ and, therefore, det $\mathcal{A}(z)$ has a $(1 - z)$ factor, which cancels the factor in the numerator. This fact, when coupled with the fact that the probabilities must sum to unity, leads to one equation in the $K + 1$ unknowns of P_0. In addition, a later exercise is to show that there are exactly K zeros of det $\mathcal{A}(z)$ in the interval $(0, 1)$ provided that det $\mathcal{M} \neq 0$. These K zeros lead to an additional K linear equations in the $K + 1$ unknowns of P_0. It turns out that the $K + 1$ linear equations are linearly independent if det $\mathcal{M} \neq 0$, so that this linear system can be used to solve for the unknown vector P_0.

Exercise 3.38 Show that det $\mathcal{A}(z)$ is a polynomial, the order of which is not greater than $2(K + 1)$.

More formally, let $\mathcal{F}_{\tilde{n}}(z) = \sum_{i=0}^{K} G_i(z)$ or in vector notation, $\mathcal{F}_{\tilde{n}}(z) = \mathcal{G}(z)\mathbf{e}$, where $\mathbf{e}$ is a column vector of 1s. Then, from (3.138), we find

$$\mathcal{F}_{\tilde{n}}(z) = \frac{1 - z}{\det \mathcal{A}(z)} P_0 \mathcal{M} \text{ adj } \mathcal{A}(z)\mathbf{e}. \qquad (3.139)$$

Based on the above discussion, we find corresponding to $z = 1$,

$$1 = \frac{1}{[\det \mathcal{A}(z)/(1 - z)]_{z=1}} P_0 \mathcal{M} \text{ adj } \mathcal{A}(z)|_{z=1}\mathbf{e}. \qquad (3.140)$$

To facilitate further discussion, we define $\mathcal{Z}^{(0,\infty)}$ to be the set of all z such that det $\mathcal{A}(z) = 0$. We partition the set $\mathcal{Z}^{(0,\infty)}$ into three sets: $\mathcal{Z}^{(0,1)}$ and $\mathcal{Z}^{(1,\infty)}$ containing those elements of $\mathcal{Z}^{(0,\infty)}$ less than and greater than unity, respectively, and the third set containing only the unity element. Thus, $\mathcal{Z}^{(0,\infty)} = \mathcal{Z}^{(0,1)} \cup \{1\} \cup \mathcal{Z}^{(1,\infty)}$. The elements of $\mathcal{Z}^{(0,1)}$ are then labeled $z_0, z_1, \ldots, z_{K-1}$; the unit element is referred to as z_K; and the elements of $\mathcal{Z}^{(1,\infty)}$ are labeled $z_{K+1}, \ldots, z_n$, where n is the total number of elements in $\mathcal{Z}^{(0,\infty)}$. We assume the elements of $\mathcal{Z}^{(0,\infty)}$ are distinct, and for convenience, we order the indexing such that $z_i < z_j$ if $i < j$.

For each $z_i \in \mathcal{Z}^{(0,1)}$, we find from (3.139) and the above argument that

$$0 = P_0 \mathcal{M} \text{ adj } \mathcal{A}(z_i)e \qquad \text{for } z_i \in \mathcal{Z}^{(0,1)}. \qquad (3.141)$$

Equations (3.140) and (3.141) then form a system of $K + 1$ linear equations through which P_0 can be determined. The result can then be substituted into (3.138) to obtain the marginal PGFs or into (3.139) to obtain the total PGF.

Note that we would usually not want to write explicit expressions for adj $\mathcal{A}(z)$ and det $\mathcal{A}(z)$ in order to formulate the linear system of equations. The entire problem can be formulated in terms of the eigenvalues and eigenvectors of a matrix, which can be specified directly from inspection of $\mathcal{A}(z)$; and the expressions for $\mathcal{F}_{\tilde{n}}n(z)$ and $\mathcal{G}(z)$ and their corresponding probabilities can be specified in a convenient manner without the need for direct manipulation of $\mathcal{A}(z)$. However, before turning to a discussion of more advanced techniques, we present a simple numerical example.

Example 3.5   A computer accesses a transmission line via a statistical multiplexer or packet switch. The computer acts as a source of traffic; in this case, arrivals of packets from the computer are analogous to arrivals of customers to a queue. The computer alternates between idle and busy periods, which have exponential durations with parameters β and δ, respectively. During busy periods, the computer generates packets at a Poisson rate λ. The service times on the transmission line form a sequence of *iid* exponential random variables with parameter μ. Compute the state probabilities and the occupancy distribution for the parameter values $\lambda = \beta = \delta = \mu = 1$.

Solution: Referring back to the model, we find $\beta_0 = \beta$, $\delta_1 = \delta$, $\lambda_0 = 0$, $\lambda_1 = \lambda$, and $\mu_0 = \mu_1 = \mu$. Thus we find

$$\mathcal{Q} = \begin{bmatrix} -\beta & \beta \\ \delta & -\delta \end{bmatrix} = \begin{bmatrix} -1 & 1 \\ 1 & -1 \end{bmatrix},$$

$$\mathcal{M} = \begin{bmatrix} \mu & 0 \\ 0 & \mu \end{bmatrix} = \begin{bmatrix} 1 & 0 \\ 0 & 1 \end{bmatrix},$$

and

$$\Lambda = \begin{bmatrix} 0 & 0 \\ 0 & \lambda \end{bmatrix} = \begin{bmatrix} 0 & 0 \\ 0 & 1 \end{bmatrix}.$$

Upon substitution of these definitions into (3.137), we find

$$\mathcal{A}(z) = \begin{bmatrix} 1 - 2z & z \\ z & z^2 - 3z + 1 \end{bmatrix},$$

$$\text{adj } \mathcal{A}(z) = \begin{bmatrix} z^2 - 3z + 1 & -z \\ -z & 1 - 2z \end{bmatrix},$$

and

$$\det \mathcal{A}(z) = 1 - 5z + 6z^2 - 2z^3$$

$$= 2(1 - z)(1 + \frac{\sqrt{2}}{2} - z)(1 - \frac{\sqrt{2}}{2} - z).$$

Thus we find that

$$\text{adj } \mathcal{A}(z)\Big|_{z=1-\frac{\sqrt{2}}{2}} = \begin{bmatrix} 0.2071068 & -0.2928932 \\ -0.2928932 & 0.4142136 \end{bmatrix},$$

$$\text{adj } \mathcal{A}(z)\Big|_{z=1} = \begin{bmatrix} -1 & -1 \\ -1 & -1 \end{bmatrix},$$

and

$$\frac{\det \mathcal{A}(z)}{(1 - z)}\Big|_{z=1} = -1.$$

Substituting these numbers into (3.140) and (3.141), we find that

$$[0 \quad 1] = P_0 \begin{bmatrix} -0.0857864 & 2 \\ +0.1213204 & 2 \end{bmatrix}.$$

Thus we find that

$$P_0 = [0.2928932 \quad 0.2071068].$$

Upon substitution of this result into (3.138), we find after some algebra that

$$\begin{bmatrix} G_0(z) \\ G_1(z) \end{bmatrix}^T = \frac{1}{1 - 0.5857864z} \begin{bmatrix} 0.2928932 - 0.0857864z \\ 0.2071068 \end{bmatrix}^T.$$

After some additional algebra, this result reduces to

$$[\,G_0(z) \quad G_1(z)\,] = [\,0.2928932 \quad 0.2071068\,]$$

$$+ \quad [\,0.1464465 \quad 0.2071068\,] \sum_{n=1}^{\infty} (0.5857864)^n z^n.$$

Thus, for $n \geq 1$, we find

$$[\,P_{n0} \quad P_{n1}\,] = [\,0.1464465 \quad 0.2071068\,](0.5857864)^n.$$

The probability generating function for the occupancy distribution can now be computed from (3.139) or by simply summing $G_0(z)$ and $G_1(z)$. We find

$$\mathcal{F}_{\tilde{n}}(z) = 0.5 + 0.3535534 \sum_{n=1}^{\infty} (0.5857864)^n z^n.$$

From this probability generating function, we find $P_0 = 0.5$ and

$$P_n \mathbf{e} = 0.3535534 \times (0.5857864)^n \qquad \text{for } n \geq 1. \quad \blacksquare$$

Exercise 3.39   Repeat the above numerical example for the parameter values $\beta = \delta = 2$, $\lambda = \mu = 1$. That is, the proportion of time spent in each phase is the same and the transition rate between the phases is faster than in the original example. Compare the results to those of the example by plotting curves of the respective complementary distributions. Compute the overall traffic intensity and compare.

Exercise 3.40   Suppose we desire to use the packet switch and transmission line of the above numerical example to serve a group of users who collectively generate packets at a Poisson rate γ, independent of the computer's activity, in addition to the computer. This is a simple example of integrated traffic. Assuming that the user packets also require exponential service with rate μ, show the impact the user traffic has on the occupancy distribution of the packet switch by plotting curves for the cases of $\gamma = 0$ and $\gamma = 0.1$.

We now turn our attention to the determination of P_0 and the specification of $\mathcal{G}(z)$ and $\mathcal{F}_{\tilde{n}}(z)$ by more advanced techniques. We shall show that all the computations required to specify these quantities can be accomplished without actually performing algebraic manipulations. With regard to (3.137), we find that[6]

$$\mathcal{G}(1)\mathcal{A}(1) = 0. \tag{3.142}$$

But from (3.136) we find that $\mathcal{A}(1) = \mathcal{Q}$. Thus we have

$$\mathcal{G}(1)\mathcal{Q} = 0. \tag{3.143}$$

That is, $\mathcal{G}(1)$ is proportional to the left eigenvector of $\mathcal{Q}$ corresponding to the eigenvalue 0 of $\mathcal{Q}$. This means that $\mathcal{G}(1)$ is the vector of ergodic probabilities of the phase process, a fact that can be readily verified by evaluation of $\mathcal{G}(1)$ using (3.130). Now, from Theorems 3.3 and 3.4, we know that the left eigenvector of $\mathcal{Q}$ corresponding to the eigenvalue zero is proportional to the rows of adj $\mathcal{Q}$, and consequently, the rows of adj $\mathcal{Q}$ are proportional to each other. But because $\mathcal{Q}$ is the infinitesimal generator for the phase process, it can be shown that not only are the rows of adj $\mathcal{Q}$ proportional to each other, but they are also *equal* to each other. Proof of this fact is left as an exercise. Thus, if we let ϕ_K denote any row of adj $\mathcal{Q}$, we find

$$\mathcal{G}(1) = \frac{1}{\phi_K e}\phi_K. \tag{3.144}$$

Exercise 3.41   Let $\mathcal{Q}$ denote the infinitesimal generator for a finite, discrete-valued, continuous-time Markov chain. Show that the rows of adj $\mathcal{Q}$ are equal.

It is left as an exercise to show that the sum of the columns of $\mathcal{A}(z)$ is equal to the column vector $(1-z)(\mathcal{M} - z\Lambda)e$. Now, summing the columns of a matrix is an elementary transformation, and the determinant of a matrix is unaffected by elementary transformations (Noble and Daniel [1977]). Therefore,

$$\lim_{z \to 1}\left[\frac{\det \mathcal{A}(z)}{1-z}\right]$$

---

[6]We liberally use notation such as G(1) and A(1) to denote the limits of these functions as z approaches 1 without the formality of stating these are limits.

is given by the inner product of the last column of the cofactor matrix of $\mathcal{A}(1)$ and $(\mathcal{M} - \Lambda)\mathbf{e}$. But the last column of the cofactor matrix of $\mathcal{A}(1)$ is exactly the transpose of the last row of adj Q, which has been defined to be ϕ_K. Therefore,

$$\lim_{z \to 1} \left[\frac{\det \mathcal{A}(z)}{1-z} \right] = \phi_K (\mathcal{M} - \Lambda)\mathbf{e}. \tag{3.145}$$

Thus, upon substituting (3.144) and (3.145) into (3.139), we find

$$1 = \frac{1}{\mathcal{G}(1)(\mathcal{M} - \Lambda)\mathbf{e}} P_0 \mathcal{M}\mathbf{e}$$

or, equivalently,

$$\mathcal{G}(1)(\mathcal{M} - \Lambda)\mathbf{e} = P_0 \mathcal{M}\mathbf{e}. \tag{3.146}$$

Thus we see that the equation corresponding to $z = 1$ can be specified without resorting to algebraic manipulation; we simply find the left eigenvector of Q corresponding to zero and normalize this eigenvector so that its components sum to unity to obtain $\mathcal{G}(1)$ and then use (3.146) to complete the specification.

Exercise 3.42   Obtain (3.146) by starting out with (3.137), differentiating both sides with respect to z, postmultiplying both sides by $\mathbf{e}$, and then taking limits as $z \to 1$.

Exercise 3.43   Show that the sum of the columns of $\mathcal{A}(z)$ is equal to the column vector $(1 - z)(\mathcal{M} - z\Lambda)\mathbf{e}$ so that $\det \mathcal{A}(z)$ has a $(1 - z)$ factor.

Equation (3.146) has an intuitively satisfying interpretation. To see this, we rearrange (3.146) as follows:

$$\mathcal{G}(1)\Lambda\mathbf{e} = [\mathcal{G}(1) - P_0]\mathcal{M}\mathbf{e}. \tag{3.147}$$

The left-hand side of (3.147) expresses the average rate at which units enter the service system, and the right-hand side expresses the average rate at which units leave the system. Thus (3.147) is a flow balance equation. A special case of (3.147) is, for example, the relationship $\lambda = (1 - P_0)\mu$ for the M/M/1 system, which can be solved to obtain $P_0 = 1 - \lambda/\mu$.

We now turn our attention to the formulation of (3.141) by non-algebraic techniques. Before proceeding to the details, we introduce some terminology (see Lancaster [1966]).

Definition 3.3 λ-Matrix.   A λ-matrix is a matrix the elements of which are polynomials in λ. $\square$

Definition 3.4   Null Value.   Let $\mathcal{A}(\lambda)$ be a λ-matrix. Then a value λ_i such that $\det \mathcal{A}(\lambda_i) = 0$ is called a null value of $\mathcal{A}(\lambda)$. For example, $(\lambda I - A)$ is a λ-matrix, and the eigenvalues of A are null values of the λ-matrix $(\lambda I - A)$. $\square$

Definition 3.5   Null Vector.   Let $\mathcal{A}(\lambda)$ be a λ-matrix, and let X_{λ_i} be a nontrivial column vector such that $\mathcal{A}(\lambda_i)X_{\lambda_i} = 0$. Then X_{λ_i} is called a *null vector* of the λ-matrix $\mathcal{A}(\lambda)$ corresponding to the null value λ_i. For example, $(\lambda I - A)$ is a λ-matrix, and the eigenvectors of the matrix A are null vectors of the λ-matrix $(\lambda I - A)$. $\square$

Definition 3.6   Left Null Vector.   Let $\mathcal{A}(\lambda)$ be a λ-matrix, and let X_{λ_i} be a nontrivial row vector such that $X_{\lambda_i}\mathcal{A}(\lambda_i) = 0$. Then X_{λ_i} is called a *left null vector* of the λ-matrix $\mathcal{A}(\lambda)$ corresponding to the null value λ_i. $\square$

From the above definitions, we see that $\mathcal{A}(\lambda)$ is a λ-matrix of order 2 because each of the elements on the major diagonal is a polynomial of order 2. In addition, we see that the zeros of $\det \mathcal{A}(\lambda)$ are equivalent to the null values of $\mathcal{A}(\lambda)$. It is left as an exercise to show that the null vector of $\mathcal{A}(\lambda)$ corresponding to the null value λ_i, $i = 0, 1, \ldots, 2K+1$ are proportional to the columns of adj $\mathcal{A}(\lambda_i)$, $i = 0, 1, \ldots, 2K+1$, respectively. Consequently, the column vectors of adj $\mathcal{A}(\lambda_i)$ are proportional to each other, and because the left-hand side of (3.141) is zero, we can replace adj $\mathcal{A}(\lambda_i)e$ in (3.141) by X_{λ_i} where X_{λ_i} is the null vector of $\mathcal{A}(\lambda)$ corresponding to λ_i. This null vector is, in turn, simply the eigenvector of $\mathcal{A}(\lambda_i)$ corresponding to the zero eigenvalue of $\mathcal{A}(\lambda_i)$. Thus, if the null values of $\mathcal{A}(\lambda)$ are known exactly, then computation of the corresponding null vectors is trivial.

Exercise 3.44   Show that the zeros of the determinant of the λ-matrix $\mathcal{A}(z)$ are all real and nonnegative. [*Hint*: First, do a similarity transformation, transforming $\mathcal{A}(z)$ into a symmetric matrix, $\hat{\mathcal{A}}(z)$. Then, form the inner product $< X_z, \hat{\mathcal{A}}(z)X_z >$, where X_z is the null vector of $\hat{\mathcal{A}}(z)$ corresponding to z. Finally, examine zeros of the resulting quadratic equation.]

Exercise 3.45   The traffic intensity for the system is defined as the probability that the server is busy at an arbitrary point in time.

1. Express the traffic intensity in terms of the system parameters and P_0.

2. Determine the average amount of time a customer spends in the system using the results of (1) and Little's result.

3. Check the result obtained in (2) for the special case $\mathcal{M} = \mu I$.

Exercise 3.46   Show that adj $\mathcal{A}(z_i)$e is proportional to the null vector of $\mathcal{A}(z)$ corresponding to z_i.

The null values and vectors of $\mathcal{A}(z)$ can be obtained from standard eigenvalue/eigenvector routines. Toward this end, consider the system $\mathcal{A}(\sigma)X_\sigma = 0$, where σ is any null value of $\mathcal{A}(z)$ and X_σ is the corresponding null vector. Define $Y_\sigma = \sigma X_\sigma$. Then, from the definition of $\mathcal{A}(z)$ given by (3.136), we find

$$\sigma \Lambda Y_\sigma - \sigma(\Lambda - Q + \mathcal{M})X_\sigma + \mathcal{M}X_\sigma = 0,$$

and, by definition,

$$Y_\sigma - \sigma X_\sigma = 0.$$

Combining these two systems, we find that

$$\left\{ \begin{bmatrix} \mathcal{M} & 0 \\ 0 & I \end{bmatrix} - \sigma \begin{bmatrix} \Lambda - Q + \mathcal{M} & -\Lambda \\ I & 0 \end{bmatrix} \right\} \begin{bmatrix} X_\sigma \\ Y_\sigma \end{bmatrix} = 0$$

or, equivalently,

$$\left\{ \begin{bmatrix} I & 0 \\ 0 & I \end{bmatrix} - \sigma \begin{bmatrix} (\Lambda - Q + M)M^{-1} & -\Lambda M^{-1} \\ I & 0 \end{bmatrix} \right\}$$

$$\begin{bmatrix} X_\sigma \\ Y_\sigma \end{bmatrix} = 0. \tag{3.148}$$

From (3.148), we see that the null values of $A(z)$ are equivalent to the inverses of the eigenvalues of the matrix

$$A_E = \begin{bmatrix} (\Lambda - Q + M)M^{-1} & -\Lambda M^{-1} \\ I & 0 \end{bmatrix}, \tag{3.149}$$

where we have used the subscript E to denote *expanded*, and where the null vectors of $A(z)$ are proportional to the upper and lower $(K + 1)$-subvectors of the eigenvectors of this same $2(K + 1)$-dimensional square matrix. Thus let $\phi_i = X_{z_i}$, $i = 0, 1, \ldots, K - 1$ where $z_i \in Z^{(0,1)}$. Then, we find that we can form the linear system of equations (3.139) and (3.140) as follows:

$$0 = P_0 M \phi_0$$
$$0 = P_0 M \phi_1$$
$$\vdots \tag{3.150}$$
$$0 = P_0 M \phi_{K-1}$$
$$G(1)(M - \Lambda)e = P_0 M e.$$

The system (3.150) can then be solved for P_0.

Having solved for P_0, we have a formal solution for $G(z)$. However, the form of $G(z)$ in its present state is not suitable for manipulation, and algebraic manipulation of $A(z)$ would be required to complete the specification. A reasonable approach at this point would be to expand $G(z)$ using partial fraction expansions. At first glance, this would appear a formidable task, but a little further investigation will show that this is not the case.

As a starting point, we repeat (3.138) putting the $(1 - z)$ factor in the denominator:

$$G(z) = \frac{1}{[\det A(z)/(1 - z)]} P_0 M \text{ adj } A(z). \tag{3.151}$$

Now, because Λ is not required to have full rank, the polynomial $\det A(z)$ may have order less than $2(K + 1)$. If so, there will be a corresponding number of eigenvalues of $\mathcal{A}_E$ which have zero values. We therefore find that

$$
\det \mathcal{A}(z) = \sum_{i=0}^{n} a_i z^i
$$

$$
= a_n \prod_{z_i \in \mathcal{Z}(0,\infty)} (z - z_i), \tag{3.152}
$$

where n is the number of eigenvalues of $\mathcal{A}_E$ having nonzero values, and where we recall that $\mathcal{Z}_p$ is the set of null values of $\mathcal{A}(z)$ corresponding to those n eigenvalues of $\mathcal{A}_E$. Thus we have

$$
\det \mathcal{A}(z)|_{z=0} = (-1)^n a_n \prod_{z_i \in \mathcal{Z}(0,\infty)} z_i. \tag{3.153}
$$

But

$$
\det \mathcal{A}(z)|_{z=0} = \det \mathcal{M}
$$

$$
= \prod_{i=0}^{K} \mu_i,
$$

so that

$$
a_n = (-1)^n \prod_{z_i \in \mathcal{Z}(0,\infty)} z_i^{-1} \prod_{i=0}^{K} \mu_i. \tag{3.154}
$$

Upon substituting (3.154) into (3.152), we find

$$
\frac{\det \mathcal{A}(z)}{(1-z)} = \prod_{i=0}^{K} \mu_i \prod_{z_i \in \mathcal{Z}(0,1) \cup \mathcal{Z}(1,\infty)} (1 - z_i^{-1} z). \tag{3.155}
$$

Substitution of (3.155) into (3.151) then yields

$$
\mathcal{G}(z) = \frac{1}{\prod_{i=0}^{K} \mu_i \prod_{z_i \in \mathcal{Z}(0,1) \cup \mathcal{Z}(1,\infty)} (1 - z_i^{-1} z)} P_0 \mathcal{M} \text{ adj } \mathcal{A}(z). \tag{3.156}
$$

We note that the zeros of det $A(z)$ in the interval $(0, 1)$ are canceled by the choice of P_0 so that the remaining zeros are the ones in the interval $(1, \infty)$. Recall that $\mathcal{Z}^{(1,\infty)}$ denotes the set of null values of $A(z)$ in $(1, \infty)$. Thus expressing (3.156) using partial fraction expansions results in

$$G(z) = C_0 + \sum_{z_{K+i} \in \mathcal{Z}^{(1,\infty)}} \frac{1}{(1 - z_{K+i}^{-1}z)} A_i, \qquad (3.157)$$

where C_0 is a row vector of constants reflecting the fact that the numerator polynomials may have degree larger than that of the denominator polynomial, and A_i is a row vector representing the residue of $G(z)$ corresponding to $z_{K+i} \in \mathcal{Z}^{(1,\infty)}$.

Upon multiplying both sides of (3.156) and (3.157) by $(1 - z_{K+i}^{-1}z)$ and taking limits as $z \to z_{K+i}^{-1}$, we find

$$A_i = \frac{1}{\prod_{i=0}^{K} \mu_i \prod_{z_i \in \mathcal{Z}^{(0,1)} \cup \mathcal{Z}^{(1,\infty)} \setminus \{z_{K+i}\}} (1 - z_j^{-1}z_{K+i})} \qquad (3.158)$$
$$P_0 M \text{ adj } A(z_{K+i}).$$

At this point, it is worthwhile to contemplate the difficulties of computation of A_i. At first glance, this computation may appear difficult because it involves evaluating adj $A(z_i)$. However, an LU decomposition approach (Press, Flannery, Teukolsky and Vetterling [1988]), which takes into account the fact that $A(z_i)$ is both tridiagonal and singular, leads to a very simple algorithm for obtaining adj $A(z_i)$ as the outer product of two vectors that are easy to obtain.

Now, from (3.157), we find that

$$G(z) = C_0 + \sum_{z_{K+i} \in \mathcal{Z}^{(1,\infty)}} A_i \sum_{j=0}^{\infty} (z_{K+i}^{-1}z)^j$$

$$= C_0 + \sum_{z_i \in \mathcal{Z}^{(1,\infty)}} A_i + \sum_{z_{K+i} \in \mathcal{Z}^{(1,\infty)}} A_i \sum_{j=1}^{\infty} (z_{K+i}^{-1}z)^j \qquad (3.159)$$

$$= P_0 + \sum_{z_{K+i} \in \mathcal{Z}^{(1,\infty)}} A_i \sum_{j=1}^{\infty} (z_{K+i}^{-1}z)^j.$$

Thus we need not obtain C_0 explicitly in order to compute the state probabilities. We find simply that

$$P_n = \sum_{z_{K+i} \in \mathcal{Z}(1,\infty)} A_i z_{K+i}^{-n} \quad \text{for } n \geq 1. \quad (3.160)$$

The marginal probabilities are obtained by simply summing the joint probabilities. We find that

$$P_n \mathbf{e} = \sum_{z_{K+i} \in \mathcal{Z}(1,\infty)} A_i \mathbf{e} z_{K+i}^{-n} \quad \text{for } j \geq 1, \quad (3.161)$$

where $P\{\tilde{n} = n\}\mathbf{e}$ is the equilibrium probability that the occupancy is n.

Example 3.6   In this example, we simply rework the previous example in which the parameter values were $\lambda = \beta = \delta = \mu = 1$, using the more advanced techniques.

Solution: From the definition of $\mathcal{A}_E$, which is given by (3.149), we find

$$\mathcal{A}_E = \begin{bmatrix} 2 & -1 & 0 & 0 \\ -1 & 2 & 0 & -1 \\ 1 & 0 & 0 & 0 \\ 0 & 1 & 0 & 0 \end{bmatrix}.$$

Then, from a standard eigenvalue/eigenvector routine, we find the eigenvalues of $\mathcal{A}_E$ to be $\{3.414214, 1.0, 0.585786, 0\}$. Thus we find $\mathcal{Z}^{(0,\infty)} = \{0.292893, 1.0, 1.707107\}$. Following our indexing scheme, we have $z_0 = 0.292893$, $z_1 = 1$, and $z_2 = 1.707107$.
    The null vectors of $\mathcal{A}(z)$ corresponding to z_0 and z_1 are found by partitioning the matrix of eigenvectors of $\mathcal{A}_E$; the results are

$$\phi_0 = \begin{bmatrix} -0.414214 \\ 0.585786 \end{bmatrix}$$

and

$$\phi_1 = \begin{bmatrix} -0.5 \\ -0.5 \end{bmatrix},$$

respectively. From (3.144), we find

$$G(1) = \begin{bmatrix} 0.5 \\ 0.5 \end{bmatrix}.$$

Thus, from (3.150), we find

$$[0 \quad 0.5] = P_0 \begin{bmatrix} -0.414214 & 0.5 \\ 0.585786 & 0.5 \end{bmatrix},$$

from which we find

$$P_0 = [0.292893 \quad 0.207107].$$

Evaluation of $A(z_2)$ yields

$$A(1.707107) = \begin{bmatrix} -2.414214 & 1.707107 \\ 1.707107 & -1.207107 \end{bmatrix},$$

from which we find

$$\text{adj } A(1.707107) = \begin{bmatrix} -1.207107 & -1.707107 \\ -1.707107 & -2.414214 \end{bmatrix}.$$

From (3.158), we find

$$A_1 = \frac{1}{(1 - z_1^{-1} z_2)} P_0 M \text{ adj } A(z_2)$$

$$= \frac{1}{(1 - 5.828429)} \begin{bmatrix} 0.292893 \\ 0.207107 \end{bmatrix}^T \begin{bmatrix} -1.207107 & -1.707107 \\ -1.707107 & -2.414214 \end{bmatrix}$$

$$= [0.146447 \quad 0.207107],$$

where the notation T denotes the matrix transpose operator. Thus, from (3.159), we find

$$G(z) = P_0 + A_1 \sum_{n=1}^{\infty} z_2^{-n} z^n$$

$$= \begin{bmatrix} 0.292893 \\ 0.207107 \end{bmatrix}^T + \begin{bmatrix} 0.146447 \\ 0.207107 \end{bmatrix}^T \sum_{n=1}^{\infty} 0.585786^n z^n.$$

Upon postmultiplication of both sides of this expression by e, we readily find

$$\mathcal{F}(z) = 0.5 + 0.353554 \sum_{n=1}^{\infty} 0.585786^n z^n.$$

so that $P_0 e = 0.5$ and $P_n e = 0.353554 \times 0.585786^n$ for $n \geq 1$, as before. ■

Example 3.7   This example provides the solution to Exercise 3.40. As in Exercise 3.40, we increase the arrival rate in each phase by 0.1 to reflect the addition of Poisson user traffic at rate 0.1 so that the resulting parameter values are $\lambda_0 = 0.1$, $\lambda_1 = 1.1$, $\beta_0 = \delta_1 = \mu_1 = \mu_2 = 1$.

Solution: Following the procedure outlined above leads to the following results:

$$\mathcal{G}(z) = P_0 + A_1 \sum_{n=1}^{\infty} z_2^{-n} z^n + A_2 \sum_{n=1}^{\infty} z_3^{-n} z^n$$

$$= [0.234605 \quad 0.165395] + [0.132521 \quad 0.170481] \sum_{n=1}^{\infty} 0.662640^n z^n$$

$$+ [0.102084 \quad -0.005086] \sum_{n=1}^{\infty} 0.047568^n z^n.$$

Upon postmultiplying both sides of the above equation by e, we find

$$\mathcal{F}(z) = 0.4 + 0.303002 \sum_{n=1}^{\infty} 0.662640^n z^n + 0.096998 \sum_{n=1}^{\infty} 0.047568^n z^n,$$

so that $P_0 e = 0.4$ and

$$P_n e = 0.303002 \times 0.662640^n + 0.096998 \times 0.047568^n \qquad \text{for } n \geq 1.$$

From the expression for the occupancy probabilities, it is easy to compute the complementary occupancy distribution. We find

$$P\{\tilde{n} > n\} = 0.595155 \times 0.662640^n + 0.004845 \times 0.047568^n.$$

Note that there are two null values of $\mathcal{A}(z)$ greater than unity. For large values of n, only the smaller of these has any significant effect upon the occupancy probabilities, marginal or otherwise. For example,

$$P\{\tilde{n} > n\} \approx 9.714 \times 10^{-3}.$$

The contribution due to the larger null value is only 2.874×10^{-16}, or roughly three parts in 10^{16}. Expressing the results in the form of a geometric sum makes it easy to see at a glance the effects of each of the null values on the occupancy probabilities for all n.   ■

The above results are now specified as a weighted sum of geometric distributions. The solution vector is then "matrix geometric." In Sec. 3.7.3 we describe a more direct approach, due to Neuts, to computing the ergodic probabilities when these probabilities are expressible in matrix geometric form. Although the approach is more direct from a descriptive point of view, the computation time for numerical solutions is not nececessarily comparable to the current method, as we will see later.

Exercise 3.47   Show that if the system described by (3.130) and (3.133) is ergodic, then there are exactly K zeros of det $\mathcal{A}(z)$ in the interval $(0, 1)$. [*Hint*: First show that this is the case if $\delta_i = 0 \; \forall \; i$. Then show that it is not possible for det $\mathcal{A}(z)/(1 - z)$ to be zero for any choice of δ_is unless $P_0 = 0$, implying no equilibrium solution exists, and that therefore, the number of zeros in $(0, 1)$ does not change when the δ_i change.]

Exercise 3.48   Beginning with (3.159) through (3.161), develop expressions for the joint and marginal complementary ergodic occupancy distributions.

Exercise 3.49   Develop an expression for adj $\mathcal{A}(z_i)$ in terms of the outer products of two vectors using LU decomposition. [*Hint*: The term in the lower right-hand corner, and consequently the last row, of the upper triangular matrix will be zero. What then is true of its adjoint?]

3.7.2   Matrix Geometric Method

Suppose there exists a matrix $\mathcal{R}$ such that

$$P_n = P_{n-1}\mathcal{R} \qquad \forall \qquad n \geq 1. \tag{3.162}$$

Then, we find by successive substitutions into (3.152) that

$$P_n = P_0\mathcal{R}^n \qquad \forall \qquad n \geq 0. \tag{3.163}$$

A solution of the form (3.163) is called a *matrix geometric* solution. The key to solving a matrix geometric system is to specify the matrix $\mathcal{R}$, the rate matrix, which we shall discuss below.

Following our probability generating approach, we find from (3.162) that

$$\sum_{n=1}^{\infty} z^n P_n = \sum_{n=1}^{\infty} z^n P_{n-1}\mathcal{R},$$

so that

$$\mathcal{G}(z) - P_0 = z\mathcal{G}(z)\mathcal{R},$$

or

$$\mathcal{G}(z)\left[I - z\mathcal{R}\right] = P_0, \tag{3.164}$$

and

$$\mathcal{G}(z) = P_0\left[I - z\mathcal{R}\right]^{-1}. \tag{3.165}$$

Thus

$$\lim_{z \to 1} \mathcal{G}(z) = P_0\left[I - \mathcal{R}\right]^{-1} \tag{3.166}$$

and

$$P_0 = \mathcal{G}(1)\left[I - \mathcal{R}\right]. \tag{3.167}$$

Also, we have from (3.129) that

$$P_{n-1}\Lambda - P_n(\Lambda - \mathcal{Q} + \mathcal{M}) + P_{n+1}\mathcal{M} = 0, \qquad n \geq 1.$$

Hence, upon substituting (3.162) into the above equation, we find

$$P_{n-1}\Lambda - P_{n-1}\mathcal{R}(\Lambda - \mathcal{Q} + \mathcal{M}) + P_{n-1}\mathcal{R}^2\mathcal{M} = 0, \qquad n \geq 1,$$

so that

$$P_{n-1}\left[\Lambda - \mathcal{R}(\Lambda - \mathcal{Q} + \mathcal{M}) + \mathcal{R}^2\mathcal{M}\right] = 0, \qquad n \geq 1. \qquad (3.168)$$

Clearly, a sufficient condition for (3.168) to hold is that $\mathcal{R}$ satisfy

$$\Lambda - \mathcal{R}(\Lambda - \mathcal{Q} + \mathcal{M}) + \mathcal{R}^2\mathcal{M} = 0. \qquad (3.169)$$

Thus, if we could solve (3.169) for $\mathcal{R}$, we could then use (3.167) to solve for P_0, having previously computed $\mathcal{G}(1)$ by normalizing the left eigenvector of $\mathcal{Q}$ corresponding to its zero eigenvalue, as described in Sec. 3.7.1. An additional check on P_0 and $\mathcal{R}$ could be obtained from the boundary condition for the system of equations as specified in (3.126). The boundary condition states that

$$P_0(\Lambda - \mathcal{Q}) - P_1\mathcal{M} = 0,$$

so that

$$P_0(\Lambda - \mathcal{Q} - \mathcal{R}\mathcal{M}) = 0. \qquad (3.170)$$

Obtaining a solution for $\mathcal{R}$ of (3.169) is not necessarily an easy task. One possibility is to specify a contraction map (Hewitt and Stromberg [1969]) on $\mathcal{R}$ based on (3.169) and then use successive approximations to obtain $\mathcal{R}$. One way to specify a contraction map is to multiply both sides of (3.138) by some positive number τ^{-1} and then add $\mathcal{R}$ to both sides of the result. This procedure yields

$$\mathcal{R} = \tau^{-1}\mathcal{R}^2\mathcal{M} + \mathcal{R}\left[I - \tau^{-1}(\mathcal{M} - \mathcal{Q} + \Lambda)\right] + \tau^{-1}\Lambda. \qquad (3.171)$$

We then set

$$\mathcal{R}_i = \tau^{-1}\mathcal{R}_{i-1}^2\mathcal{M} + \mathcal{R}_{i-1}\left[I - \tau^{-1}(\mathcal{M} - \mathcal{Q} + \Lambda)\right] + \tau^{-1}\Lambda \qquad (3.172)$$

and iterate on i, starting with some suitable value for $\mathcal{R}_0$, until $\mathcal{R}_i$ converges. One possibility is to set $\mathcal{R}_0 = \mathrm{diag}(1/(K + 1), 1/(K + 1), \ldots, 1/(K + 1))$.

An alternative contraction map is one specified by Neuts [1981a]. It is obtained simply by solving (3.169) for $\mathcal{R}$ and then introducing subscripts. The result is

$$\mathcal{R}_j = \Lambda(\Lambda - \mathcal{Q} + \mathcal{M})^{-1} + \mathcal{R}_{j-1}^2\mathcal{M}(\Lambda - \mathcal{Q} + \mathcal{M})^{-1} \quad \text{for } j \geq 1. \qquad (3.173)$$

The idea is to start with $\mathcal{R}_0 = 0$ and then compute successive approximations to $\mathcal{R}$ using (3.173). Neuts [1981] has shown that the sequence $\{\mathcal{R}_0, \mathcal{R}_1, \mathcal{R}_2, \ldots\}$ is a monotonically increasing sequence that converges to the minimal nonnegative solution to (3.169), and that this solution is the solution that uniquely provides the rate matrix $\mathcal{R}$ that satisfies (3.162).

This approach, called the *matrix geometric* approach, is elegantly described in Neuts [1981]. In its most general form, Neuts describes the quasi-birth–death (QBD) process as a Markov chain on $\{(n, i), n \geq 0, 0 \leq i \leq K\}$ having an infinitesimal generator of the form

$$
\tilde{Q} = \begin{bmatrix}
B_0 & A_0 & 0 & \cdots & \cdots \\
B_1 & A_1 & A_0 & \cdots & \cdots \\
0 & A_2 & A_1 & A_0 & \cdots \\
0 & 0 & A_2 & A_1 & \cdots \\
0 & 0 & 0 & A_2 & \cdots \\
0 & 0 & 0 & 0 & \cdots
\end{bmatrix},
$$

where $(B_0 + A_0)e = 0$, $(B_1 + A_1 + A_0)e = 0$, $(A_0 + A_1 + A_2)e = 0$, and the matrix $A = A_0 + A_1 + A_2$ is a finite generator.

In Neuts's terminology, we have

$$
\begin{aligned}
B_0 &= -(\Lambda - Q) \\
B_1 &= \mathcal{M} \\
A_0 &= \Lambda \\
A_1 &= -(\Lambda - Q + \mathcal{M}) \\
A_2 &= \mathcal{M},
\end{aligned}
$$

so that our system matches Neuts's definition of a QBD process.[7]

Neuts [1981a] presents the following theorem relevant to the analysis of such systems.

Theorem 3.6   The process $\tilde{Q}$ is positive recurrent[8] if and only if the

---

[7]The term *quasi-birth–death process* seems to have been first applied to this type of system by Evans [1967].

[8]The phrase "the process $\tilde{Q}$" is interpreted as "the process whose infinitesimal generator is $\tilde{Q}$."

minimal nonnegative solution $\mathcal{R}$ to the matrix quadratic equation

$$\mathcal{R}^2 A_2 + \mathcal{R} A_1 + A_0 = 0$$

has all of its eigenvalues inside the unit disk and the finite system of equations

$$P_0(B_0 + \mathcal{R} B_1) = 0,$$

$$P_0(I - \mathcal{R})^{-1} e = 1,$$

has a unique positive solution P_0.

If the matrix $A\ (= A_2 + A_1 + A_0)$ is irreducible, then $\text{sp}(\mathcal{R}) < 1$ if and only if $\pi A_2 e > \pi A_0 e$, where π is the stationary probability vector of A.[9]

The stationary probability vector $x = [P_0, \ P_1, \ \ldots]$ of $\tilde{Q}$ is given by $P_i = P_0 \mathcal{R}^i$ for $i \geq 0$.

The (equivalent) equalities

$$(\mathcal{R} A_2 - A_0)e = (\mathcal{R} B_1 - B_0)e = 0$$

hold.   □

The equation $P_0(B_0 + \mathcal{R} B_1) = 0$ is equivalent to (3.170), and the equation $P_0(I - \mathcal{R})^{-1} e = 1$ can be obtained from (3.167) by postmultiplying both sides by e. The condition $\pi A_2 e > \pi A_0 e$ is equivalent to $\mathcal{G}(1)\mathcal{M}e > \mathcal{G}(1)\Lambda e$, which states that the maximum average rate at which service can be rendered must exceed the average arrival rate.

Matrix geometric techniques are very powerful—their use is not limited to the analysis of QBD processes. The literature contains many applications of matrix geometric techniques to the solution of problems. An application of this method to a non-Markovian queueing system is presented in Daigle and Langford [1985,1986], and an application of this method to analysis of Ethernet-based local area networks is presented in Coyle and Liu [1985].

---

[9]The expression $\text{sp}(\mathcal{R})$ denotes the *spectral radius* of the matrix $\mathcal{R}$, which is defined as the magnitude of the largest eigenvalue of $\mathcal{R}$. A plot of $\text{sp}(\mathcal{R})$ as a function of overall traffic intensity is sometimes called the *caudal characteristic curve* for the system.

In addition, the results obtained via matrix geometric techniques are not limited to occupancy distributions. Ramaswami and Lucantoni [1985] discuss the application of matrix geometric techniques to obtaining stationary waiting-time distributions in QBD and other systems. Additional results along these lines are given in Daigle and Lucantoni [1990]. Note that it is also possible to obtain such distributions using the PGF approach described in Sec. 3.7.1, but the development is more cumbersome.

Example 3.8   Provide the solution in matrix geometric form to the problem solved in Example 3.7.

Solution: Upon substituting the parameters from Example 3.7 into (3.172), we find

$$\mathcal{R}_i = \tau^{-1}\mathcal{R}_{i-1}^2 + \mathcal{R}_{i-1}\left[I - \tau^{-1}\begin{pmatrix} 2.1 & -1.0 \\ -1 & 3.1 \end{pmatrix}\right] + \tau^{-1}\begin{bmatrix} 0.1 & 0.0 \\ 0.0 & 1.1 \end{bmatrix},$$

which will be solved iteratively for $\mathcal{R}$.

We arbitrarily choose $\tau = 3$, and the iteration process yields

$$\mathcal{R} = \begin{bmatrix} 0.070500 & 0.029500 \\ 0.460291 & 0.639709 \end{bmatrix}.$$

We next determine the equilibrium phase probabilities by any of the methods previously described, all of which are simple to apply. We find

$$\mathcal{G}(1) = \begin{bmatrix} 0.5 & 0.5 \end{bmatrix}.$$

Substituting this result into (3.167), we get

$$P_0 = \begin{bmatrix} 0.5 & 0.5 \end{bmatrix}\left[I - \begin{pmatrix} 0.070500 & 0.029500 \\ 0.460291 & 0.639709 \end{pmatrix}\right]$$

$$= \begin{bmatrix} 0.234605 & 0.165395 \end{bmatrix}.$$

The solution expressed in matrix geometric form as in (3.163) is then

$$P_n = P_0\mathcal{R}^n$$

$$= \begin{bmatrix} 0.234605 & 0.165395 \end{bmatrix}\begin{bmatrix} 0.070500 & 0.029500 \\ 0.460291 & 0.639709 \end{bmatrix}.$$

We see from this example that the behavior of the tail probabilities is somewhat less obvious than it is in the form of the previous example, where the geometric quantities are expressed in scalar form.   ∎

Exercise 3.50   Solve for the equilibrium state probabilities for Example 3.8 using the matrix geometric approach. Specify the results in terms of the matrix $\mathcal{R}$. Determine numerically the range of values of τ for which (3.171) converges. Also, verify numerically that the results are the same as those obtained above.

Exercise 3.51   Solve Exercise 3.39 using the matrix geometric approach. Compare the relative difficulty of using the matrix geometric approach to that of using the probability generating function approach.

3.7.3   Rate Matrix Computation via Eigenanalysis

We now turn our attention to a discussion of the relationship between the probability generating function and the matrix geometric approaches discussed in the previous subsections. To begin our discussion, let $\nu \neq 0$ be an eigenvalue of $\mathcal{R}$, and let V_ν be a left eigenvector of $\mathcal{R}$ corresponding to ν. Then, by the defining relationship between eigenvalues and eigenvectors, we have

$$V_\nu \mathcal{R} = V_\nu \nu. \tag{3.174}$$

Also, upon premultiplying (3.169) by V_ν, we find that

$$V_\nu \left[\Lambda - \mathcal{R}(\Lambda - \mathcal{Q} + \mathcal{M}) + \mathcal{R}^2 \mathcal{M}\right] = 0.$$

Substitution of (3.174) into the previous equation yields

$$V_\nu \left[\Lambda - \nu(\Lambda - \mathcal{Q} + \mathcal{M}) + \nu^2 \mathcal{M}\right] = 0. \tag{3.175}$$

Then, upon substituting $\sigma = 1/\nu$ into (3.175) and multiplying both sides by σ^2, we find

$$V_\nu \left[\Lambda \sigma^2 - (\Lambda - \mathcal{Q} + \mathcal{M})\sigma + \mathcal{M}\right] = 0. \tag{3.176}$$

But this expression is exactly

$$V_\nu \mathcal{A}(\sigma) = 0. \tag{3.177}$$

This means that if V_ν is a left eigenvector of $\mathcal{R}$ corresponding to ν, then V_ν is a left null vector of $\mathcal{A}(z)$ corresponding to its null value $1/\nu$. It is obvious from (3.163) that, for a stable system, all the eigenvalues of $\mathcal{R}$ have magnitudes less than unity; therefore, the null values of $\mathcal{A}(z)$ which are of interest are those that have magnitudes greater than unity, that is, those in the set $\mathcal{Z}^{(1,\infty)}$. Analogous to the case of Sec. 3.7.2, these eigenvalues and left eigenvectors can be found via a standard eigenanalysis of the matrix

$$\mathcal{A}'_E = \begin{bmatrix} (\Lambda - Q^T + \mathcal{M})\mathcal{M}^{-1} & -\Lambda\mathcal{M}^{-1} \\ I & 0 \end{bmatrix}, \qquad (3.178)$$

where the only difference between (3.149) and (3.178) is that the matrix Q is transposed.

Now, the matrix $\mathcal{A}'_E$ may have zero eigenvalues. In fact, it is easy to show (Daigle and Lucantoni [1990]) that the number of zero eigenvalues of this matrix is exactly the same as the number of terms that are zero on the major diagonal of Λ. Following an elementary transformation to transform $\mathcal{A}(z)$ into a symmetric λ-matrix, we can write the quadratic form of the transformed symmetric λ-matrix, which has the same null values as the original matrix, as

$$V_\nu \hat{\mathcal{A}}(\sigma) V_\nu^T = \ell\sigma^2 - (\ell - q + m)\sigma + m = 0,$$

where ℓ, m, and q are nonnegative, positive, and nonpositive, respectively. The discriminant of the solution of this quadratic equation is readily found to be $(\ell - m)^2 - 2q(\ell + m) + q^2$, which is always nonnegative. Therefore, all null values of $\mathcal{A}(z)$ are real. It is also easy to see that the null values of $\mathcal{A}(z)$ are nonnegative. But as the value of ℓ becomes smaller and smaller, the value of the null value corresponding to V_ν becomes larger and larger, and its inverse becomes smaller and smaller. In the limit, the null value becomes infinity and its inverse becomes zero. In effect, the matrix $\mathcal{A}$ has one less null value, but the inverse of this "null value at infinity" shows up as a zero eigenvalue of $\mathcal{A}_E$.

From (3.173), it is easy to see that if $\lambda_i = 0$ for some i, then the corresponding row of the $\mathcal{R}$ matrix will be zero; this can be seen by simply doing successive substitutions in (3.173) starting with $\mathcal{R}_0 = 0$. Thus, if we define the $(K + 1) \times 1$ column vector whose ith element is 1 with all other elements being 0 by e_i, then it is easy to see that

e_i is a left eigenvector of $\mathcal{R}$.

Now, suppose there are n values of i for which $\lambda_i = 0$. Then there will be n rows of $\mathcal{R}$ which will be identically 0. Define $\mathcal{T}$ to be the elementary transformation such that $\mathcal{T}\Lambda\mathcal{T}$ is a diagonal matrix in which the 0 values of λ_i appear as the first n diagonal elements. Then, the first n rows of the matrix $\mathcal{T}\mathcal{R}\mathcal{T}$ will be identically 0, and the row vectors e_i, $0 \le i < n$, will be left eigenvectors of this matrix. Next, we denote the matrix formed by the collection of the remaining left eigenvectors of $\mathcal{T}\mathcal{R}\mathcal{T}$ by $\hat{V}$ and partition this matrix into the matrix $\left[\hat{V}_1 \hat{V}_2\right]$, where $\hat{V}_1$ contains the first n columns of $\hat{V}$. Then, we can readily verify that

$$\begin{bmatrix} I & 0 \\ \hat{V}_1 & \hat{V}_2 \end{bmatrix} \mathcal{T}\mathcal{R}\mathcal{T} = \begin{bmatrix} 0 & 0 \\ 0 & \hat{\mathcal{N}} \end{bmatrix} \begin{bmatrix} I & 0 \\ \hat{V}_1 & \hat{V}_2 \end{bmatrix}, \qquad (3.179)$$

where $\hat{\mathcal{N}}$ is the diagonal matrix of the nonzero eigenvalues of $\mathcal{R}$. The form of (3.179) indicates that if the matrix of left eigenvectors spans the $(K + 1)$-dimensional eigenspace, then the matrix $\hat{V}_2$ is nonsingular. Thus we find

$$\mathcal{R} = \mathcal{T} \begin{bmatrix} 0 & 0 \\ \hat{V}_2^{-1}\hat{\mathcal{N}}\hat{V}_1 & \hat{V}_2^{-1}\hat{\mathcal{N}}\hat{V}_2 \end{bmatrix} \mathcal{T}. \qquad (3.180)$$

The implication of the above discussion is that a zero-valued eigenvalue of $\mathcal{R}$ having multiplicity greater than one simplifies, rather than complicates, computation of $\mathcal{R}$.

The computation of the matrix of left eigenvectors of $\mathcal{R}$ is quite straightforward using standard eigenanalysis packages. First, we formulate the matrix $\mathcal{A}'_E$ and obtain its eigenvalues and corresponding eigenvectors. We then select the set of eigenvalues that are less than unity together with their corresponding eigenvectors. The last $K + 1$ elements of the eigenvector of $\mathcal{A}'_E$ corresponding to each eigenvalue of $\mathcal{A}'_E$ which is less than unity are then transformed by $\mathcal{M}^{-1}$ to yield the elements of the left eigenvector of $\mathcal{R}$ corresponding to the same eigenvalue. If the diagonal matrix whose diagonal elements are the eigenvalues of $\mathcal{R}$ is denoted by $\mathcal{N}$, and the matrix of corresponding left eigenvectors is denoted by $\mathcal{V}$, then we compute $\mathcal{R}$ from

$$\mathcal{R} = \mathcal{V}^{-1}\mathcal{N}\mathcal{V}. \qquad (3.181)$$

Once we know $\mathcal{R}$, we can solve for P_0 using (3.167), and then we can compute P_n for $n \geq 1$ via (3.163). Note that the computational effort required to compute P_0 via (3.181) and (3.167) is roughly equal to that required to compute P_0 via (3.150). Note also that computation of a particular power of $\mathcal{R}$ is readily accomplished by making use of the identity

$$\mathcal{R}^n = \mathcal{V}^{-1}\mathcal{N}^n\mathcal{V}.$$

We now turn to the computation of the survivor function and the moments of the occupancy distribution. With regard to the survivor functions, define the joint (occupancy, phase) survivor function as

$$\Sigma_n = \sum_{m=n+1}^{\infty} P_m. \tag{3.182}$$

Then due to (3.163), we find

$$\begin{aligned}
\Sigma_n &= \sum_{m=n+1}^{\infty} P_0\mathcal{R}^m \\
&= P_0[I - \mathcal{R}]^{-1}\mathcal{R}^{n+1} \\
&= \mathcal{G}(1)\mathcal{R}^{n+1}.
\end{aligned} \tag{3.183}$$

Thus we can readily see that the values of the vector Σ_n for successive values of n can be obtained via a simple postmultiplication by $\mathcal{R}$. The marginal survivor function for the queue occupancy can then be obtained by summing the elements of Σ_n or, equivalently, by postmultiplication by e. Also, the terms of the conditional survivor functions for the queue occupancy can be obtained by dividing the ith element of Σ_n by the ith element of $\mathcal{G}(1)$.

By using the final form of (3.183) and the well known result that the expected value of a nonnegative random variable is given by the integral of its survivor function, we find

$$\begin{aligned}
E[\tilde{n}] &= \sum_{n=0}^{\infty} \Sigma_n\mathbf{e} \\
&= \mathcal{G}(1)[I - \mathcal{R}]^{-1}\mathcal{R}\mathbf{e}.
\end{aligned}$$

But, because our technique for computing $\mathcal{R}$ yields the eigenvalues and eigenvectors, the expectation can be computed using these quantities. In particular, by using (3.181) and modest algebraic manipulation, we find

$$E[\tilde{n}] = \mathcal{G}(1)\mathcal{V}^{-1}$$
$$\text{diag}\,[\,\nu_0/1 - \nu_0 \quad \nu_1/1 - \nu_1 \quad \cdots \quad \nu_K/1 - \nu_K\,]\,\mathcal{V}\text{e} \tag{3.184}$$

Computational forms for higher factorial moments can be easily derived along the same lines. The resulting formulae are

$$\mathcal{G}^{(n)}(1)\text{e} = \frac{d^n}{dz^n}\mathcal{G}(z)\Big|_{z=1}\text{e}$$
$$= \mathcal{G}(1)\mathcal{V}^{-1}\,\text{diag}\,[\,(\nu_0/1 - \nu_0)^n$$
$$\cdots \quad (\nu_K/1 - \nu_K)^n\,]\,\mathcal{V}\text{e}. \tag{3.185}$$

Formulae for the above quantities based on the partial fraction expansion representation of the occupancy distribution can be readily developed, the most complicated operation being the summing of a geometric series.

Exercise 3.52   Prove the result given by (3.185) for the nth factorial moment of $\tilde{n}$.

An alternative matrix geometric approach for solving QBD models, based on the notion of *complete level crossing information*, is described by Beuerman and Coyle [1989]. Beuerman and Coyle first expand the state space so that the resulting model has *complete level crossing information*, and then they describe a technique for obtaining an alternative rate matrix, W, that is completely specified analytically. In addition, Zhang and Coyle [1989] describe a procedure, based on transform analysis, to determine the time-dependent state probabilities for QBD processes. These results will not be commented upon further here, but the reader interested in solutions to QBD models is encouraged to consult the references.

3.8   SERVICE-TIME DISTRIBUTIONS OF THE PHASE TYPE AND OTHER VARIATIONS

At this point we have just begun to scratch the surface concerning systems having matrix geometric solutions. In this section, we make minor modifications to the model of the preceding section and show how more general service-time distributions may be considered via matrix geometric methods. In particular, our modifications serve to introduce distributions of the *phase type*, a broad class of distributions that are covered in detail in Neuts [1981a].

The essence of our modification is that we allow both the level and the phase of the process to change simultaneously. In particular, we express the infinitesimal generator of the phase process as

$$Q = S + S^0 b, \qquad (3.186)$$

where S is a nonsingular $(K+1) \times (K+1)$ matrix representing phase changes within the same level, S^0 is a nonnegative $(K+1)$-column vector equal to $-Se$, b is a nonnegative $(K+1)$-row vector such that $be = 1$, and $S^0 b$ is a $(K+1) \times (K+1)$ matrix representing phase changes that result in a level decrease, that is, a service completion.

Since $S^0 b$ represents phase changes that are simultaneously level decreases, the net effect of corresponding transitions of this nature is service completion. Thus we let

$$M = S^0 b. \qquad (3.187)$$

In addition, we restrict the arrival process so that the arrival rate is independent of the phase, so that

$$\Lambda = \lambda I. \qquad (3.188)$$

Then, substituting (3.186) through (3.188) into (3.126) and (3.129), we get

$$P_0(\lambda I - S - S^0 b) - P_1 S^0 b = 0, \qquad (3.189)$$

$$P_{n-1}\lambda I - P_n(\lambda I - S) + P_{n+1}S^0 b = 0, \quad \text{for } n \geq 1. \qquad (3.190)$$

We now modify the behavior of the system so that the state of the system following a service completion from level 1 is always $(0, 0)$, and the state of the system following an arrival from level 0 is $(1, i)$ with probability b_i, $i = 0, 1, \ldots, K$. Then we find that

$$P_0 = [p_{00} \quad 0 \quad \cdots \quad 0],$$

equations analogous to (3.189) and (3.190) for this special case are

$$P_{00}\lambda - P_1 S^0 = 0, \tag{3.191}$$

$$P_{00}\lambda b - P_1(\lambda I - S) + P_2 S^0 b = 0, \tag{3.192}$$

and

$$P_{n-1}\lambda - P_n(\lambda I - S) + P_{n+1}S^0 b = 0, \qquad \text{for } n \geq 2. \tag{3.193}$$

Neuts [1981a], pp. 83–86, shows, using very elementary arguments, that the system of equations (3.190) through (3.193) has the unique solution

$$P_{00} = 1 - \rho,$$
$$P_n = (1 - \rho)b\mathcal{R}^n, \qquad \text{for } n \geq 1, \tag{3.194}$$

where

$$\mathcal{R} = \lambda[\lambda I - \lambda eb - S]^{-1}, \tag{3.195}$$

and

$$\rho = -\lambda b S^{-1} e. \tag{3.196}$$

Note that the matrix $\mathcal{R}$ is given explicitly, so that the state distribution can be determined in closed form modulo a matrix inversion. This demonstrates that it is worthwhile to attempt to find an analytic solution to a problem even though it may at first appear difficult.

A little thought will reveal that the system we have just analyzed is a queueing system having Poisson arrivals; identically, but not exponentially, distributed service times; and infinite waiting capacity. In short, the system is a special case of the M/G/1 queueing system.

The special case is the one in which the service-time distribution is of the *phase type*.

For service-time distributions of the phase type, each time service is begun the phase of the process is initiated in phase i with probability b_i, $i = 0$, 1, ..., K, with $be = 1$. Changes in the phase process are then governed by the infinitesimal generator

$$\tilde{Q} = \begin{bmatrix} S & S^0 \\ 0 & 0 \end{bmatrix}, \tag{3.197}$$

where S and S^0 are defined as above, 0 is a $(K + 1)$-row vector of zeros, and 1 is a scalar. A transition to phase $K + 1$ represents absorption of the process or, equivalently, the end of the current service time.

In forming our system of equations, we represent absorption by a level change, or service completion, so that phase $(K + 1)$ is not needed. The column vector S^0 represents the rate at which the process changes levels, and the vector b is the vector of probabilities determining the phase of the process immediately following a service completion. Equivalently, b is the vector of probabilities determining the phase of the process at the beginning of the service time, and consequently it is needed to specify the phase of the process following an arrival from the empty state, only one of which is needed since the joint probability $P_{0i} = 0$ for $i \neq 0$.

If the infinitesimal generator matrix $Q = S + S^0 b$ is irreducible, then Neuts [1981a], pp. 48–51, shows that the resulting service-time distribution will be

$$F_{\tilde{x}}(x) = 1 - be^{Sx}e, \tag{3.198}$$

and the moments of the distribution are readily shown to be given by

$$E[\tilde{x}^n] = (-1)^n b S^{-n} e. \tag{3.199}$$

A broad class of distributions can be described by judicious choice of the terms of Q. For example, these terms can be easily chosen so that the resulting distribution is exponential, or Erlang-k. But the representation of a given distribution is not unique. For example, two representations for the exponential distribution with parameter μ follow. First we choose to let Q be a scalar. Then,

$S = -\mu$, $S^0 = \mu$, and $b = 1$. Second, we choose

$$S = \begin{bmatrix} -(\mu + \alpha) & \alpha \\ \beta & -(\mu + \beta) \end{bmatrix}, \quad S^0 = \begin{bmatrix} \mu \\ \mu \end{bmatrix}, \quad b = [p_0 \quad p_1], \quad (3.200)$$

where α and β are any nonnegative constants and p_0 and p_1 are any two nonnegative numbers such that $p_0 + p_1 = 1$. The interested reader is urged to consult Neuts [1981a] for a superb treatment of distributions of the phase type.

Modifications to the basic model of phase-dependent arrival and service rates can be made to model both *iid* arrival and service times of the phase type; such models are classified as PH/PH/1. Neuts [1981a] covers the analysis of PH/PH/1 models, which have matrix geometric solutions, as well as numerous other models. We defer further coverage of models having the matrix geometric solution to Chapter 5 and turn to the analysis of other models at this time.

Exercise 3.53   Starting with (3.198) as given, prove the validity of (3.199).

Exercise 3.54   Suppose

$$S = \begin{bmatrix} -\mu & \mu \\ 0 & -\mu \end{bmatrix} \quad S^0 = \begin{bmatrix} 0 \\ \mu \end{bmatrix}, \quad \text{and } P_t(0) = [1 \quad 0].$$

Find $F_{\tilde{x}}(t) = P\{\tilde{x} \le t\}$ and $f_{\tilde{x}}(t)$, and identify the form of $f_{\tilde{x}}(t)$. [*Hint*: First solve for $P_0(t)$, then for $P_1(t)$, and then for $P_2(t) = P_a(t)$. There is never a need to do matrix exponentiation.]

Exercise 3.55   Consider a single-server queueing system having Poisson arrivals. Suppose upon entering service, each customer initially receives a type 1 service increment. Each time a customer receives a type 1 service increment, the customer leaves the system with probability $(1 - p)$ or else receives a type 2 service increment followed by an additional type 1 service increment. Suppose type 1 and type 2 service increment times are each drawn independently from exponential distributions with parameters μ_1 and μ_2, respectively. Define the phase of the system to be 1 if a customer in service is receiving a type 2 service increment. Otherwise, the system is in phase 0. Define the state of the system to be 0 when the system is empty and by the pair (i, j) where $i > 0$ is the system occupancy and $j = 0, 1$

is the phase of the service process. Define $P_i = [\, P_{i0} \quad P_{i1} \,]$ for $i > 0$ and P_0, a scalar. Draw the state diagram, and determine the matrix Q, the infinitesimal generator for the continuous-time Markov chain defining the occupancy process for this system.

3.9 SUPPLEMENTARY PROBLEMS

1. Messages arrive to a statistical multiplexing system according to a Poisson process having rate λ. Message lengths, denoted by $\tilde{m}$, are specified in octets, groups of eight bits, and are drawn from an exponential distribution having mean $1/\mu$. Messages are multiplexed onto a single trunk having a transmission capacity of C bits per second according to a FCFS discipline.

   (a) Let $\tilde{x}$ denote the time required for transmission of a message over the trunk. Show that $\tilde{x}$ has the exponential distribution with parameter $\mu C/8$.

   (b) Let $E[\tilde{m}] = 128$ octets and $C = 56$ kilobits per second (Kbps). Determine $\lambda_{\max}$, the maximum message-carrying capacity of the trunk.

   (c) Let $\tilde{n}$ denote the number of messages in the system in stochastic equilibrium. Under the conditions of (b), determine $P\{\tilde{n} > n\}$ as a function of λ. Determine the maximum value of λ such that $P\{\tilde{n} > 50\} < 10^{-2}$.

   (d) For the value of λ determined in part (c), determine the maximum value of s such that $P\{\tilde{s} > s\} < 10^{-2}$, where $\tilde{s}$ is the total amount of time a message spends in the system.

   (e) Using the value of λ obtained in part (c), determine the minimum value of K, the system capacity, such that $P_B(K) < 10^{-2}$.

2. A finite population, K, of users attached to a statistical multiplexing system operate in a continuous cycle of *think, wait, service*. During the think phase, the length of which is denoted by $\tilde{t}$, the user generates a message. The message then waits in a queue behind any other messages, if any, that may be awaiting transmission. Upon reaching the head of the queue, the user receives service and the corresponding message is transmitted over

a communication channel. Message service times, $\tilde{x}$, and think times, $\tilde{t}$, are drawn from exponential distributions with rates μ and λ, respectively. Let the state of the system, defined as the total number of users waiting and in service, be denoted by $\tilde{n}$.

(a) The first passage time from state i to state $i-1$ is the total amount of time the system spends in all states from the time it first enters state i until it makes its first transition to the state $i-1$. Let $\tilde{s}_i$ denote the total cumulative time the system spends in state i during the first passage time from state i to state $i-1$. Determine the distribution of $\tilde{s}_i$.

(b) Determine the distribution of the number of visits from state i to state $i+1$ during the first passage time from state i to $i-1$.

(c) Show that $E[\tilde{y}_K]$, the expected length of a busy period, is given by the following recursion:

$$E[\tilde{y}_K] = \frac{1}{\mu}\left(1 + \lambda(K-1)E\left[\tilde{y}_{K-1}\right]\right) \quad \text{with } E\left[\tilde{y}_0\right] = 0.$$

[*Hint*: Use the distribution found in part (b) in combination with the result of part (a) as part of the proof.]

(d) Let $P_0(K)$ denote the stochastic equilibrium probability that the communication channel is idle. Determine $P_0(K)$ using ordinary birth–death process analysis.

(e) Let $E[\tilde{i}_K]$ denote the expected length of the idle period for the communication channel. Verify that $P_0(K)$ is given by the ratio of the expected length of the idle period to the sum of the expected lengths of the idle and busy periods, that is,

$$P_0(K) = \frac{E[\tilde{i}_K]}{E[\tilde{i}_K] + E[\tilde{y}_K]},$$

which can be determined iteratively by

$$P_0(K) = \frac{1}{1 + [(K\lambda)/\mu]\,\{1 + (K-1)\lambda\,E[\tilde{y}_{K-1}]\}}.$$

That is, show that $P_0(K)$ computed by the formula just stated is identical to that obtained in part (d).

3. *Traffic engineering with finite population.* Ten students in a certain graduate program share an office that has four telephones. The students are always busy doing one of two activities: *doing queueing homework* (work state) or *using the telephone* (service state); no other activities are allowed—ever. Each student operates continuously as follows: The student is initially in the work state for an exponential, rate β, period of time. The student then attempts to use one of the telephones. If all telephones are busy, then the student is blocked and returns immediately to the work state. If a telephone is available, the student uses the telephone for a length of time drawn from an exponential distribution with rate μ and then returns to the work state.

(a) Define an appropriate state space for this service system.

(b) Draw a state diagram for this system showing all transition rates.

(c) Write the balance equations for the system.

(d) Specify a method of computing the ergodic blocking probability for the system—that is, the proportion of attempts to join the service system that will be blocked—in terms of the system parameters and the ergodic state probabilities.

(e) Specify a formula to compute the average call generation rate.

(f) Let $\mu = 1/3$ calls per minute; that is, call holding times have a mean of three minutes. Compute the call blocking probability as a function of β for $\beta \in (0, 30)$.

(g) Compare the results of part (f) to those of the Erlang loss system having four servers and total offered traffic equal to that of part (f). That is, for each value of β, there is a total offered traffic rate for the system specified in this problem. Use this total offered traffic to obtain a value of λ, and then obtain the blocking probability that would result in the Erlang loss system, and plot this result on the same graph as the results obtained in (f). Then compare the results.

4. A company has six employees who use a leased line to access a database. Each employee has a *think* time which is exponentially distributed with parameter λ. Upon completion of the think time,

the employee needs the database and joins a queue along with other employees who may be waiting for the leased line to access the database. Holding times are exponentially distributed with parameter μ. When the waiting employee reaches a level 2, use of an auxiliary line is authorized. The time required for the employee to obtain the authorization is exponentially distributed with rate τ. If the authorization is completed when there are less than three employees waiting, or if the number of employees waiting drops below two at any time while the extra line is in use, the extra line is immediately disconnected.

(a) The set $\{0, 1, 2, 3, 3r, 3a, 4r, 4a, 5r, 5a\}$, where the numbers indicate the number of employees waiting and in service, the letter r indicates that authorization has been requested, and the letter a indicates that the auxiliary line is actually available for service, is a suitable state space for this process.

(b) The situation in state 4r is that there are employees waiting and in service and an authorization has been requested. With the repair process in state 4r at time t_0, list the events that would cause a change in the state of the process.

(c) Compute the probability that each of the possible events listed in part (a) would actually cause the change of state, and specify the new state of the process following the event.

(d) What is the distribution of the amount of time the system spends in state 4r on each visit? Explain.

(e) Draw the state transition-rate diagram.

(f) Write the balance equations for the system.

5. Consider the M/M/2 queueing system, the system having Poisson arrivals, exponential service, two parallel servers, and an infinite waiting room capacity.

(a) Determine the expected first passage time from state 2 to state 1. [*Hint*: How does this period of time compare to the length of the busy period for an ordinary M/M/1 queueing system?]

(b) Determine the expected length of the busy period for the ordinary M/M/2 queueing system by conditioning on whether or not an arrival occurs before the first service completion of the busy period and by using the result from part (a).

(c) Define $\tilde{c}$ as the length of time between successive entries into busy periods, that is, as the length of one busy/idle cycle. Determine the probability that the system is idle at an arbitrary point in time by taking the ratio of the expected length of an idle period to the expected length of a cycle.

(d) Determine the total expected amount of time the system spends in state 1 during a busy period. Determine the probability that there is exactly one customer in the system by taking the ratio of the expected amount of time that there is exactly one customer in the system during a busy period to the expected length of a cycle.

(e) Check the results of parts (c) and (d) using classical birth–death analysis.

(f) Determine the expected sojourn time, $E[\tilde{s}]$, for an arbitrary customer by conditioning on whether an arbitrary customer finds either zero, one, two or more customers present. Consider the nonpreemptive last-come-first-serve discipline together with Little's result and the fact that the distribution of the number of customers in the system is not affected by order of service.

6. Messages arrive to a statistical multiplexer at a Poisson rate λ for transmission over a communication line having a capacity of C in octets per second. Message lengths, specified in octets, are exponentially distributed with parameter μ. When the waiting messages reach a level 3, the capacity of the transmission line is increased to C_e by adding a dial-up line. The time required to set up the dial-up line to increase the capacity is exponentially distributed with rate τ. If the connection is completed when there are less than three messages waiting or if the number of messages waiting drops below two at any time while the additional capacity is in use, the extra line is immediately disconnected.

(a) Define a suitable state space for this queueing system.

(b) Draw the state transition-rate diagram.

(c) Organize the state vector for this system according to level,

where the level corresponds to the number of messages waiting and in service, and write the vector balance equations
for the system.

(d) Determine the infinitesimal generator for the underlying
Markov chain for this system and comment on its structure
relative to matrix geometric solutions.

7. Let Q be an $(m+1)$ square matrix representing the infinitesimal
generator for a continuous-time Markov chain with state space
$\{0, 1, \ldots, m\}$. Let

$$\tilde{Q} = \begin{bmatrix} T & T^0 \\ 0 & 0 \end{bmatrix},$$

where T is an m-square matrix, T^0 is an $m \times 1$ column vector,
and the remaining terms are chosen to conform, be a matrix
obtained by replacing any row of Q by a row of zeros and then
exchanging rows so that the final row is a vector of zeros. Let
$P(t) = [P_t(t) \quad P_a(t)]$ denote the state probability vector for the
Markov chain for which $\tilde{Q}$ is the infinitesimal generator, with
$P_t(t)$ a row vector of dimension m and $P_a(t)$ a scalar.

(a) Argue that if Q is the infinitesimal generator for an irreducible Markov chain, then the states $0, 1, \ldots, m-1$ of
the modified chain are all transient, and state m is an ab-
sorbing state.

(b) Prove that if Q is the infinitesimal generator for an irreducible Markov chain, then the matrix T must be nonsingular. [*Hint*: Solve for $P_t(t)$, then prove by contradiction.
Make use of the fact that if T is singular, then T has a zero
eigenvalue.]

(c) Show that $P_a(t) = 1 - P_t(0) \exp\{Tt\}\mathbf{e}$. [*Hint*: $P_t(t)\mathbf{e}$ is the
probability that the state of the modified Markov chain is in
the set $\{0, \ldots, m-1\}$ at time t.]

(d) Let $\tilde{x}$ be the time required for the modified Markov chain
to reach state m given an initial probability vector $P(0) =
[P_t(0) \quad 0]$, that is, with $P_t(0)\mathbf{e} = 1$. Argue that $P\{\tilde{x} \leq t\} =
P_a(t)$, that is, $P\{\tilde{x} \leq t\} = 1 - P_t(0) \exp\{Tt\}\mathbf{e}$.

(e) Argue that if Q is the infinitesimal generator for an irreducible Markov chain, then the matrix $\tilde{T} = T + T^0 P_t(0)$ is the infinitesimal generator for an irreducible Markov chain with state space $\{0, 1, \ldots, m - 1\}$.

8. Consider an m-server queueing system having Poisson arrivals. Suppose upon entering service, each customer initially receives a type 1 service increment. Each time a customer receives a type 1 service increment, the customer leaves the system with probability $(1 - p)$ or else receives a type 2 service increment followed by an additional type 1 service increment. Suppose type 1 and type 2 service increment times are each drawn independently from exponential distributions with parameters μ_1 and μ_2, respectively. With the service process defined as in Problem 7, suppose there are m servers. Define the phase of the system to be j if there are j customers receiving a type 2 service increment, $j = 0, 1, \ldots, m$. Define the state of the system to be the 0 when the system is empty and by the pair (i, j) where $i \geq 0$ is the system occupancy and $j = 0, \ldots, i$ is the phase of the service process. Define $P_i = [P_{i0} \quad P_{i1} \quad \cdots \quad P_{i,\min\{i,m\}}]$ for $i > 0$ and P_0, a scalar.

   (a) Draw the state-transition diagram for the special case of $m = 3$.

   (b) Write the matrix balance equations for the special case of $m = 3$.

   (c) Write the matrix balance equations for the case of general values of m.

   (d) Determine the matrix Q, the infinitesimal generator for the continuous-time Markov chain defining the occupancy process for this system.

   (e) Comment on the structure of the matrix Q relative to that for the phase-dependent arrival and service rate queueing system and to the M/PH/1 system. What modifications in the solution procedure would you have to make to solve this problem? [*Hint*: See Neuts [1981a], pp. 24–26.

C H A P T E R

$$\boxed{4}$$

The M/G/1 Queueing System and Variants

In the previous chapters we made extensive use of the memoryless properties of the exponential distribution to study the dynamics of the M/M/1 and other queueing systems as well as the service-time distributions and interarrival time distributions, which were exponentially distributed. Due to the memoryless property of the exponential distribution, the evolution of such systems from any point in time forward is independent of past history. Thus, the memoryless property allowed us to specify the state of the system at an arbitrary point in time and to write equations describing the system dynamics conveniently.

If the service system has service times drawn from a general distribution, then the memoryless property is lost; it is then necessary to choose observation times carefully in order that the state of the system at the observation times can be easily specified. That is, if we choose the observation times carefully, we may be able to specify the state of the system conveniently, and further, we may succeed in having the evolution of the process from that point forward be independent of past history. Suppose, for example, that we choose our observation times as those instants in time when a customer has just completed service. At those points in time, both the arrival process,

159

which is memoryless, and the service process, which is not necessarily memoryless, start over again. Thus, in order to determine the future evolution of the system, it is necessary to know only the number of customers left in the system immediately following customer departures.

Define $\{\tilde{q}_n,\ n \geq 1\}$ to be the number of customers left in the system by the nth departing customer. Then, according to our previous observations, the process $\{\tilde{q}_n,\ n \geq 1\}$ is Markovian. We call $\{\tilde{q}_n,\ n \geq 1\}$ an embedded Markov chain, and we say that we have "embedded a Markov chain at the points of customer departure." Following our notation of the previous chapters, we denote the number of customers in the system, including the one in service, if any, by $\tilde{n}(t)$. The process $\{\tilde{n}(t),\ t \geq 0\}$ does not have the Markovian property. That is, unlike for the M/M/1 case, the future evolution of the process depends on the length of time the system has been in the present state. However, the process does have the Markov property at instants of time just after customer departures. Thus, the process $\{\tilde{n}(t),\ t \geq 0\}$ is called a semi-Markov process.

The analytical tools used to study queueing systems of this type are fundamentally the same as those used to study Markovian models, but their application is quite different. The notion of balance equations in non-Markovian systems, for example, can still be applied, but the application is much more difficult (see Daigle and Whitehead [1985]). Thus different approaches are used to examine non-Markovian systems. In this chapter, we present basic tools that are found to be useful in the analysis of non-Markovian systems. Our presentation is accomplished through the development of many of the classical results for the M/G/1 system and some of its variants, in addition to presentation of some nontraditional approaches and results.

In Section 4.1, we begin our study of the M/G/1 queueing system with a classical development of the Pollaczek–Khintchine transform equation, or probability generating function, for the occupancy distribution. In the same section, we develop the Laplace–Stieltjes transforms for the ergodic waiting time, sojourn time, and busy-period distributions.

In Section 4.2, we address inversion of the occupancy distributions probability generating function developed in the first section.

Two methods are presented. The first method is based on Fourier analysis (Daigle [1989]), and the second approach, due to Keilson and Servi [1989], is recursive. The latter approach appears to be useful when only a few terms of the distribution are required; while the former appears to be more appropriate when the entire distribution is desired. Both approaches are applicable to systems other than the ordinary M/G/1.

We next turn our attention to the direct computation of average waiting and sojourn times for the M/G/1 queueing system. Our development follows that for the M/M/1 system to the point at which the consequences of not having the Markovian property surfaces. At this point, a little renewal theory is introduced so that the analysis can be completed. Additional insight into the properties of the M/G/1 system is also introduced at this point. Following completion of the waiting- and sojourn-time development, we introduce alternating renewal theory and use a basic result of alternating renewal theory to compute the average length of the M/G/1 busy period directly.

Based on the results of Section 4.3, it will be seen that the Pollaczek–Khintchine waiting and sojourn times can be expressed as geometrically weighted sums of random variables. This characteristic has long eluded logical explanation but has finally been explained in terms of the unfinished work for the M/G/1 system under the last-come-first-serve (LCFS) service discipline. This explanation, due to Kelly [1979] and Cooper and Niu [1986], is provided in Section 4.4. The material can be skipped on first reading, but it is included primarily because it illustrates the analytical advantage of substituting a seemingly difficult queueing-system question for a relatively easy one that has the same solution.

In Section 4.5, we analyze the M/G/1 queueing system with exceptional first service; that is, the service times of all customers except the first customer of each busy period are chosen independently from a common distribution $F_{\tilde{x}}$, whereas the service time of the first customer of each busy period is chosen independently from the distribution $F_{\tilde{x}_e}$. We begin our development by deriving the Pollaczek–Khintchine transform equation of the occupancy distribution using the same argument by which Fuhrmann–Cooper decomposition was derived (Fuhrmann and Cooper [1985]); this approach avoids the difficulties of writing and solving difference equations. We then derive the probability generating function of the occupancy distribution for the M/G/1 queueing system with exceptional first service, again using the ideas of Fuhrmann–Cooper decomposition. Finally, we derive the probability generating function of the occupancy distribution for the M/G/1 queueing system with set-up as a variant of the M/G/1 queueing system with exceptional first service.

The techniques explored in the study of the M/G/1 queueing system with exceptional first service are used in Section 4.6 to study the M/G/1 queueing system with externally assigned priorities and head-of-the-line service. That is, the customers arriving belong to a certain priority group, where the arrival processes of the various classes are Poisson with parameter dependent on the class. There are K classes, and the service times for the class i customers are drawn independently of everything from the distribution $F_{\tilde{x}_i}$, $1 \leq i \leq K$. Transform equations are developed for the occupancy, waiting-time and sojourn-time distributions.

In Section 4.7, we develop expressions for the average waiting and sojourn times for the M/G/1 queueing system under both preemptive and nonpreemptive priority disciplines. This section is basically an extension of Section 4.3.

4.1 M/G/1 QUEUEING SYSTEM TRANSFORM EQUATIONS

In this section we examine the behavior of the ordinary M/G/1 queueing system. We develop the probability generating function for the occupancy distribution, and then we use this result to develop the Laplace–Stieltjes transforms for the ergodic waiting-time, sojourn-time, and busy-period distributions.

Recall that we have defined $\{\tilde{q}_n, \ n \geq 1\}$ to be the number of customers left in the system by the nth departing customer. Now, it is easy to see that the number of customers left by the $(n+1)$th departing customer is equal to the number of customers who arrive during the $(n+1)$th service plus either zero or one fewer than the number left by the nth departing customer, whichever is greater. Thus, we define $\tilde{v}_n$ to be the number of arrivals that occur during the nth customer's service. Then, we find according to the above discussion that

$$\tilde{q}_{n+1} = (\tilde{q}_n - 1)^+ + \tilde{v}_{n+1}, \qquad (4.1),$$

where

$$(a)^+ = \max\{a, 0\}. \qquad (4.2)$$

We shall solve (4.1) by making use of probability generating functions and Laplace–Stieltjes transforms. In particular, we shall develop an expression for the probability generating functions for the sequence of random variables $\tilde{q}_n$, and then we will obtain the ergodic probability generating function by taking limits.

Observation of (4.1) reveals that $\tilde{q}_{n+1}$ is the sum of two independent random variables, $(\tilde{q}_n - 1)^+$ and $\tilde{v}_{n+1}$. Each of these random variables has a generic form, which will occur in later analysis. In addition, we will constantly be encountering sums of independent random variables. Therefore, before proceeding to the analysis of (4.1), we present the following three theorems, which will be useful both in the current analysis and in later analyses.

Theorem 4.1   Let $\tilde{x}$ and $\tilde{y}$ be two independent, nonnegative, integer-valued random variables. Then

$$\mathcal{F}_{\tilde{x}+\tilde{y}}(z) = \mathcal{F}_{\tilde{x}}(z)\mathcal{F}_{\tilde{y}}(z),$$

where $\mathcal{F}_{\tilde{x}}(z) \triangleq E[z^{\tilde{x}}]$.

Proof   The proof follows directly from the fact that $z^{\tilde{x}}$ and $z^{\tilde{y}}$ are independent random variables and consequently $E[z^{\tilde{x}}z^{\tilde{y}}] = E[z^{\tilde{x}}]E[z^{\tilde{y}}]$. □

Theorem 4.2   Let $\tilde{x} \sim F_{\tilde{x}}(x)$ denote a random period of time, and let $F_{\tilde{x}}^*(s)$ denote the Laplace–Stieltjes transform of $F_{\tilde{x}}(x)$; that is, $F_{\tilde{x}}^*(x) = \int_0^\infty e^{-st}dF_{\tilde{x}}(t)$. Further, let $\{\tilde{n}(t), t \geq 0\}$ be a Poisson process with rate λ, and let $\tilde{y}$ denote the number of events from $\{\tilde{n}(t), t \geq 0\}$ that occur during the period of time $\tilde{x}$. Then, $\mathcal{F}_{\tilde{y}}(z) = F_{\tilde{x}}^*(\lambda[1 - z])$. That is, the probability generating function for the number of events from a Poisson process that occur during a random period of time is given by the Laplace–Stieltjes transform for the distribution of the length of the period of time with the transform variable, s, evaluated at the point $\lambda[1 - z]$.

Proof

$$\mathcal{F}_{\tilde{y}}(z) = \int_0^\infty E[z^{\tilde{y}} | \tilde{x} = x] dF_{\tilde{x}}(x).$$

But

$$E[z^{\tilde{y}} | \tilde{x} = x] = \sum_{y=0}^\infty E[z^{\tilde{y}} | \tilde{x} = x, \ \tilde{y} = y] P\{\tilde{y} = y | \tilde{x} = x\}$$

$$= \sum_{y=0}^\infty z^y \frac{(\lambda x)^y}{y!} e^{-\lambda x}$$

$$= e^{-\lambda(1-z)x}.$$

Thus we have

$$\mathcal{F}_{\tilde{y}}(z) = \int_0^\infty e^{-\lambda(1-z)x} dF_{\tilde{x}}(x)$$

$$= \int_0^\infty e^{-sx} dF_{\tilde{x}}(x) \Big|_{s=\lambda(1-z)}.$$

That is,

$$\mathcal{F}_{\tilde{y}}(z) = F_{\tilde{x}}^*(\lambda[1-z]). \qquad \square$$

Exercise 4.1   With $\tilde{x}$, $\{\tilde{n}(t), \ t \geq 0\}$, and $\tilde{y}$ defined as in Theorem 4.2, show that $E[\tilde{y}(\tilde{y}-1)\cdots(\tilde{y}-n+1)] = \lambda^n E[\tilde{x}^n]$.

Theorem 4.3   Let $\tilde{x}$ be a nonnegative integer valued random variable with probability generating function $\mathcal{F}_{\tilde{x}}(z)$. Then

$$\mathcal{F}_{(\tilde{x}-1)^+}(z) = (1 - \frac{1}{z})P\{\tilde{x} = 0\} + \frac{1}{z}\mathcal{F}_{\tilde{x}}(z). \qquad \square$$

Exercise 4.2   Prove Theorem 4.3.

We now turn to the analysis of (4.1). As before, we let $\tilde{x}_n$ denote the service time of the nth customer, and we assume $\{\tilde{x}_n, \ n \geq 1\}$ to be a sequence of *iid* random variables with mean

$$\frac{1}{\mu} = \int_0^\infty x \ dF_{\tilde{x}}(x),$$

where $\tilde{x}$ represents a generic $\tilde{x}_i$. Clearly, $\tilde{v}_{n+1}$ is independent of $(\tilde{q}_n - 1)^+$ because the number of arrivals during the $(n+1)$th service time does not depend on the number of customers left in the system by the nth departing customer. Therefore, by Theorem 4.1,

$$\mathcal{F}_{\tilde{q}_{n+1}}(z) = \mathcal{F}_{(\tilde{q}_n - 1)^+}(z)\mathcal{F}_{\tilde{v}_{n+1}}(z).$$

But according to Theorem 4.2, we find that

$$\mathcal{F}_{\tilde{v}_{n+1}}(z) = F^*_{\tilde{x}_{n+1}}(\lambda[1 - z]),$$

and by Theorem 4.3,

$$\mathcal{F}_{(\tilde{q}_n - 1)^+} = \left(1 - \frac{1}{z}\right)P\{\tilde{q}_n = 0\} + \frac{1}{z}\mathcal{F}_{\tilde{q}_n}(z).$$

Thus we have

$$\mathcal{F}_{\tilde{q}_{n+1}}(z) = \left[\left(1 - \frac{1}{z}\right)P\{\tilde{q}_n = 0\} + \frac{1}{z}\mathcal{F}_{\tilde{q}_n}(z)\right]F^*_{\tilde{x}_{n+1}}(\lambda[1 - z]). \quad (4.3)$$

In the limit as $n \to \infty$, $\tilde{q}_n \to \tilde{q}$, and $\tilde{x}_n \to \tilde{x}$, so we get

$$\mathcal{F}_{\tilde{q}}(z) = \left[\left(1 - \frac{1}{z}\right)P\{\tilde{q} = 0\} + \frac{1}{z}\mathcal{F}_{\tilde{q}}(z)\right]F^*_{\tilde{x}}(\lambda[1 - z]). \quad (4.4)$$

Upon solving (4.4), we find that

$$\mathcal{F}_{\tilde{q}}(z) = \frac{(1 - z)P\{\tilde{q} = 0\}F^*_{\tilde{x}}(\lambda[1 - z])}{F^*_{\tilde{x}}(\lambda[1 - z]) - z}. \quad (4.5)$$

It remains to specify $P\{\tilde{q} = 0\}$, the probability that a departing customer leaves no customers in the system. It is straightforward to determine this unknown probability by using the facts that $F^*_X(0) = 1$, $\mathcal{F}_X(1) = 1$, and other properties of the Laplace–Stieltjes transform and probability generating function that we have previously discussed. By taking limits on both sides of (4.5), applying L'Hôpital's rule, and then using the properties of Laplace transforms and probability generating functions, we find that

$$P\{\tilde{q} = 0\} = 1 - \frac{\lambda}{\mu} = 1 - \rho, \quad (4.6)$$

where $\rho = \lambda/\mu$ is the server utilization as defined in Chapter 3. Thus we find that

$$\mathcal{F}_{\tilde{q}}(z) = \frac{(1-z)(1-\rho)F_{\tilde{x}}^*(\lambda[1-z])}{F_{\tilde{x}}^*(\lambda[1-z]) - z}. \tag{4.7}$$

Exercise 4.3   Starting with (4.5), use the properties of Laplace transforms and probability generating functions to establish (4.6).

Exercise 4.4   Establish (4.6) directly by using Little's result.

Now, in the M/G/1 queueing system, the probability that a departing customer leaves n customers in the system is the same as the probability that an arriving customer finds n customers in the system when the system is in stochastic equilibrium. A little thought will show that this must be true in order for an equilibrium distribution to exist. In addition, we have pointed out earlier that the Poisson arrival's view of the system is exactly the same as that of a random observer. Thus we find that

$$P\{\tilde{n} = n\} = P\{\tilde{q} = n\} = P\{\tilde{q}' = n\},$$

where $\tilde{q}'$ is the number of customers found in the system by an arbitrary arrival when the system is in stochastic equilibrium, and $\tilde{n}$ is the number of customers found in the system by an arbitrary random observer. Thus we find

$$\mathcal{F}_{\tilde{n}}(z) = \frac{(1-z)(1-\rho)F_{\tilde{x}}^*(\lambda[1-z])}{F_{\tilde{x}}^*(\lambda[1-z]) - z}. \tag{4.8}$$

Definition 4.1   **Squared Coefficient of Variation**. For any nonnegative random variable $\tilde{x}$ with $E[\tilde{x}] > 0$, the *squared coefficient of variation* for the random variable $\tilde{x}$ is defined to be the quantity

$$C_{\tilde{x}}^2 = \frac{\text{Var}(\tilde{x})}{E^2[\tilde{x}]}. \quad \square \tag{4.9}$$

Exercise 4.5   Using the properties of the probability generating function, show that

$$E[\tilde{n}] = \rho + \frac{\lambda\rho}{1 - \rho}\frac{E[\tilde{x}^2]}{2E[\tilde{x}]}$$

$$= \rho\left(1 + \frac{\rho}{1 - \rho}\frac{C_{\tilde{x}}^2 + 1}{2}\right). \tag{4.10}$$

[*Hint*: The algebra will be greatly simplified if (4.8) is first rewritten as

$$\mathcal{F}_{\tilde{n}}(z) = \alpha(z)/\beta(z),$$

where

$$\alpha(z) = (1 - \rho)F_{\tilde{x}}^*(\lambda[1 - z])$$

and

$$\beta(z) = 1 - \frac{1 - F_{\tilde{x}}^*(\lambda[1 - z])}{1 - z}.$$

Then, in order to find

$$\lim_{z \to 1}\frac{d}{dz}\mathcal{F}_{\tilde{n}}(z),$$

first find the limits as $z \to 1$ of $\alpha(z)$, $\beta(z)$, $d\alpha(z)/dz$, and $d\beta(z)/dz$, and then substitute these limits into the formula for the derivative of a ratio. Alternatively, multiply on both sides of (4.8) to clear fractions and then differentiate and take limits.]

Exercise 4.6   Let $\delta_n = 1$ if $\tilde{q}_n = 0$, and let $\delta_n = 0$ if $\tilde{q}_n > 0$, so that $\tilde{q}_{n+1} = \tilde{q}_n - 1 + \delta_n + \tilde{v}_{n+1}$. Starting with this equation, find $E[\delta_\infty]$ and $E[\tilde{n}]$. Interpret $E[\delta_\infty]$. [*Hint*: To find $E[\tilde{n}]$, start off by squaring both sides of the equation for $\tilde{q}_{n+1}$.]

Exercise 4.7   Batch Arrivals. Suppose arrivals to the system occur in batches of size $\tilde{b}$, and the batches occur according to a Poisson process at rate λ. Develop an expression equivalent to (4.5) for this case. Be sure to define all variables carefully.

4.1.1   Sojourn Time for the M/G/1 System

Recall that $s_n \to \tilde{s}$ is the total amount of time spent in the system by an arbitrary customer. Thus

$$F_{\tilde{s}}^*(s) = \int_0^\infty e^{-st} dF_{\tilde{s}}(t)$$

is the Laplace–Stieltjes transform of the distribution of the total amount of time that an arbitrary customer spends in the system. From Theorem 4.2, we therefore find that the probability generating function for the number of customers that arrive during the time a customer spends in the system is given by $F_{\tilde{s}}^*(\lambda[1 - z])$. But, for a FCFS system, the number of customers that arrive while a customer is in the system is exactly the same as the number of customers left behind by that customer. So

$$\mathcal{F}_{\tilde{q}}(z) = F_{\tilde{s}}^*(\lambda[1 - z]). \tag{4.11}$$

From this we conclude that

$$F_{\tilde{s}}^*(s) = \mathcal{F}_{\tilde{q}}(z)\Big|_{z=1-(s/\lambda)}. \tag{4.12}$$

Thus, from (4.8), we find that

$$F_{\tilde{s}}^*(s) = \frac{(1 - z)(1 - \rho)F_{\tilde{x}}^*(\lambda[1 - z])}{F_{\tilde{x}}^*(\lambda[1 - z]) - z}\Big|_{z=1-(s/\lambda)}. \tag{4.13}$$

After a little algebra, (4.13) reduces to the Pollaczek–Khintchine transform equation for the sojourn time, which is

$$F_{\tilde{s}}^*(s) = \frac{(1 - \rho)s F_{\tilde{x}}^*(s)}{s - \lambda[1 - F_{\tilde{x}}^*(s)]}. \tag{4.14}$$

An alternative presentation of (4.14), which we will find useful later, is

$$F_{\tilde{s}}^*(s) = \frac{(1 - \rho)F_{\tilde{x}}^*(s)}{1 - \rho\{[1 - F_{\tilde{x}}^*(s)]/(sE[\tilde{x}])\}}. \tag{4.15}$$

In principle, $F_{\tilde{s}}^*(s)$ can be inverted to obtain $d/dt\, P\{\tilde{s} \leq t\}$, which is the density of the sojourn time. This can be done fairly easily if $F_{\tilde{x}}^*(s)$ is rational (that is, if it is a ratio of polynomials) by using partial fraction expansions. The above expression can also be differentiated to obtain moments, for example,

$$E[\tilde{s}] = -\frac{d}{ds}F_{\tilde{s}}^*(s)|_{s=0}.$$

Exercise 4.8   Using (4.14) and the properties of the Laplace transform, show that

$$E[\tilde{s}] = \frac{\rho}{1-\rho}\frac{E[\tilde{x}^2]}{2E[\tilde{x}]} + E[\tilde{x}]$$

$$= \left(\frac{\rho}{1-\rho}\frac{C_{\tilde{x}}^2+1}{2} + 1\right)E[\tilde{x}]. \tag{4.16}$$

Combine this result with that of Exercise 4.5 to verify the validity of Little's result when applied to the M/G/1 queueing system. [*Hint*: Use (4.15) rather than (4.14) as a starting point, and use the hint for Exercise 4.5.]

4.1.2   Waiting Time for the M/G/1 System

Recall that $w_n \to \tilde{w}$ refers to the amount of time a customer spends in the queue waiting for service to begin. This means that $\tilde{s} = \tilde{w} + \tilde{x}$. Because the service time for a customer does not depend on the amount of time the customer waits for service to begin, $\tilde{w}$ and $\tilde{x}$ are independent, and consequently, $F_{\tilde{s}}^*(s) = F_{\tilde{w}}^*(s)F_{\tilde{x}}^*(s)$. It therefore follows from (4.14) and (4.15) that

$$F_{\tilde{w}}^*(s) = \frac{(1-\rho)s}{s - \lambda[1 - F_{\tilde{x}}^*(s)]}$$

$$= \frac{(1-\rho)}{1 - \rho\{[1 - F_{\tilde{x}}^*(s)]/(sE[\tilde{x}])\}}. \tag{4.17}$$

Exercise 4.9   Using (4.17) and the properties of the Laplace transform, show that

$$E[\tilde{w}] = \frac{\rho}{1-\rho}\frac{C_{\tilde{x}}^2+1}{2}E[\tilde{x}]. \tag{4.18}$$

Combine this result with the result of Exercise 4.5 to verify the validity of Little's result when applied to the waiting line for the M/G/1 queueing system.

Platzman, Ammons, and Bartholdi [1988] describe an approximate method for inverting transforms such as those for the waiting and sojourn time. Experience has shown that this method works quite well, especially for the tail of the distribution.

4.1.3   Busy Period for the M/G/1 Queueing System

In this section, we will determine the Laplace–Stieltjes transform for the distribution of the length of the busy period for the M/G/1 queueing system. As before, we let $\tilde{y}$ denote the length of an M/G/1 busy period, and we let $F_{\tilde{y}}^*(s)$ denote the Laplace–Stieltjes transform of the distribution of $\tilde{y}$; that is, $F_{\tilde{y}}^*(s) = E[e^{-s\tilde{y}}]$. Further, denote the length of service time for the first customer in the busy period by $\tilde{x}$, and let $\tilde{v}$ denote the number of arrivals during the service time of this customer. Then

$$F_{\tilde{y}}^*(s) = \int_0^\infty E[e^{-s\tilde{y}} \mid \tilde{x} = x]dF_{\tilde{x}}(x). \tag{4.19}$$

Also

$$E[e^{-s\tilde{y}} \mid \tilde{x} = x] = \sum_{v=0}^\infty E[e^{-s\tilde{y}} \mid \tilde{x} = x, \; \tilde{v} = v]P\{\tilde{v} = v \mid \tilde{x} = x\}.$$

Now, if $\tilde{v}$ customers arrive during x, then at the end of x there will be $\tilde{v}$ customers in the system, none of whom have begun service. Because order of service does not affect the length of the busy period, the remainder of the busy period has length $\tilde{y}_0 + \tilde{y}_1 + \tilde{y}_2 + \cdots + \tilde{y}_v$, where $\tilde{y}_j$ denotes the length of the sub-busy period due to the jth customer who arrived during x and $\tilde{y}_0 = 0$ with probability 1. Thus

$$E[e^{-s\tilde{y}} \mid \tilde{x} = x] = \sum_{v=0}^\infty E[e^{-s(x+\sum_{i=0}^v \tilde{y}_i)}]\frac{(\lambda x)^v}{v!}e^{-\lambda x}$$

$$= \sum_{v=0}^\infty e^{-sx} E\left[\prod_{i=0}^v e^{-s\tilde{y}_i}\right]\frac{(\lambda x)^v}{v!}e^{-\lambda x}.$$

But, for $i \geq 1$, the $\tilde{y}_i$s are *iid* random variables with common distribution $F_{\tilde{y}}$, so

$$E\left[\prod_{i=0}^{v} e^{-s\tilde{y}_i}\right] = [F_{\tilde{y}}^*(s)]^v,$$

where we have used the fact that $E[e^{-s\tilde{y}_0}] = E[e^{-s0}] = 1$. Thus

$$E[e^{-s\tilde{y}} \mid \tilde{x} = x] = \sum_{v=0}^{\infty} \frac{[F_{\tilde{y}}^*(s)]^v(\lambda x)^v}{v!} e^{-\lambda x} \tag{4.20}$$

$$= e^{-[\lambda - \lambda F_{\tilde{y}}^*(s)]x}.$$

Substitution of (4.20) into (4.19) then yields

$$F_{\tilde{y}}^*(s) = \int_0^{\infty} e^{-[s+\lambda-\lambda F_{\tilde{y}}^*(s)]x} dF_{\tilde{x}}(x) \tag{4.21}$$

$$= F_{\tilde{x}}^*[s + \lambda - \lambda F_{\tilde{y}}^*(s)].$$

Equation (4.21) is a functional relationship defining $F_{\tilde{y}}^*(s)$. This functional relationship can be used to determine moments for the length of the busy period.

Exercise 4.10   Using properties of the Laplace transform, show that

$$E[\tilde{y}] = \frac{E[\tilde{x}]}{1 - \rho}. \tag{4.22}$$

We point out in passing that busy-period analysis is an extremely important tool in the analysis of priority queueing systems. Often delays can be specified entirely in terms of busy periods, as will be shown later on. One variant of the M/G/1 system which is useful in analysis of complicated systems is the M/G/1 with exceptional first service. In this system, the service time for the first customer in each busy period is drawn from the service-time distribution $F_{\tilde{x}_e}(x)$, and the remaining service times in each busy period are drawn from the general distribution $F_{\tilde{x}}(x)$. The length of the busy period for this system is denoted by $\tilde{y}_e$. We leave it as an exercise to show that

$$E[\tilde{y}_e] = \frac{E[\tilde{x}_e]}{1 - \rho}, \tag{4.23}$$

where we retain the definition $\rho = \lambda E[\tilde{x}]$. Thus the expected length of the busy period is proportional to the expected length of the first service time. In addition, it is easy to see that if $F_{\tilde{x}_e}(x) = F_{\tilde{x}}(x)$, then (4.23) reduces to (4.22).

Exercise 4.11 For the ordinary M/G/1 queueing system, determine $E[\tilde{y}]$ without first solving for $F_{\tilde{y}}(s)$. [*Hint*: Condition on the length of the first customer's service and the number of customers that arrive during that period of time.]

Exercise 4.12 **M/G/1 with Exceptional First Service.** A queueing system has Poisson arrivals with rate λ. The service time for the first customer in each busy period is drawn from the service time distribution $F_{\tilde{x}_e}(x)$, and the remaining service times in each busy period are drawn from the general distribution $F_{\tilde{x}}(x)$. Let $\tilde{y}_e$ denote the length of the busy period for this system. Show that

$$E[\tilde{y}_e] = \frac{E[\tilde{x}_e]}{1 - \rho},$$

where $\rho = \lambda E[\tilde{x}]$.

Exercise 4.13 For the M/G/1 queueing system with exceptional first service, as defined in the previous exercise, show that $F_{\tilde{y}_e}^*(s) = F_{\tilde{x}_e}^*(s + \lambda - \lambda F_{\tilde{y}}^*(s))$.

Exercise 4.14 Comparison of the formulas for the expected waiting time for the M/G/1 system and the expected length of a busy period for the M/G/1 system with the formula for exceptional first service reveals that they both have the same form; that is, the expected waiting time in an ordinary M/G/1 system is the same as the length of the busy period of an M/G/1 system in which the expected length of the first service is given by

$$E[\tilde{x}_e] = \rho \frac{E[\tilde{x}^2]}{2E[\tilde{x}]}.$$

Explain why these formulas have this relationship. What random variable must $\tilde{x}_e$ represent in this form? [*Hint*: Consider the operation of the M/G/1 queueing system under a nonpreemptive, LCFS, service discipline and apply Little's result, taking into account that an arriving customer may find the system empty.]

4.2   ERGODIC OCCUPANCY DISTRIBUTION FOR M/G/1

We have previously pointed out that the ergodic occupancy distribution can be calculated by using (4.8) and the properties of probability generating functions. Because this process requires differentiation of fractions and numerous applications of L'Hôpital's rule, the process of generating the occupancy distribution in this manner is tedious at best. In this section, we present two alternative methods of computing the occupancy distribution. The first method is based on discrete Fourier transform analysis, and the second approach, due to Keilson and Servi [1989], is based on a recursion.

4.2.1   Discrete Fourier Transform Approach to Ergodic Occupancy Computation

In this subsection, we describe an approach to inversion of the probability generating function for the occupancy distribution which is based upon Fourier analysis (Daigle [1989]). We first show that a tracing of the PGF around the unit circle describes the *characteristic function* (Feller [1971]) for the occupancy distribution in the form of a complex Fourier series in which the coefficients are the probability masses. Approximate values for these Fourier coefficients are then expressed via finite Riemann sums, where the resulting approximations are a finite set of $K + 1$ discrete Fourier transform (DFT) coefficients. It turns out that, if K is properly chosen, then the $K + 1$ DFT coefficients can be used to obtain approximations for all of the probability masses. A finite number of coefficients is sufficient because the tail of the occupancy distribution decreases geometrically; this fact can be used both to convert the DFT coefficients into probability estimates and to generate the tail probabilities. We also present an algorithm for choosing an appropriate value of K.

Briefly stated, our objective in this section is as follows. Starting with the definition of the PGF,

$$\mathcal{F}_{\tilde{n}}(z) = E[z^{\tilde{n}}] = \sum_{n=0}^{\infty} p_n z^n, \tag{4.24}$$

we shall develop a simple computational technique based upon DFTs to compute

$$p_n = P\{\tilde{n} = n\} \qquad \text{for } n \geq 0$$

from $\mathcal{F}_{\tilde{n}}(z)$. The methodology developed here is useful for inversion of PGFs for a large class of distributions—namely, those having geometrically decreasing tails.

To begin our development, we define

$$\Psi_{\tilde{n}}(\alpha) = \mathcal{F}_{\tilde{n}}\left(e^{-j2\pi\alpha}\right) = \sum_{n=0}^{\infty} p_n e^{-j2\pi n\alpha}, \tag{4.25}$$

where $j = \sqrt{-1}$ and α is a real variable. That is, $\Psi_{\tilde{n}}(\alpha)$ is the *Fourier–Stieltjes integral* (Feller [1971]), or *characteristic function*, of the cumulative distribution function $F_{\tilde{n}}$. We note that $\Psi_{\tilde{n}}(\alpha)$ is always periodic in α with period 1, and that $\Psi_{\tilde{n}}(\alpha)$ is expressed in (4.25) as a complex Fourier series (Churchill and Brown [1987]); that is, it is expressed as a Fourier series in which the basis set (Hewitt and Stromberg [1969]) is $\{\phi_n(\alpha), \ n = 0, \pm 1, \pm 2, \ldots\}$, where $\phi_n(\alpha) = e^{-j2\pi n\alpha}$. Indeed, the Fourier coefficients are simply the probability masses.

As usual, the Fourier coefficients are given by the integral, averaged over one period, of the product of the function in question and the complex conjugate of the basis function for the coefficient in question; that is,

$$p_n = \int_0^1 \Psi_{\tilde{n}}(\alpha)\phi_n^*(\alpha)d\alpha, \tag{4.26}$$

where $\phi_n^*(\alpha)$ denotes the complex conjugate of $\phi_n(\alpha)$. To perform the integration indicated in (4.26) numerically, we partition the interval $[0, 1]$ into $K+1$ equal subintervals. We denote the approximate value of the integral thus obtained by $c_{n,K}$, and we find that

$$c_{n,K} = \sum_{k=0}^{K} \Psi_{\tilde{n}}(\alpha_k)\phi_n^*(\alpha_k)\Delta\alpha$$

$$= \frac{1}{K+1} \sum_{k=0}^{K} \mathcal{F}_{\tilde{n}}(e^{-j[(2\pi k)/(K+1)]}) \; e^{j[(2\pi nk)/(K+1)]}, \qquad (4.27)$$

where $\alpha_k = k/(K+1)$ and $\Delta\alpha = 1/(K+1)$. The right-hand side of (4.27) is the *inverse discrete Fourier transform* (IDFT) (Nussbaumer [1982]) of the finite sequence $\{\mathcal{F}_{\tilde{n}}(e^{(j2\pi k)/(K+1)}),\; 0 \le k \le K\}$. It is easily verified by substituting $n + m(K+1)$ for n that the resulting $c_{n,K}$ sequence is periodic with period $K+1$. However, we shall think of the $c_{n,K}$ as being defined for $0 \le n \le K$ only.

The exact relationship between the probability masses, p_n and $c_{n,K}$ for $0 \le n \le K$, can be obtained by substituting the definition of $\Psi_{\tilde{n}}(\alpha)$ into (4.27) and performing the indicated summation. We find that

$$c_{n,K} = \frac{1}{K+1} \sum_{k=0}^{K}\sum_{\ell=0}^{\infty} p_\ell e^{-j[(2\pi k\ell)/(K+1)]} \; e^{j[(2\pi nk)/(K+1)]}$$

$$= \frac{1}{K+1} \sum_{k=0}^{K}\sum_{\ell=0}^{\infty} p_\ell e^{-j\{[2\pi k(\ell-n)]/(K+1)\}} \qquad (4.28)$$

$$= \frac{1}{K+1} \sum_{\ell=0}^{\infty} p_\ell \sum_{k=0}^{K} e^{-j\{[2\pi k(\ell-n)]/(K+1)\}}.$$

The final summation on the right-hand side of (4.28) is the sum of a finite number of terms from a geometric series. It is easily shown that the sum is $K+1$ if $\ell = (K+1)m + n$ and zero otherwise. Therefore,

$$c_{n,K} = p_n + \sum_{m=1}^{\infty} p_{m(K+1)+n} \qquad \text{for } 0 \le n \le K. \qquad (4.29)$$

Clearly, $\sum_{n=0}^{K} c_{n,K} = \sum_{n=0}^{\infty} p_n$. Thus the $c_{n,K}$ sum to unity for each K. As an example, if we choose $K = 255$, then

$$c_{0,255} = p_0 + p_{256} + p_{512} + p_{768} + \cdots$$
$$c_{1,255} = p_1 + p_{257} + p_{513} + p_{769} + \cdots$$
$$\vdots$$
$$c_{255,255} = p_{255} + p_{511} + p_{767} + p_{1023} + \cdots .$$

Exercise 4.15 Show that the final summation on the right-hand side of (4.28) is $K + 1$ if $\ell = (K + 1)m + n$ and zero otherwise.

The lack of equality between $c_{n,K}$ and p_n in this particular form is called *aliasing*, and it is a direct result of approximating the integral (4.25) by a finite sum. It will be pointed out later in this subsection that tail probabilities in queueing systems decrease geometrically. Thus it is clear by observation of (4.29) that the error due to aliasing can be reduced to any desired degree by increasing K. But this practice results in round-off error and, in addition, still does not yield tail probabilities.

We now develop an approach that takes advantage of the fact that the tail probabilities decay geometrically. This approach simultaneously addresses aliasing error and round-off error and, in addition, provides values for p_n for $n \geq K + 1$.

From (4.8), we find

$$\mathcal{F}_{\tilde{n}}(z) = \frac{(1 - \rho)(z - 1)}{z - F_{\tilde{x}}^*(\lambda[1 - z])} F_{\tilde{x}}^*(\lambda[1 - z]). \tag{4.30}$$

It can be shown that the denominator of the right-hand side of (4.30) has only one zero for $z > 1$; call this zero z_0. Then, the geometric rate at which the tail probabilities decrease is given by the inverse of z_0. This fact follows directly from the Laurent series expansion (Churchill [1960]) of $\mathcal{F}_{\tilde{n}}(z)$ about its singularity at z_0. Indeed, the *principle part* of $\mathcal{F}_{\tilde{n}}(z)$ is given by the quantity $b_1/(z - z_0)$, where

$$
\begin{aligned}
b_1 &= \lim_{z \to z_0} (z - z_0)\mathcal{F}_{\tilde{n}}(z) \\
&= \left[\frac{(1 - \rho)(z - 1)F_{\tilde{x}}^*(\lambda[1 - z])}{1 - d/dz\, F_{\tilde{x}}^*(\lambda[1 - z])} \right]_{z=z_0}.
\end{aligned}
\tag{4.31}
$$

Thus the principle part of $\mathcal{F}_{\tilde{n}}(z)$ is given in power series form by the expression

$$-b_1 \sum_{n=0}^{\infty} z_0^{-(n+1)} z^n.$$

It turns out that for large n, the values of the coefficients of z^n in the Laurent series expansion of $\mathcal{F}_{\tilde{n}}(z)$ are dominated by the principle part. Thus the principle part can be used to obtain very close estimates of the tail probabilities, as in Woodside and Ho [1987]. Two obvious disadvantages of this method of computing tail probabilities are that the singularity z_0 must usually be found numerically, and the derivative of $F_{\tilde{x}}^*(\lambda[1 - z])$ must be evaluated at z_0. Sometimes neither of these operations is straightforward, but so long as it is possible to evaluate the denominator of (4.30), it is easy to bound the difference between z_0^{-1} and r_0, as determined by the algorithm defined below.

Remark. Discussions of Laurent series expansions are sometimes quite difficult to follow. The Laurent series in this particular case can be related to the Taylor series in the following way. First, define a function $\xi(z)$ such that $(z - z_0)\mathcal{F}_{\tilde{n}}(z) = \xi(z)$. Then $\xi(z)$ has no singularities and has a Taylor series. That is,

$$\xi(z) = \sum_{i=0}^{\infty} \frac{\xi^{(i)}(z_0)}{i!} (z - z_0)^i,$$

where $\xi^{(i)}(z_0)$ denotes the ith derivative of $\xi(z)$ evaluated at z_0. Now divide the Taylor series of $\xi(z)$, term by term, by the quantity $z - z_0$; the result is the Laurent series for $\mathcal{F}_{\tilde{n}}(z)$. More on Laurent series can be found in Churchill [1960].

Exercise 4.16 Argue the validity of the expression for b_1 in (4.31).

Exercise 4.17 Show that the denominator of the right-hand side of the expression (4.30) for the probability generating function of the occupancy distribution has only one zero for $z > 1$. [*Hint:* From Theorem 4.2, we know that $F_{\tilde{x}}^*(\lambda[1 - z])$ is the probability generating function for the number of arrivals during a service time. Therefore, $F_{\tilde{x}}^*(\lambda[1 - z])$ can be expressed as a power series in which the coefficients are probabilities and therefore are nonnegative. The function and all of its derivatives are therefore nonnegative for non-negative z, and so on. Now compare the functions $f_1(z) = z$ and $f_2(z) = F_{\tilde{x}}^*(\lambda[1-z])$, noting that the expression $\mathcal{F}_{\tilde{n}}(z)$ can have poles neither inside nor on the unit circle. (Why?)]

Let n_g denote the occupancy level at and above which the tail probabilities are geometrically decreasing to within computational accuracy, and let r_0 denote the geometric rate of decay; that is, $r_0 = z_0^{-1}$. Then, with $K \geq n_g$, for each n, $0 \leq n \leq K$, the sequence $\{p_{m(K+1)+n}, \ m \geq 1\}$, is geometrically decreasing at rate $r_0^{(K+1)}$. Thus, in general,

$$p_{i+n} \approx p_i r_0^n \quad \text{for } i \geq n_g \tag{4.32}$$

and, in particular, with $i = K + 1$,

$$p_{K+1+n} \approx p_K r_0^{n+1}. \tag{4.33}$$

By using (4.32) in (4.29), one can find after a moderate amount of algebraic manipulation that

$$r_0 \approx \frac{c_{0,K} - p_0}{c_{K,K}}, \tag{4.34}$$

and

$$p_n \approx c_{n,K} - (c_{0,K} - p_0)r_0^n \quad \text{for } 1 \leq n \leq K. \tag{4.35}$$

Finally, from (4.24), we have that

$$p_0 = \mathcal{F}_{\tilde{n}}(0). \tag{4.36}$$

Thus, to the extent that K has been chosen sufficiently large so that the tail probabilities are actually decaying geometrically, we see that (4.33) through (4.36) can be used to obtain approximations for p_n, $n \geq 0$, in which aliasing has been removed and only round-off error affects the results. Having selected a value of K, we first compute the $c_{n,K}$, $0 \leq n \leq K$ using either (4.27) or, more likely, a fast Fourier transform (FFT) algorithm (Nussbaumer [1982]), then compute p_0 using (4.36). Next, compute r_0 using (4.34). Finally, compute the probability masses using (4.35) for $1 \leq n \leq K$ and (4.33) for $n > K$.

Exercise 4.18   Starting with (4.29) and (4.32), establish the validity of (4.33) through (4.36).

We now turn our attention to specifying a method of choosing K. There are two conflicting objectives. On the one hand, the larger the value of K, the more likely it is that the probability masses are geometrically decreasing at least starting with p_K, thus satisfying the assumption leading to (4.35). On the other hand, the larger the selected value of K, the larger the round-off error will be in the computations leading to the specifications of the $c_{n,K}$. Since the FFT yields round-off errors of equal magnitude for all coefficients, the most serious effect of this round-off error will be upon the accuracy of $c_{K,K}$. This will obviously lead to inaccuracies in the computation of r_0, which is the key to the generation of tail probabilities. Thus the appropriate choice of K is the minimum for which the tail probabilities are geometrically decreasing.

The value for K should be chosen algorithmically so that one can passively use the computational technique. Toward this end, we note that under the assumption that the quantity n_g is large enough so that the tail probabilities are decreasing, it follows that

$$c_{n,K} = \frac{p_n}{1 - r_0{}^{K+1}} \quad \text{for } n_g \leq n \leq K. \tag{4.37}$$

That is, in our choice of K, we insist that K be sufficiently large to assure that the tail probabilities are geometrically decreasing beginning at n_g, which is in turn less than K. If so, then we also have that $p_{n+1} = r_0 p_n$ for all $n \geq n_g$. Thus, from (4.35), it is readily seen that $c_{n,K}/c_{n-1,K} = r_0$ for $n_g < n \leq K$. We therefore have two ways of computing r_0: first, using (4.35) and second, taking ratios of successive coefficients. An algorithm for choosing K based on these observations is as follows:

1. For a candidate K, let $n_g = K - \lfloor K/4 \rfloor$.

2. Compute $c_{n,K}, 0 \leq n \leq K$ using (4.27) and r_0 using (4.35).

3. Compute $r_{n,K} = c_{n,K}/c_{n-1,K}$ for $n_g < n \leq K$.

4. Compute $a_K = \max_{n_g < n \leq K} |(r_0 - r_{n,K})/r_0|$.

5. Let $K' = 2(K + 1) - 1$.

6. Compute $a_{K'}$ as in (a), (b), (c), and (d).

7. If $a_{K'} < a_K$, then replace K' by K and repeat (e) and (f), else use the computations based on the current value of K in the final results.

The values a_K are a measure of the maximum deviation of the calculated ratios for the last one-fourth of the coefficients from the computed value of the ratio r_0 based on (4.35). Thus, a_K can be viewed as a measure of the accuracy of the assumption that K is large enough to assure geometrically decreasing tail probabilities.

We note that the above development was discussed in terms of the M/G/1 queueing system, but that the techniques are applicable to the inversion of any PGF for which the tail probabilities are geometrically decreasing. Queueing systems having these properties include the G/G/c system as reported in Tijms [1986] and many priority queueing systems that we shall discuss later. We also note that once the ergodic occupancy distribution is known for the case of infinite capacity, it is straightforward to obtain the ergodic occupancy distribution for the case of the finite waiting room by methods outlined in Cooper [1972, 1981] and Keilson and Servi [1989].

The above technique is more fully described and evaluated with respect to computation of M/G/1 occupancy distributions in Daigle [1989], which shows that satisfactory results can be obtained with very few coefficients, especially if traffic intensity is high. An example of the type of results that might be obtained using the techniques is given below.

Definition 4.2   Erlang-k Distribution. The distribution of $\tilde{x}$ is said to be *Erlang-k* with mean $1/\mu$ if $\tilde{x}$ is the sum of k independent exponentially distributed random variables each of which has mean $1/(k\mu)$. □

Example 4.1   Compare the survivor functions for the occupancy distribution of the M/G/1 queueing system for the following service-time distributions:

- M/D/1, the ordinary M/G/1 queueing system having deterministic, unit, service time. The squared coefficient of variation of the service time distribution is 0, and the Laplace–Stieltjes transform of the service time distribution is $F_{\tilde{x}}^*(s) = e^{-s}$.

- M/E$_2$/1, the ordinary M/G/1 queueing system having Erlang-2, unit mean, service times. The squared coefficient of variation of the service-time distribution is 0.5, and the Laplace–Stieltjes transform (LST) of the service-time distribution is $F_{\tilde{x}}^*(s) = [2/(s+2)]^2$.

- M/M/1, the ordinary M/G/1 queueing system having exponential, unit mean, service time. The squared coefficient of variation of the service-time distribution is 1.0, and the LST of the service-time distribution is $F_{\tilde{x}}^*(s) = 1/(s+1)$.

- M/B$_{1.5}$/1, the ordinary M/G/1 queueing system having a two-phase, unit mean, branching Erlang, service-time distribution. The particular branching Erlang distribution used here is the one given in Chandy and Sauer [1981] for specifying distributions whose squared coefficient of variation is greater than 1. The LST for that distribution is

$$F_{\tilde{x}}^*(s) = \frac{\mu_1}{s + \mu_1} \frac{vs + \mu_2}{s + \mu_2},$$

where

$$\mu_1 = 1 + \sqrt{1 - \frac{2}{1 + C_{\tilde{x}}^2}},$$

$$\mu_2 = 1 - \sqrt{1 - \frac{2}{1 + C_{\tilde{x}}^2}},$$

and

$$v = C_{\tilde{x}}^2 \mu_2,$$

and $C_{\tilde{x}}^2$ is the squared coefficient of variation of the distribution of $\tilde{x}$. In our example, the squared coefficient of variation was chosen to be 1.5.

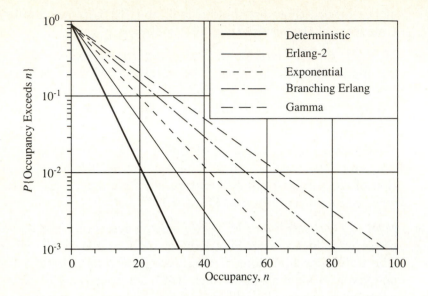

Figure 4.1 Survivor functions with deterministic, Erlang-2, exponential, branching Erlang and gamma service-time distributions at $\rho = 0.9$.

- $M/G_2/1$, the ordinary M/G/1 queueing system having service times drawn from a gamma distribution. The LST for the gamma distribution is $F_{\tilde{x}}^*(s) = (1 + \beta s)^{-\alpha}$ (Hogg and Craig [1978]). In this case, $E[\tilde{x}] = \alpha\beta$ and $\text{Var}(\tilde{x}) = \alpha\beta^2$, so that the parameter values for which the service-time distribution has unit mean and a squared coefficient of variation of 2, we find $\beta = 2$ and $\alpha = 0.5$.

Solution: The results are shown in Figure 4.1, which shows that the occupancy probabilities are greatly affected by the form of the service-time distribution. For example, the probability that the queue length exceeds 60 is about 10 times as large for the case in which service times are drawn from the gamma distribution as it is for the case in which service times are drawn from the exponential distribution. ∎

Example 4.2   Message Lengths Having Truncated Geometric Distribution. In analyzing communication systems, it is common to represent the distribution of message lengths as geometric. For example, the number of characters in a typed line may be represented as having a geometric distribution with mean 30. It is clear that the distribution cannot actually be geometric because the number of characters in a typed line on an 80-character screen cannot exceed 80 characters. Consider a communication system in which messages are transmitted over a communication line having a capacity of 2400 bits/sec or, equivalently, 300 characters/sec. Suppose the message lengths are drawn from a geometric distribution having a mean of 30 characters, but truncated at a and b characters on the lower and upper ends of the distribution, respectively. That is, message lengths are drawn from a distribution characterized as follows:

$$P\{\tilde{m} = m\} = k\theta(1 - \theta)^{m-1} \quad \text{for } a \le m \le b,$$

where $\tilde{c}$ is the number of characters in a message and k is a normalizing constant. We wish to determine the survivor function for several different values of a and b at a traffic utilization of 95%, assuming a transmission capacity of 30 characters/sec.

Solution: Curves showing the desired results and additional results are presented in Figure 4.2. The pair of numbers shown beside each curve gives the points at which the geometric distribution is truncated. Note that the survivor function is an increasing function of the spread between the lower and upper truncation points. For example, if $a = 29$ and $b = 32$, then the survivor function is very nearly that of the M/D/1 system. On the other hand, if $a = 1$ and $b = 5000$, then the service-time distribution is very nearly geometric, and we expect the survivor function to approach that of the M/M/1 system. The program used by the author to generate the curves is given in the Appendix.   ■

Exercise 4.19   Approximate the distribution of the service time for the previous example by an exponential distribution with an appropriate mean. Plot the survivor function for the corresponding M/M/1

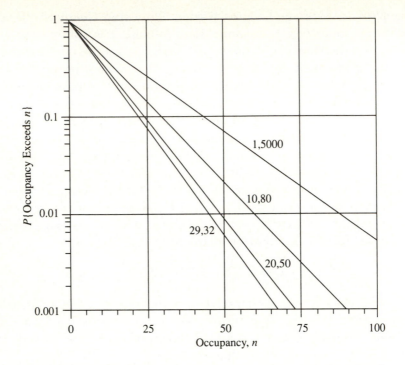

Figure 4.2 Survivor functions for system occupancy with message lengths drawn from truncated geometric distributions at $\rho = 0.95$.

system at 95% utilization. Compare the result to those shown in Figure 4.2.

An important consideration in the design of communication systems is the blocking probability. As stated in Chapter 3, the blocking probability is defined as the proportion of the customers seeking admission to the queueing system who are denied admission. We assume a finite waiting room of capacity K. As in the case of the general birth–death model covered in Chapter 3, ergodicity exists for the finite K model even when it does not exist for the case of the infinite waiting room. For the special case in which ergodicity exists for the case of the unbounded waiting room, Keilson and Servi [1989] present a simple relationship between the ergodic occupancy probabilities and the blocking probabilities for the finite case. The following is their result, which we state without proof:

$$P_B(K) = \frac{1-\rho}{1 - \rho S_{K-1}} S_{K-1}, \qquad (4.38)$$

where ρ has the usual definition and $S_{K-1} = P\{\tilde{n} > K-1\}$. Table 4.1 illustrates the drastic difference between $P\{\tilde{n} > K - 1\} = P\{\tilde{n} \geq K\}$ and the blocking probability at $\rho = 0.9$. Again, the reader is cautioned against using survivor function and blocking probabilities interchangeably.

In case ergodicity does not exist for the case of the unbounded waiting room (that is, $\rho \geq 1$), the blocking probability is more difficult to compute. The interested reader is referred to Langford [1990] and also Niu and Cooper [1989] for a treatment of the more general case.

4.2.2   Recursive Approach to Ergodic Occupancy Computation

In this section, we present an alternative method of computing the occupancy distribution which is based on the paper by Keilson and Servi [1989], although our approach is somewhat different and the results are stated in a slightly different form.

Table 4.1

	$K = 10$		$K = 30$	
SYSTEM	S_{K-1}	$P_B(K)$	S_{K-1}	$P_B(K)$
M/D/1	0.17795	0.021188	0.002825	0.000283
M/E$_2$/1	0.29806	0.040733	0.018246	0.001855
M/M/1	0.38742	0.059482	0.047101	0.004919
M/B$_{1.5}$/1	0.45117	0.075961	0.085055	0.009211
M/G$_2$/1	0.50514	0.092622	0.145434	0.016734

To begin our development, we rewrite (4.14) as follows:

$$F_{\tilde{s}}^*(s) = \frac{(1-\rho)s}{s - \lambda[1 - F_{\tilde{x}}^*(s)]} \, F_{\tilde{x}}^*(s).$$

We shall show in the next section that the expression

$$\frac{1 - F_{\tilde{x}}^*(s)}{s \, E[\tilde{x}]}$$

is the Laplace–Stieltjes transform of the distribution of a random variable, which we shall denote by $\tilde{x}_r$ and refer to as the residual life of $\tilde{x}$. Therefore we define

$$F_{\tilde{x}_r}^*(s) = \frac{1 - F_{\tilde{x}}^*(s)}{s \, E[\tilde{x}]}. \tag{4.39}$$

From (4.15) and (4.40), we therefore find that the Laplace–Stieltjes transform of the sojourn-time distribution can be written as

$$F_{\tilde{s}}^*(s) = \frac{(1-\rho)F_{\tilde{x}}^*(s)}{1 - \rho F_{\tilde{x}_r}^*(s)}. \tag{4.40}$$

In turn, (4.40) can be rewritten as

$$F_{\tilde{s}}^*(s) = (1-\rho)F_{\tilde{x}}^*(s) \sum_{i=0}^{\infty} \left[\rho F_{\tilde{x}_r}^*(s) \right]^i. \tag{4.41}$$

After some minor algebra, this equation can be rearranged as

$$F_{\tilde{s}}^*(s) = (1-\rho)F_{\tilde{x}}^*(s) + \rho F_{\tilde{x}_r}^*(s)F_{\tilde{s}}^*(s). \tag{4.42}$$

Using (4.42) as a starting point, we will specify a convenient method of generating the occupancy distribution for the M/G/1 system.

We have previously argued that $\mathcal{F}_{\tilde{n}}(z) = F_{\tilde{s}}^*(\lambda[1 - z])$; that is, the probability generating function for the occupancy distribution is given by the Laplace–Stieltjes transform for the sojourn-time distribution evaluated at the point $\lambda(1 - z)$. For consistency of notation, we shall specify the probability generating function for the number of arrivals that occur from a Poisson process with rate λ during a random period of time $\tilde{x}$ by

$$F_{\tilde{x}}^*(\lambda[1-z]) = \sum_{i=0}^{\infty} z^i P_{\tilde{x},i}. \tag{4.43}$$

Then, from (4.42), we find

$$\sum_{i=0}^{\infty} z^i P_{\tilde{s},i} = (1-\rho) \sum_{i=0}^{\infty} z^i P_{\tilde{x},i} + \rho \left[\sum_{i=0}^{\infty} z^i P_{\tilde{x}_r,i} \right] \left[\sum_{i=0}^{\infty} z^i P_{\tilde{s},i} \right]$$

or, equivalently,

$$\sum_{i=0}^{\infty} z^i P_{\tilde{s},i} = (1-\rho) \sum_{i=0}^{\infty} z^i P_{\tilde{x},i} + \rho \sum_{i=0}^{\infty} z^i \left[\sum_{n=0}^{i} P_{\tilde{x}_r,n} P_{\tilde{s},i-n} \right]. \tag{4.44}$$

Upon matching coefficients of z^i in (4.44), we find that

$$P_{\tilde{s},i} = (1-\rho) P_{\tilde{x},i} + \rho \sum_{n=0}^{i} P_{\tilde{x}_r,n} P_{\tilde{s},i-n}. \tag{4.45}$$

Equation (4.45) can then be solved for $P_{\tilde{s},i}$. We find

$$P_{\tilde{s},i} = \frac{(1-\rho) P_{\tilde{x},i} + \rho \sum_{n=1}^{i} P_{\tilde{x}_r,n} P_{\tilde{s},i-n}}{1 - \rho P_{\tilde{x}_r,0}}. \tag{4.46}$$

Now it is straightforward to show that

$$P_{\tilde{x}_r,i} = \frac{1}{\rho} \left[1 - \sum_{n=0}^{i} P_{\tilde{x},n} \right]. \tag{4.47}$$

Substituting (4.47) into (4.46), we find

$$P_{\tilde{s},0} = 1 - \rho \tag{4.48}$$

and for $i \geq 1$,

$$P_{\tilde{s},i} = \frac{(1-\rho) P_{\tilde{x},i} + \sum_{n=1}^{i} \left(1 - \sum_{m=0}^{n} P_{\tilde{x},n} \right) P_{\tilde{s},i-n}}{P_{\tilde{x},0}}. \tag{4.49}$$

Exercise 4.20 Starting with (4.39), demonstrate the validity of (4.47).

Clearly, $P_{\tilde{s},i}$ can be determined recursively from (4.49). The number of terms of the form $P_{\tilde{x},i}$ which must be computed is limited to the number of occupancy probabilities that the analyst is interested in computing for the particular problem at hand. As we have noted in Section 4.1, $P_{\tilde{s},i}$ is equivalent to $P_i = P\{\tilde{n} = i\}$. Thus we find

$$P_i = \frac{(1 - \rho)P_{\tilde{x},i} + \sum_{n=1}^{i} \left(1 - \sum_{m=0}^{n} P_{\tilde{x},n}\right) P_{i-n}}{P_{\tilde{x},0}}. \tag{4.50}$$

In addition, as we have seen earlier in this subsection, the ratio $P_i/(P_{i-1})$ converges to a constant as i increases for all $F_{\tilde{x}}(x)$ of practical interest. Thus (4.50) offers a practical method for calculating occupancy probabilities so long as the $P_{\tilde{x},i}$ can be computed readily. In general, the computation of these quantities is straightforward if the Laplace–Stieltjes transform for the service-time distribution is rational or if the service-time distribution can be adequately approximated by a discrete distribution. On the other hand, for more general distributions, this task, in and of itself, is more difficult to accomplish than is the direct computation of the occupancy distribution using the methods presented in the previous section.

Exercise 4.21   Evaluate $P_{\tilde{x},i}$ for the special case in which $\tilde{x}$ has the exponential distribution with mean $1/\mu$. Starting with (4.50), show that the ergodic occupancy distribution for the M/M/1 system is given by $P_i = (1 - \rho)\rho^i$, where $\rho = \lambda/\mu$.

Exercise 4.22   Evaluate $P_{\tilde{x},i}$ for the special case in which $P\{\tilde{x} = 1\} = 1$. Use (4.50) to calculate the occupancy distribution. Compare the complementary occupancy distribution $(P\{N > i\})$ for this system with that of the M/M/1 system with $\mu = 1$.

Exercise 4.23   Evaluate $P_{\tilde{x},i}$ for the special case in which $P\{\tilde{x} = \frac{1}{2}\} = P\{\tilde{x} = \frac{3}{2}\} = \frac{1}{2}$. Use (4.50) to calculate the occupancy distribution. Compare the complementary occupancy distribution $(P\{N > i\})$ for this system with that of the M/M/1 system with $\mu = 1$.

4.3   EXPECTED VALUES FOR M/G/1 VIA RENEWAL THEORY

In this section, we present methodology for direct computation of expected waiting and sojourn times as well as busy-period lengths.

We begin our presentation by reviewing our approach to computing the expected waiting time for the M/M/1 system and showing where this approach fails when applied to the M/G/1 system. At that point, we introduce renewal processes and present a few elementary but useful results from renewal theory. These results are then used to complete the derivation of the expected waiting time for the M/G/1 system. Next, we turn to the direct computation of the expected length of the busy period. At this point, we introduce alternating renewal processes and state a major result from the theory of alternating renewal processes in the form of a theorem. The theorem is then used to compute the expected length of the busy period directly.

4.3.1   Expected Waiting Times and Renewal Theory

We indicated earlier via an exercise that the expected waiting and sojourn times for the M/M/1 queueing system can be computed directly by applying Little's result in combination with the memoryless property of the exponential distribution. In particular, we suggested that the waiting time is the sum of the waiting time due to the customers in the queue, $\tilde{w}_q$, and the waiting time due to the customers in service, $\tilde{w}_s$, if any. That is,

$$E[\tilde{w}] = E[\tilde{w}_q] + E[\tilde{w}_s]. \tag{4.51}$$

Now, because the service times of the customers in the queue are independent of the number of customers in the queue, then

$$E[\tilde{w}_q] = E[\tilde{n}_q]E[\tilde{x}], \tag{4.52}$$

where $\tilde{n}_q$ denotes the expected number of customers in the queue. Also,

$$E[\tilde{w}_s] = \rho E[\tilde{x}_s] \tag{4.53}$$

where ρ is the probability that there is a customer in service at an arbitrary point in time and $\tilde{x}_s$ denotes the remaining service time for the customer in service, if any. Using $E[\tilde{n}_q] = \lambda E[\tilde{w}_q]$ in (4.52) and then substituting the result together with (4.53) into (4.51) leads to

$$E[\tilde{w}] = \frac{\rho E[\tilde{x}_s]}{1 - \rho}. \tag{4.54}$$

Because of the memoryless property of the exponential distribution, $E[\tilde{x}_s] = E[\tilde{x}] = 1/\mu$. Thus, for the M/M/1 system, we find

$$E[\tilde{w}] = \frac{\rho/\mu}{1 - \rho}. \tag{4.55}$$

Exercise 4.24   Use a busy-period argument to establish the validity of (4.54). [*Hint*: Consider the M/G/1 system under the nonpreemptive LCFS service discipline.]

A little thought reveals that (4.51) through (4.54) are still valid for the M/G/1 queueing system but that (4.55) is no longer valid. That is, the service-time distribution is not memoryless, so that the distribution of remaining time for the customer in service, if any, is not equal to the ordinary service-time distribution.

Since Poisson arrivals see the system in stochastic equilibrium, it is natural to conjecture that the expected length of time until the customer in service completes service would be one-half of the expected length of an ordinary service interval. But we know that this quantity is equal to the entire expected length of a service interval if the service times are exponentially distributed. Thus there seems to be paradox here. The paradox, called the inspection paradox, is resolved by noting that the probability that random observers are more likely to observe longer intervals is higher than the probability that these longer intervals occur. The following example illustrates the paradox.

Suppose that $P\{\tilde{x} = 1\} = \frac{3}{4}$ and $P\{\tilde{x} = 2\} = \frac{1}{4}$. Now suppose we draw four customers at random without replacement from a group of thousands of customers and that the lengths of the service times corresponding to these customers are $x_{292} = 1$, $x_{2085} = 1$, $x_{1605} = 2$, and $x_{3176} = 1$. So we have been lucky: We have drawn the customers such that the proportion of service times of each length in the sample are in exact proportion to their probabilities of occurrence. We now string these four intervals out in time and pick an arbitrary point in time in the interval covered by all four intervals, as shown in Figure 4.3. If the point falls in an interval of length 2, we say that we "observe an interval of length 2." Because the total proportion of the line covered by intervals of length 2 is $\frac{2}{5}$, the probability that the interval observed has length 2 is $\frac{2}{5}$. If we let $\tilde{x}_o$ denote the length of the observed intervals, we find that $P\{\tilde{x}_o = 1\} = \frac{3}{5}$ and $P\{\tilde{x}_o = 2\} = \frac{2}{5}$. Thus $E[\tilde{x}_o] = \frac{7}{5}$ and $E[\tilde{x}] = \frac{5}{4}$. We see that, in this particular example, $E[\tilde{x}_o] > E[\tilde{x}]$; that is, the expected length of the service times of the *observed* customers is greater than the expected service time taken over *all* customers.

It turns out that, in the general case, the expected length of the observed intervals is greater than or equal to the expected length taken over all intervals with equality holding if and only if the intervals have fixed length.

Definition 4.3 Renewal Process. Let $\{\tilde{z}_i, \ i \geq 1\}$ denote a sequence of independent and identically distributed nonnegative random variables with $P\{\tilde{z} > 0\} > 0$ so that $E[\tilde{z}] > 0$, where $\tilde{z}$ denotes a generic $\tilde{z}_i$. Let $\tilde{s}_n = \sum_{i=1}^{n} \tilde{z}_i$ and $\tilde{s}_0 = 0$ with probability 1, and let $\{\tilde{n}(t), \ t \geq 0\} = \sup\{n | \tilde{s}_n \leq t\}$. Then the counting process $\{\tilde{n}(t), \ t \geq 0\}$ is called a renewal process, $\tilde{z}$ is called the renewal interval, and $\tilde{s}_n$ is called the time of the nth renewal. $\square$

For a general renewal process, it is intuitive that the probability that an interval of a particular length is observed is proportional to both the length in question and the probability of occurrence of an interval of the given length. That is,

$$P\{z \leq \tilde{z}_o \leq z + dz\} = K z P\{z \leq \tilde{z} \leq z + dz\}, \qquad (4.56)$$

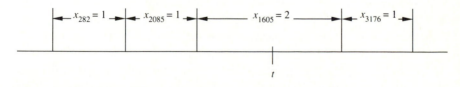

Figure 4.3 A sample of service times.

where $\tilde{z}_o$ denotes the length of the observed interval. Upon integrating both sides of (4.56), we find that $K = E[\tilde{z}]$ so that

$$\frac{d}{dz}F_{\tilde{z}_o}(z) = \frac{1}{E[\tilde{z}]}z\frac{d}{dz}F_{\tilde{z}}(z). \tag{4.57}$$

Now, from (4.57), we find that

$$E[\tilde{z}_o] = \frac{E[\tilde{z}^2]}{E[\tilde{z}]}. \tag{4.58}$$

Because $\text{Var}(\tilde{z}) = E[\tilde{z}^2] - E^2[\tilde{z}]$ and $\text{Var}(\tilde{z}) \geq 0$, we see that in general,

$$E[\tilde{z}_o] \geq E[\tilde{z}], \tag{4.59}$$

as we had observed earlier in our special case.

Based on the above definition of the renewal process, we see that $\tilde{n}(t)$ is the number of renewals up to time t. This means that the time of the last renewal up to time t is given by $\tilde{s}_{\tilde{n}(t)}$, and the time of the first renewal after time t is given by $\tilde{s}_{\tilde{n}(t)+1}$. The interval $(\tilde{s}_{\tilde{n}(t)}, \tilde{s}_{\tilde{n}(t)+1}]$ is the observed interval, as shown in Figure 4.4. Returning to the computation of the expected waiting time for the M/G/1 system, we note that if we condition on the system being busy, then the sequence of service times for the M/G/1 queueing system has the properties needed to form a renewal process. A little thought reveals that because the Poisson arrival observes the state of the system in exactly the same way as a random observer does, then $E[\tilde{x}_s] = E[\text{length of } (t, \tilde{s}_{\tilde{n}(t)+1}]]$, and

$$E[\tilde{w}_s] = \rho\, E\left[\text{length of } (t, \tilde{s}_{\tilde{n}(t)+1}]\right].$$

That is, given that there is a customer in service upon an arbitrary customer's arrival, the expected waiting time due to the customer in service is given by the expected amount of time from the observance time until the customer in service completes service. One would guess that the expected length of this interval would be one-half the expected length of the observed interval. After the following definitions, we shall specify the distribution of the length of this interval, and we shall see that this is indeed the case.

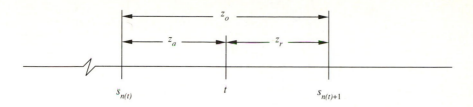

Figure 4.4 An observed interval of a renewal process.

Definition 4.4   Forward Recurrence Time (Residual Life). The forward recurrence time, or residual life, for the renewal process $\{\tilde{n}(t),\ t \geq 0\}$ is defined as the interval $(t,\ \tilde{s}_{\tilde{n}(t)+1}]$. If $\tilde{z}$ denotes the length of a renewal interval, then the forward recurrence time for the renewal process will be denoted by $\tilde{z}_r$.   □

Based upon the above discussion, we see that $\tilde{x}_s$ of (4.54) is equivalent to the forward recurrence time of the renewal process whose underlying renewal interval is $\tilde{x}$. Thus

$$E[\tilde{w}] = \frac{\rho E[\tilde{x}_r]}{1 - \rho}. \tag{4.60}$$

Definition 4.5   Backward Recurrence Time (Age). The interval $(\tilde{s}_{\tilde{n}(t)},\ t]$ is called the backward recurrence time or age, for the renewal process $\{\tilde{n}(t),\ t \geq 0\}$. If $\tilde{z}$ denotes the length of a renewal interval, then the backward recurrence time for the renewal process will be denoted by $\tilde{z}_a$.   □

Now, $P\{\tilde{z}_r \leq r \mid \tilde{z}_o = z\} = r/z$ for $r \leq z$ because the point t is selected at random during the interval $\tilde{z}_o$. Thus, for $z \leq r$, we find

$$f_{\tilde{z}_r|\tilde{z}_o}(r \mid \tilde{z}_o = z) = \frac{d}{dr}P\{\tilde{z}_r \leq r \mid \tilde{z}_o = z\} = \frac{1}{z}.$$

The density function for $\tilde{z}_r$ is then given by

$$f_{\tilde{z}_r}(r) = \int_r^\infty \frac{d}{dr} P\{\tilde{z}_r \le r \mid \tilde{z}_o = z\} dF_{\tilde{z}_o}(z)$$

$$= \int_r^\infty \frac{1}{z} \frac{z f_{\tilde{z}}(z)}{E[\tilde{z}]} dz \qquad (4.61)$$

$$f_{\tilde{z}_r}(z) = \frac{[1 - F_{\tilde{z}}(z)]}{E[\tilde{z}]}.$$

Exercise 4.25 Show that the Laplace–Stieltjes transform for the distribution of the residual life for the renewal process having renewal intervals of length $\tilde{z}$ is given by

$$F_{\tilde{z}_r}^*(s) = \frac{1 - F_{\tilde{z}}^*(s)}{s\, E[\tilde{z}]}. \qquad (4.62)$$

We note $E[\tilde{z}] = \int_0^\infty [1 - F_{\tilde{z}}(z)] dz$ for $\tilde{z}$ a nonnegative random variable so that $f_{\tilde{z}_r}(z)$ is indeed a density function. Turning to the computation of the expected value of the residual service life, we find

$$E[\tilde{z}_r] = \int_0^\infty r f_{\tilde{z}_r}(r) dr$$

$$= \int_0^\infty r \left[\int_r^\infty \frac{1}{z} \frac{z f_{\tilde{z}}(z)}{E[\tilde{z}]} dz \right] dr$$

$$= \frac{1}{E[\tilde{z}]} \int_0^\infty r \left[\int_r^\infty f_{\tilde{z}}(z) dz \right] dr$$

$$= \frac{1}{E[\tilde{z}]} \int_0^\infty \left[\int_0^z r dr \right] f_{\tilde{z}}(z) dz$$

$$= \frac{1}{E[\tilde{z}]} \int_0^\infty \frac{z^2}{2} f_{\tilde{z}}(z) dz.$$

Thus,

$$E[\tilde{z}_r] = \frac{E[\tilde{z}^2]}{2E[\tilde{z}]}. \qquad (4.63)$$

Comparing (4.58) and (4.63), we see that

$$E[\tilde{z}_r] = \frac{1}{2} E[\tilde{z}_o]$$

as we would expect intuitively.

It is sometimes useful to express $E[\tilde{z}_r]$ in terms of the coefficient of variation of $F_{\tilde{z}}(z)$, which we shall denote by $C_{\tilde{z}}$, where

$$C_{\tilde{z}} \triangleq \frac{\sqrt{\mathrm{Var}(\tilde{z})}}{E(\tilde{z})}.$$

Because $E[\tilde{z}^2] = \mathrm{Var}(\tilde{z}) + E^2[\tilde{z}]$, we find that

$$E[\tilde{z}_r] = \frac{E[\tilde{z}](1 + C_{\tilde{z}}^2)}{2}. \tag{4.64}$$

Then, substituting (4.64) into (4.60) with $\tilde{z} = \tilde{x}$, we find for the M/G/1 system that

$$E[\tilde{w}] = \frac{\rho\, E[\tilde{z}]}{1 - \rho} \left[\frac{1 + C_{\tilde{z}}^2}{2} \right]. \tag{4.65}$$

It is reasonable to question the general applicability of the theorems and definitions stated above. For example, the renewal intervals for a renewal process must all be drawn independently from the same distribution. One might ask, "What about processes for which the first renewal interval or the first several renewal intervals are drawn from a distribution other than the common distribution from which the length of all remaining intervals are drawn? Does this affect the stochastic equilibrium distribution of the length of observed intervals and backward and forward recurrence times?" The answer is that processes that are defective in this way behave in the same way as nondefective processes once they reach stochastic equilibrium. In this book, we take these results for granted, but we proceed carefully. These results can be found in any good text on stochastic processes (see, for example, Ross [1983]).

Exercise 4.26   For an arbitrary nonnegative random variable, $\tilde{x}$, show that

$$E\left[\tilde{x}_r^n\right] = \frac{E\left[\tilde{x}^{n+1}\right]}{(n + 1)E[\tilde{x}]}. \tag{4.66}$$

Exercise 4.27   For the M/G/1 system, suppose that $\tilde{x} = \tilde{x}_1 + \tilde{x}_2$, where $\tilde{x}_1$ and $\tilde{x}_2$ are independent, exponentially distributed random variables with parameters μ_1 and μ_2, respectively. Show that $C_{\tilde{x}}^2 \leq 1$ for all μ_1, μ_2 such that $E[\tilde{x}] = 1$.

Exercise 4.28 Compute the expected waiting time for the M/G/1 system with unit mean, deterministic service times and for the M/G/1 system with service times drawn from the unit mean, Erlang-2 distribution. Plot on the same graph $E[\tilde{w}]$ as a function of ρ for these two distributions and for the M/M/1 queueing system with $\mu = 1$. Compare the results.

Exercise 4.29 For the M/G/1 system, suppose that $\tilde{x}$ is drawn from the distribution $F_{\tilde{x}_1}(x)$ with probability p and from $F_{\tilde{x}_2}(x)$ otherwise, where $\tilde{x}_1$ and $\tilde{x}_2$ are independent, exponentially distributed random variables with parameters μ_1 and μ_2, respectively. Let $E[\tilde{x}] = 1$. Show that $C_{\tilde{x}}^2 \geq 1$ for all $p \in [0, 1]$.

Exercise 4.30 With $\tilde{x}$ and p defined as in Exercise 4.29, let $p = \frac{1}{2}$. Find μ_1 and μ_2 such that $C_{\tilde{x}}^2 = 2$. Would it be possible to determine p, μ_1, and μ_2 uniquely for a given value of $C_{\tilde{x}}^2$? Explain.

4.3.2   Busy Periods and Alternating Renewal Theory

We now turn to the direct computation of the expected length of the busy period for the M/G/1 queueing system. We introduce alternating renewal processes and a major result from the theory of alternating renewal processes as a tool for approaching this computation. It will be seen that formulating problems in terms of alternating renewal processes provides a very powerful conceptual framework for dealing with important aspects of the behavior of complicated stochastic processes.

  Alternating renewal processes are special types of renewal processes. In particular, an alternating renewal process is a renewal process in which the renewal interval comprises two subintervals. For example, consider the ordinary M/G/1 queueing system. Periods of time alternate between idle periods and busy periods. If we define a *cycle* to be the period of time between successive entries into idle periods, then the process that counts the number of cycles completed up to time t is an alternating renewal process.

Alternating renewal theory provides a useful framework through which to conceptualize the functioning of more advanced queueing systems. In this subsection, we shall present a formal definition of an alternating renewal process, state a basic theorem from the theory of alternating renewal processes, and compute the average length of a busy period by using the basic theorem. The theorem will not be proved, but an intuitive explanation of why it is true will be provided.

Definition 4.6   Alternating Renewal Process. Let $\{\tilde{x}_i, \ i \geq 1\}$ and $\{\tilde{y}_i, \ i \geq 1\}$ denote sequences of independent and identically distributed nonnegative random variables, but with $\tilde{x}_i$ and $\tilde{y}_i$ not necessarily independent. Let $\tilde{x}$ and $\tilde{y}$ denote generic random variables for $\tilde{x}_i$ and $\tilde{y}_i$, respectively; and let $P\{\tilde{x} > 0\} > 0$ and $P\{\tilde{y} > 0\} > 0$ so that $E[\tilde{x}] > 0$ and $E[\tilde{y}] > 0$. Define $\tilde{z}_i = \tilde{x}_i + \tilde{y}_i$, and let $\tilde{z}$ denote a generic $\tilde{z}_i$. Further, define $\tilde{s}_n = \sum_{i=1}^{n} \tilde{z}_i$ and $\tilde{s}_0 = 0$ with probability 1, and let $\{\tilde{n}(t), \ t \geq 0\} = \sup\{n | \tilde{s}_n \leq t\}$. Then the counting process $\{\tilde{n}(t), \ t \geq 0\}$ is called an alternating renewal process, $\tilde{z}$ is called the renewal interval, and $\tilde{s}_n$ is called the time of the nth renewal.   □

We envision the alternating renewal process as alternating between x-periods and y-periods, and we think of each completion of an *x-period* followed by a *y-period* as the completion of a cycle. That is, time evolves as a succession of intervals as follows: $\tilde{x}_1, \ \tilde{y}_1, \ \tilde{x}_2, \ \tilde{y}_2, \ \dots$. The following is a useful theorem from the theory of alternating renewal processes.

Theorem 4.4   Let $\{\tilde{n}(t), \ t \geq 0\}$ be an alternating renewal process that alternates between x-periods and y-periods as defined above. Then, the probability that the process is in an x-period at an arbitrary point in time is given by the ratio of the expected length of the x-period to the expected cycle length. That is,

$$P_x = \frac{E[\tilde{x}]}{E[z]}$$

$$= \frac{E[\tilde{x}]}{E[\tilde{x}] + E[\tilde{y}]},$$

where

$$P_x = \lim_{t \to \infty} P\{\text{system is a } x\text{-period at time } t\}.$$

Similarly,

$$P_y = \frac{E[\tilde{y}]}{E[\tilde{x}] + E[\tilde{y}]},$$

where

$$P_y = \lim_{t \to \infty} P\{\text{system is a } y\text{-period at time } t\}.$$

Proof   (Bogus) The truth of this theorem follows directly from the theory of Markov chains. We can define the process to be in state 0 whenever it is in an x-period and state 1 otherwise. Then, because the system alternates between x-periods and y-periods, it is clear that the proportion of transitions into each state is one-half. Then, from the theory of Markov chains, the proportion of time spent in state 0 is simply

$$\frac{(1/2)E[\tilde{x}]}{(1/2)E[\tilde{x}] + (1/2)E[\tilde{y}]} = \frac{E[\tilde{x}]}{E[\tilde{x}] + E[\tilde{y}]},$$

and the proportion of time spent in state 1 is

$$\frac{E[\tilde{y}]}{E[\tilde{x}] + E[\tilde{y}]}. \qquad \square$$

We shall make use of the above theorem extensively in our study of priority queueing systems. Here, we use this theorem to determine the expected length of the busy period for the ordinary M/G/1 queueing system. As pointed out above, if we consider the idle periods as x-periods and the busy periods as y-periods, then the counting process that counts the number of cycles completed by time t is an alternating renewal process. Thus the probability that the process is in a busy period is given simply as the ratio of the expected length of the busy period to the expected length of the cycle. But the expected length of the cycle is simply the sum of the expected lengths of the idle and busy periods. Therefore,

$$P\{\text{busy}\} = \frac{E[\tilde{y}]}{E[\tilde{\imath}] + E[\tilde{y}]}.$$

But the expected length of the idle period is $1/\lambda$, and by application of Little's result the probability that the server is busy is found to be $\rho = \lambda E[\tilde{x}]$. Thus

$$\rho = \frac{E[\tilde{y}]}{1/\lambda + E[\tilde{y}]}.$$

Upon solving the above equation for $E[\tilde{y}]$, we readily find that

$$E[\tilde{y}] = \frac{1/\mu}{1 - \rho},$$

as we previously determined in at least two other ways.

Thus we see that parameters of interest can sometimes be computed very simply by application of Theorem 4.4. In addition, the proof of the theorem explains why the expected length of the busy period is not affected by the form of the service-time distribution. The basic reason for this is simply that the probability that the server is busy is a time-averaged probability. For time period prior to time t, the proportion of time spent in the busy period is simply the sum of the amount of time spent in the busy state divided by t. So long as there is at least one visit to the busy state, both numerator and denominator can be divided by the number of visits by time t, which is a random variable. An application of the strong law of large numbers and the elementary renewal theorem (see Wolff [1989]) then produces the desired result.

Exercise 4.31   Formalize the informal discussion of the previous paragraph.

It should be noted again that the truth of Theorem 4.4 does not depend upon independence of the length of x-periods and y-periods of the same cycle. The lengths of the x-periods must be drawn independently of each other from a common distribution, and the lengths of the y-periods must be drawn independently of each other from a common distribution; but there is no requirement that the lengths of the x-period and y-period of the same cycle be drawn independently of each other. For this particular example, however, the busy and idle periods are independent of each other.

One can begin to appreciate the power of the seemingly trivial Theorem 4.4 by working a slightly more complicated example. The following exercise provides such an example.

Exercise 4.32   (Ross[1989]) Consider an ordinary renewal process with renewal interval $\tilde{z}$. Choose a real number c arbitrarily. Now suppose the renewal process is observed at a random point in time, t_0. If the age of the observed interval is less than c, define the system to be in an x-period; else define the system to be in a y-period. Thus the expected cycle length is $E[\tilde{z}]$, and the expected length of the x-period is $E[\min\{c, \tilde{z}\}]$. Show that

$$E[\min\{c, \tilde{z}\}] = \int_0^c [1 - F_{\tilde{z}}(z)]dz$$

so that

$$\frac{d}{dz}F_{\tilde{z}_a}(z) = \frac{1 - F_{\tilde{z}}(z)}{E[\tilde{z}]},$$

as was shown in the previous subsection.

As in the case of ordinary renewal process and defective renewal processes, if the lengths of the initial cycles have a distribution other than that of the common distribution from which all remaining intervals are chosen, the above theorem is still valid. In addition, if the lengths of the x-periods and y-periods are drawn independently of each other, then it does not matter how one thinks of grouping the intervals of a cycle so long as a cycle consists of an x-period and a y-period. For example, one can think of a cycle as being y_i then x_i, x_i then y_i, or y_i then x_{i+1}. We shall see that this property makes the theory even more useful in conceptualizing, from a mathematical point of view, the behavior of complicated systems.

4.4   M/G/1 UNDER LAST-COME-FIRST-SERVED, PREEMPTIVE-RESUME DISCIPLINE

Under the last-come-first-served, preemptive-resume (LCFS-PR) service discipline, newly arriving customers immediately enter into service. If there is currently a customer in service, that customer's service is suspended until service for the newly arrived customer and his descendants is completed. Then, service for the suspended customer is resumed. Clearly, the sojourn time for a customer has the same distribution as the length of the busy period in an ordinary (FCFS) M/G/1 system. That is,

$$F^*_{\tilde{s}_{\text{LCFS−PR}}}(s) = F^*_{\tilde{y}}(s), \tag{4.67}$$

where $\tilde{s}_{\text{LCFS−PR}}$ is the sojourn time for the M/G/1 under the LCFS-PR discipline and $F^*_{\tilde{y}}(s) = F^*_{\tilde{x}}[s + \lambda - \lambda F^*_{\tilde{y}}(s)]$.

Exercise 4.33   Argue the validity of (4.67).

Exercise 4.34   Derive an expression for the Laplace–Stieltjes transform of the sojourn-time distribution for the M/G/1 system under the LCFS-PR discipline conditional on the customer's service-time requirement. [*Hint*: See Exercise 4.13.]

Exercise 4.35   Compare the means and variances of the sojourn times for the ordinary M/G/1 system and the M/G/1 system under the LCFS-PR discipline.

Two other quantities of interest in this system are the unfinished work, $\tilde{u}$, and the occupancy distribution. Clearly the unfinished work for the LCFS-PR discipline is equivalent to the waiting time for the ordinary M/G/1 system. That is, the unfinished work in any work-conserving system is independent of order of service (Wolff [1970]), and because the Poisson arrival sees the system in stochastic equilibrium, the waiting time for the ordinary M/G/1 system is the same as the unfinished work for that system. Thus, for the M/G/1 system under the LCFS-PR discipline, $\tilde{u} = \tilde{w}$, and from (4.41), we find,

$$F^*_{\tilde{u}}(s) = F^*_{\tilde{w}}(s) = (1 - \rho) \sum_{i=0}^{\infty} [\rho F^*_{\tilde{x}_r}(s)]^i. \tag{4.68}$$

The observation represented by (4.68) is attributed to Kelly [1979] in Cooper and Niu [1986].

We now turn to the computation of the occupancy distribution, for which purpose we follow Cooper and Niu [1986]. Clearly, the customers left in the system by any customer are exactly the same as the ones found in the system by that customer. Thus the distribution of the number of customers seen by a departing customer is certainly the same as the distribution of the number of customers found by an arriving customer. Consequently, the distribution of the number of customers left in the system by an arbitrary departing customer is the same as the stochastic equilibrium occupancy distribution.

Now, the customers in the queue at an arbitrary point in time have all been preempted at least once. Indeed, they have been preempted only while in service and then only by customers arriving from a Poisson process. Clearly, the remaining service time for all customers in the queue is independent and identically distributed. One would suspect that the distribution of the remaining service time for the customers in the queue is the same as the distribution of the residual service-life variables because the interrupting (observing) process is Poisson. Thus we shall denote the remaining service time for the customers in the queue by $\tilde{x}_r$.

Let $P_j = P\{j$ customers in the system at an arbitrary point in time$\}$. Then, clearly, from Little's result, $P_0 = 1 - \rho$. Also, for $j > 1$, an arbitrary customer who arrives at time t_0 (call this customer "tagged") will find j customers in the system if and only if one of the following two conditions holds:

1. the most recent epoch prior to t_0 was an arrival that found $j - 1$ customers in the system, or

2. the most recent epoch prior to t_0 was a departure that left j customers in the system.

We have argued that the arrival, departure, and stochastic equilibrium occupancy distributions are identical, so we find

$$P_j = P_{j-1}P\{\tilde{t} \leq \tilde{x}\} + P_j P\{\tilde{t} \leq \tilde{x}_r\}, \qquad (4.69)$$

where $\tilde{t}$ is the interarrival time. Thus

$$P_j = P_{j-1} \int_0^\infty (1 - e^{-\lambda x}) dF_{\tilde{x}}(x) + P_j \int_0^\infty (1 - e^{-\lambda x}) dF_{\tilde{x}_r}(x), \quad (4.70)$$

or

$$P_j = P_{j-1}[1 - F_{\tilde{x}}^*(\lambda)] + P_j[1 - F_{\tilde{x}_r}^*(\lambda)]. \qquad (4.71)$$

After collecting terms, we find

$$P_j = \frac{1 - F_{\tilde{x}}^*(\lambda)}{F_{\tilde{x}_r}^*(\lambda)} P_{j-1} \tag{4.72}$$

or

$$P_j = \left(\frac{1 - F_{\tilde{x}}^*(\lambda)}{F_{\tilde{x}_r}^*(\lambda)} \right)^j P_0. \tag{4.73}$$

From the requirement that the probabilities sum to unity, we find that

$$P_0 = 1 - \frac{1 - F_{\tilde{x}}^*(\lambda)}{F_{\tilde{x}_r}^*(\lambda)} \tag{4.74}$$

But, because $P_0 = 1 - \rho$, (4.74) implies

$$\rho = \frac{1 - F_{\tilde{x}}^*(\lambda)}{F_{\tilde{x}_r}^*(\lambda)}. \tag{4.75}$$

Substitution of (4.75) into (4.73) yields the occupancy distribution

$$P_j = (1 - \rho)\rho^j. \tag{4.76}$$

From (4.76), we see that the occupancy distribution for the M/G/1 with LCFS-PR discipline is independent of the service-time distribution and identical to that of the ordinary M/M/1 system. In addition, we find from (4.75) that

$$F_{\tilde{x}_r}^*(\lambda) = \frac{1 - F_{\tilde{x}}^*(\lambda)}{\lambda E[\tilde{x}]}, \tag{4.77}$$

where $\rho = \lambda E[\tilde{x}] < 1$. Substituting s for λ in (4.77) yields

$$F_{\tilde{x}_r}^*(s) = \frac{1 - F_{\tilde{x}}^*(s)}{s E[\tilde{x}]}. \tag{4.78}$$

This expression holds for all s for which $F_{\tilde{x}}^*(s)$ is defined by the analytic continuity property of regular functions. Since (4.78) and (4.62) are identical, the remaining service times for the customers in the queue for the M/G/1 with LCFS-PR discipline are indeed given by the residual service time as conjectured; that is, $\tilde{z}_r = \tilde{x}_r$.

Having determined the occupancy distribution and the distribution of the remaining service time for the customer in the system, we can readily determine the distribution for the unfinished work at an arbitrary point in time. We find

$$F_{\tilde{u}}(u) = (1 - \rho) \sum_{i=0}^{\infty} \rho^i [F_{\tilde{x}_r}(u)^{(i)}]. \tag{4.79}$$

where $[F_{\tilde{x}_r}(u)^{(j)}]$ denotes the j-fold convolution of $F_{\tilde{x}_r}(u)$ with itself, and $[F_{\tilde{x}_r}(u)^{(0)}] = 1$. Upon taking the Laplace–Stieltjes transform of both sides of (4.79) and comparing to (4.68), we readily find that $F_{\tilde{u}}^*(s) = F_{\tilde{w}}^*(s)$, as expected. We note in passing that the result given in (4.79) is valid for any work-conserving system.

Thus the behavior of the M/G/1 system under the LCFS-PR discipline provides an intuitive explanation for (4.68) as follows. The waiting-time distribution for the ordinary M/G/1 system is the same as the unfinished work in the M/G/1 system under the LCFS-PR discipline. The occupancy distribution under the LCFS-PR discipline is independent of service-time distribution and identical to the occupancy distribution for the ordinary M/M/1 system. The remaining service times for the customers in the system are independent and identically distributed, and their distribution is the same as that of the residual service time. The unfinished work is then just the geometrically weighted sum of the j-fold convolutions of the residual service-time distribution.

4.5   M/G/1 SYSTEM WITH EXCEPTIONAL FIRST SERVICE

In this section, we develop transform equations for the M/G/1 queueing system with exceptional first service—that is, an M/G/1 system in which the first customer served in each busy period has a special service time, $\tilde{x}_e$, and all other customers have service time $\tilde{x}$. The M/G/1 queueing system with exceptional first service is interesting in its own right, but it is also a useful tool in understanding priority queueing systems, which are in turn valuable in examining the behavior of many practical systems.

In this section we discuss four basic models. First, we present a very simple method for specifying the PGF for the number of customers left by an arbitrary departing customer in an ordinary M/G/1 queueing system. Our development is based on a decomposition principle similar to that used by Fuhrmann and Cooper [1985] to examine the M/G/1 queueing system with vacations (which we shall discuss later). This approach is more direct than the method presented earlier in this text because it does not require the specification and manipulation of recursive equations. Next, we use the decomposition principle to develop the PGF for the occupancy distribution for the M/G/1 queueing system with exceptional first service; the LSTs for the waiting- and sojourn-time distributions are left as exercises. We then consider the M/G/1 queueing system with set-up times, which is a special case of exceptional first service. Finally, we consider the M/G/1 queueing system with multiple vacations.

We begin our development for the M/G/1 system with exceptional first service by presenting an alternative derivation for the PGF of the occupancy distribution of the ordinary M/G/1 system. The development is more direct than that previously presented in that it does not involve solving recursive equations. In addition, the alternative development has the advantage of introducing powerful analysis techniques in a simple setting.

The idea exploited is very simple; namely, the number of customers left in the queue by an arbitrary departing customer—which we shall again refer to as the *tagged customer*—is independent of the order of service so long as the order of service is not based on the service-time requirement. Thus we simply arrange the order of service in a conceptually simple way, and the Pollaczek–Kinchine transform equation magically appears.

In a manner parallel to Fuhrmann and Cooper [1985], we organize servicing in the following way. First, we classify customers as belonging to one of the following two types:

1. Type 2 customers are those who arrive during the busy period but after the expiration of the first service of the busy period.

2. Type 1 customers are all customers that are not type 2, including those who arrive when the server is idle (and therefore start busy periods).

Let $\tilde{x}_1$ denote the service time of the first service of the busy period.

Then upon expiration of $\tilde{x}_1$, the system contains 0 or more type 1 customers and no type 2 customers. If there are 0 type 1 customers, the busy period ends. Otherwise, service of customers during the remainder of the busy period is organized as a sequence of type 2 *sub-busy periods*, each of which is initiated by a type 1 customer. That is, following $\tilde{x}_1$, for the remainder of the busy period, we begin service for a type 1 customer only when there are no type 2 customers waiting. Type 2 customers can then arrive and generate a sub-busy period. Upon expiration of the first sub-busy period, we select another type 1 customer, if any are left, and we initiate another sub-busy period, which again has the same statistics as the first sub-busy period. We continue this process until all type 1 customers have been served. The busy period ends upon expiration of the sub-busy period of the last type 1 customer.

We note that the dynamics of the system during each of these type 2 sub-busy periods is identical to that of an ordinary M/G/1 busy period. Thus, the PGF for the number of type 2 customers left in the system by an arbitrary departing customer during the sub-busy period, $\tilde{n}_2$, is the same as that for the ordinary M/G/1 system:

$$\mathcal{F}_{\tilde{n}_2}(z) = \mathcal{F}_{\tilde{n}}(z), \tag{4.80}$$

which we assume to be unknown.

Now, the tagged customer may arrive either during a busy period or not. Because arrivals are Poisson, the probability that the tagged customer arrives during a busy period is given by the probability that the server is busy at an arbitrary point in time. By Little's result, this quantity is readily computed to be $\rho = \lambda E[\tilde{x}]$.

If the tagged customer arrives during the idle period, then the number of type 2 customers left in the system by the tagged customer is identically zero. Also, the number of type 1 customers left in the system under this condition is equal to the number of customers that arrive during $\tilde{x}_1$, the PGF for which is found to be $F_{\tilde{x}}^*(\lambda[1 - z])$ by Theorem 2, because $\tilde{x}_1$ is drawn from $F_{\tilde{x}}$.

If the tagged customer arrives during the busy period, then the tagged customer may leave both type 1 and type 2 customers in the system upon departure. Because the statistics of the sub-busy period are identical to those of the ordinary M/G/1 system, the

PGF for $\tilde{n}_2$—the number of type 2 customers left in the system by the tagged customer given that the tagged customer arrived during a busy period—is given by (4.80).

We now consider the number of type 1 customers, $\tilde{n}_1$, left by the tagged customer given that that customer arrived during a busy period. Because only one type 1 customer is served in any sub-busy period, these customers are exactly the type 1 customers left behind by the departing type 1 customer who started the sub-busy period in which the tagged customer is serviced. In turn, these type 1 customers are exactly the ones who arrived during $\tilde{x}_1$ but after the type 1 customer who started the sub-busy period in which the tagged customer is serviced.

Now, the sequence of first service times of the busy periods constitutes a sequence of renewal intervals in a renewal process. Thus the distribution of the remaining service time that an arbitrary type 1 customer sees is simply the distribution of the residual life of $\tilde{x}_1$. This quantity is given by $F_{\tilde{x}_r}(x)$, and the PGF for the number of type 1 customers who arrive during this period is thus given by $\mathcal{F}_{\tilde{n}_1}(z) = F^*_{\tilde{x}_r}(\lambda[1-z])$, where $\tilde{n}_1$ denotes number of type 1 customers left in the system by the tagged customer given that the tagged customer arrived during a busy period.

Because $\tilde{n}_1$ is independent of $\tilde{n}_2$, the PGF for the total number of customers left in the system by the tagged customer given that the tagged customer arrived during the busy period is given by

$$F^*_{\tilde{x}_r}(\lambda[1-z])\mathcal{F}_{\tilde{n}}(z).$$

We therefore find, by conditioning upon whether or not the tagged customer arrived during a busy period, that

$$\mathcal{F}_{\tilde{n}}(z) = (1-\rho)F^*_{\tilde{x}}(\lambda[1-z]) + \rho F^*_{\tilde{x}_r}(\lambda[1-z])\mathcal{F}_{\tilde{n}}(z). \qquad (4.81)$$

Solving this last equation for $\mathcal{F}_{\tilde{n}}(z)$, we find

$$\mathcal{F}_{\tilde{n}}(z) = \frac{(1-\rho)F^*_{\tilde{x}}(\lambda[1-z])}{1 - \rho F^*_{\tilde{x}_r}(\lambda[1-z])}. \qquad (4.82)$$

Of course, (4.82) is also the PGF for the distribution of the number of customers found in the system by an arbitrary arriving customer and the stochastic equilibrium occupancy distribution.

We now turn to the determination of the PGF for the stochastic equilibrium occupancy distribution for the M/G/1 system with exceptional first service. Our reasoning is identical to that used to obtain (4.81), but there are two differences. First, the probability that an arriving customer finds the system busy in stochastic equilibrium is no longer given by our previously defined ρ; and second, the initial service time is drawn from the distribution $F_{\tilde{x}_e}$ rather than from $F_{\tilde{x}}$.

Let P_{busy} denote the probability that the tagged customer arrives during the busy period. We then find that the PGF for the total number of customers left in the system in the case of exceptional first service is given by

$$\mathcal{F}_{\tilde{n}_e}(z) = (1 - P_{\text{busy}})F_{\tilde{x}_e}^*(\lambda[1-z]) + P_{\text{busy}}F_{\tilde{x}_{er}}^*(\lambda[1-z])\mathcal{F}_{\tilde{n}}(z). \quad (4.83)$$

We now develop an expression for P_{busy} by using results from alternating renewal theory. From Takàcs [1962], and also from Exercise 4.12, we know that the expected length of the busy period in which the expected initial backlog is $E[\tilde{x}_e]$ is given by

$$\frac{E[\tilde{x}_e]}{1 - \rho,} \quad (4.84)$$

where $\rho = \lambda E[\tilde{x}]$ and the expected length of the idle period is given by $1/\lambda$. Because the busy and idle periods form an alternating renewal process and the Poisson arrivals observe the system in stochastic equilibrium, we find that the probability that an arbitrary arriving customer finds the system busy is given simply by the ratio of the expected length of the busy period to the expected length of the renewal cycle; that is,

$$
\begin{aligned}
P_{\text{busy}} &= \frac{E[\tilde{x}_e]/(1 - \rho)}{1/\lambda + E[\tilde{x}_e]/(1 - \rho)} \\
&= \frac{\rho_e}{1 - \rho + \rho_e}
\end{aligned}
\quad (4.85)
$$

where ρ_e is defined to be $\lambda E[\tilde{x}_e]$.

Substituting (4.84) into (4.83), we find

$$
\begin{aligned}
\mathcal{F}_{\tilde{n}_e}(z) = {} & \frac{1-\rho}{1-\rho+\rho_e} F^*_{\tilde{x}_e}(\lambda[1-z]) \\
& + \frac{\rho_e}{1-\rho+\rho_e} F^*_{\tilde{x}_{er}}(\lambda[1-z])\mathcal{F}_{\tilde{n}}(z).
\end{aligned}
\tag{4.86}
$$

A special case of exceptional first service is the M/G/1 queueing system with set-up times, which was studied by Levy and Kleinrock [1986]. For this system, we assume $\tilde{x}_e = \tilde{x}_s + \tilde{x}$, where $\tilde{x}_s$ represents a *set-up* time independent of $\tilde{x}$. For this special case, $\rho_e = \rho + \rho_s$, where $\rho_s = \lambda \tilde{x}_s$, and (4.85) reduces to

$$
P_{\text{busy}} = \frac{\rho_e}{1+\rho_s},
\tag{4.87}
$$

where ρ_e is defined to be $\lambda E[\tilde{x}_e]$. Because $\tilde{x}_s$ and $\tilde{x}$ are independent, we find that $F^*_{\tilde{x}_e}(s) = F^*_{\tilde{x}}(s)F^*_{\tilde{x}_s}(s)$ and

$$
\begin{aligned}
F^*_{\tilde{x}_{er}}(s) &= \frac{\rho}{\rho_e} F^*_{\tilde{x}_r}(s)F^*_{\tilde{x}_s}(s) + \frac{\rho_s}{\rho_e} F^*_{\tilde{x}_{sr}}(s) \\
&= \frac{\rho}{\rho_e} F^*_{\tilde{x}_r}(s) + \frac{\rho_s}{\rho_e} F^*_{\tilde{x}_{sr}}(s)F^*_{\tilde{x}}(s).
\end{aligned}
\tag{4.88}
$$

The expression (4.88) can be obtained as follows. We consider an alternating renewal process for which the renewal interval is $\tilde{x} + \tilde{x}_s$. The forward recurrence time for the process can then be obtained by conditioning on whether a random observer observes the system during an $\tilde{x}$ period or during an $\tilde{x}_s$ period, the probabilities of which are $E[\tilde{x}]/\{E[\tilde{x}] + E[\tilde{x}_s]\}$ and $E[\tilde{x}_s]/\{E[\tilde{x}] + E[\tilde{x}_s]\}$, respectively. These probabilities can be rewritten as ρ/ρ_e and ρ_s/ρ_e by multiplying numerator and denominator by λ. Now, if the observer observes an $\tilde{x}$ period in progress, then the time until the end of the cycle is $\tilde{x}_r + \tilde{x}_s$, the LST of the distribution of which is given by $F^*_{\tilde{x}_r}(s)F^*_{\tilde{x}_s}(s)$. On the other hand, if the observer finds the system in an $\tilde{x}_s$ interval, then the time until the end of the cycle is $\tilde{x}_{sr}$, the residual life of $\tilde{x}_s$, the LST of the distribution of which is $F^*_{\tilde{x}_{sr}}(s)$. We note that it is natural to think of $\tilde{x}_s$ as preceding $\tilde{x}$, but the distribution of the remaining time in the cycle is the same as that with $\tilde{x}$ preceding $\tilde{x}_s$.

The PGF for the equilibrium occupancy distribution for the M/G/1 queueing system with set-up times can now be obtained by substituting (4.88) into (4.86). We find

$$\mathcal{F}_{\tilde{n}_s}(z) = \frac{1-\rho}{1+\rho_s} F_{\tilde{x}}^*(\lambda[1-z]) F_{\tilde{x}_s}^*(\lambda[1-z]) + \frac{\rho_e}{1+\rho_s}$$

$$\left(\frac{\rho}{\rho_e} F_{\tilde{x}_r}^*(\lambda[1-z]) F_{\tilde{x}_s}^*(\lambda[1-z]) \right. \qquad (4.89)$$

$$\left. + \frac{\rho_s}{\rho_e} F_{\tilde{x}_{sr}}^*(\lambda[1-z]) \right) \mathcal{F}_{\tilde{n}}(z),$$

which, with a minimum of algebra, can be reduced to

$$\mathcal{F}_{\tilde{n}_s}(z) = \left(\frac{1}{1+\rho_s} F_{\tilde{x}_s}^*(\lambda[1-z]) + \frac{\rho_s}{1+\rho_s} F_{\tilde{x}_{sr}}^*(\lambda[1-z]) \right) \mathcal{F}_{\tilde{n}}(z).$$
$$(4.90)$$

The form of (4.90) suggests that the number of customers left in the system by an arbitrary departing customer can be obtained as the sum of two independent random variables as pointed out by Fuhrmann and Cooper [1985]. We modify our definition of type 1 and type 2 customers to facilitate the explanation: type 1 customers are those who arrive before the first service of the busy period begins; all other customers are of type 2. The $\mathcal{F}_{\tilde{n}}(z)$ part of the expression then corresponds to the number of type 2 customers left in the system. The grouped term of (4.90) corresponds to the number of type 1 customers and has a simple interpretation.

Interpretation of the grouped term of (4.90) is as follows. Note that the distribution of the number of type 1 customers left in the system by an arbitrary departing customer is the same as the distribution of the number of type 1 customers left by an arbitrary departing type 1 customer, there being one type 1 customer for each sub-busy period. Now, if a type 1 customer arrives to find the system empty, then the number of type 1 customers left by that customer is exactly the number that arrive during the set-up time. If, on the other hand, the type 1 customer arrives while the set-up is in progress, then the number of type 1 customers left is the number that arrive during the forward recurrence time of the renewal process in which the underlying renewal interval is $\tilde{x}_s$, because the type 1 customer arrivals are Poisson. The relative probabilities of these two events are readily obtained by setting up an alternating renewal process over the intervals of time during which type 1 customers arrive. The underlying renewal interval is then the length of an idle period plus the length of the set-up interval. Hence the probability that a random observer finds the system in an idle interval is the ratio of the expected length of an idle period to the expected length of a cycle,

$$\frac{1/\lambda}{1/\lambda + E[\tilde{x}_s]} = \frac{1}{1 + \rho_s}.$$

Also, the probability that a random observer finds the system in a set-up interval is the ratio of the expected length of a set-up period to the expected length of a cycle, which is

$$\frac{\rho_s}{1 + \rho_s}.$$

(The proportion of type 1 customers that arrive while the system is in a set-up period is also given by this ratio.) Thus the PGF for the number of type 1 customers left in the system by an arbitrary customer is

$$\frac{1}{1 + \rho_s} F_{\tilde{x}_s}^*(\lambda[1 - z]) + \frac{\rho_s}{1 + \rho_s} F_{\tilde{x}_{sr}}^*(\lambda[1 - z]).$$

Alternative forms for the expressions (4.86) and (4.90) that use only the ordinary service-time distributions rather than both ordinary distributions and residual life distributions are now given. Recall that for any nonnegative random variable, $\tilde{x}$,

$$F_{\tilde{x}_r}^*(s) = \frac{1 - F_{\tilde{x}}^*(s)}{sE[\tilde{x}]}. \tag{4.91}$$

In particular,

$$F_{\tilde{x}_{er}}^*(s) = \frac{1 - F_{\tilde{x}_e}^*(s)}{sE[\tilde{x}_e]}, \tag{4.92}$$

and

$$F_{\tilde{x}_{sr}}^*(s) = \frac{1 - F_{\tilde{x}_s}^*(s)}{sE[\tilde{x}_s]}. \tag{4.93}$$

If we substitute (4.92) and (4.93) into (4.86) and (4.90), respectively and substitute (4.8) into the result, the following alternative expressions can be obtained from simple algebra:

$$\mathcal{F}_{\tilde{n}_e}(z) = \frac{1 - \rho}{1 - \rho + \rho_e} \frac{z F_{\tilde{x}_e}^*(\lambda[1 - z]) - F_{\tilde{x}}^*(\lambda[1 - z])}{z - F_{\tilde{x}}^*(\lambda[1 - z])}, \qquad (4.94)$$

and

$$\mathcal{F}_{\tilde{n}_s}(z) = \frac{\rho_s}{1 + \rho_s} \frac{1 - z F_{\tilde{x}_s}^*(\lambda[1 - z])}{\lambda[1 - z] E[\tilde{x}_s]} \\ \frac{(1 - \rho)(z - 1) F_{\tilde{x}}^*(\lambda[1 - z])}{z - F_{\tilde{x}}^*(\lambda[1 - z])}. \qquad (4.95)$$

As we have pointed out in our discussion of (4.90), the product of the first two fractions of (4.95) is the probability generating function for the number of type 1 customers left in the system by an arbitrary departing customer. The third fraction is the familiar Pollaczek–Kintchine transform equation for the occupancy of the ordinary M/G/1 system, which is in turn the probability generating function for the number of type 2 customers left in the system by an arbitrary departing customer.

An interesting and useful variation of the M/G/1 system with set-up times is the M/G/1 system with server vacations (Cooper [1972, 1981]). In the simplest version of this system, the server takes a *vacation* each time the queue becomes empty. Upon return from each vacation, the server begins a busy period if any customers are waiting; otherwise, the server takes another vacation (this model is called the *multiple vacation model*, as opposed to the *single vacation model*, in which the server remains idle once having returned from vacation if there are no customers present). The duration of each vacation is a random variable $\tilde{x}_v$ drawn from the distribution $F_{\tilde{x}_v}$.

If we now define the type 1 customers as those who arrive during vacation periods, we can readily see that the distribution of the number of type 1 customers left by an arbitrary departing customer is the same as the distribution of the number of customers who arrive from the Poisson process during the residual life of the vacation period. The primary distinction between this simple vacation model and the set-up time model is that for the vacation model *all* of the type 1 customers arrive during the server vacation, whereas for the set-up time model all type 1 customers except the first arrive during the server set-up time (and the first customer arrives during the idle period). From (4.90) and (4.91), we find that the probability generating function for the number of customers left in the system by an arbitrary departing customer is, therefore,

$$
\mathcal{F}_{\tilde{n}_v}(z) = \frac{1 - F^*_{\tilde{x}_v}(\lambda[1-z])}{\lambda[1-z]E[\tilde{x}_v]} \frac{(1-\rho)(z-1)F^*_{\tilde{x}}(\lambda[1-z])}{z - F^*_{\tilde{x}}(\lambda[1-z])}. \quad (4.96)
$$

Vacation models have a number of interesting applications. For example, consider a variation of the M/G/1 queue in which the server works as in the following way (Wortman and Disney [1990]).

> The server works on an auxiliary task for a period of time $\tilde{v}$ and then checks the system occupancy. If there are at least K customers waiting, the server serves a batch of K customers and then returns to the auxiliary task, regardless of the queue length. If there are less than K customers waiting, the server immediately returns to the auxiliary task.

Note that in the general analysis of vacation systems, the successive vacation periods are not required to be mutually independent. Some interesting applications of server vacation models include the study of server breakdowns and polling systems. The reader is referred to Doshi [1986,1990], Levy and Sidi [1990], and Takagi [1987a, 1987b, 1990] for recent articles that survey the application of vacation models.

This concludes our discussion of the M/G/1 queueing system with exceptional first service and its variants. We shall use the ideas presented here later in the development of the transform equations for priority queueing systems. Note that $\mathcal{F}_{\tilde{n}_e}(z)$ and $\mathcal{F}_{\tilde{n}_s}(z)$ can be readily inverted using the methods based on discrete Fourier transforms, which were presented earlier in this chapter to obtain the distributions of $\tilde{n}_e$ and $\tilde{n}_s$, respectively.

4.6   M/G/1 WITH HEAD-OF-THE-LINE PRIORITY

We now turn our attention to the analysis of queueing systems having externally assigned priorities—that is, priorities assigned prior to or upon entry into the system. We assume that there is an integer number, I, of customer classes. Class i, $1 \le i \le I$, customers arrive to the system according to a Poisson process with rate λ_i, and their service times are drawn independently from the distribution $F_{\tilde{x}_i}(x)$. Class i customers have priority over class j customers if $i < j$. Upon arrival, a customer joins the queue ahead of all customers whose priority is lower than that of the arriving customer and behind all customers whose priority is at least as high as that of the arriving customer. The service discipline is illustrated in Figure 4.5.

There are two primary variations of this service discipline: non-preemptive and preemptive resume. In the nonpreemptive version, denoted by HOL, servicing of a customer is never interrupted. That is, once servicing of a given customer begins, the server serves the customer to completion independent of the arrival process. Upon service completions, the server begins service on behalf of the customer who is currently at the head of the line.

In the case of preemptive resume, denoted by HOL-PR, an entering customer whose priority is higher than that of the customer currently in service immediately gains access to the server. Servicing of the preempted customer resumes from the point at which it was preempted as soon as there is no longer a customer present in the system whose priority exceeds that of the interrupted customer. Thus, under the HOL-PR discipline, customers of a given priority

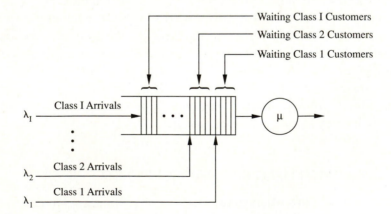

Figure 4.5 HOL service discipline.

never receive service while any higher priority customer is in the
system. There may be no more than one customer of a given priority
preempted at any given time, and the maximum possible number of
preempted customers is $I - 1$.

We analyze the ordinary HOL system for the special case of
$I = 2$, and we leave extension to the case of arbitrary I and the
HOL-PR discipline to the exercises. We derive probability generating
functions for the occupancy distribution of each customer class, and
then we use these distributions to specify the Laplace–Stieltjes transforms for the waiting- and sojourn-time distributions. Our derivation
is based on a variation of the Fuhrmann–Cooper decomposition principle discussed earlier in combination with results on alternating renewal processes from Section 4.3 and exceptional first service from
Section 4.5. Customers with higher and lower priorities are examined in separate subsections in hopes of avoiding confusion about
definitions of types and classes for the different points of view we
will take.

4.6.1   Customers with Higher Priority

As we did in the case of the ordinary M/G/1 analysis using the principles of Fuhrmann–Cooper decomposition, we shall obtain the probability generating function for the ergodic occupancy distribution by
computing the probability generating function for the distribution of
the number of customers left in the system by an arbitrary departing
customer in stochastic equilibrium, because these two distributions
are equal. We shall designate an arbitrary customer as the tagged
customer. Because arrivals are Poisson, the tagged customer sees the
system in stochastic equilibrium, as we stated earlier.

To begin our development, we note that at any given time, the
server is in one of three possible states: idle, busy serving a class 1
customer, or busy serving a class 2 customer—the respective ergodic
probabilities are $1 - \rho_1 - \rho_2$, ρ_1, and ρ_2, where $\rho_i = \lambda_i E[\tilde{x}_i]$. We
separate the class 1 customers into two groups as follows:

1. Type 1 customers are those class 1 customers who arrive to the
   system either during an idle period or during a period during
   which a class 2 customer is being serviced, and

2. Type 2 customers are those class 1 customers who arrive to the system while a class 1 customer is being serviced.

As in the case of the ordinary M/G/1 queueing system, we envision all servicing as being organized as a series of sub-busy periods, all of which are started by type 1 customers, are generated by type 2 customers, and are statistically identical to ordinary M/G/1 busy periods in which the arrival rate is λ_1 and the service times are drawn from the distribution $F_{\tilde{x}_2}$.

Let $\tilde{n}_{11}$ and $\tilde{n}_{12}$ denote the number of type 1 and type 2 customers, respectively, left in the system by an arbitrary departing class 1 customer, and let $\tilde{n}_1 = \tilde{n}_{11} + \tilde{n}_{12}$. Because all class 1 customers depart the system during one of the sub-busy periods just defined and all of the sub-busy periods are statistically identical, the distributions of $\tilde{n}_{11}$ and $\tilde{n}_{12}$ are the same as the distributions of the numbers of type 1 and type 2 customers left in the system by an arbitrary customer departing during an arbitrary sub-busy period. Thus we can study the system by studying an arbitrary sub-busy period.

Because type 1 and type 2 customers arrive according to a Poisson process over nonoverlapping intervals of time, $\tilde{n}_{11}$ and $\tilde{n}_{12}$ are statistically independent. Thus by Theorem 4.1 we see that

$$\mathcal{F}_{\tilde{n}_1}(z) = \mathcal{F}_{\tilde{n}_{11}}(z)\mathcal{F}_{\tilde{n}_{11}}(z). \qquad (4.97)$$

We shall compute $\mathcal{F}_{\tilde{n}_{11}}(z)$ and $\mathcal{F}_{\tilde{n}_{12}}(z)$ separately in the following paragraphs and then combine the result to obtain $\mathcal{F}_{\tilde{n}_1}(z)$.

From the definitions of type 1 and type 2 customers and the remark following their definition, it is clear that the distribution of the number of type 2 customers left in the system by an arbitrary departing customer is identically the same as that of an ordinary M/G/1 system in which the arrival rate is λ_1 and the service times are drawn from the distribution $F_{\tilde{x}_1}(x)$. Thus we find from the Pollaczek–Khintchine transform equation for the occupancy distribution,

$$\mathcal{F}_{\tilde{n}}(z) = \frac{(1-\rho)F_{\tilde{x}}^*(\lambda[1-z])}{1 - \rho F_{\tilde{x}_r}^*(\lambda[1-z])},$$

that

$$\mathcal{F}_{\tilde{n}_{12}}(z) = \frac{(1 - \rho_1)F_{\tilde{x}_1}^*(\lambda_1[1 - z])}{1 - \rho_1 F_{\tilde{x}_{1r}}^*(\lambda_1[1 - z])}. \tag{4.98}$$

It remains to specify $\mathcal{F}_{\tilde{n}_{11}}(z)$. We note that the type 1 customers left by an arbitrary departing customer during a sub-busy period are identically those type 1 customers left by the first departing customer from the sub-busy period. But the first departing customer from an arbitrary sub-busy period is simply an arbitrary type 1 customer. Hence we define the tagged type 1 customer to be the type 1 customer who started the busy period during which the tagged customer is served. Then, the distribution of the number of type 1 customers left by the tagged class 1 customer is the same as the distribution of the number of type 1 customers left by the tagged type 1 customer. These are, in turn, the same as the type 1 customers who arrive while an arbitrary type 1 customer is in the system.

If the tagged type 1 customer arrives while the server is idle, the number of type 1 customers left by the tagged type 1 customer upon departure is 0 with probability 1, and the probability generating function for this distribution is identically 1. This is because the tagged type 1 customer immediately begins service so that all class 1 customers who arrive during the time the customer is in the system are of type 2.

If, on the other hand, the tagged type 1 customer arrives while the server is serving a class 2 customer, then the period of time over which type 1 customers arrive following the arrival of the tagged type 1 customer is the same as the distribution of the forward recurrence time of the renewal process in which the lengths of the renewal intervals are drawn from the distribution $F_{\tilde{x}_2}(x)$. This is because the tagged type 1 customer is drawn arbitrarily from a Poisson stream.[1] Therefore, by Theorem 4.2, the probability generating function for the number of type 1 customers left by the tagged type 1 customer

---

[1]The class 1 arrival process is Poisson and thus has stationary and independent increments. Thus, if we observe the arrival process over only those intervals during which class 2 customers are being serviced, the observed arrival process will still have stationary and independent increments, and the probability of an arrival over an interval of length h will still be $\lambda_1 h$; hence the arrival process will still be Poisson with rate λ_1.

given that the tagged type 1 customer arrived during a class 2 service period is given by $F^*_{\tilde{x}_{2r}}(\lambda_1[1-z])$, where $\tilde{x}_{2r}$ denotes the residual life of $\tilde{x}_2$.

Combining the results of the previous two paragraphs, we find that

$$\mathcal{F}_{\tilde{n}_{11}}(z) = \frac{1-\rho_1-\rho_2}{1-\rho_1} + \frac{\rho_2}{1-\rho_1} F^*_{\tilde{x}_{2r}}(\lambda_1[1-z]), \qquad (4.99)$$

where it is easily seen that

$$\frac{1-\rho_1-\rho_2}{1-\rho_1}$$

is the conditional probability that the server is idle given that the server is either idle or serving class 2 customers, and

$$\frac{\rho_2}{1-\rho_1}$$

is the conditional probability that the server is serving class 2 customers given that the server is either idle or serving class 2 customers. Combining (4.97) through (4.99), we find

$$\mathcal{F}_{\tilde{n}_1}(z) = \left(\frac{1-\rho_1-\rho_2}{1-\rho_1} + \frac{\rho_2 F^*_{\tilde{x}_{2r}}(\lambda_1[1-z])}{1-\rho_1} \right) \frac{(1-\rho_1) F^*_{\tilde{x}_1}(\lambda_1[1-z])}{1-\rho_1 F^*_{\tilde{x}_{1r}}(\lambda_1[1-z])}. \qquad (4.100)$$

Exercise 4.36   Compare the probability generating function for the class 1 occupancy distributions for the HOL system to that of the M/G/1 system with set-up times discussed in Section 4.5. Do they have exactly the same form? Explain why or why not intuitively.

Because the class 1 customers left in the HOL system by the departing class 1 customers are identically the customers who arrive during the class 1 sojourn time, we find directly from Theorem 4.2 that

$$F^*_{\tilde{s}_1}(s) = \left(\frac{1-\rho_1-\rho_2}{1-\rho_1} + \frac{\rho_2 F^*_{\tilde{x}_{2r}}(s)}{1-\rho_1} \right) \frac{(1-\rho_1) F^*_{\tilde{x}_1}(s)}{1-\rho_1 F^*_{\tilde{x}_{1r}}(s)}, \qquad (4.101)$$

where $\tilde{s}_1$ denotes the Laplace–Stieltjes transform of the class 1 sojourn time. Similarly,

$$F_{\tilde{w}_1}^*(s) = \left(\frac{1 - \rho_1 - \rho_2}{1 - \rho_1} + \frac{\rho_2 F_{\tilde{x}_{2r}}^*(s)}{1 - \rho_1} \right) \frac{(1 - \rho_1)}{1 - \rho_1 F_{\tilde{x}_{1r}}^*(s)}. \qquad (4.102)$$

where $\tilde{w}_1$ denotes the Laplace–Stieltjes transform of the class 1 waiting time.

4.6.2   Customers with Lower Priority

We now turn our attention to the determination of the PGF for the class 2 occupancy distribution and the corresponding class 2 sojourn time. The mathematics for obtaining the desired probability generating function is quite simple, but the logic behind it is a little complicated due to the number of concepts that have to be juggled simultaneously. We shall therefore approach the problem in a roundabout way. First, we shall examine the queueing behavior of the system only during those busy periods started by a class 2 customer. We shall then be in a position to examine the queueing behavior during all busy periods during which class 2 customers are served.

Consider the evolution of the service system during busy periods started by class 2 customers. For reasons that will become clear later, we shall refer to this type of busy period as a "type 2 busy period," and we shall denote its length by $\tilde{y}_{22}$. Initially, the server is idle. Upon arrival of a class 2 customer, service begins immediately. During servicing of the class 2 customer, class 1 and class 2 customers may arrive. But, in any event, the server will not be available to service the second class 2 customer until the service of the first class 2 customer is complete and there are no class 1 customers in the system. The distribution of the length of time between the start of service of the first class 2 customer of the busy period and the second class 2 customer of the same busy period, if any, is identical to the distribution of the length of a class 1 busy period started by a class 2 customer. This period of time is called the "class 2 completion time," and we denote its length by $\tilde{x}_{2c}$. From the results of our analysis of M/G/1 queueing systems with exceptional first service, we find

$$F^*_{\tilde{x}_{2c}}(s) = F^*_{\tilde{x}_2}(s + \lambda_1 - \lambda_1 F^*_{\tilde{y}_{11}}(s)), \qquad (4.103)$$

where $\tilde{y}_{11}$ denotes the length of a class 1 busy period started by a class 1 customer,[2] which we shall refer to as a "type 1 busy period," and $F^*_{\tilde{y}_{11}}(s)$ satisfies the functional equation

$$F^*_{\tilde{y}_{11}}(s) = F^*_{\tilde{x}_1}(s + \lambda_1 - \lambda_1 F^*_{\tilde{y}_{11}}(s)). \qquad (4.104)$$

From this discussion, it is clear that the busy period started by a class 2 customer evolves as a sequence of class 2 completion times. The waiting time of a class 2 customer served in a type 2 busy period therefore has the same distribution as that of an ordinary M/G/1 queueing system in which the service times are drawn from the distribution $F_{\tilde{x}_{2c}}$. Consequently, the probability generating function for the distribution of the number of class 2 customers left in the system at the time an arbitrary class 2 service is completed is given by the Laplace–Stieltjes transform of the waiting-time distribution evaluated at $\lambda_2(1 - z)$. In addition, the number of class 2 customers left in the system by a departing class 2 customer is simply the sum of the number in the system at the time the customer entered service and the the number who arrive while the class 2 customer is in service. The probability generating function for the distribution of the latter quantity is given by the Laplace–Stieltjes transform of the service time distribution evaluated at $\lambda_2(1 - z)$. Thus, if we denote by n_{22} the number of class 2 customers left in the system by a departing class 2 customer during a class 2 busy period started by a class 2 customer, we find

$$\mathcal{F}_{\tilde{n}_{22}}(z) = \frac{(1 - \lambda_2 E[\tilde{x}_{2c}]) F^*_{\tilde{x}_2}(\lambda_2[1 - z])}{1 - \lambda_2 E[\tilde{x}_{2c}] F^*_{\tilde{x}_{2cr}}(\lambda_2[1 - z])}, \qquad (4.105)$$

where $\tilde{x}_{2cr}$ denotes the residual life of $\tilde{x}_{2c}$. Paralleling our definition of ρ, we define

$$\gamma_2 = \lambda_2 E[\tilde{x}_{2c}], \qquad (4.106)$$

---

[2] That is $\tilde{y}_{11}$ would be the length of the busy period if the system served only class 1 customers.

and upon substituting (4.106) into (4.105), we find

$$\mathcal{F}_{\tilde{n}_{22}}(z) = \frac{(1 - \gamma_2)F^*_{\tilde{x}_2}(\lambda_2[1-z])}{1 - \gamma_2 F^*_{\tilde{x}_{2cr}}(\lambda_2[1-z])}. \tag{4.107}$$

Now consider the evolution of a busy period for class 2 customers started by a class 1 customer. Initially, the server is idle. Then, upon arrival of a class 1 customer, the busy period starts. First, the server serves an initial busy period of class 1 customers, the length of which is $\tilde{y}_{11}$. Just as in the case of the ordinary M/G/1 system, we can think of the remainder of this busy period as evolving as a sequence of type 2 sub-busy periods, all of which have the same distribution as an ordinary type 2 busy period. Thus we see that for any busy period during which class 2 customers are served, the periods over which class 2 customers are served can be thought of as evolving as a sequence of type 2 busy periods.

Corresponding to our definition of type 1 and type 2 jobs above, we classify type 1 customers as those class 2 customers who arrive prior to the start of service of the first class 2 customer served in a busy period, and we classify all other class 2 customers as type 2. Without affecting the distribution of the number of class 2 customers left in the system by an arbitrary departing class 2 customer, we may think of the order of service of the type 1 and type 2 customers as being the same as in Section 4.5. Then each sub-busy period behaves in exactly the same way as the type 2 busy period described above. It is then easy to see that the PGF for the number of type 2 customers left in the system by an arbitrary departing type 2 customer is given by $\mathcal{F}_{\tilde{n}_{22}}$.

The PGF for number of type 1 jobs left by the tagged class 2 job can be obtained in a manner analogous to the explanation of the bracketed term of (4.101). To begin with, we consider only that portion of the time line during which type 1 jobs arrive. During that portion of the time line, the system behaves as though the class 2 customers never enter the system; they are merely observers. Periods of time under this condition alternate between class 1 idle periods, the lengths of which are drawn from an exponential distribution with parameter λ_1, and ordinary class 1 busy periods, the lengths of which are drawn from the distribution $F_{\tilde{y}_{11}}(y)$.[3]

A random observer who arrives during this portion of the time line, and consequently an arbitrary type 1 arrival, finds the system idle with probability

$$\frac{1/\lambda_1}{1/\lambda_1 + E[\tilde{y}_{11}]} = \frac{1}{1 + \lambda_1 E[\tilde{y}_{11}]} = \frac{1}{1 + \gamma_1},$$

where we have defined $\gamma_1 = \lambda_1 E[\tilde{y}_{11}]$, and busy with probability one minus that quantity.

If the observer finds the server idle during these periods, then the number of type 1 jobs left will be identically zero; otherwise, the number of type 1 class 2 customers left will be equal to the number that arrive during the residual life of $\tilde{y}_{11}$, which we denote by $\tilde{y}_{11r}$. Thus the PGF for the distribution of the number of type 1 jobs left in the system by the tagged class 2 job, $\tilde{n}_{21}$, is given by

$$\mathcal{F}_{\tilde{n}_{21}}(z) = \frac{1}{1 + \gamma_1} + \frac{\gamma_1}{1 + \gamma_1} F^*_{\tilde{y}_{11r}}(\lambda_2[1 - z]). \tag{4.108}$$

Because $\mathcal{F}_{\tilde{n}_2}(z) = \mathcal{F}_{\tilde{n}_{21}}(z)\mathcal{F}_{\tilde{n}_{22}}(z)$, we find from (4.107) and (4.108) that

$$\mathcal{F}_{\tilde{n}_2}(z) = \left(\frac{1}{1 + \gamma_1} + \frac{\gamma_1 F^*_{\tilde{x}_{2cr}}(\lambda_2[1 - z])}{1 + \gamma_1} \right) \frac{(1 - \gamma_2) F^*_{\tilde{x}_2}(\lambda_2[1 - z])}{1 - \gamma_2 F^*_{\tilde{x}_{2cr}}(\lambda_2[1 - z])}. \tag{4.109}$$

Using the general relationship between the LST of the distribution

---

[3]The validity of this assertion is not necessarily obvious, but it can be reasoned as follows. Due to the properties of the exponential distribution, the length of each idle period is drawn independently from an exponential distribution with parameter $\lambda_1 + \lambda_2$, which is the distribution of the minimum of two independent exponential distributions having parameters λ_1 and λ_2, respectively. In addition, each idle period is terminated, independently of its length, by a class 2 customer with probability $\lambda_2/(\lambda_1 + \lambda_2)$. Thus the total amount of the idle time observed before an idle period is terminated by a class 1 customer is the geometric, parameter $\lambda_2/(\lambda_1 + \lambda_2)$, sum of idle periods whose lengths are drawn independently from an exponential distribution having parameter $\lambda_1 + \lambda_2$. The overall length of this idle period is then exponentially distributed with parameter λ_1.

of random variable and that of its residual,

$$F_{\tilde{x}_r}^*(s) = \frac{1 - F_{\tilde{x}}^*(s)}{s E[\tilde{x}]}, \tag{4.110}$$

in (4.109), we find, after rearranging terms, that

$$\mathcal{F}_{\tilde{n}_2}(z) = \frac{1 - \gamma_2}{1 + \gamma_1}$$
$$\left(\frac{(1 - z) + (\lambda_1/\lambda_2)\{1 - F_{\tilde{y}_{11}}^*(\lambda_2[1 - z])\}}{F_{\tilde{x}_{2c}}^*(\lambda_2[1 - z]) - z} \right) \tag{4.111}$$
$$F_{\tilde{x}_2}^*(\lambda_2[1 - z]).$$

Because the class 2 customers left in the system are precisely those who arrive during the sojourn time of the class 2 customer, it follows from Theorem 4.2 that $\mathcal{F}_{\tilde{n}_2}(z) = F_{\tilde{s}_2}^*(\lambda_2[1 - z])$. Thus, from (4.111), we find

$$F_{\tilde{s}_2}^*(s) = \frac{1 - \gamma_2}{1 + \gamma_1} \left[\frac{s + \lambda_1\{1 - F_{\tilde{y}_{11}}^*(s)\}}{s - \lambda_2 + \lambda_2 F_{\tilde{x}_{2c}}^*(s)} \right] F_{\tilde{x}_2}^*(s). \tag{4.112}$$

Exercise 4.37   Derive the expression for $\mathcal{F}_{\tilde{n}_2}(z)$ for the case of the HOL-PR discipline with $I = 2$.

Exercise 4.38   Derive expressions for $\mathcal{F}_{\tilde{n}_1}(z)$, $\mathcal{F}_{\tilde{n}_2}(z)$, and $\mathcal{F}_{\tilde{n}_3}(z)$ for the ordinary HOL discipline with $I = 3$. Extend the analysis to the case of arbitrary I.

Exercise 4.39   Extend the analysis of the previous case to the case of the HOL-PR discipline.

4.7   EXPECTED WAITING TIMES AND SOJOURN TIMES FOR M/G/1 WITH HOL PRIORITY

As in Section 4.6, we shall compute the average waiting time and average sojourn time for each customer class under two service disciplines: head of the line (HOL) and HOL-preemptive resume (HOL-PR). Under the ordinary HOL discipline, class i customers arriving to the system join the service queue ahead of all customers of lower priority and behind all customers whose priorities are at least as high. The HOL-PR discipline is similar except that a newly arriving customer goes directly into service if the server is serving a customer of lower priority than the new customer.

We shall again compute the delays by examining the system from the point of view of an arbitrary class i customer, whom we shall refer to as the "tagged class i" customer. Owing to the Poisson arrivals, the tagged class i customer observes the system in stochastic equilibrium, so that the average delay observed by the tagged class i customer is the same as that for an arbitrary class i customer.

Suppose the tagged class i customer arrives to the system at time t_0. The waiting time in the queue that this customer experiences can then be thought of as resulting from two basic customer groups: early arrivals and late arrivals. The early arrivals are those customers who arrived to the system prior to t_0; the late arrivals are those customers who arrive to the system prior to t_0.

Let $\tilde{w}_{i,e_j}$ and $\tilde{w}_{i,\ell_j}$ denote the delay suffered by the tagged class i customer due to early and late class j customers, respectively. Then, we find that

$$\tilde{w}_i = \sum_{j=1}^{I} \tilde{w}_{i,e_j} + \sum_{j=1}^{I} \tilde{w}_{i,\ell_j}, \qquad (4.113)$$

where $\tilde{w}_i$ denotes the waiting time for the class i customers. Now, the waiting time due to early arrivals can be further subdivided into the delay due to customers in the queue and the delay due to customers whose service has already begun at time t_0, which we shall denote as $\tilde{w}_{i,q_j}$ and $\tilde{w}_{i,s_j}$, respectively. Thus (4.113) can be rewritten as

$$\tilde{w}_i = \sum_{j=1}^{I} \tilde{w}_{i,q_j} + \sum_{j=1}^{I} \tilde{w}_{i,s_j} + \sum_{j=1}^{I} \tilde{w}_{i,\ell_j}. \qquad (4.114)$$

Clearly, under the HOL discipline, $\tilde{w}_{i,q_j} = 0$ if $j > i$ and $\tilde{w}_{i,\ell_j} = 0$ if $j \geq i$. But delays due to customers who may be in service at time t_0 depend on whether or not the service discipline is preemptive. Under HOL-PR, $\tilde{w}_{i,s_j} = 0$ for $j > i$, but under ordinary HOL, $\tilde{w}_{i,s_j}$ may be nonzero for all j. Based on the above discussions, we find

$$\tilde{w}_i = \sum_{j=1}^{i} \tilde{w}_{i,q_j} + \sum_{j=1}^{i-1} \tilde{w}_{i,\ell_j} + \sum_{j=1}^{I} \tilde{w}_{i,s_j}. \qquad (4.115)$$

so that

$$E[\tilde{w}_i] = \sum_{j=1}^{i} E[\tilde{w}_{i,q_j}] + \sum_{j=1}^{i-1} E[\tilde{w}_{i,\ell_j}] + \sum_{j=1}^{I} E[\tilde{w}_{i,s_j}]. \qquad (4.116)$$

Clearly, $E[\tilde{w}_{i,q_j}] = E[N_{q_j}]E[\tilde{x}_j]$ for $j \leq i$ where N_{q_j} denotes the number of class j customers in the queue at time t_0. Due to Little's result, $E[N_{q_j}] = \lambda_j E[\tilde{w}_j]$. Thus,

$$E[\tilde{w}_{i,q_j}] = \rho_j E[\tilde{w}_j] \qquad \text{for } j \leq i. \qquad (4.117)$$

As for the late arrivals, the tagged class i customer will be delayed in the queue by any class j late arrivals, $j < i$, who arrive while the tagged class i customer is still in the queue. That is, all class j, $j < i$, customers who arrive during $\tilde{w}_i$ will delay the tagged class i customer in the queue. Because class j arrivals are Poisson with rate λ_j and service times are drawn independently of everything, we find $E[\tilde{w}_{i,\ell_j}] = \lambda_j E[\tilde{w}_i]E[\tilde{x}_j]$ or, equivalently,

$$E[\tilde{w}_{i,\ell_j}] = \rho_j E[\tilde{w}_i] \qquad \text{for } j < i. \qquad (4.118)$$

Since $E[\tilde{w}_{i,s_j}]$ is dependent on the service discipline, we shall defer specifying a formula for its computation for the time being, and we solve (4.116) for the general case. Substitution of (4.117) and (4.118) into (4.116) yields

$$E[\tilde{w}_i] = \sum_{j=1}^{i} \rho_j E[\tilde{w}_j] + \sum_{j=1}^{i-1} \rho_j E[\tilde{w}_i] + \sum_{j=1}^{I} E[\tilde{w}_{i,s_j}]. \qquad (4.119)$$

Now, define

$$\sigma_i = \sum_{j=1}^{i-1} \rho_j. \qquad (4.120)$$

Then we can rewrite (4.119) in the following two versions:

$$(1 - \sigma_{i-1})E[\tilde{w}_i] = \sum_{j=1}^{i} \rho_j E[\tilde{w}_j] + \sum_{j=1}^{I} E[\tilde{w}_{i,s_j}] \qquad (4.121)$$

and

$$(1 - \sigma_i)E[\tilde{w}_i] = \sum_{j=1}^{i-1} \rho_j E[\tilde{w}_j] + \sum_{j=1}^{I} E[\tilde{w}_{i,s_j}]. \qquad (4.122)$$

Comparing (4.121) and (4.122), we find

$$(1 - \sigma_i)E[\tilde{w}_i] = (1 - \sigma_{i-2})E[\tilde{w}_{i-1}] + E[\tilde{w}_{i0}] - E[\tilde{w}_{i-1,0}], \qquad (4.123)$$

where we have defined

$$\tilde{w}_{i0} = \sum_{j=1}^{I} \tilde{w}_{i,s_j} \qquad (4.124)$$

and $\tilde{w}_{i0} = 0$ for $i \leq 0$. Thus, we find

$$E[\tilde{w}_i] = \frac{(1 - \sigma_{i-2})E[\tilde{w}_{i-1}] + E[\tilde{w}_{i0}] - E[\tilde{w}_{i-1,0}]}{(1 - \sigma_i)}. \qquad (4.125)$$

4.7.1   HOL Discipline

Recall that $\tilde{w}_{i0}$ is the total delay suffered by the class i tagged customer due to customers whose service is in progress at time t_0. This quantity is clearly a function of the service discipline. Under the ordinary HOL discipline, $\tilde{w}_{i0} = \tilde{w}_{j0}$ for all $i, j \geq 1$, because customers who are in service remain in service regardless of the class to which the tagged customer belongs. Thus, for the HOL discipline, we find by solving (4.125) recursively that

$$E[\tilde{w}_i] = \frac{E[\tilde{w}_{i0}]}{(1 - \sigma_i)(1 - \sigma_{i-1})}. \qquad (4.126)$$

It remains to specify $E[\tilde{w}_{i0}]$. From (4.124) we find

$$E[\tilde{w}_{i0}] = \sum_{j=1}^{I} E[\tilde{w}_{i,s_j}].$$

By conditioning on whether or not a class j customer is in service at time t_0, we find

$$E[\tilde{w}_{i0}] = \sum_{j=1}^{I} E[\tilde{w}_{i,s_j}| \text{ class } j \text{ in service at } t_0] \tag{4.127}$$

$$P\{\text{class } j \text{ in service at } t_0\}.$$

Clearly, the delay a class i customer suffers due to a class j customer in service at time t_0 is equal to the residual service time for a class j customer and the probability that a class j customer is in service is ρ_j. Thus, (4.127) reduces to

$$E[\tilde{w}_{i0}] = \sum_{j=1}^{I} \rho_j E[\tilde{x}_{r_j}] \tag{4.128}$$

or, equivalently,

$$E[\tilde{w}_{i0}] = \sum_{j=1}^{I} \rho_j \left(\frac{1 + C_{\tilde{x}_j}^2}{2} \right) E[\tilde{x}_j]. \tag{4.129}$$

Upon substituting (4.120) and (4.129) into (4.126), we find

$$E[\tilde{w}_i] = \frac{\sum_{j=1}^{I} \rho_j \left[(1 + C_{\tilde{x}_j}^2)/2 \right] E[\tilde{x}_j]}{(1 - \sigma_i)(1 - \sigma_{i-1})}. \tag{4.130}$$

4.7.2   HOL-PR Discipline

Under the HOL-PR discipline, $\tilde{w}_{i0}$ is different for each i because class i customers are delayed by class j customers only if $j \leq i$. Thus, under this discipline,

$$\tilde{w}_{i0} = \sum_{j=1}^{i} \tilde{w}_{i,s_j}. \tag{4.131}$$

In addition class j customers are preempted by all higher priority customers who arrive while they are in service. As a result, the time required to complete service for a class j customer is the same as the length of a busy period started by a customer whose service time is $\tilde{x}_j$ and generated by all traffic having priority higher than class j. This period, called a "class j completion time," is denoted by $\tilde{x}_{c_j}$.

Thus

$$E[\tilde{x}_{c_j}] = \frac{E[\tilde{x}_j]}{1 - \sigma_{j-1}}. \tag{4.132}$$

Now, at time t_0, a class j customer whose service has begun may be either preempted or actually in service. In either case, that customer's remaining service time is given by $\tilde{x}_{r_j}$. Also, the probability that there is a class j customer either in service or preempted at time t_0 is readily computed by applying Little's result. We find

$$P\{\text{class } j \text{ service in progress at } t_0\} = \frac{\lambda_j E[\tilde{x}_j]}{1 - \sigma_{j-1}}$$

or

$$P\{\text{class } j \text{ service in progress at } t_0\} = \frac{\rho_j}{1 - \sigma_{j-1}}. \tag{4.133}$$

Applying (4.133) and our remaining service-time observation to (4.131) and conditioning, we find

$$E[\tilde{w}_{i0}] = \sum_{j=1}^{i} \frac{\rho_j E[\tilde{x}_{r_j}]}{1 - \sigma_{j-1}}. \tag{4.134}$$

Substitution of (4.134) into (4.125) yields

$$E[\tilde{w}_i] = \frac{(1 - \sigma_{1-2})E[\tilde{w}_{i-1}] + \{(\rho_i E[\tilde{x}_{ri}])/(1 - \sigma_{i-1})\}}{(1 - \sigma_i)} \tag{4.135}$$

or, equivalently,

$$E[\tilde{w}_i] = \frac{(1 - \sigma_{i-1})(1 - \sigma_{i-2})E[\tilde{w}_{i-1}] + \rho_i E[\tilde{x}_{ri}]}{(1 - \sigma_i)(1 - \sigma_{i-1})}. \tag{4.136}$$

Solving recursively, we find

$$E[\tilde{w}_i] = \frac{\sum_{j=1}^{i} \rho_j E[\tilde{x}_{ri}]}{(1 - \sigma_i)(1 - \sigma_{i-1})}. \tag{4.137}$$

Thus we find that for the HOL-PR service discipline,

$$E[\tilde{w}_i] = \frac{\sum_{j=1}^{i} \rho_j \left[(1 + C_{\tilde{x}_j}^2)/2\right] E[\tilde{x}_j]}{(1 - \sigma_i)(1 - \sigma_{i-1})}. \tag{4.138}$$

Comparison of (4.138) to (4.130) reveals that the only difference between the waiting times for HOL and HOL-PR is accounted for by the difference in perception of the delay due to the customer who may be in service at time t_0. Customers of all classes are relevant in the case of HOL, whereas for HOL-PR, only customers having priority at least as high as that of the customer in question appear in the result. This is intuitively satisfying in that the only effect of preemption for customers who are serviced during the tagged customer's waiting time is to rearrange the order in which service is rendered. Additionally, from the tagged customer's point of view, the customer preempted at time t_0 has a lower priority and for all intents and purposes doesn't exist.

The sojourn time under the HOL discipline is obtained by simply adding the service time to the waiting time, whereas that for the HOL-PR system is obtained by adding the completion time to the waiting time. Thus we find, for the HOL discipline,

$$E[\tilde{s}_i] = \frac{\sum_{j=1}^{I} \rho_j \left[(1 + C_{\tilde{x}_j}^2)/2\right] E[\tilde{x}_j]}{(1 - \sigma_i)(1 - \sigma_{i-1})} + E[\tilde{x}_i], \tag{4.139}$$

and for the HOL-PR discipline,

$$E[\tilde{s}_i] = \frac{\sum_{j=1}^{i} \rho_j \left[(1 + C_{\tilde{x}_j}^2)/2\right] E[\tilde{x}_j]}{(1 - \sigma_i)(1 - \sigma_{i-1})} + \frac{E[\tilde{x}_i]}{1 - \sigma_{i-1}}. \tag{4.140}$$

Exercise 4.40   Suppose that the service time of the customers in an M/G/1 system are drawn from the distribution $F_{\tilde{x}_i}(x)$ with probability p_i such that $\sum_{i=1}^{I} p_i = 1$. Determine $E[\tilde{w}]$ for this system.

Exercise 4.41   Conservation Law (Kleinrock [1976]). Under the conditions of Exercise 4.40, suppose the customers whose service times are drawn from the distribution $F_{\tilde{x}_i}(x)$ are assigned priority i. Show that $\sum_{i=1}^{I} \rho_i E[\tilde{w}_i] = \rho E[\tilde{w}]$ where $E[\tilde{w}]$ is as determined in Exercise

4.9. Explain the implications of this result. Does the result imply that the expected waiting time is independent of the priority assignment? Why or why not? If not, under what conditions would equality hold?

4.8 SUPPLEMENTARY PROBLEMS

1. Consider a communication system in which messages are transmitted over a communication line having a capacity of C octets/sec. Suppose the messages have length $\tilde{m}$ (in octets), and the lengths are drawn from a geometric distribution having a mean of $E[\tilde{m}]$ octets, but truncated at a and b characters on the lower and upper ends of the distribution, respectively. That is, message lengths are drawn from a distribution characterized as follows:

$$P\{\tilde{m} = m\} = k\theta(1 - \theta)^{m-1} \quad \text{for } a \leq m \leq b,$$

where $\tilde{m}$ is the number of characters in a message and k is a normalizing constant.

(a) Given that

$$P\{\tilde{m} = m\} = k\theta(1 - \theta)^{m-1} \quad \text{for } a \leq m \leq b,$$

show that

$$k = \left[(1 - \theta)^{a-1} - (1 - \theta)^{b}\right]^{-1},$$

$$E[z^{\tilde{m}}] = z^{(a-1)} \frac{\theta z}{1 - (1 - \theta)z} \frac{1 - [(1 - \theta)z]^{(b-[a-1])}}{1 - (1 - \theta)^{(b-[a-1])}}$$

and

$$E[\tilde{m}] = a - 1 + \frac{1}{\theta} - \frac{(b - [a - 1])(1 - \theta)^{(b-[a-1])}}{1 - (1 - \theta)^{(b-[a-1])}}.$$

(b) Rearrange the expression for $E[\tilde{m}]$ given above by solving for θ^{-1} to obtain an equation of the form

$$\frac{1}{\theta} = f(E[\tilde{m}], \ a, \ b, \ \theta),$$

and use this expression to obtain a recursive expression for θ of the form

$$\frac{1}{\theta_{i+1}} = f(E[\tilde{m}], \ a, \ b, \ \theta_i).$$

(c) Write a simple program to implement the recursive relation-ship defined in part (b) to solve for θ in the special case of $a = 10$, $b = 80$, and $E[\tilde{m}] = 30$. Use $\theta_0 = E^{-1}[\tilde{m}]$ as the starting value for the recursion.

(d) Argue that $F_{\tilde{x}}^*(s) = F_{\tilde{m}}^*(s/C)$, where C is the transmission capacity in octets/sec.

(e) Using the computer program given in the Appendix, obtain the complementary occupancy distribution for the transmis-sion system under its actual message length distribution at a traffic utilization of 95%, assuming a transmission capacity of 30 characters/sec.

(f) Compare this complementary distribution to one obtained under the assumption that the message lengths are drawn from an ordinary geometric distribution. Comment on the suitability of making the geometric assumption.

2. Using the properties of the probability generating function, de-termine a formula for $E[\tilde{n}^2]$, the second moment of the occupancy distribution for the ordinary M/G/1 system, in terms of the first three moments of $F_{\tilde{x}}(x)$, the service time distribution. Verify the formula for $E[\tilde{n}]$ along the way. [*Hint*: The algebra will be greatly simplified if (4.8) is first rewritten as

$$\mathcal{F}_{\tilde{n}}(z) = \alpha(z)/\beta(z),$$

where

$$\alpha(z) = (1 - \rho)F_{\tilde{x}}^*(\lambda[1 - z])$$

and

$$\beta(z) = 1 - \rho F_{\tilde{x}_r}^*(\lambda[1 - z]),$$

and

$$\beta(z) = 1 - \rho F_{\tilde{x}_r}^*(\lambda[1 - z]),$$

where $F_{\tilde{x}_r}(x)$ is the distribution for the forward recurrence time of the service time. Then, in order to find

$$\lim_{z \to 1} \frac{d^2}{dz^2} \mathcal{F}_{\tilde{n}}(z),$$

first find the limits as $z \to 1$ of $\alpha(z)$, $\beta(z)$, $d\alpha(z)/dz$, $d\beta(z)/dz$, $d^2\alpha(z)/dz^2$, and $d^2\beta(z)/d^2z$, and then substitute these limits into the formula for the second derivative of the ratio.]

3. Consider a queueing system in which ordinary customers have service times drawn from a general distribution with mean $1/\mu$. There is a special customer who receives immediate service whenever she enters the system, her service time being drawn, independently on each entry, from a general distribution, $F_{\tilde{x}_s}(x)$, which has mean $1/\alpha$. Upon completion of service, the special customer departs the system and then returns after an exponential, rate β, length of time. Let $\tilde{x}_{si}$ denote the length of the ith interruption of an ordinary customer by the special customer, and let $\tilde{n}$ denote the number of interruptions. Also, let $\tilde{c}$ denote the time that elapses from the instant an ordinary customer enters service until the instant the ordinary customer departs.

(a) Suppose that service time for the ordinary customer is chosen once. Following an interruption, the ordinary customer's service resumes from the point of interruption. Determine $P\{\tilde{n} = n | \tilde{x} = x\}$ and $\mathcal{F}_{\tilde{n}}(z)$, the probability generating function for the number of interruptions suffered by the ordinary customer.

(b) Determine $F_{\tilde{c}}^*(s)$, the Laplace–Stieltjes transform for $\tilde{c}$ under this policy. [*Hint*: Condition on the the length of the service time of the ordinary customer and the number of service interruptions that occur.]

(c) Compare the results of part (b) with the Laplace–Stieltjes transform for the length of the M/G/1 busy period. Explain the relationship between these two results.

(d) Determine $E[\tilde{c}]$ and $E[\tilde{c}^2]$.

(e) Determine the probability that the server will be busy at an arbitrary point in time in stochastic equilibrium, and determine the stability condition for this system.

4. Jobs arrive to a single server system at a Poisson rate λ. Each job consists of a random number of tasks, $\tilde{m}$, drawn from a general distribution $F_{\tilde{m}}(m)$, independent of everything. Each task requires a service time drawn from a common distribution, $F_{\tilde{x}_t}$, independent of everything.

(a) Determine the Laplace–Stieltjes transform of the job service-time distribution.

(b) Determine the mean forward recurrence time of the service-time distribution using the result of part (a) and transform properties.

(c) Determine the stochastic equilibrium mean sojourn time for jobs in this system.

(d) Determine the mean number of tasks remaining for a job in service at an arbitrary point in time, if any.

5. For the M/G/∞ queueing system, it is well known that the stochastic equilibrium distribution for the number of busy servers is Poisson with parameter $\lambda E[\tilde{x}]$, where λ is the arrival rate and $\tilde{x}$ is the holding time.

(a) Suppose that $\tilde{x} = i$ with probability p_i for $i = 1$, 2, 3 with $p_1 + p_2 + p_3 = 1$. Determine the equilibrium distribution of the number of servers that are busy serving jobs of length i for $i = 1$, 2, 3, and the distribution of the number of servers that are busy serving all jobs.

(b) Determine the probability that a job selected at random from all of the jobs in service at an arbitrary point in time in stochastic equilibrium will have service time i, $i = 1, 2, 3$.

(c) Calculate the mean length of an arbitrary job that is in service at an arbitrary point in time in stochastic equilibrium.

(d) Suppose that job service times are drawn from an arbitrary distribution $F_{\tilde{x}}(x)$. Repeat part (c).

(e) What can be concluded about the distribution of remaining service time of a customer in service at an arbitrary point in time in stochastic equilibrium for the $M/G/\infty$ system?

6. Consider a queueing system that services customers from a finite population of K identical customers. Each customer, while not being served or waiting, *thinks* for an exponentially distributed length of time with parameter λ and then joins a FCFS queue to wait for service. Service times are drawn independently from a general service time distribution $F_{\tilde{x}}(x)$.

(a) Given the expected length of the busy period for this system, describe a procedure through which you could obtain the expected waiting time. [*Hint*: Use alternating renewal theory.]

(b) Given the expected length of the busy period with $K = 2$, describe a procedure for obtaining the expected length of the busy period for the case of $K = 3$.

5

Embedded Markov Chain Analysis: The M/G/1 and G/M/1 Paradigms

In the previous chapter of this book, we discussed the M/G/1 queueing system and some of its variants. We have seen that the occupancy process $\{\tilde{n}(t),\ t \geq 0\}$ is a semi-Markov process, and we analyzed the system by first embedding a Markov chain, $\{\tilde{q}_n,\ n = 0,\ 1,\ 2,\ \ldots\}$, at instants of customer departure. Although we identified the process $\{\tilde{q}_n,\ n = 0,\ 1,\ 2,\ \ldots\}$ as a discrete-parameter Markov chain on the nonnegative integers, we did not explicitly present its transition probability matrix. In fact, such a specification was unnecessary because our analysis technique avoided this issue.

In this chapter, we provide a brief introduction to the G/M/1 and M/G/1 paradigms, which have been found to be useful in solving practical problems and have been discussed at length in Neuts [1981a] and [1989], respectively. These paradigms are natural extensions of the ordinary M/G/1 and G/M/1 systems. In particular, the structure of the one-step transition probability matrices for the embedded Markov chains for these systems are simply matrix versions of the one-step transition probability matrices for the embedded Markov chains of the elementary systems.

In Section 5.1 we introduce the M/G/1 and G/M/1 paradigms. We first present a concise development of the one-step transition probability matrix for the embedded Markov chain of the M/G/1 system. Next, for the G/M/1 system, we define the embedded Markov chain $\{\tilde{q}'_n, \ n = 0, \ 1, \ 2, \ \ldots\}$, where $\tilde{q}'_n$ denotes the number of customers found in the system by the nth arriving customer, and we specify its one-step transition probability matrix. Markov chains of the M/G/1 and G/M/1 type are then defined.

The general solution procedure for models of the G/M/1 type is then discussed in Section 5.2. This presentation is brief because of the extensive coverage of similar methodology presented in Chapter 3. In Section 5.3, a solution procedure for models of the M/G/1 type is presented. In Section 5.4, application of M/G/1 paradigm ideas to statistical multiplexing is discussed by way of examples. Finally, additional applications are discussed and conclusions are drawn in Section 5.5.

As mentioned earlier, an entire book each is devoted to the solution procedures for models of the M/G/1 and G/M/1 type, respectively. There is no attempt here to provide complete coverage of the solution methodologies that have been developed over the last 20 years. Rather, we satisfy ourselves with a presentation of the main ideas and direct our readers to the appropriate references.

5.1   THE M/G/1 AND G/M/1 PARADIGMS

Recall that for the M/G/1 system, $\tilde{q}_n$, $n = 0, \ 1, \ 2, \ \ldots$, denotes the number of customers left in the system by the nth departing customer. From (4.1), we have

$$\tilde{q}_{n+1} = (\tilde{q}_n - 1)^+ + \tilde{v}_{n+1}, \tag{5.1}$$

where $(a)^+ = \max\{a, \ 0\}$ and $\tilde{v}_n$ is defined as the number of arrivals that occur during the nth customer's service.

As we have pointed out, the process $\{\tilde{q}_n, \ n = 0, \ 1, \ 2, \ \ldots\}$ is a discrete-parameter Markov chain on the nonnegative integers. Recall that for such Markov chains, the probability of being in state j after the $(n + 1)$th state change given that the system was in state i after the nth state change is called the *one-step transition probability* from state i to state j. The matrix of these transition probabilities, $P_{ij} =$

$P\{\tilde{q}_{n+1} = j | \tilde{q}_n = i\}$, is called the *one-step transition probability matrix*.

Upon conditioning on $\tilde{q}_n$, we find

$$P\{\tilde{q}_{n+1} = j\} = \sum_{i=0}^{\infty} P\{\tilde{q}_{n+1} = j | \tilde{q}_n = i\} P\{\tilde{q}_n = i\}. \tag{5.2}$$

Then, substitution of (5.1) into (5.2) yields

$$P\{\tilde{q}_{n+1} = j\} = \sum_{i=0}^{\infty} P\{(\tilde{q}_n - 1)^+ + \tilde{v}_{n+1} = j | \tilde{q}_n = i\} P\{\tilde{q}_n = i\}. \tag{5.3}$$

Because $\tilde{v}_{n+1}$ is independent of $\tilde{q}_n$, (5.3) is readily reduced to

$$P\{\tilde{q}_{n+1} = j\} = \sum_{i=0}^{\infty} P\{\tilde{v}_{n+1} = j - (i - 1)^+\} P\{\tilde{q}_n = i\}. \tag{5.4}$$

Now, departures occur only one at a time. Therefore, the infinite summation of (5.4) can be replaced by the finite summation

$$P\{\tilde{q}_{n+1} = j\} = \sum_{i=0}^{j+1} P\{\tilde{v}_{n+1} = j - (i - 1)^+\} P\{\tilde{q}_n = i\}. \tag{5.5}$$

Because the service times are a sequence of *iid* random variables with distribution $F_{\tilde{x}}(x)$, we see that the one-step transition probability of going from state i to state j is simply

$$P\{\tilde{q}_{n+1} = j | \tilde{q}_n = i\} = P\{\tilde{v} = j - (i - 1)^+\},$$

where $\tilde{v}$ is the number of arrivals that occur during a service time, and that these are nonzero for only $i + 1$ entries. We define $a_k = P\{\tilde{v} = k\}$, and because arrivals occur according to a Poisson process with parameter λ, we find

$$a_k = \int_0^{\infty} \frac{(\lambda x)^k}{k!} e^{-\lambda x} dF_{\tilde{x}}(x). \tag{5.6}$$

The one-step transition probability matrix for the embedded Markov chain for the M/G/1 system is then

$$
\mathcal{P}_{\mathrm{MG}} =
\begin{bmatrix}
a_0 & a_1 & a_2 & a_3 & \cdots \\
a_0 & a_1 & a_2 & a_3 & \cdots \\
0 & a_0 & a_1 & a_2 & \cdots \\
0 & 0 & a_0 & a_1 & \cdots \\
\cdots & \cdots & \cdots & \cdots & \cdots
\end{bmatrix}.
\tag{5.7}
$$

In case first service times are exceptional, the distribution of the number of arrivals that occur during the first service time of each busy period is different from the distribution of the number of arrivals that occur during service times other than the first. In this case, we define b_k as the probability that k arrivals occur during the exceptional first service, and we find

$$
b_k = \int_0^\infty \frac{(\lambda x)^k}{k!} e^{-\lambda x} dF_{\tilde{x}_e}(x),
\tag{5.8}
$$

where $\tilde{x}_e$ denotes the length of the exceptional first service. The one-step transition probability matrix is then

$$
\mathcal{P}_{\mathrm{MG}} =
\begin{bmatrix}
b_0 & b_1 & b_2 & b_3 & \cdots \\
a_0 & a_1 & a_2 & a_3 & \cdots \\
0 & a_0 & a_1 & a_2 & \cdots \\
0 & 0 & a_0 & a_1 & \cdots \\
\cdots & \cdots & \cdots & \cdots & \cdots
\end{bmatrix}.
\tag{5.9}
$$

If we now define $\pi_j = \lim_{n \to \infty} P\{\tilde{q}_n = j\}$ and $\pi = [\pi_0 \quad \pi_1 \quad \cdots]$, then, at least in principle, we can obtain π by solving the matrix equations

$$
\pi = \pi \mathcal{P}_{\mathrm{MG}}, \quad \pi e = 1
$$

simultaneously. The limiting solution is known to exist so long as the service rate exceeds the arrival rate. But the solution is not necessarily easily obtained, as we have already seen in Chapter 4. In addition, the entries of the matrices $\mathcal{P}_{\mathrm{MG}}$ must also be calculated; this, in itself, is nontrivial for most distributions unless a special form such as a weighted sum of exponentials or a collection of point masses is assumed for the service time distribution.

Remark. We use the notation π rather than P for these probabilities to emphasize that the stationary probability vector is for a

discrete-parameter Markov chain rather than for a continuous-time
Markov chain. Therefore, the individual probabilities represent the
proportion of entries to or exits from a given state rather than the
time-averaged probability that the system is in the given state. For
systems having Poisson arrivals, such as the ordinary M/G/1 system,
these probabilities are equal, but they are not equal in the general
case.

Exercise 5.1   Suppose that $P\{\tilde{x} = 1\} = 1$, that is the service time is
deterministic with mean 1. Determine $\{a_k,\ k = 0,\ 1,\ \ldots\}$ as defined
by (5.6).

Exercise 5.2   Suppose that $\tilde{x}$ is a discrete valued random variable having support set $\mathcal{X} = \{x_0,\ x_1,\ \ldots,\ x_K\}$, where K is an integer. Define $\alpha_k = P\{\tilde{x} = x_k\}$ for $x_k \in \mathcal{X}$. Determine $\{a_k,\ k = 0,\ 1,\ \ldots\}$ as
defined by (5.6). In order to get started, let $dF_{\tilde{x}}(x) = \sum_{x \in \mathcal{X}} \alpha_k \delta(x -
x_k)$, where $\delta(x)$ is the Dirac delta function.

Exercise 5.3   Suppose that $\tilde{x}$ is an exponential random variable with
parameter μ. Determine $\{a_k,\ k = 0,\ 1,\ \ldots\}$ as defined by (5.6).

Exercise 5.4   Suppose that $\tilde{x} = \tilde{x}_1 + \tilde{x}_2$, where $\tilde{x}_1$ and $\tilde{x}_2$ are exponential random variables with parameter μ_1 and μ_2, respectively.
Determine $\{a_k,\ k = 0,\ 1,\ \ldots\}$ as defined by (5.6).

Similar to the case of the M/G/1 system, the G/M/1 system
can be analyzed by embedding a Markov chain at points in time
just prior to customer arrivals. As before, we denote the embedded
Markov chain by $\{\tilde{q}'_n,\ n = 0,\ 1,\ 2,\ \ldots\}$. The state of this Markov
chain is then defined as the number of customers found in the system
by the nth arriving customer. It is easy to see that

$$\tilde{q}'_{n+1} = \tilde{q}'_n + 1 - \tilde{v}'_{n+1}, \tag{5.10}$$

where $\tilde{v}'_n$ denotes the number of service completions that occur during the nth interarrival interval. From (5.10), we can easily determine
that

$$P\{\tilde{q}'_{n+1} = j\} = \sum_{i=0}^{\infty} P\{\tilde{v}' = i + 1 - j\}P\{\tilde{q}'_n = i\}.$$

Since arrivals occur only one at a time, this equation can be rewritten as

$$P\{\tilde{q}'_{n+1} = j\} = \sum_{i=(j-1)^+}^{\infty} P\{\tilde{v}' = i+1-j\}P\{\tilde{q}'_n = i\}. \qquad (5.11)$$

From (5.11), we see that the one-step transition probability from state i to state j is given by $P\{\tilde{v}' = i+1-j\}$. Computation of these transition probabilities is slightly more involved than in the M/G/1 case because we have to distinguish between whether or not all customers present are served prior to the next arrival—that is, whether the system is left empty or not. If we let $\tilde{x}_k$ denote the service time of the ith customer served during the $(n+1)$th interarrival time, then we find

$$P\{\tilde{v}' = i+1-j\} = \begin{cases} P\{\sum_{k=1}^{i+1} \tilde{x}_k < \tilde{t}\} & \text{for } j = 0, \\ P\{\sum_{k=1}^{i+1-j} \tilde{x}_k < \tilde{t}, \sum_{k=1}^{i+1-j} \tilde{x}_k > \tilde{t}\} & \text{for } j > 0, \end{cases}$$

$$(5.12)$$

where $\tilde{t}$ denotes the interarrival time.

We therefore define b_k to be the probability that k customers are served during the $(n + 1)$th interarrival time if the system is found empty by the $(n + 1)$th arriving customer and a_k to be the corresponding probability otherwise. Because service times are exponential and the sum of $K + 1$ independent exponentially distributed random variables has the gamma distribution with parameters K and μ or, equivalently, the Erlang-$(K + 1)$ distribution, it is easy to see that

$$b_k = \int_0^{\infty} \frac{\mu(\mu x)^k}{k!} e^{-\mu x} F_{\tilde{t}}^c(x)dx \quad \text{for } k = 0, 1, \dots. \qquad (5.13)$$

Owing to the exponential services and the properties of the Poisson process, it is easy to see that a_k is simply the probability that exactly k arrivals from a Poisson process occur during the $(n + 1)$th interarrival time. Thus,

$$a_k = \int_0^\infty \frac{(\mu x)^k}{k!} e^{-\mu x} dF_{\tilde{t}}(x) \quad \text{for } k = 0,\ 1,\ \dots. \tag{5.14}$$

The one-step transition probability matrix for the embedded Markov chain for the G/M/1 system is then

$$\mathcal{P}_{GM} = \begin{bmatrix} b_0 & a_0 & 0 & \cdots & \cdots \\ b_1 & a_1 & a_0 & 0 & \cdots \\ b_2 & a_2 & a_1 & a_0 & \cdots \\ b_3 & a_3 & a_2 & a_1 & \cdots \\ \cdots & \cdots & \cdots & \cdots & \cdots \end{bmatrix}. \tag{5.15}$$

As in the case of the M/G/1 system, if we define $\pi_j = \lim_{n\to\infty} P\{\tilde{q}'_n = j\}$ and $\pi = [\pi_0 \quad \pi_1 \quad \cdots]$, then we can obtain π by solving the matrix equations

$$\pi = \pi \mathcal{P}_{MG}, \quad \pi e = 1$$

simultaneously. Again, the limiting solution is known to exist so long as the service rate exceeds the arrival rate. Unlike the case of the M/G/1 system, the solution to the embedded Markov chain for the G/M/1 system has a very simple form, namely,

$$\pi_j = (1 - \omega)\omega^j \quad \text{for } j \geq 0, \tag{5.16}$$

where ω is the unique (real) solution inside the unit circle to the functional equation

$$\omega = F_{\tilde{t}}^*(\mu[1 - \omega]). \tag{5.17}$$

The value of ω can be obtained iteratively from the mapping

$$\omega_{i+1} = F_{\tilde{t}}^*(\mu[1 - \omega_i]) \quad \text{with } 0 \leq \omega_0 < 1, \tag{5.18}$$

as is shown in Takàcs [1962].

The waiting time for an arbitrary arriving customer, given that there is at least one customer present, is then simply the geometric sum of *iid* exponential variables and is consequently exponential with parameter $(1 - \omega)\mu$. Because the probability that an arriving customer finds at least one customer present is ω, we find

$$P\{\tilde{w} > t\} = \omega e^{-(1-\omega)\mu t}. \tag{5.19}$$

We note in passing that the expression on the right-hand side of (5.17) is, according to Theorem 4.2, the probability generating function for the number of arrivals that occur from a Poisson process having rate μ over a random period of time having distribution $F_{\tilde{t}}(t)$, where the arrival process is independent of $\tilde{t}$. By contrast, in the case of the M/G/1 system, the tail probabilities are approximately geometrically decreasing with the decay rate r_0, where r_0 is the inverse of the unique (real) solution outside the unit circle, z_0, to the functional equation

$$z = F_{\tilde{x}}^*(\lambda[1 - z]). \tag{5.20}$$

The general form of the occupancy distribution for the M/G/1 system is much more complicated than that of the G/M/1 system seen in Chapter 4.

Markov chains whose one-step transition probability matrices have the structures of (5.9) and (5.15) are said to be *Markov chains of the M/G/1 type* and *Markov chains of the G/M/1 type*, respectively. The idea has been generalized by Neuts[1981a] to the cases in which these one-step transition matrices have block-partitioned structures of similar forms, as follows:

$$\mathcal{P}_{\mathrm{MG}} = \begin{bmatrix} B_0 & B_1 & B_2 & B_3 & \cdots \\ A_0 & A_1 & A_2 & A_3 & \cdots \\ 0 & A_0 & A_1 & A_2 & \cdots \\ 0 & 0 & A_0 & A_1 & \cdots \\ \cdots & \cdots & \cdots & \cdots & \cdots \end{bmatrix} \tag{5.21}$$

and

$$\mathcal{P}_{\mathrm{GM}} = \begin{bmatrix} B_0 & A_0 & 0 & \cdots & \cdots \\ B_1 & A_1 & A_0 & 0 & \cdots \\ B_2 & A_2 & A_1 & A_0 & \cdots \\ B_3 & 0 & A_2 & A_1 & \cdots \\ \cdots & \cdots & \cdots & \cdots & \cdots \end{bmatrix}. \tag{5.22}$$

In this case, as in the cases covered in Chapter 3, the states of the Markov chain are denoted by (i, j), $i \geq 0$, and $0 \leq j \leq K$, where i denotes the occupancy (or level) and j denotes an abstract auxiliary descriptor that we refer to as the *phase*. The states are ordered lexicographically; that is, we define $\pi_i = [\pi_{i0} \quad \pi_{i1} \quad \cdots \quad \pi_{iK}]$ and $\pi = [\pi_0 \quad \pi_1 \quad \pi_2 \quad \pi_3 \quad \cdots]$. The Markov chains $\{\tilde{q}_n, n = 0, 1, 2, \ldots\}$

and $\{\tilde{q}_n', \ n = 0, \ 1, \ 2, \ \ldots\}$ are then interpreted as vector-valued Markov chains.

Remark. As has been our practice throughout this book, we avoid inventing special notation to distinguish between scalar and vector quantities unless there is a specific gain to be made in the particular problem under consideration. In this case, there does not appear to be any.

5.2   G/M/1 SOLUTION METHODOLOGY

We saw in Chapter 3 that some queueing systems have matrix-geometric solutions. Note that all positive-recurrent Markov chains of the G/M/1 type have matrix-geometric solutions. That is, the occupancy probabilities have the form

$$\pi_{i+1} = \pi_i R \quad \text{for } i \geq 0,$$

or, equivalently,

$$\pi_i = \pi_0 R^i \quad \text{for } i \geq 0. \tag{5.23}$$

This result is given in the following theorem from Neuts [1981a, pp. 10–11]:

Theorem 5.1   (Neuts) If the Markov chain $\mathcal{P}_{\mathrm{GM}}$ is positive recurrent, then

1. for $i \geq 0$, we have $\pi_{i+1} = \pi_i \mathcal{R}$, the eigenvalues of $\mathcal{R}$ lie inside the unit disk of the complex plane,

2. the matrix

$$B(\mathcal{R}) = \sum_{k=0}^{\infty} \mathcal{R}^k B_k$$

is stochastic,[1] and

---

[1] That is, the elements of the matrix are nonnegative and the elements of each row sum to unity.

4. the vector π_0 is a positive, left invariant eigenvector of $B(\mathcal{R})$ normalized by $\pi_0(I - \mathcal{R})^{-1}e = 1$.   □

Neuts [1981a] is devoted to the algorithmic solution of Markov chains of the G/M/1 type. He shows that the matrix $\mathcal{R}$ can be obtained by solving the matrix equation

$$\mathcal{R} = \sum_{k=0}^{\infty} \mathcal{R}^k A_k \tag{5.24}$$

for its minimal nonnegative solution, and that the minimal nonnegative solution can be obtained by solving the equation

$$\mathcal{R} = \left(\sum_{\substack{k=0 \\ k \neq 1}}^{\infty} \mathcal{R}^k A_k \right) (I - A_1)^{-1}$$

by successive substitutions starting with $\mathcal{R} = 0$. Note that (5.24) is simply a matrix version of (5.18) because

$$F_{\tilde{t}}^*(\mu[1 - \omega]) = \sum_{k=0}^{\infty} w^k a_k. \tag{5.25}$$

That is, $F_{\tilde{t}}^*(\mu[1 - \omega])$ is simply the probability generating function for the number of arrivals that occur from a Poisson process having rate μ during a period of time of length $\tilde{t}$.

Some researchers have suggested that it is easier to solve the Markov chain $\mathcal{P}_{GM}$ directly by truncating the state space and approximating the probabilities; such an approach certainly has some advantages if the goal of the analysis is to obtain occupancy distributions only. However, the rate matrix, $\mathcal{R}$, obtained via the matrix geometric approach, as we have seen in Chapter 3, is a fundamental parameter of a given Markov chain. As such, the matrix $\mathcal{R}$ can be used to obtain much more than the occupancy distribution. For example, just as the scalar ω allows one to determine the FCFS waiting time in the ordinary G/M/1 system, the matrix $\mathcal{R}$ allows us to determine the waiting-time distribution from many points of view for queues of the G/M/1 type, as is shown in Ramaswami and Lucantoni [1985] and Daigle and Lucantoni [1990].

5.3   M/G/1 SOLUTION METHODOLOGY

We turn now to the M/G/1 system. Analogous to our discussion of the ordinary M/G/1 system, we define the vector generating function

$$\mathcal{F}_{\tilde{q}}(z) = \sum_{j=0}^{\infty} z^j \pi_j. \tag{5.26}$$

Then, based on (5.21), it is easy to show that

$$\mathcal{F}_{\tilde{q}}(z)[Iz - \mathcal{A}(z)] = \pi_0[z\mathcal{B}(z) - \mathcal{A}(z)], \tag{5.27}$$

where $\mathcal{A}(z)$ and $\mathcal{B}(z)$ are defined as

$$\mathcal{A}(z) = \sum_{j=0}^{\infty} A_j z^j \quad \text{and} \quad \mathcal{B}(z) = \sum_{j=0}^{\infty} B_j z^j. \tag{5.28}$$

The scalar version of (5.27) is given in (4.94) and is

$$\mathcal{F}_{\tilde{n}_e}(z) = \frac{1-\rho}{1-\rho+\rho_e} \frac{z F_{\tilde{x}_e}^*(\lambda[1-z]) - F_{\tilde{x}}^*(\lambda[1-z])}{z - F_{\tilde{x}}^*(\lambda[1-z])}, \tag{5.29}$$

where the correspondence between the terms of (5.27) and (5.29) are obvious.

Just as in the case of the scalar version of the M/G/1 system, there are two difficulties: solving for the unknown constant (vector) π_0, and inverting the transform. Both of these operations are somewhat more involved than in the scalar case. A brief sketch of the techniques developed by Lucantoni, Neuts, and Ramaswami is given below. The reader is referred to Neuts [1989] for a thorough pedagogical presentation, and to Lucantoni [1991] for a current and thorough reformulation of the solution methodology and some additional new results.

We first discuss the technique for computing π_0 and then present Ramaswami's technique for determining π_j, for $j = 1,\ 2,\ \ldots$, for the general case of the M/G/1 paradigm. We then consider a special case in which simplified algorithms can be developed. The special case has application to statistical multiplexing systems and the results of this section are used as a starting point in the next section, which discusses an application.

Determination of the vector π_0 is accomplished through the clever application of elementary Markov chain theory. Toward this end, let $\wp_n$ denote the phase of the system at the instant of the nth return to level 0. Then, due to the memoryless property of the arrival process, the stochastic process $\{\wp_n,\ n = 0,\ 1,\ \ldots\}$ is a discrete parameter Markov chain on the space $\{0,\ 1,\ \ldots,\ K\}$. Let $\mathcal{P}_\wp$ denote the one-step transition probability matrix for this embedded Markov chain, and let κ denote its stationary probability vector.

From elementary Markov chain theory, it is well known that the proportion of transitions into level 0 is simply the inverse of the expected number of transitions between entries to level 0. Let κ_i^* denote the expected number of transitions between entries to level 0 given that the system enters level 0 in phase i, and let κ^* denote the column vector $[\,\kappa_0\quad \kappa_1\ \cdots\ \kappa_K\,]^T$. Then it is easy to see that

$$\pi_0 = (\kappa\kappa^*)^{-1}\kappa. \tag{5.30}$$

It remains to specify $\mathcal{P}_\wp$, κ, and κ^*. Toward this end, we begin by considering the first passage time between successive entries to level 0 of the Markov chain $\mathcal{P}_{\mathrm{MG}}$ in stochastic equilibrium. In the first transition from level 0, the Markov chain makes a transition to level j with probability B_j. Having entered level j, the system cannot return to level 0 without having first passed through each level between j and 0.

Observation of the matrix $\mathcal{P}_{\mathrm{MG}}$ reveals that the number of transitions required to decrease the level from j to $j - 1$ is independent of j. Thus the number of transitions required in the first passage time from level j to level 0 is simply the sum of j iid discrete valued random variables. Define $G(z)$ to be the (matrix) generating function for the first passage time from level 1 to level 0.[2] The (matrix) generating function for the first passage time from level j to level 0 is then $[G(z)]^j$.

---

[2] That is, the number of transitions of the Markov chain $\mathcal{P}_{\mathrm{MG}}$ in the first passage time from phase i of level 1 to level 0 is a discrete random variable. If the probability masses for this discrete random variable are partitioned according to the phase entered upon entry to level 0, and then the generating function is taken on the set of partitioned probability masses, then the result is a matrix of generating functions. If the elements of any row of the resulting matrix are summed, the result is a *probability* generating function in the ordinary sense.

Remark.   We distinguish between generating functions and probability generating functions. The idea of a generating function is to represent an arbitrary sequence of numbers $\{s_0,\ s_1,\ \ldots\}$, finite or infinite, by a power series, $\sum_{i=0}^{\infty} s_i z^i$, which may or may not be expressible in closed form. In the case of a probability generating function, the sequence in question is a probability mass function; that is, the s_i are probability masses for a discrete random variable.

By conditioning on the outcome of the first transition from level 1, we readily find that

$$G(z) = \sum_{j=0}^{\infty} z A_j [G(z)]^j. \tag{5.31}$$

Also, let $\mathcal{K}(z)$ denote the (matrix) generating function for the number of transitions between successive entries to level 0. Then, by conditioning on the outcome of the first transition from level 0, we find that

$$\mathcal{K}(z) = \sum_{j=0}^{\infty} z B_j [G(z)]^j. \tag{5.32}$$

We then find that $\mathcal{K}(1)$ is the one-step transition probability matrix for the Markov chain $\{\wp_n,\ n = 0,\ 1,\ \ldots\}$ defined above; that is,

$$\mathcal{P}_\wp = \mathcal{K}(1) = \sum_{j=0}^{\infty} B_j G^j, \tag{5.33}$$

where $G = G(1)$ is the unique *stochastic matrix solution* to the equation

$$G = \sum_{i=0}^{\infty} A_i G^j, \tag{5.34}$$

which is obtained by substituting $z = 1$ into (5.31). For consistency with Neuts's notation, from now on we will refer to $\mathcal{P}_\wp$ as $\mathcal{K}(1)$. We emphasize that G is the unique stochastic solution to (5.34) because, in general, (5.34) does not have a unique solution. For example, recall that in the scalar case, (5.34) has exactly the form $z = F_{tx}^*(\lambda[1 - z])$.

We have already seen that this functional equation has a solution $z = 1$, which is a 1×1 stochastic matrix, and an additional real-valued solution, z_0, the inverse of which determines the rate at which the tail of the occupancy distribution decreases.

In addition, using standard properties of probability generating functions, we readily find that

$$\kappa^* = \lim_{z \to 1} \frac{d}{dz} K(z)\mathbf{e} = K'(1)\mathbf{e}. \tag{5.35}$$

The desired solution for G can be obtained by solving (5.34) by successive substitutions, starting with $G = 0$. The transition matrix $K(1)$ can then be obtained from (5.32), and then κ can be obtained by any of a number of techniques such as those described in Chapter 3. A normalizing constant $\kappa \kappa^*$ is needed to compute π_0 in (5.30). The usual technique for obtaining this normalizing constant is to differentiate (5.31) and (5.32) directly and then take advantage of the special structure of the problem at hand to develop a reasonable computational formula. This involves a certain level of creativity on the part of the analyst, as may be seen from some of the published literature and our discussion here.

Ramaswami [1988a, 1988b] has devoted substantial energy to developing workable algorithms to solve for the stationary probability vector P of the Markov chain $\mathcal{P}_{MG}$. A primary theorem resulting from his work is quoted below for continuity, but the interested reader is encouraged to consult Ramaswami [1988b].

Theorem 5.2   (Ramaswami) For $i \geq 1$,

$$\pi_i = \left[\pi_0 \bar{B}_i + \sum_{j=1}^{i-1} \pi_j \bar{A}_{i+1-j} \right] (I - \bar{A}_1)^{-1}, \tag{5.36}$$

where $\bar{B}_i = \sum_{j=i}^{\infty} B_j G^{j-i}$ and $\bar{A}_i = \sum_{j=i}^{\infty} A_j G^{j-i}$. $\square$

The key to finding the unknown probabilities in this approach is to determine the matrix G and then to find the unknown vector of probabilities π_0. Beginning with π_0, Ramaswami's algorithm can be applied to find the remaining probabilities. Although Ramaswami has shown that a computational algorithm based on Theorem 5.2 is numerically stable, Lucantoni [1991] has pointed out that in practice it has not been feasible to implement the algorithm in its full generality.

Lucantoni [1991] has considered a special case of considerable interest called the BMAP/G/1 queueing system, where BMAP stands for *batch Markovian arrival process*. He has developed new algorithms that allow for general implementation in terms of "canned computer programs." The BMAP includes all the models discussed in this section. A general discussion of Lucantoni's methodology is beyond the scope of the current text, but the reader is urged to consult this reference for an up-to-date treatment of queueing systems in this class.

5.4   AN APPLICATION TO STATISTICAL MULTIPLEXING

A significant issue in the design of computer communications is the analysis of the occupancy distribution in statistical multiplexing systems. Specifically, we envision a collection of individual users whose traffic is multiplexed onto a single high-capacity trunk. Traffic from individual users arrives to the statistical multiplexer over access lines, which may have lower capacity than the trunk. The users tend to transmit messages, whereas the statistical multiplexers tend to transfer data as fixed length packets. This gives rise to a high degree of correlation in the packet-arrival process of individual users. This correlation among individual users and the arrival process as a whole can be captured to a very high degree through the introduction of a discrete-time Markov chain, called the phase process, that characterizes the state of the arrival process. The distribution of the number of packets that arrive during a slot is then dependent solely on the phase of the arrival process and the distribution of the number of arrivals per slot given the phase.

Under these conditions, the matrices $\mathcal{B}(z)$ and $\mathcal{A}(z)$ of (5.27) are then equal and have the form $\mathcal{P}\mathcal{F}_{\tilde{a}}(z)$, where $\mathcal{P}$ is the one-step transition probability matrix for the phase process and $\mathcal{F}_{\tilde{a}}(z)$ is a diagonal matrix in which the ith diagonal element is a probability generating function. For this special case, it is possible to obtain a simplified algorithm for obtaining results.

We begin by making the substitutions in (5.27) to obtain

$$\mathcal{F}_{\tilde{q}}(z)[Iz - \mathcal{P}\mathcal{F}_{\tilde{a}}(z)] = \pi_0[z - 1]\mathcal{P}\mathcal{F}_{\tilde{a}}(z). \tag{5.37}$$

Then differentiating on both sides, postmultiplying by e, and taking limits as $z \to 1$, leads to

$$[1 - \mathcal{F}_{\tilde{q}}(1)\mathcal{P}\mathcal{F}_{\tilde{a}}^{(1)}(1)e] = \pi_0 e. \tag{5.38}$$

We then note that (5.31) and (5.32) are identical under the restricted case. This means that $G(1)$ and $\mathcal{K}(1)$ are equal. Thus we can solve for $\mathcal{K}(1)$ by solving the fixed-point matrix equation

$$\mathcal{K}(1) = \sum_{j=0}^{\infty} B_j \mathcal{K}(1)^j. \tag{5.39}$$

Once $\mathcal{K}(1)$ is determined, we can solve for its stationary probability vector, which is denoted by κ.

Exercise 5.5   Show that the quantity $\mathcal{F}_{\tilde{q}}(1)$ corresponds to the stationary probability vector for the phase process.

Exercise 5.6   Derive equation (5.38).

Now, the implication of (5.30) is that π_0 is proportional to κ. But we know the value of $\pi_0 e$ from (5.38), so that we can readily determine the constant of proportionality. That is, we have

$$\pi_0 = \gamma \kappa, \tag{5.40}$$

where γ is an unknown constant. Thus

$$\pi_0 e = \gamma \kappa e = \gamma,$$

where the final equality of the previous equation follows because κ is a stationary probability vector. Therefore, we have

$$\pi_0 = [1 - \mathcal{F}_{\tilde{q}}(1)\mathcal{F}_{\tilde{a}}^{(1)}(1)e]\kappa. \tag{5.41}$$

An interesting special case is the one in which there are N statistically identical users, each of whose arrival process is governed by a phase process having M phases. In this case, the specifications of $\mathcal{P}$ and $\mathcal{F}_{\tilde{a}}(z)$ are not unique. It is easy to show that if we take $\mathcal{P}$ and

$\mathcal{F}_{\tilde{a}}(z)$ to be the n-fold Kronecker products of $\mathcal{P}_s$ and $\mathcal{F}_{\tilde{a}_s}(z)$, respectively, then the resulting arrival process correctly characterizes the system. However, the description would contain redundant phases. For a system having N independent sources, each of which has M phases, it is relatively straightforward to show that the minimum dimension of the combined phase process is $\binom{N+M-1}{N}$, whereas a straightforward Kronecker product formulation would lead to $\mathcal{A}(z)$ having a dimension of M^N.

For example, if $M = 3$, then the minimum dimension for the phase process is $(N + 2)(N + 1)/2$, and the dimension of the phase process, not taking redundancies into account, is 3^N. To put this in perspective, if $N = 5$, then $3^N = 243$ and $(N + 2)(N + 1)/2 = 21$; and if $N = 50$, then $3^N \approx 7.2 \times 10^{23}$ and $(N + 2)(N + 1)/2 = 1326$.

Exercise 5.7 Suppose there are N identical traffic sources, each of which has an arrival process that is governed by an M-state Markov chain. Suppose the state of the combined phase process is defined by an M-vector in which the ith element is the number of sources currently in phase i. First, argue that this state description completely characterizes the phase of the arrival process. Next, show that the number of states of the phase process is given by $\binom{N+M-1}{N}$.

To illustrate the power of this approach, we present the analysis of a problem that has received much attention, but for which exact results do not seem to have been presented as of this time. Specifically, we show how to obtain the matrices $\mathcal{P}$ and $\mathcal{F}_{\tilde{a}}(z)$ for the special case in which there are N identical individual users, each of whom has an access line that has exactly one-half the capacity of the trunk line onto which it is being statistically multiplexed. Following Example 5.1, we discuss the solution of the resulting model.

Example 5.1 Consider a collection of N identical and independently operating sources. Suppose that each source alternates between inactive and active periods. During an active period, the source generates a packet every second time slot, and the number of packets generated during an active period is geometrically distributed with mean $1/(1 - \alpha)$. The lengths of inactive periods, in time slots, are geometrically distributed with mean $1/(1 - \beta)$. We wish to specify $\mathcal{P}$ and $\mathcal{F}_{\tilde{a}}(z)$.

Solution: We find that the Markov chain governing the phase of each source is

$$
\mathcal{P}_s = \begin{bmatrix} \beta & 1-\beta & 0 \\ 0 & 0 & 1 \\ 1-\alpha & \alpha & 0 \end{bmatrix}
$$

and the probability generating function for the number of arrivals in each slot is

$$
\mathcal{F}_{\tilde{a}_s}(z) = \begin{bmatrix} 1 & 0 & 0 \\ 0 & 1 & 0 \\ 0 & 0 & z \end{bmatrix}.
$$

Clearly, the arrival process can be described in the form

$$
\mathcal{A}(z) = \mathcal{P}\mathcal{F}_{\tilde{a}}(z),
$$

and the methods described above can be used to obtain the unknown probability vector and then the occupancy distribution.

As mentioned above, the total number of phases required to characterize the phase of the combined arrival process is $\binom{N+M-1}{N}$. For the special case under discussion, $M = 3$ so that $(N + 2)(N + 1)/2$ phases are required. For example, if $N = 2$, we define the six required phases as shown in Table 5.1.

For the given phase definitions, $\mathcal{F}_{\tilde{a}}(z) = \text{diag}\,(1, \; 1, \; 1, \; z, \; z, \; z^2)$. This indicates that in the first three phases of the aggregate process, no packets would arrive; during the fourth and fifth phases,

Table 5.1

Aggregate Phase	Phases of Individual Sources
0	both sources in phase 0
1	one source in phase 0, one source in phase 1
2	both sources in phase 1
3	one source in phase 0, one source in phase 2
4	one source in phase 1, one source in phase 2
5	both sources in phase 2

one packet would arrive; and in the sixth phase, two packets would arrive. It is straightforward to generate an algorithm to define the minimum set of phases for arbitrary M and N.

Given the state definitions as defined in Table 5.1, the resulting one-step probability transition matrix for the phase process, $\mathcal{P}$, is given by

$$
\begin{bmatrix}
\beta^2 & 2\beta(1-\beta) & (1-\beta)^2 & 0 & 0 & 0 \\
0 & 0 & 0 & \beta & (1-\beta) & 0 \\
0 & 0 & 0 & 0 & 0 & 1 \\
\beta(1-\alpha) & \beta\alpha+(1-\beta)(1-\alpha) & \alpha(1-\beta) & 0 & 0 & 0 \\
0 & 0 & 0 & (1-\alpha) & \alpha & 0 \\
(1-\alpha)^2 & 2\alpha(1-\alpha) & \alpha^2 & 0 & 0 & 0
\end{bmatrix}
$$

This completes the basic description of the model.   ■

Exercise 5.8   Define the matrices $\mathcal{P}$ and $\mathcal{F}_{\tilde{a}}(z)$ for the model defined in Example 5.1 for the special case of $N = 3$, where the states of the phase process have the interpretations shown in Table 5.2. In the table, if the phase vector is ijk, then there are i sources in phase 0, j sources in phase 1, and k sources in phase 2.

In consideration of the form of $\mathcal{F}_{\tilde{a}}(z)$ and the process through which $K(1)$ is obtained using (5.32), it is easy to see that column i of $K(1)$ is nonzero if and only if the ith diagonal element of $\mathcal{F}_{\tilde{a}}(z)$

Table 5.2

Aggregate Phase	Phase Vector
0	3 0 0
1	2 1 0
2	1 2 0
3	0 3 0
4	2 0 1
5	1 1 1
6	0 2 1
7	1 0 2
8	0 1 2
9	0 0 3

is equal to 1. This fact is also made obvious by considering that $K(1)$ is the one-step transition matrix for the Markov chain whose state is the phase of the arrival process upon entries of the queueing process to level 0. Level 0 can be entered only if there are no arrivals during a slot, and the latter condition is satisfied only if there are no arrivals to the system during the slot. Because the condition for no arrivals during a slot is that the number of arrivals is equal to unity with probability 1, the generating function for the number of arrivals during the slot is equal to 1. Thus, an efficient algorithm can be devised to compute $K(1)$. From this, κ can be determined and then the result normalized as in (5.41).

Exercise 5.9   In the previous example, we specified $\mathcal{F}_{\tilde{a}}(z)$ and $\mathcal{P}$. From these specifications, we have

$$\mathcal{P}\mathcal{F}_{\tilde{a}}(z) = \sum_{i=0}^{2} A_i z^i.$$

Therefore

$$K(1) = \sum_{i=0}^{2} A_i [K(1)]^i,$$

with

$$A_0 = \begin{bmatrix} \beta^2 & 2\beta(1-\beta) & (1-\beta)^2 & 0 & 0 & 0 \\ 0 & 0 & 0 & 0 & 0 & 0 \\ 0 & 0 & 0 & 0 & 0 & 0 \\ \beta(1-\alpha) & \beta\alpha + +(1-\beta)(1-\alpha) & \alpha(1-\beta) & 0 & 0 & 0 \\ 0 & 0 & 0 & 0 & 0 & 0 \\ (1-\alpha)^2 & 2\alpha(1-\alpha) & \alpha^2 & 0 & 0 & 0 \end{bmatrix},$$

$$A_1 = \begin{bmatrix} 0 & 0 & 0 & 0 & 0 & 0 \\ 0 & 0 & 0 & \beta & (1-\beta) & 0 \\ 0 & 0 & 0 & 0 & 0 & 0 \\ 0 & 0 & 0 & 0 & 0 & 0 \\ 0 & 0 & 0 & (1-\alpha) & \alpha & 0 \\ 0 & 0 & 0 & 0 & 0 & 0 \end{bmatrix},$$

and

$$A_2 = \begin{bmatrix} 0 & 0 & 0 & 0 & 0 & 0 \\ 0 & 0 & 0 & 0 & 0 & 0 \\ 0 & 0 & 0 & 0 & 0 & 1 \\ 0 & 0 & 0 & 0 & 0 & 0 \\ 0 & 0 & 0 & 0 & 0 & 0 \\ 0 & 0 & 0 & 0 & 0 & 0 \end{bmatrix}.$$

Now, suppose we compute $\mathcal{K}(1)$ iteratively; that is, we use the formula

$$\mathcal{K}_j(1) = \sum_{i=0}^{2} A_i [\mathcal{K}_{j-1}(1)]^i \quad \text{for } j \geq 1, \tag{5.42}$$

with $\mathcal{K}_0(1) = 0$. Prove that the final three columns of $\mathcal{K}_j(1)$ are zero columns for all j.

Exercise 5.10   Suppose $\mathcal{K}(1)$ has the form

$$\mathcal{K}(1) = \begin{bmatrix} \mathcal{K}_{00} & 0 \\ \mathcal{K}_{10} & 0 \end{bmatrix}, \tag{5.43}$$

where $\mathcal{K}_{00}$ is a square matrix. Bearing in mind that $\mathcal{K}(1)$ is stochastic, prove that $\mathcal{K}_{00}$ is also stochastic and that κ has the form $[\kappa_0 \quad 0]$, where κ_0 is the stationary probability vector for $\mathcal{K}_{00}$.

Theorem 5.3   Consider the algorithm

$$\mathcal{K}_j(1) = \sum_{i=0}^{\infty} A_i [\mathcal{K}_{j-1}(1)]^i \quad \text{for } j \geq 1. \tag{5.44}$$

Suppose that any stochastic matrix is chosen for $\mathcal{K}_0(1)$. Then $\sum_{i=0}^{\infty} A_i$ is stochastic, $[\mathcal{K}_0(1)]^i$ is stochastic for every $i \geq 0$, and $\mathcal{K}_j(1)$ is stochastic for every $j \geq 0$.   □

Exercise 5.11   Prove Theorem 5.3.

The implication of Theorem 5.3 and Exercises 5.9, 5.10 and 5.11 is that the initial condition for the recursion

$$\mathcal{K}_j(1) = \sum_{i=0}^{\infty} A_i [\mathcal{K}_{j-1}(1)]^i \quad \text{for } j \geq 1$$

need not necessarily be chosen to be 0. In fact, experience has shown that convergence is especially slow when 0 is chosen as the initial condition. As an example, in working with the system discussed above, we defined $\mathcal{K}_0(1)$ in the following way:

1. each row of $\mathcal{K}_0(1)$ is exactly the same as the rows of A_0 when the corresponding row of A_0 is not zero, and

2. each row of $\mathcal{K}_0(1)$ has a 1 in its first column when the corresponding row of A_0 is a row of zeros.

For example, with $N = 2$, we chose $\mathcal{K}_0(1)$ as

$$
\begin{bmatrix}
\beta^2 & 2\beta(1-\beta) & (1-\beta)^2 & 0 & 0 & 0 \\
1 & 0 & 0 & 0 & 0 & 0 \\
1 & 0 & 0 & 0 & 0 & 0 \\
\beta(1-\alpha) & \beta\alpha + +(1-\beta)(1-\alpha) & \alpha(1-\beta) & 0 & 0 & 0 \\
1 & 0 & 0 & 0 & 0 & 0 \\
(1-\alpha)^2 & 2\alpha(1-\alpha) & \alpha^2 & 0 & 0 & 0
\end{bmatrix}. \qquad (5.45)
$$

For the case of $N = 4$, when $\mathcal{K}_0(1)$ was chosen according to the above procedure, the iterative algorithm converged to an acceptable level of accuracy in roughly 300 iterations; the same algorithm required more than 1700 iterations to converge when $\mathcal{K}_0(1)$ was chosen to be 0. The algorithm, of course, converged to the same values in either case. However, this illustrates that when multiple runs are to be made, it is worthwhile to experiment with initial conditions.

An alternative approach to obtaining the level probabilities, $\pi_j e$, is to obtain π_0 as described above first, and then to use the discrete Fourier transform approach described in Chapter 4. Specifically, once π_0 is known, we can use (5.27) or (5.37) directly to solve for the value of the $\mathcal{F}_{\tilde{q}}(z)e$ at points around the unit circle of the complex plane and then use the IFDT to obtain the marginal or joint level probabilities. This procedure, of course, involves solving the complex linear system

$$
\mathcal{F}_{\tilde{q}}(z_k)[Iz - \mathcal{P}\mathcal{F}_{\tilde{a}}(z_k)] = \pi_0[z_k - 1]\mathcal{A}(z_k), \qquad (5.46)
$$

where $z_k = e^{-j[(2\pi k)/(K+1)]}$ for $1 \leq k \leq K$, where $K = 2^n - 1$ for some integer-valued n.

Example 5.2   (Example 5.1 continued) Consider a statistical multi-plexing system described in Example 5.1. Suppose it is known that the mean message length of the individual users is eight packets. We wish to determine the probability that the system occupancy will exceed a certain number of packets at a traffic load of $\rho = 0.9$ during an arbitrary slot in stochastic equilibrium as a function of the number of individual users served.

Solution: Each source operates independently according to an alternating renewal process, so the proportion of time each source spends in the active period is given by the ratio of the expected length of the active period to the expected length of the cycle. Because a source delivers a geometric number of packets with mean $1/(1 - \alpha)$ during an active period, and because packets arrive only on alternate slots beginning with the second, the expected length of an active period in slots is $2/(1 - \alpha)$. Similarly, the expected length of the idle period is $1/(1 - \beta)$. Therefore the proportion of time each source spends in the active period is given by

$$\frac{2(1 - \beta)}{(1 - \alpha) + 2(1 - \beta)}.$$

Because packets are generated at rate 0.5 during active periods by each source and the service time of a packet is one slot, the traffic intensity is

$$\rho = \frac{N(1 - \beta)}{(1 - \alpha) + 2(1 - \beta)}.$$

For fixed ρ and $(1 - \alpha)$, we can then solve for

$$\beta = 1 - \frac{(1 - \alpha)\rho}{N - 2\rho}.$$

The average message length is eight packets, so $(1 - \alpha) = 0.125$. This, then, completely specifies the parameters for the model.

The recursion of (5.42) with $\mathcal{K}_0(1)$ as defined in (5.45) is then used to determine $\mathcal{K}(1)$ and its stationary probability vector, κ, is determined by solving the system $\kappa_0 = \kappa_0 \mathcal{K}_{00}$, $\kappa_0 e = 1$. Then, $\mathcal{F}_{\tilde{q}}(1)$ is determined by solving the system $\mathcal{F}_{\tilde{q}}(1) = \mathcal{F}_{\tilde{q}}(1)\mathcal{K}_{00}$, $\mathcal{F}_{\tilde{q}}(1)e = 1$. Next, (5.41) is used to obtain π_0. Finally, (5.46) and the IDFT

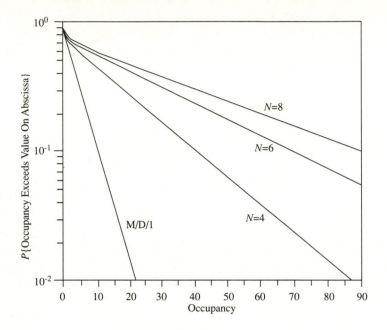

Figure 5.1 Survivor function for the occupancy distribution for statistical multiplexing system with 0.5 to 1 speed conversion.

procedure described in Chapter 4 are used to obtain the occupancy distribution. Numerical results are presented in Figure 5.1 and Table 5.3. ∎

With reference to Figure 5.1, we see that the survivor function is an increasing function of the number of independent sources that generate the traffic to the statistical multiplexer. This demonstrates that the often-cited claim that traffic arriving from a large number of sources can be treated as a Poisson arrival process must be carefully examined. In fact, often, as in the current case, exactly the opposite is true—a larger number of sources delivers traffic that is more bursty than that delivered by an ordinary Poisson process. This can be seen by observation of Figure 5.1, where the survivor function for the occupancy distribution for the M/D/1 system at a traffic intensity of 0.9 is also presented. Obviously, an M/D/1 approximation for the current system would miss the mark considerably.

Table 5.3 presents the mean and second moment of the occupancy distribution for several values of N. As a check on the accuracy of the PGF inversion routine, the mean values computed on the basis of the occupancy distribution were compared to the mean values computed analytically. The percent difference between the results of the two calculations is presented in the table. The table shows that the PGF inversion process works quite well. The general formula for the mean occupancy, derived in Daigle, Lee, and Magalhães [1990] following the parallel development in Lucantoni, Meier-Hellstern, and Neuts [1990], is

$$E[\tilde{q}] = \mathcal{F}_{\tilde{q}}^{(1)}(1)\mathbf{e}$$
$$= \frac{1}{1-\rho}\left\{\frac{1}{2}\mathcal{F}_{\tilde{q}}(1)\mathcal{F}_{\tilde{a}}^{(2)}(1)\mathbf{e} + \pi_0\mathcal{P}\mathcal{F}_{\tilde{a}}^{(1)}(1)\mathbf{e} \right.$$
$$+ \left[\pi_0\mathcal{P} - \mathcal{F}_{\tilde{q}}(1)[I - \mathcal{F}_{\tilde{a}}^{(1)}(1)]\right] \tag{5.47}$$
$$\left. [I - \mathcal{P} + \mathbf{e}\mathcal{F}_{\tilde{q}}(1)]^{-1}\mathcal{P}\mathcal{F}_{\tilde{a}}^{(1)}(1)\mathbf{e}\right\}.$$

The development is rather involved and is deferred to the Supplementary Problems. We consider here only one aspect of the formula shown in (5.47). Note that the right-hand side of the equation contains the expression $[I - \mathcal{P} + \mathbf{e}\mathcal{F}_{\tilde{q}}(1)]^{-1}$. The expression is called the fundamental matrix for the Markov chain whose one-step transition

Table 5.3 Multiplexing with Line Speed Conversion

N	$E[\tilde{n}]$	% difference	$E[\tilde{n}^2]$	r_k
2	1.1025	2.9502E-17	1.5075	0.0196
4	15.9627	9.2715E-14	631.87702	0.9514
6	26.9358	1.0751E-13	1836.14439	0.9714
8	33.5743	1.1819E-13	2865.30967	0.9771

probability matrix is $\mathcal{P}$ (see Hunter [1983]). For irreducible Markov chains, the fundamental matrix is always nonsingular. In addition, $e\mathcal{F}_{\tilde{q}}(1)[I - \mathcal{P} + e\mathcal{F}_{\tilde{q}}(1)] = e\mathcal{F}_{\tilde{q}}(1)$, the proof of which is to be obtained in Exercise 5.12.

Exercise 5.12 Suppose that $\mathcal{P}$ is the one-step transition probability matrix for an irreducible discrete-valued, discrete-parameter Markov chain. Define ϕ to be the stationary probability vector for the Markov chain. Prove that $e\phi[I - \mathcal{P} + e\phi] = e\phi$ and that, therefore, $e\phi = e\phi[I - \mathcal{P} + e\phi]^{-1}$.

Further simplification in the computational technique for π_0 is readily obtained if the traffic arrival process for multiplexing system under study has only one phase during which 0 packets can arrive. That is, the distribution of the number of packets that arrive during a slot is dependent on the phase of the arrival process. The phase is, in turn, governed by a discrete-time Markov chain. Now, suppose that the probability generating function for the number of arrivals during a slot, given the phase, is arbitrary except that the number of packets delivered during a time slot can be zero if and only if the phase of the arrival process is zero. Under that condition, the unknown probability vector, π_0, is trivially computed as described in the following paragraph.

In (5.38), the quantity $\mathcal{F}_{\tilde{q}}(1)$ corresponds to the stationary vector for the phase process, as is readily seen by taking limits on both sides of (5.37) as $z \to 1$. Now, $\pi_0 = [\pi_{00} \quad \pi_{10} \quad \cdots \quad \pi_{N0}]$. But π_{j0} represents the probability that the phase process is in phase j and zero packets are present at the end of the slot. Hence, $\pi_{j0} = 0$ except for $j = 0$. Thus, $\pi_{00} = [1 - \mathcal{F}_{\tilde{q}}(1)\mathcal{P}\mathcal{F}_{\tilde{a}}^{(1)}(1)e]$.

As in Example 5.2, such an arrival process is useful in modeling the traffic arising from a collection of independently operating sources in an integrated services environment. This is shown in Example 5.3.

Example 5.3 Consider a collection of N identical and independently operating sources. Suppose that each source alternates between inactive and active periods. During an active period, the source generates a packet every time slot, and the number of packets generated during an active period is geometrically distributed with mean $1/(1 - \alpha)$.

The lengths of inactive periods, in time slots, are geometrically distributed with mean $1/(1-\beta)$. We wish to specify $\mathcal{P}$ and $\mathcal{F}_{\tilde{a}}(z)$, and to determine the occupancy distribution for the statistical multiplexing system as a function of N with $\rho = 0.9$ and $1/(1-\alpha) = 8$.

Solution: The solution is similar to that of Example 5.1. We find that the Markov chain governing the phase of each source and the probability generating function for the number of arrivals in each slot are as follows:

$$\mathcal{P}_s = \begin{bmatrix} \beta & 1-\beta \\ 1-\alpha & \alpha \end{bmatrix} \quad \text{and} \quad \mathcal{F}_{\tilde{a}_s}(z) = \begin{bmatrix} 1 & 0 \\ 0 & z \end{bmatrix},$$

respectively. Clearly, the arrival process can be described in the form

$$\mathcal{A}(z) = \mathcal{P}\mathcal{F}_{\tilde{a}}(z),$$

and the methods described above can be used to obtain the unknown probability vector and then the occupancy distribution.

Packets arrive during every time slot when a source is active, so the state of the phase process can be defined simply as the number of sources in the active state. Thus the total number of phases required to characterize the phase of the combined arrival process is $N+1$.

It is relatively easy to show that the phase transition probabilities are obtained from the expression

$$\mathcal{P}_{mk} = \sum_{i=(k-[N-n])+}^{\min\{k,n\}} \binom{n}{i}\binom{N-n}{k-i} \alpha^i (1-\alpha)^{n-i}(1-\beta)^{k-i}\beta^{(N-n-k+i)}.$$

For the given phase definitions, $\mathcal{F}_{\tilde{a}}(z) = \text{diag}(1, z, z^2, \ldots, z^N)$. This indicates that in the first phase of the aggregate process, no packets would arrive. This completes the basic description of the model.

By following the development of Example 5.2, we can readily find that the proportion of time each source spends in the active period is given by

$$\sigma = \frac{(1-\beta)}{(1-\alpha)+(1-\beta)}$$

and that the traffic intensity is given by

$$\rho = \frac{N(1-\beta)}{(1-\alpha)+(1-\beta)}.$$

For fixed ρ and $(1-\alpha)$, we can then solve for

$$\beta = 1 - \frac{(1-\alpha)\rho}{N-\rho}.$$

Because the average message length is eight packets, $(1-\alpha) = 0.125$. This, then, completely specifies the parameters for the model.

We could obtain $\mathcal{F}_{\tilde{q}}(1)$ by solving the system $\mathcal{F}_{\tilde{q}}(1) = \mathcal{F}_{\tilde{q}}(1)P$, $\mathcal{F}_{\tilde{q}}(1)e = 1$. However, because each of the sources operates according to an alternating renewal process, we can readily see that the equi-

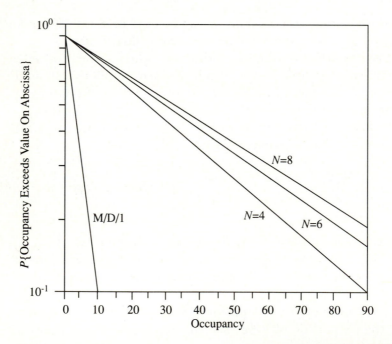

Figure 5.2 Survivor function for the occupancy distribution for statistical multiplexing system with equal line and trunk capacities.

Table 5.4 Multiplexing with No Line Speed Conversion

N	$E[\tilde{n}]$	% difference	$E[\tilde{n}^2]$	r_k
2	1.1025	2.9502E − 17	1.5075	0.0196
4	35.5275	9.3871E − 14	3020.63366	0.9769
6	43.4250	2.3726E − 13	4532.70825	0.9811
8	47.6775	2.6868E − 13	5473.48123	0.9828
10	50.3262	2.2786E − 13	6104.22453	0.9837
12	52.1325	2.2243E − 13	6554.07506	0.9843
14	53.4426	2.4292E − 13	6890.33668	0.9847

librium number of active sources has the binomial distribution with parameters N and σ. Thus, $\mathcal{F}_{\tilde{q}}(1)$ is simply the vector of the equilibrium probabilities. Also, π_0 is trivially determined as $[\rho, 0, \ldots, 0]$. Thus it remains only to use (5.46) and the IDFT procedure described in Chapter 4 to obtain the occupancy distribution. Numerical results are presented in Figure 5.2 and Table 5.4. ∎

As in Example 5.2, we can see from Figure 5.2 that the survivor function is an increasing function of N. In fact, the departure from the survivor function for the M/D/1 system having equal traffic intensity is even more pronounced than in Example 5.2. This is because the line speeds of the individual sources are higher than in Example 5.2, thus giving rise to more bursty traffic. The differences among the M/D/1, the N-source model with transmission-speed conversion, and the N-source model without transmission-speed conversion are highlighted in Figure 5.3, where numerical results are presented for the special case of $N = 8$.

5.5   CONCLUDING REMARKS

In this chapter, we have presented a brief description of M/G/1 and G/M/1 paradigms and the solution techniques of Lucantoni, Neuts, and Ramaswami. Again, the interested reader is referred to the two excellent books by Neuts, the papers of Ramaswami, and especially to Lucantoni [1991] for more thorough treatments of the current model. For a treatment of the M/G/1 model extended to the M/G/1 with vacations and a broad class of interarrival time distributions, the reader is referred to Lucantoni, Meier-Hellstern, and Neuts [1990].

The phase-dependent arrival and service model of Chapter 3, which is a quasi-birth and death (QBD) model, is a special case in which the model is of both the M/G1 and G/M/1 types. As we have seen earlier, when models have a special structure, we can develop special techniques to solve the model efficiently.

We have seen that solving for the stationary probabilities of Markov chains of the M/G/1 type is substantially more complicated than solving QBD models. It is worth mentioning that sometimes one may obtain a model of the QBD type that approximates the behavior of a system that is naturally modeled by a Markov chain

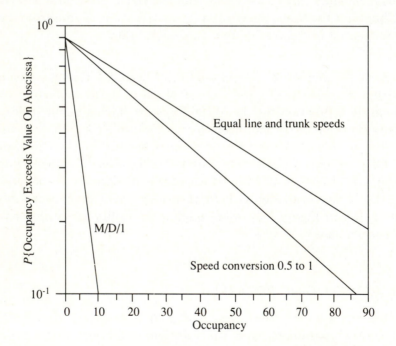

Figure 5.3 Survivor function for the occupancy distribution for statistical multiplexing system with and without line-speed conversion.

of the M/G/1 type. An example of an analysis based on such an approximation is given in Chipalkatti, Kurose, Towsley [1989] and the references therein.

We have shown that the methodology described in this chapter is useful in analyzing many types of queueing problems related to computer communications. There are many other applications in addition to the statistical multiplexing systems described in Section 5.4. We now discuss some of those briefly.

One rather unusual application on a topic of current interest that uses M/G/1 paradigm techniques is Chandramouli, Neuts, and Ramaswami [1989]. In that paper, the authors analyze a meteor-burst packet-communication system. In meteor-burst communications, successful message transmission is dependent on the level of ionization in the upper atmosphere. The quality of the channel during a given slot is modeled as a discrete-parameter, discrete-valued Markov chain, and the probability of successful message transmission depends on the state of the Markov chain, thus giving rise to a Markov chain of the M/G/1 type.

The procedures presented above can be altered to handle multiserver queues if service time is deterministic. Neuts [1981b] is an example of work along these lines. In that paper, Neuts discusses the analysis of the discrete time c-server queueing system having the equivalent of BMAP arrivals; the current notation for this model would be the BMAP/D/c queueing system. Neuts presents formulae and algorithms for both occupancy and waiting-time distributions and moments. No numerical results are presented there, however.

Li [1990] presents an analysis of a special case in which the arrival process is as described in Daigle, Lee, and Magalhães [1990], but there are multiple servers and there is a one-to-one correspondence between the phase of the arrival process and the number of packets that arrive during a slot; that is, each active source generates one packet during a slot. Li presents mean occupancies for a variety of parameter sets. Although Li's analysis could have been carried out using the methods described here, Li chose to approach the problem by spectral decomposition instead. His methods are quite interesting, and the reader is encouraged to investigate his approach.

Other work of interest along the same lines as presented here are Stavrakakis [1990] and van Arem [1990]. Both consider discrete time queues. Stavrakakis considers a single-server system having an arrival process similar to that of Li's, and van Arem's arrival process has the same form for $\mathcal{F}_{\tilde{a}}(z)$ but an arbitrary form for $\mathcal{P}$. Both present mean values only.

More recently, Daigle and Tang [1991] have considered the c-server queueing system in which $\mathcal{P}$ has a general form and $\mathcal{F}_{\tilde{a}}$ has the same form as Li [1990]; that is, $\mathcal{F}_{\tilde{a}}(z) = \text{diag}(1,\ z,\ z^2,\ \ldots,\ z^N)$. They developed solution methodology for the queue length distribution in terms of partial fraction expansions using eigenanalysis along the same lines as presented in Chapter 3. Extensions of that work to the case of more general $\mathcal{F}_{\tilde{a}}(z)$ are currently underway at the time of this writing.

As a final note, we point out that some researchers have suggested that the stationary probabilities for the embedded Markov chains could be obtained more efficiently by solving for these probabilities directly; that is, one could simply solve the matrix equations $\pi = \pi\mathcal{P}$, $\pi e = 1$ numerically without regard for the structure of $\mathcal{P}$. Related to this topic, a state-of-the-art workshop on the numerical solution of Markov chains was held in January of 1990. The papers presented during the workshop contain many interesting ideas and form the chapters of Stewart [1991]; the reader interested in this topic is strongly urged to consult Stewart.

5.6   SUPPLEMENTARY PROBLEMS

1. Consider a slotted-time, single-server queueing system having unit service rate. Suppose the arrival process to the system is a Poisson process modulated by a discrete-time Markov chain on $\{0,\ 1\}$ that has the following one-step transition probability matrix:

$$\mathcal{P} = \begin{bmatrix} \beta & 1 - \beta \\ 1 - \alpha & \alpha \end{bmatrix}.$$

While the arrival process is in phase i, arrivals to the system occur according to a Poisson process with rate λ_i, $i = 0,\ 1$.

(a) Argue that $\mathcal{A}(z) = \mathcal{B}(z)$ for this system.

(b) Show that

$$A(z) = \begin{bmatrix} \beta & 1-\beta \\ 1-\alpha & \alpha \end{bmatrix} \begin{bmatrix} e^{-\lambda_0(1-z)} & 0 \\ 0 & e^{-\lambda_1(1-z)} \end{bmatrix}.$$

(c) Show that

$$A(z) = \begin{bmatrix} \beta & 1-\beta \\ 1-\alpha & \alpha \end{bmatrix} \begin{bmatrix} e^{-\lambda_0(1-z)} & 0 \\ 0 & e^{-\lambda_1(1-z)} \end{bmatrix}.$$

(d) Determine A_i for all $i \geq 0$.

(e) Suppose that at the end of a time slot, the system occupancy level is zero and the phase of the arrival process is i, $i = 0$, 1. Determine the probability that the system occupancy level at the end of the following time slot will be k, $k = \{0, 1, \ldots\}$ and the phase of the arrival process will be j, $j = 0$, 1.

(f) Suppose that at the end of a time slot, the system occupancy level is $k > 0$ and the phase of the arrival process is i, $i = 0$, 1. Determine the probability that the system occupancy level at the end of the following time slot will be ℓ, $\ell = \{k-1, k, k+1\}$ and the phase of the arrival process will be j, $j = 0$, 1.

(g) Let $\alpha = 0.5$, $\beta = 0.75$, $\lambda_0 = 1.2$, and $\lambda_1 = 0.3$. Determine the equilibrium probability vector for the phase process and ρ for the system.

(h) Write a computer program to determine $K(1)$ for the parameters given in part (g), and then determine the equilibrium probability vector for the Markov chain for which $K(1)$ is the one-step transition probability matrix.

(i) Compute $E[\tilde{q}]$, the expected number of packets in the system at the end of an arbitrary time slot. Compare the result to the equivalent mean value $E[\tilde{q}]$ for the system in which $\lambda_0 = \lambda_1 = \rho$ as computed in part (g). What can be said about the effect of burstiness on the average system occupancy?

2. The objective of this problem is to develop a closed-form expression for the mean queue length, $E[\tilde{q}]$, for the slotted M/D/1 system having phase-dependent arrivals and unit service times.

Our point of departure is the expression for the generating function for the occupancy distribution as given in (5.37), which is now repeated for continuity:

$$\mathcal{F}_{\tilde{q}}(z)[Iz - P\mathcal{F}_{\tilde{a}}(z)] = \pi_0[z - 1]P\mathcal{F}_{\tilde{a}}. \qquad (5.48)$$

(a) Differentiate both sides of (5.48) to obtain

$$\mathcal{F}_{\tilde{q}}(z)[I - P\mathcal{F}_{\tilde{a}}^{(1)}(z)] + \mathcal{F}_{\tilde{q}}^{(1)}(z)[Iz - P\mathcal{F}_{\tilde{a}}(z)]$$
$$= \pi_0[z - 1]P\mathcal{F}_{\tilde{a}}^{(1)}(z) + \pi_0 P\mathcal{F}_{\tilde{a}}(z). \qquad (5.49)$$

(b) Take limits of both sides of (5.49) as $z \to 1$ to obtain

$$\mathcal{F}_{\tilde{q}}^{(1)}(1)[I - P] = \pi_0 P - \mathcal{F}_{\tilde{q}}(1)[I - P\mathcal{F}_{\tilde{a}}^{(1)}(1)]. \qquad (5.50)$$

(c) Define ρ to be the marginal probability that the system is not empty at the end of a slot. Postmultiply both sides of (5.50) by e, and show that $\rho = \mathcal{F}_{\tilde{q}}(1)\mathcal{F}_{\tilde{a}}^{(1)}(1)e$.

(d) Add $\mathcal{F}_{\tilde{q}}^{(1)}(1)e\mathcal{F}_{\tilde{q}}(1)$ to both sides of (5.50), solve for $\mathcal{F}_{\tilde{q}}^{(1)}(1)$, and then postmultiply by $P\mathcal{F}_{\tilde{a}}^{(1)}(1)e$ to obtain

$$\mathcal{F}_{\tilde{q}}^{(1)}(1)P\mathcal{F}_{\tilde{a}}^{(1)}(1)e = \mathcal{F}_{\tilde{q}}^{(1)}(1)e\rho$$
$$+ \left\{ \pi_0 P - \mathcal{F}_{\tilde{q}}(1)\left[I - \mathcal{F}_{\tilde{a}}^{(1)}(1)\right] \right\} \quad (5.51)$$
$$[I - P + e\mathcal{F}_{\tilde{q}}(1)]^{-1}.$$

Use the fact that $e\mathcal{F}_{\tilde{q}}(1)[I - P + e\mathcal{F}_{\tilde{q}}(1)] = e\mathcal{F}_{\tilde{q}}(1)$, as shown in Exercise 5.12 in Section 5.3.

(e) Differentiate both sides of (5.49) with respect to z, postmultiply both sides by e, take limits on both sides as $z \to 1$, and then rearrange terms to find

$$\mathcal{F}_{\tilde{q}}^{(1)}(1)P\mathcal{F}_{\tilde{a}}^{(1)}(1)e = \mathcal{F}_{\tilde{q}}^{(1)}(1)e - \frac{1}{2}\mathcal{F}_{\tilde{q}}^{(1)}(1)\mathcal{F}_{\tilde{a}}^{(1)}(1)e$$
$$- \pi_0 P\mathcal{F}_{\tilde{a}}^{(1)}(1)e. \qquad (5.52)$$

(f) Equate right-hand sides of (5.51) and (5.52), and then solve for $\mathcal{F}_{\tilde{q}}^{(1)}(1)e$ to obtain

$$E[\tilde{q}] = \mathcal{F}_{\tilde{q}}^{(1)}(1)\mathbf{e}$$

$$= \frac{1}{1-\rho}\left\{\frac{1}{2}\mathcal{F}_{\tilde{q}}(1)\mathcal{F}_{\tilde{a}}^{(2)}(1)\mathbf{e} + \pi_0\mathcal{P}\mathcal{F}_{\tilde{a}}^{(1)}(1)\mathbf{e}\right.$$

$$+ \left(\pi_0\mathcal{P} - \mathcal{F}_{\tilde{q}}(1)[I - \mathcal{F}_{\tilde{a}}^{(1)}(1)]\right)$$

$$\left. \times \; [I - \mathcal{P} + \mathbf{e}\mathcal{F}_{\tilde{q}}(1)]^{-1}\mathcal{P}\mathcal{F}_{\tilde{a}}^{(1)}(1)\mathbf{e}\right\}.$$

C H A P T E R

$\boxed{6}$

Conclusions

In this chapter, we summarize our presentation and point out a few related topics in queueing theory of immediate interest within the telecommunications area.

Throughout, our approach has been directed toward the development of an intuitive understanding of how queueing systems work. In most cases, we have carried our development far enough to obtain numerical results. Our thrust has been to provide the reader with sufficient background to be able to appreciate the major papers currently appearing in the applications literature, and numerous references to applications have been cited.

In Chapters 1 and 2, we presented background material of an elementary nature and developed useful properties of the Poisson process and the exponential distribution while simultaneously developing a few useful analytical techniques. These properties and techniques were then exploited in Chapter 3, in which we discussed analysis of systems modeled by birth and death models and quasi-birth and death models. We discussed both classical models and a number of variations that are of particular interest to the applications communities, especially communications.

We also introduced distributions of the phase type in Chapter 3. This rich class of distributions finds broad application in the computer communications area, especially in defining interarrival times for integrated communication systems. In addition, if distributions are approximated by those of the phase type, then it is possible to analyze the system via conventional continuous-time Markov chain

271

analysis. Sometimes, such approximation leads to a QBD model, and sometimes analysis yields an explicit formula for the rate matrix.

In Chapter 4, we examined the M/G/1 queueing system and some of its variants. Our analysis, although primarily based on transforms, was oriented toward development of an intuitive understanding of the underlying processes. We developed the concept of busy-period analysis and introduced a few key results from renewal theory early in the chapter. We then exploited these results from renewal theory and used busy-period analysis to introduce Fuhrmann–Cooper decomposition. We obtained the Pollaczek–Khinchine transform equation for the occupancy distribution using the basic ideas behind Fuhrmann–Cooper decomposition, and then we exploited this concept to develop major results for the M/G/1 system with exceptional first service, the M/G/1 system with set-up overhead, the M/G/1 system with vacations, and the M/G/1 system with head-of-the-line (HOL) priority. In addition, we introduced a technique based on the discrete Fourier transform for obtaining mass probabilities from probability generating functions that is applicable to all of the variants of the M/G/1 system covered in the chapter as well as to many others.

In Chapter 5, we discussed the M/G/1 and G/M/1 paradigms. We provided several examples that illustrate how the M/G/1 paradigm can be used to obtain fundamental insight about the behavior of slotted-time queueing systems that represent statistical multiplexing systems.

From a communications perspective, it appears that there are two major characteristics of communication systems that will in the future drive requirements for analytical tools. The first of these is the fundamental change in the transmission methodology brought about by the advent of BISDN in general, and the asynchronous transport mode in particular. This will increase the demand for understanding how services sharing the same transmission facilities affect each others' performance from the perspective of the user. The second characteristic of these is a fundamental shift in the underlying information infrastructure that will result in the migration of the majority of the communication software to the network edges.

The many articles on integrated voice/data services that have recently appeared in the literature (e.g., Sriram and Lucantoni [1989]) take steps in recognizing this fundamental change in transmission strategy. As line capacities increase, databases become more usable,

and complete articles begin to be readily obtainable in electronic
form from optical disk libraries. Due to this trend, user transmission
rates are likely to increase dramatically. When this happens, the user
will want the capability to run simultaneous sessions with a number of remote applications in much the same way as is done in the
Macintosh Hypercard environment on a single machine today.

The software overhead required to control several sessions simultaneously, at high speeds, in a remote hypermedia environment will
be astronomical. To achieve this goal, a fundamental understanding
of the relationship between the software structure within the system
and system performance will have to be achieved. This will require
the development of priority queueing models that have sufficient flexibility to capture the essential features of the software under a variety
of competing structures. The task-oriented queueing model (Daigle
[1986]) is a step in the direction of the development of the required
tools.

There are more fundamental issues in the network design area as
well. The baseline document describing broadband aspects of ISDN
(Sinha [1990]), for example, is loaded with statements of uncertainty
about how the network will be controlled, how resources will be
allocated, how new calls will be admitted to the network, and so
on. In addition, the quality of service achievable as a function of
offered load is an issue of serious concern. As an example, a serious
concern in the design of an ATM switch is the issue of where ATM
cells should be buffered. Another concern is how many cells need
to be buffered in order to achieve an acceptable cell-loss probability.
Another problem is whether buffers can be shared among the various
output lines or whether each output line should be provided with its
own set of buffers. If buffers are shared, how can the buffer sharing
algorithm be implemented so as not to bog down the system?

An interesting aspect of these concerns is that the buffering requirements are very sensitive to correlation in the arrival process.
With ATM, correlation is a serious issue because the cells derive from
DLC frames. There is, then, a problem regarding how cells should
be scheduled to enter the originating ATM switch. For example, if
the cells from different frames are interleaved, then at succeeding
switches correlation will be less significant because successive cells
would then more likely be switched to different output lines. In addition, the number of cells of the same frame that are affected by

a burst of errors on the transmission system is likely to be smaller than if the cells are not interleaved. Thus interleaving of cells may result in both a smaller proportion of frame retransmissions and an easing of buffering requirements at ATM switching nodes.

The design issues in BISDN that need to be addressed via queueing theory are numerous, as are the issues in many other areas, including communications for flexible manufacturing. It is hoped that the material covered in this book has provided a thorough introduction to queueing theory that will prove useful in appreciating the issues addressed in current literature, formulating appropriate models to address current and future design issues, and solving the models to obtain useful results.

$\boxed{\text{A}}$

PGF Inversion
Program Listing

This appendix provides a listing of the computer program used in Chapter 4 to compute the occupancy distribution for the M/G/1 queueing system for the special case in which message lengths are drawn from a truncated geometric distribution. In order to modify the program for use with a different service-time distribution, an alternative routine must be substituted for eval_pgf_trunc(), which evaluates the Pollaczek–Khintchine transform equation at points around the unit circle. This routine, in turn, calls the routine eval_trunc_Lst(), which evaluates the Laplace–Stieltjes transform of the service-time distribution at a point in the complex plane. This routine must also be replaced. The routine eval_cx2_dx3(), which computes the second and third central moments of the service-time distribution, must also be replaced if it is desired to verify the results of the computations against theoretical values of the first and second moments of the queue length distributions. In addition, parameters specific to the service-time distribution must be specified. All other routines are generic.

```
#define _MC68881_
#include <math.h>
#include <stdio.h>
#include <unix.h>
#include <storage.h>
#include <strings.h>
#include <util.h>
#include <complex_util.h>

#define J_max (int)512 /* maximum # points for DFT */
#define J_min (int)8 /* minimum # points for DFT */
#define JM_max (int)(2*J_max)
/* twice maximum number of points for DFT */
/* FFT inversion routine expects real and imaginary
   components in even and odd positions of arrays */
#define n_max (int)200 /* maximum number of points of
       distribution to list in output file */
#define lambda (double)0.95 /* arrival rate */
#define mu (double)1.0 /* average service rate */
#define service_mean_value (double)1.0/mu
/* average service time */
#define false 1 #define true 0 #define debug true
/* set equal to true for verbose printout during
       execution */
#define pi PI #define TINY (double)1.0e-20
#define file_out "test_run_trunc_29_32_95"
/* output file in which to store results */
#define avg_msg_length (double)30
#define a_cutoff (int)29
#define b_cutoff (int)32
#define line_capacity (double)30

void gen_coef_array(), double test_eval(),
     double sqr(); eval_pgf_trunc(), eval_theta_k(),
     eval_cx2_dx3();
/* Last 3 routines are special to current service
       time distribution changes. */
```

```c
main()
{
  int J, J_final, outcome, first_pass;
  c_rect *f_n_z; c_polar *polar_prob;
  double new_error, old_error, ratio_K, p_0;
  int low, high; double ec, theta, k, cx2, dx3;
  polar_prob = c_polar_vector(0,J_max-1);
   f_n_z = c_rect_vector(0,J_max-1);
  ec = avg_msg_length; low=a_cutoff; high=b_cutoff;
  eval_theta_k(ec,low,high,&theta,&k);
  eval_cx2_dx3(ec,low,high,theta,k,&cx2,&dx3);
  eval_pgf_trunc(J_max,theta, k, f_n_z);
    J = J_min; J_final = J_min; old_error = 1;
    first_pass = true; outcome = false;
    while (outcome == false) {
        if (first_pass == true) first_pass = false;
        else J = J*2;
        if (J <= J_max) {
          gen_coef_array (J,f_n_z,polar_prob);
          new_error = test_eval(J, polar_prob);
          if (new_error < old_error) {
            if (J != J_min)
              printf("%4d ' points provides an
              improvement over ' %4d 'points'\n", J,
                                      J_final);
              old_error = new_error; J_final = J;
          } else {
              outcome = true;
              printf("%4d ' points does not provide an
              improvement over ' %4d 'points'\n", J,
                                      J_final);
              gen_coef_array(J_final,f_n_z,
                                      polar_prob);
              output_stats(J_final, polar_prob,
                                  old_error, cx2,dx3);
          }
        } else {
          printf(" 'J exceeds J_max =' %5d\n",
                                      J_max);
          outcome = true;
        }
    }
}
```

```
double sqr(x) double x;
{
    double y;
    y = x*x;
    return(y);
}


void eval_theta_k(ec,low,high,theta,k)
    double ec, *theta, *k; int low, high;
/* routine evaluates theta and k parameters for the
   truncated geometric distribution. */
{
    double eval_theta(), eval_mean(), eval_k();
    double temp, dif;
    double mean;

    *theta = 1/ec; temp = *theta; dif = 0.5;

    /* Iterative procedure to compute theta. */
    while (fabs((dif)/(*theta)) > TINY)
        {
        *theta = eval_theta(ec,low,high,*theta);
        dif = temp - *theta;
        temp = *theta;
        }
    printf("\n %18.16f\n", *theta);

    *k = eval_k(low,high,*theta);
    printf("\n %18.16f\n", *k);

    /* Check the computed value of the mean. */
    mean = eval_mean(low,high,*k,*theta);
    printf("\n %18.16f\n", mean);


}
```

```
double eval_k(low,high,theta)
                          int low,high; double theta;
/* Given theta, computes the value k for the
   truncated geometric distribution. */
{
    double temp;
    temp = exp(((double)low-1)*log(1-theta))
    return (1/temp);
}


void eval_cx2_dx3(ec,low,high,theta,k,cx2,dx3)
double ec, theta, k, *cx2, *dx3; int low, high;
/*
computes coefficient of variation for the truncated
 geometric message length distribution which is equal
 to that for the service time distribution.
 Similarly for the normalized third central moment.
*/
{
double k_hat; int b_hat;
double a_p, a_pp, a_ppp, b_p,b_pp,b_ppp, var_m,
        dar_m, m_1, m_2, m_3, m_1_2, m_1_3;
b_hat = high - (low - 1);
k_hat = k*exp((double)(low-1)*log(1-theta));
b_p   = - ((double)b_hat*k_hat) * exp((double)(b_hat)
          *log(1.0-theta));
b_pp  = b_p*((double)(b_hat-1));
b_ppp = b_pp*((double)(b_hat-2));
a_p   = 1/theta;
a_pp  = 2.0*a_p*(1.0-theta)/theta;
a_ppp = 3.0*a_pp*(1.0-theta)/theta;
m_1 = a_p + b_p;
m_2 = a_pp + 2.0*a_p*b_p + b_pp;
m_3 = a_ppp + 3.0*a_pp*b_p + 3.0*a_p*b_pp + b_ppp;
m_1_2 = m_1*m_1;
m_1_3 = m_1_2*m_1;
var_m = m_2 + m_1 - m_1*m_1;
dar_m = m_3 + 3.0*m_2*(1-m_1) + 2.0*m_1_3 - 3.0*m_1_2 + m_1;
*cx2 = var_m/(ec*ec);
*dx3 = dar_m/(ec*ec*ec);
}
```

```
c_rect eval_trunc_Lst(sr,low,high,theta,k,C)
c_rect sr; int low,high;double theta,k,C;

/*
function evaluates the Laplace-Stieltjes transform of
the service time when message lengths are drawn from a
geometric distribution truncated at low and high and
 distribution at a complex point sp, the result being
 returned in the complex structure fp by address.
*/

{
c_polar g_polar, g_polar_a, g_polar_b;
c_rect g_rect, g_rect_a, g_rect_b, temp_rect,
        one_minus_g_rect;
double multiplier;

g_polar.mag = (1-theta)*exp(-1.0*sr.re/C);
g_polar.arg = -1.0*sr.im/C;

g_rect = polar_to_rect(g_polar);
one_minus_g_rect.re = 1.0-g_rect.re;
one_minus_g_rect.im = -1.0*g_rect.im;

g_polar_a.mag = exp((double)low*log(g_polar.mag));
g_polar_a.arg = (double)low*g_polar.arg;
g_polar_b.mag = exp((double)(high+1)
                *log(g_polar.mag));
g_polar_b.arg = (double)(high+1)*g_polar.arg;

g_rect_a = polar_to_rect(g_polar_a);
g_rect_b = polar_to_rect(g_polar_b);

temp_rect = c_div(c_sub(g_rect_a,g_rect_b),
                            one_minus_g_rect);
multiplier = (k*theta)/(1.0-theta);
temp_rect.re *= multiplier;
temp_rect.im *= multiplier;
return temp_rect;

}
```

```
double eval_mean(low,high,k,theta)
   int low,high; double k, theta;
/* Computes value of mean for truncated geometric
   distribution as a check on routine for computing
   theta and k. */
{
   double temp;

   temp = k*exp(((double)low-1)*log(1-theta))*
       ((1/theta)*(1.0 - exp(((double)high-
       (double)low+1)*log(1-theta))) - (double)high
       *exp(((double)high-(double)low+1)*log(1-theta))
       + ((double)low-1));
   return (temp);
}

double eval_theta(ec,low,high,theta)
   double ec, theta; int low,high;
/* Computes next value of theta in iterative routine.
*/
{
   double temp;

   temp = ec*(1.0 - exp(((double)high-(double)low+1)
       *log(1-theta))) + ((double)high+1/theta)
       *exp(((double)high-(double)low+1)
       *log(1-theta)) - ((double)low-1.0);
   return (1/temp);
}
```

```
void eval_pgf_trunc(n, theta, k, pgf_eval)
     int n; double theta, k; c_rect *pgf_eval;
/*
 Evaluates P-K queue length transform equation at
 points around the unit circle.
*/

{
  int index;
  c_rect z, s, lst_eval, one, one_minus_z, denom,
                                              num;
  double two_pi_by_n, rho;
  double ec, C; int low, high;

  ec = avg_msg_length; low=a_cutoff; high=b_cutoff;
  C=line_capacity;

  two_pi_by_n    = 2*PI/ (double) n;
  rho = lambda / mu;
  one.re = 1.0; one.im = 0.0;
  pgf_eval[0] = one;

  for (index = 1; index <= n-1; index++) {
      z.re = cos(two_pi_by_n*index);
      z.im = sin(two_pi_by_n*index);
      s.re = lambda * (1 - z.re);
      s.im = -1.0 * lambda * z.im;
      lst_eval = eval_trunc_Lst(s,low,high,theta,k,C);
      /*  previous line dependent upon particular
          service time distribution. */
      denom = c_sub(lst_eval,z);
      one_minus_z = c_sub(one,z);
      num = c_mul(one_minus_z,lst_eval);
      num.re *= (1.0 - rho);
      num.im *= (1.0 - rho);
      pgf_eval[index] = c_div(num,denom);
  }
}
```

```
void gen_coef_array (n, pgf_eval,coef_array)
int n; c_rect *pgf_eval; c_polar *coef_array;
/* Selects a subset of the total number of points
   evaluated around unit circle to obtain the
   distribution based on less than the maximum
   number of coefficients considered. */
{
  c_rect coef;
  double *x_array;
  int step_size, index, index1;
  x_array = dvector(0,2*n-1);

  step_size = floor((J_max)/(n)+0.5);
  for(index=0;index<=2*n-1;index++)
                                  x_array[index] = 0.0;
  for(index=0;index<=J_max-1;index++) {
  coef_array[index].mag = 0;
  coef_array[index].arg = 0;
  }
  for (index = 0; index <= n-1; index++) {
     x_array[2*index] = pgf_eval[step_size*index].re;
     x_array[2*index+1] =
                          pgf_eval[step_size*index].im;
     }
  FFT(n,-1,x_array-1);
  for (index = 0; index <= n-1; index++) {
     coef.re = x_array[2*index]/(n);
     coef.im = x_array[2*index+1]/(n);
     coef_array[index] = rect_to_polar(coef);
     }
  free_dvector(x_array,0,2*n-1);

}
```

```
FFT(nn,isign,data) int nn,isign; double *data;
/*
Routine adapted from Press et. al. [1988]
*/
{  /* procedure FFT */

   int n,mmax,m,j,istep,i;
   double temp,wtemp,wr,wpr,wpi,wi,theta,tempr,tempi;

   n = nn*2;
   j = 1;

   /* c for statement follows */
   i = 1;
   while (i < n) {
      if (j>i) {
          temp = data[i];
          data[i] = data[j];
          data[j] = temp;
          temp = data[i+1];
          data[i+1] = data[j+1];
          data[j+1] = temp;
          }
      m = n >>1;
      while ((m>=2) && (j>m)) {
          j = j - m;
          m >>= 1;
          }
      j = j + m;
      i = i + 2;
      }
   /* c for statement ends */
```

```
  mmax = 2;
  while (n > mmax) {
     istep = 2 * mmax;
     theta = 2*pi/(isign*mmax);
     wtemp = sin(0.5 * theta);
     wpr = -2.0*wtemp*wtemp;
     wpi = sin(theta);
     wr = 1.0;
     wi = 0.0;

     /* c for statement follows */
     m = 1;
     while (m<mmax) {

        /* c for statement follows */
        i = m;
        while (i <= n) {
           j = i + mmax;
           tempr = wr*data[j] - wi*data[j+1];
           tempi = wr*data[j+1] + wi*data[j];
           data[j] = data[i] - tempr;
           data[j+1] = data[i+1]- tempi;
           data[i] = data[i] + tempr;
           data[i+1] = data[i+1] + tempi;
           i = i + istep;
           }
        /* c for statement ends */

        wtemp = wr;
        wr = wr*wpr-wi*wpi + wr;
        wi = wi*wpr + wtemp*wpi+wi;
        m = m+2;
        }
     /* c for statement ends */

     mmax = istep;
     }
} /* procedure fft */
```

```
double test_eval(n, coef) int n; c_polar *coef;
/* Routine to determine disagreement between rate
   of decrease in tail probability computed two ways. */


{
  int index, k_min;
  double p, rho, eps, computed_error, error, r;

  rho = lambda*service_mean_value;
  p = 1 - rho;
  eps = coef[0].mag - p;
  r = eps/coef[n-1].mag;
  k_min = (n-1) - floor(n/4);
  error = 0.0;
  for (index = k_min; index <= n-1; index++) {
     computed_error = fabs((coef[index].mag
                       /coef[index-1].mag-r)/r);
     if (computed_error > error)
                          error = computed_error;
     }
  return error;
}

output_stats(n, coef, err, C_x_2,D_x_3)
int n; double  err,C_x_2,D_x_3; c_polar *coef;
/* Outputs data to text file for easy handling with
   graphics package and for producing tables in
    textures. */
{

  int index;
  double rho, current_error, r_to_power_K_plus_1,
     prob_check, E_n, next_prob, p, eps, r, E_n_2,
     E_n1, E_n2, E_n1_2, E_n2_2, E_n_theor,
     E_n_2_theor, prob_mass_fcn[n_max],
     surv_fcn[n_max], temp_prob[J_max],
                            temp_surv[J_max];
  FILE *fopen(), *fp;
```

```
rho = lambda*service_mean_value;
p = 1-rho;
eps = coef[0].mag - p;
/* theoretical calculations follow */
/* first moment */
E_n1 = rho*(rho*(1 + C_x_2)/2)/(1-rho);
E_n2 = rho;
E_n_theor = E_n1 + E_n2;
/* second moment */
E_n1_2 = E_n1*(2*E_n1 + 1 + 2* rho) +
         rho*(rho*(rho/(1-rho)))*((D_x_3-2)/3);
E_n2_2 = rho*rho*(1+C_x_2) + rho;
E_n_2_theor = E_n1_2 + E_n2_2 + 2* E_n1 * E_n2;
r = eps/coef[n-1].mag;
current_error = eps;
temp_prob[0] = coef[0].mag - current_error;
prob_check = temp_prob[0];
temp_surv[0] = 1.0 - temp_prob[0];
E_n = temp_surv[0];
E_n_2 = 0.0;
for (index = 1; index <= n-1; index++) {
    current_error = current_error * r;
    temp_prob[index] = coef[index].mag -
                                current_error;
    prob_check = prob_check + temp_prob[index];
    temp_surv[index] = temp_surv[index-1] -
                                temp_prob[index];
    E_n = E_n + temp_surv[index];
    E_n_2 = E_n_2 + (double)index*temp_prob[index]
                                *(double)index;
    }
r_to_power_K_plus_1 = exp((n)*log(r));
next_prob = eps * (1-r_to_power_K_plus_1);
prob_check = prob_check + next_prob*r/(1-r);
E_n = E_n + (next_prob*r/(1-r))/(1-r);
E_n_2 = E_n_2 + (next_prob/(1-r)) *
                    (r*((1+r)/(1-r) + 2*(n))/(1-r)
                        + sqr((double)(n)));
printf("'second moment is ' %16.6e\n",E_n_2);
fp = fopen(file_out,"w");
fprintf(fp,"'*'\n");
```

```
    fprintf(fp, " '{\\rm System}' \t  '&'   \t   'K'
                          \t '&' \t  '\\rho' ");
    fprintf(fp, " \t  '&'  \t '{\\rm accuracy}'
                        \t  '&'  \t '\\epsilon_K' ");
    fprintf(fp,    " \t  '&'  \t  'r_k'  \t  '&'
                        \t 'E[\\tilde n]'  \t  '&' ") ;
    fprintf(fp,   " \t 'E[\\tilde n^2]' '&' \t
                      'E[\\tilde n_{\\rm act}]' \t ");
    fprintf(fp,   " '&' \t 'E[\\tilde n^2_{\\rm act}]'
                               \t '\\cr' \n");
    fprintf(fp," 'M/G_2/1' \t '&' \t %4d \t '&' \t
        %6.3f \t '&' \t %11.6e \t'&' \t %11.6e \t '&'
        \t %7.5f \t'&' \t %7.5f \t '&' \t   %7.5f \t
        '&' \t %7.5f \t '&' \t %7.5f \t '\\cr' \n",
      n, rho,err,eps,r,E_n,E_n_2,E_n_theor,
         E_n_2_theor);
    if (n >= n_max) for (index = 0; index <= n_max; in
dex++)
        fprintf(fp, "%16.12e \t %16.12e \n",
                  temp_prob[index], temp_surv[index]);
    else {
       for (index = 0; index <= n-1; index++)
          fprintf(fp, "%16.12e \t %16.12e \n",
          temp_prob[index], temp_surv[index]);
       for (index = n; index <= n_max; index++) {
          fprintf(fp,"%16.12e \t %16.12e \n",
                      next_prob, next_prob*r/(1-r));
          next_prob = next_prob * r;
          }
       }

    fclose(fp);

}
```

The following is the collection of utilities that should be placed in a file and linked to the main program at run time. The include file names may need to be changed if the program is not run under Lightspeed C.

```c
#define _MC68881_
#include <math.h>
#include <stdio.h>
#include <unix.h>
#include <storage.h>
#include <strings.h>
#include <trunc_util.h>

c_polar *c_polar_vector(nl,nh)
int nl,nh;
/* Allocates a vector of complex structures
   with range [nl..nh]. */
{
    c_polar *v;

    v = calloc((nh-nl+1),sizeof(c_polar));
    if (!v) nrerror("allocation failure in
                            complex_vector()");
    return v-nl;
}

void free_c_polar_vector(v,nl,nh)
                          c_polar *v; int nl,nh;
/* Frees a complex vector allocated by dvector(). */
{
free((char*) (v+nl));
}

c_rect *c_rect_vector(nl,nh)
int nl,nh;
/* Allocates a vector of complex structures with
   range [nl..nh]. */
{
 c_rect *v;

 v = calloc((nh-nl+1),sizeof(c_rect));
 if (!v) nrerror("allocation failure in
                            c_rect_vector()");
 return v-nl;
}
```

```
void free_c_rect_vector(v,nl,nh)
c_rect *v; int nl,nh;
/* Frees a complex vector allocated by dvector(). */
{
free((char*) (v+nl));
}

double mag_c_rect(r) c_rect r;

/* magnitude of a complex number currently
                    stored in rectangular form */

{
   double h,rr,ri;
   rr=r.re;ri=r.im;
   rr = fabs(rr); ri = fabs(ri);
   if(ri > rr) {
       h = rr; rr = ri; ri = h;
   }
   if(ri != 0.0) { h = ri/rr; h *= ri/rr;
               h += 1.0; ri = sqrt(h); rr *= ri; }
   return(rr);
}

c_rect polar_to_rect(p) c_polar p;

{
   c_rect r;
   r.re = (p.mag) * cos(p.arg);
    r.im = (p.mag) * sin(p.arg);
    return(r);
}

c_rect c_sub(x,y) c_rect x,y;
/* return dif x-y as z */
{
   c_rect z;
   z.re = x.re - y.re;
   z.im = x.im - y.im;
   return(z);
}
```

```
c_polar rect_to_polar(r) c_rect r;
{
int outcome;
double   x, y, mag;
c_polar p;

    x = fabs(r.re);
    y = fabs(r.im);
    (p.mag) = mag_c_rect(r);
    if ((r.re == 0) && (r.im == 0)) outcome = 0;
    if ((r.re == 0) && (r.im > 0))  outcome = 1;
    if ((r.re == 0) && (r.im < 0))  outcome = 2;
    if ((r.re > 0) && (r.im == 0))  outcome = 3;
    if ((r.re > 0) && (r.im > 0))  outcome = 4;
    if ((r.re > 0) && (r.im < 0))  outcome = 5;
    if ((r.re < 0) && (r.im == 0))  outcome = 6;
    if ((r.re < 0) && (r.im > 0))  outcome = 7;
    if ((r.re < 0) && (r.im < 0))  outcome = 8;
    switch (outcome) {
        case 0: case 3 : p.arg = 0.0; break;
        case 1 : p.arg = PI/2; break;
        case 2 : p.arg = 3*PI/2; break;
        case 4 : p.arg = atan(y/x); break;
        case 5 : p.arg = - atan(y/x); break;
        case 6 : p.arg = PI; break;
        case 7 : p.arg = PI - atan(y/x); break;
        case 8 : p.arg = PI + atan(y/x); break;
    }
    return(p);
}


c_rect c_mul(x,y) c_rect x,y;
/* return product x*y as z */
{
    c_rect z;
    z.re = x.re * y.re - x.im * y.im;
    z.im = x.re * y.im + x.im * y.re;
    return(z);
}
```

```
c_rect c_div(x,y) c_rect x,y;
/* return quotient x/y as z */
{
 c_rect z;
 double r, den;
 if(fabs(y.re) >= fabs(y.im)) {
    r = y.im/y.re;
    den = y.re + r * y.im;
    z.re = (x.re + r * x.im)/den;
    z.im = (x.im - r * x.re)/den;
  } else {
    r = y.re/y.im;
    den = y.im + r * y.re;
    z.re = (x.re * r + x.im)/den;
    z.im = (x.im * r - x.re)/den;
  }
     return (z);
}

void nrerror(error_text) char error_text[];
/* Numerical recipes standard error handler.
   Adopted from Press et. al. [1988]. */
{
    void exit();
    fprintf(stderr,"Numerical Recipes run-time
    fprintf(stderr,"%s\n",error_text);
    fprintf(stderr,"... Now exiting system ...\n");
    exit(1);
}

double *dvector(nl,nh)
int nl,nh;
/* Allocates a double vector with range [nl..nh].
   Adopted from Press et. al. [1988]. */
{
double *v;

v = calloc((nh-nl+1),sizeof(double));
if (!v) nrerror("allocation failure in dvector()");
return v-nl;
}
```

```
void free_dvector(v,nl,nh)
double *v;
int nl,nh;
/* Frees a double vector allocated by dvector().
   Adopted from Press et. al. [1988] */
{
if(free((char *)(v+nl))==-1) nrerror("free failure in
free_dvector()");
}
```

The following is the include file named at the beginning of the previous collection of utilities. To be compatible with the above, the file must be named trunc_util.c.

```
typedef struct C_Rect {double re, im;} c_rect;
typedef struct C_Polar {double mag, arg;} c_polar;

extern void nrerror(char *);
extern double *dvector(int,int);
/* From Press et. al. [1988] */
extern void free_dvector(double *,int,int);

extern c_rect c_sub(c_rect,c_rect);
      /* dif x-y, x,y,rect */
extern c_rect c_mul(c_rect,c_rect);
      /* product x*y, x,y,rect */
extern c_rect c_div(c_rect,c_rect);
      /* quotient x/y , x, y,rect */
extern c_rect *c_rect_vector(int,int);
   /* Allocates a vector of complex rect
        structures with range [nl..nh]. */
extern c_polar *c_polar_vector(int,int);
   /* Allocates a vector of complex polar
        structures with range [nl..nh]. */
extern double mag_c_rect(c_rect);
    /* magnitude of a rect complex number */
extern c_polar rect_to_polar(c_rect);
    /* convert rect to polar */
extern c_rect polar_to_rect(c_polar);
    /* convert polar to rect */
```

R E F E R E N C E S

Abate, J., and W. Whitt. 1988 Transient Behavior of the M/M/1 Queue via Laplace Transforms. *Advances in Applied Probability* **20:1**, 145–178.

Abate, J., and W. Whitt. 1989 Calculating Time-Dependent Performance Measures for the M/M/1 Queue. *IEEE Trans. on Commun.* **37:10**, 1102–1104.

Ackroyd, M. H. 1980. Computing the Waiting Time Distribution for the G/G/1 Queue by Signal Processing Methods. *IEEE Trans. on Commun.* **28:1**, 52–58.

Bertsekas, D., and R. Gallager. 1987. *Data Networks.* Prentice-Hall, Englewood Cliffs, N. J.

Beuerman, S. L., and E. J. Coyle. 1987. The Delay Characteristics of CSMA/CD Networks. *IEEE Trans. on Commun.* **36:5**, 553–563.

Beuerman, S. L., and E. J. Coyle. 1989. State Space Expansions and the Limiting Behavior of Quasi-Birth and Death Processes. *Advances in Applied Probability* **21:2**, 284–314.

Bhargava, A., and M. G. Hluchyj. 1990. Frame Losses Due to Buffer Overflows in Fast Packet Networks, *Proc. of IEEE INFOCOM '90*, 132–139, San Francisco.

Bruneel, H. 1988. Queueing Behavior of Statistical Multiplexers with Correlated Inputs. *IEEE Trans. on Commun.* **36:12**, 1339–1341.

Burke, P. J. 1956. The Output of a Queuing System. *Ops. Res.* **4**, 699–704.

Chandramouli, Y., M. F. Neuts, and V. Ramaswami. 1989. A Queueing

Model for Meteor Burst Communication Systems. *IEEE Trans. on Commun.* **37:10**, 1024–1030.

Chandy, K. M., and C. H. Sauer. 1981. *Computer Systems Performance Modelling.* Prentice-Hall, Englewood Cliffs, N. J.

Chipalkatti, R., J. F. Kurose, and D. Towsley. 1989. Scheduling Policies for Real-Time and Non-Real-Time Traffic in a Statistical Multiplexer. *Proc. IEEE INFOCOM '89.* 774–783, Ottawa.

Churchill, R. V. 1960. *Complex Variables and Applications.* McGraw-Hill, New York.

Churchill, R. V., and J. W. Brown. 1987. *Fourier Series and Boundary Value Problems, 4th Ed.* McGraw-Hill, New York.

Cinlar, E. 1975. *Introduction to Stochastic Processes.* Prentice-Hall, Englewood Cliffs, N. J.

Cohen, J. W. 1969. *The Single Server Queue.* Wiley Interscience, New York.

Cooper, R. B. 1972. *Introduction to Queueing Theory.* Macmillan, New York.

Cooper, R. B. 1981. *Introduction to Queueing Theory, 2nd Ed.* North-Holland, New York. Republished 1990 by CEEPress, The George Washington University, Washington, D. C.

Cooper, R. B. 1990. Queueing Theory. Chapter 10 in *Stochastic Models*, D. P. Heyman and M. J. Sobel, eds. Volume 2 in the Series Handbooks of Operations Research and Management Science, North-Holland, New York.

Cooper, R. B., and S. C. Niu. 1986. Beneš's Formula for M/G/1-FIFO Explained by Preemptive-Resume LIFO. *J. Appl. Prob.* **23:2**, 350–354.

Coyle, E., and B. Liu. 1985. A Matrix Representation of CSMA/CD Networks. *IEEE Trans. on Commun.* **33:1**, 53–64.

Daigle, J. N. 1977a. Queueing Analysis of a Packet Switching Node with Markov-Renewal Arrival Process. *Proc. IEEE Int. Commun. Conf.* 1, 279–283. Chicago.

Daigle, J. N. 1977b. "Queueing Analysis of a Packet Switching Node in a Data Communication System." Doctoral Dissertation, Columbia University.

Daigle, J. N. 1986. Task Oriented Queueing: A Design Tool for Communications Software Design. *IEEE Trans. on Commun.* **34:12**, 250–256.

Daigle, J. N. 1989. Queue Length Distributions from Probability Generating Functions via Discrete Fourier Transforms. *Ops. Res. Letters* **8**, 229–236.

Daigle, J. N., and J. D. Langford. 1985. Queueing Analysis of a Packet Voice Communication System. *Proc. IEEE INFOCOM '85.* 18–26. Washington, D. C.

Daigle, J. N., and J. D. Langford. 1986. Models for Analysis of Packet Voice Communication Systems. *IEEE Journal of Selected Areas in Communications* **4:6**, 847–855.

Daigle, J. N., Y. Lee, and M. N. Magalhães. 1990. Discrete Time Queues with Phase Dependent Arrivals. *Proc. of IEEE INFOCOM'90*, 728–732.

Daigle, J. N., and D. M. Lucantoni. 1990. Queueing Systems Having Phase-Dependent Arrival and Service Rates. *First International Workshop on the Numerical Solutions of Markov Chains*, 375–395. Raleigh, N. C. Also Chapter 10 of Stewart [1991].

Daigle, J. N., and M. N. Magalhães. 1991. Transient Behavior of $M/M^{ij}/1$ Queues. To appear in *Queueing Systems: Theory and Applications*.

Daigle, J. N., and S. Tang. 1991. Numerical Methods for Discrete Time Queues with Phase Dependent Arrivals. Manuscript in preparation.

Daigle, J. N., and S. D. Whitehead. 1985. A Balance Equation Approach to Non-Markovian Queueing Systems. University of Rochester, W. E. Simon Graduate School of Business Administration, Working Paper, Series QM-8629.

Disney, R. L., and P. C. Kiessler. 1987. *Traffic Processes in Queueing Networks: A Markov Renewal Approach*. The Johns Hopkins University Press, Baltimore.

Disney, R. L., D. C. McNickle, and B. Simon. 1980. The M/G/1 Queue with Instantaneous Feedback. *Naval Res. Log. Qrt.* **27**, 635–644.

Doshi, B. T. 1986. Queueing Systems with Vacations—A Survey. *Queueing Systems.* **1:1**, 29–66.

Doshi, B. T. 1990. Single Server Queues with Vacations. *Stochastic Analysis of Computer and Communication Systems* (H. Takagi, ed.). North-Holland, New York, pp. 217–265.

Evans, R. V. 1967. Geometric Distributions in Some Two Dimensional Queueing Systems. *Operations Research* **15:5**, 830–846.

Feller, W. 1968. *An Introduction to Probability Theory and Its Applications* **I**, John Wiley, New York.

Feller, W. 1971. *An Introduction to Probability Theory and Its Applications* **II**, John Wiley, New York.

Fuhrmann, S. W., and R. B. Cooper. 1985. Stochastic Decomposition in the M/G/1 Queue with Generalized Vacations. Ops. Res. 33:5, 1091–1099.

Gavish, B., and K. Altinkemer. 1990. Backbone Design Tools with Economic Tradeoffs. *ORSA Journal on Computing* **2:3**, 236–251.

Gavish, B., and I. Neuman. 1986. Capacity and Flow Assignment in Large Computer Networks. *Proceedings of IEEE INFOCOM'86*. 275–284, Miami.

Gelenbe, E., and G. Pujolle. 1987. *Introduction to Queueing Networks*. John Wiley, New York.

Giffin, W. C. 1978. *Queueing: Basic Theory and Applications*. Grid, Inc., (Reprinted by Books on Demand, UMI, Ann Arbor, MI).

Gordon, J. J. 1990. The Evaluation of Normalizing Constants in Closed Queueing Networks. *Operations Research* **38:5**, 863–869.

Gordon, W. L., and G. F. Newell. 1967. Closed Queuing Systems with Exponential Servers. *Operations Research* **15:2**, 254–265.

Grassmann, W. K. 1990. Finding Transient Solutions in Markovian Event Systems Through Randomization. *First International Workshop on the Numerical Solutions of Markov Chains*, 179–211. Raleigh, N. C.

Green, L., and B. Melamed. 1990. An Anti-PASTA Result for Markovian Systems. *Ops. Res.* **38:1**, 173–175.

Hahne, E. L., A. K. Choudhury, and N. F. Maxemchuk. 1990. Improving the Fairness of Distributed Queue-Dual-Bus Networks. *Proceedings of IEEE INFOCOM'90*, 175–184, San Francisco.

Hammond, J. L., and P. J. P. O'Reilly. 1986. Performance Analysis of Local Computer Networks. Addison-Wesley, Reading.

Harrison, M. 1985. On Normalizing Constants in Queueing Networks. *Ops. Res.* **33:2**, 464–468.

Hewitt, E., and K. Stromberg. 1969. *Real and Abstract Analysis*. Springer-

Verlag, New York.

Hogg, R. V., and A. T. Craig. 1978. *Introduction to Mathematical Statistics.* Macmillan, New York.

Hunter, J.J. 1983. *Mathematical Techniques of Applied Probability. Volume 1, Discrete Time Models: Basic Theory.* Academic Press, New York.

Iliadis, I., and W. E. Denzel. 1990. Performance of Packet Switches with Input and Output Queueing. *Proceedings of IEEE ICC'90*, 747–753, Atlanta.

Jackson, J. R. 1957. Networks of Waiting Lines. *Ops. Res.* **5**, 518–521.

Jackson, J. R. 1963. Jobshop-like Queueing Systems. *Management Science* **10**, 131–142.

Jensen, A. 1953. Markoff Chains as an Aid in the Study of Markoff Processes. *Skandinavisk Aktuarietidskrift.* **36**, 87–91.

Jewell, W. S. 1967. A Simple Proof of: $L = \lambda W$. *Ops. Res.* **15:6**, 1109–1116.

Jiang, I., and J. S. Meditch. 1990. A Queueing Model for ATM-based Multi-Media Communication Systems. *Proceedings of IEEE ICC'90*, 264–267, Atlanta.

Keilson, J. 1979. *Markov Chain Models—Rarity and Exponentiality.* Springer-Verlag, New York.

Keilson, J., and L. Servi. 1988. A Distributional Form of Little's Law. *Ops. Res. Let.* **7:5**, 223–227.

Keilson, J., and L. Servi. 1989. Blocking Probability for M/G/1 Vacation Systems with Occupancy Level Dependent Schedules. *Ops. Res.* **37:1**, 134–140.

Keilson, J., and D.M.G. Wishart. 1965. A Central Limit Theorem for Process Defined on a Finite Markov Chain. *Proc. Cam. Phil. Soc.* **60**, 547–567.

Kelly, F. P. 1979. *Reversibility and Stochastic Networks.* John Wiley, New York.

Kendall, D. G. 1953. Stochastic Processes Occurring in the Theory of Queues and Their Analysis by the Method of Imbedded Markov Chains. *Ann. Math. Statist.* **24**, 338–354.

Kim, H. S., and A. Leon-Garcia. 1990. Performance of Self-Routing ATM

Switch under Nonuniform Traffic Pattern. *Proceedings of IEEE INFO-COM'90*, 140–145, San Francisco.

Kleinrock, L. 1975. *Queueing Systems: Volume 1, Theory.* John Wiley, New York.

Kleinrock, L. 1976. *Queueing Systems: Volume 2, Computer Applications.* John Wiley, New York.

Kobayashi, H. 1978. *Modeling and Analysis: An Introduction to System Performance Evaluation Methodology.* Addison-Wesley, Reading, Mass.

Lam, S.S. In progress. Addison-Wesley, Reading, Mass.

Lancaster, P. 1966. *Lambda Matrices and Vibrating Systems.* Pergamon Press, London.

Langford, J. D. 1990. "Queueing Delays in Systems Having Batch Arrivals and Setup Times." Doctoral Dissertation, University of Rochester.

Lazowska, D. E., J. Zahorjan, G. S. Graham, and K.C. Sevcik. 1984. *Quantitative System Performance: Computer System Analysis Using Queueing Network Models.* Prentice-Hall, N. J.

Lazowska, D. E., J. Zahorjan, and K.C. Sevcik. 1986. Computer System Performance Evaluation Using Queueing Network Models. *Ann. Rev. Comput. Sci.* **1**, 107–137.

Lea, C.-T. 1990. Design and Evaluation of Unbuffered Self-Routing Networks for Wideband Packet Switching, *Proceedings of IEEE INFO-COM'90*, 148–156, San Francisco.

Leon-Garcia, A. 1989. *Probability and Random Processes for Electrical Engineering.* Addison-Wesley, Reading, Mass.

Levy, H., and L. Kleinrock. 1986. A Queue with Startup and a Queue with Vacations: Delay Analysis by Decomposition. *Ops. Res.* **34:3**, 426–436.

Levy, H., and M. Sidi. 1990. Polling Systems: Applications, Modeling, and Optimization. *IEEE Trans. on Commun.* **38:10**, 1750–1760.

Li, S.-Q. 1990. A General Solution Technique for Discrete Queueing Analysis of Multi-Media Traffic on ATM. *Proceedings of IEEE INFOCOM'90*, 1144–1155, San Francisco.

Little, J. D. C. 1961. A Proof of the Queuing Formula $L = \lambda W$. *Operations Research* **9**, 383–387.

Lucantoni, D. M. 1991. New Results on the Single Server Queue with a

Batch Markovian Arrival Process. *Stochastic Models*, **7**:1, 1-46.

Lucantoni, D. M., K. S. Meier-Hellstern, and M. F. Neuts. 1990. A Single Server Queue with Server Vacations and a Class of Non-Renewal Arrival Processes. *Adv. in Appl. Prob.* **22:3**, 676–705.

Melamed, B., and W. Whitt. 1990. On Arrivals that See Time Averages. *Ops. Res.* **38:1**, 156–172.

Moler, C., and C. F. van Loan. 1978. Nineteen Dubious Ways to Compute the Exponential of a Matrix. *SIAM Review* **20:4**, 801–835.

Neuts, M. F. 1981a. *Matrix Geometric Solutions in Stochastic Models*. The Johns Hopkins University Press, Baltimore.

Neuts, M. F. 1981b. The c-Server Queue with Constant Service Times and a Versatile Markovian Arrival Process. *Applied Probability—Computer Science: The Interface*, **1**, pp. 31–67.

Neuts, M. F. 1989. *Structured Stochastic Matrices of the M/G/1 Type and Their Applications*. Marcel-Dekker, New York.

Niu, S.-C., and R. B. Cooper. 1989. Transform-Free Results for the M/G/1 Finite- and Infinite-Capacity Queues, with Generalizations. Unpublished manuscript.

Noble, B., and J. W. Daniel. 1977. *Applied Linear Algebra*. Prentice-Hall, Englewood Cliffs, N. J.

Nussbaumer, H. J. 1982. *Fast Fourier Transforms and Convolution Algorithms*. Springer-Verlag, New York.

Platzman, L. K., J. C. Ammons, and J. J. Bartholdi, III. 1988. A Simple and Efficient Algorithm to Compute Tail Probabilities from Transforms. *Ops. Res.* **36:1**, 137–144.

Press, W. H., B. P. Flannery, S. A. Teukolsky, and W. T. Vetterling. 1988. *Numerical Recipes in C—The Art of Scientific Computing*. Cambridge University Press, Cambridge, England.

Ramaswami, V. 1988a. A Stable Recursion for the Steady State Vector in Markov Chains of the M/G/1 Type. *Stochastic Models* **4**, 183–188.

Ramaswami, V. 1988b. Nonlinear Matrix Equations in Applied Probability—Solution Techniques and Open Problems. *SIAM Rev.* **30**, 256–263.

Ramaswami, V., and D. M. Lucantoni. 1985. Stationary Waiting Time Distributions in Queues with Phase-Type Service and in Quasi-Birth–Death Processes. *Stochastic Models* **1:2**, 125–134.

Ross, S. M. 1983. *Stochastic Processes.* John Wiley, New York.

Ross, S. M. 1989. *Introduction to Probability Models,* 4th ed., Academic Press, New York.

Saha, A., and M. D. Wagh. 1990. Performance Analysis of Banyan Networks Based on Buffers of Various Sizes. *Proceedings of IEEE INFOCOM'90,* 157–164, San Francisco.

Schwartz, M. 1987. *Telecommunications Networks: Protocols, Modeling and Analysis.* Addison-Wesley, Reading, Mass.

Shanthikumar, J. G. 1984. On a software reliability model: A review. *Microelectronics and Reliability,* **23**, 903–943.

Sinha, R. 1990. Baseline Document: T1S1 Technical Sub-Committee on Broadband Aspects of ISDN. Joint Report of AT&T, Bellcore, Bell-South Services, GTE-Telops, and Northern Telecom.

Spragins, J. D. 1991. *Telecommunications: Protocols and Design.* Addison-Wesley, Reading, Mass.

Sriram, K., and D. M. Lucantoni. 1989. Traffic Smoothing Effects of Bit Dropping in a Packet Voice Multiplexer. *IEEE Trans. on Commun.* **37:7**, 703–712.

Stallings, W. 1990a. *Handbook of Computer-Communications Standards: The Open Systems Interconnection (OSI) Model and OSI-Related Standards.* Macmillan, New York.

Stallings, W. 1990b. *Handbook of Computer-Communications Standards: Local Network Standards.* Macmillan, New York.

Stallings, W. 1990c. *Handbook of Computer-Communications Standards: Department of Defense (DOD) Protocol Standards.* Macmillan, New York.

Stavrakakis, I. 1990. Analysis of a Statistical Multiplexer under a General Input Traffic Model. *Proceedings of IEEE INFOCOM'90,* 1220–1225, San Francisco.

Stern, T. E. 1979. Approximations of Queue Dynamics and Their Application to Adaptive Routing in Computer Communication Networks. *IEEE Trans. on Commun.* **27:9**, 1331–1335.

Stern, T. E. 1983. A Queueing Analysis of Packet Voice. *Proc. Global Tele. Conf.* **1**, 71–76. San Diego.

Stewart, W. J. 1991. *Numerical Solution of Markov Chains,* Marcel-Dekker,

New York.

Stidham, S., Jr. 1974. A Last Word on $L = \lambda W$. *Operations Research* **22:2**, 417–421.

Sumita, U., and J. G. Shanthikumar. 1986. A Software Reliability Model with Multiple Error Introduction and Removal. *IEEE Trans. on Reliability* R–35, 459–462.

Takàcs, L. 1962. *Introduction to the Theory of Queues.* Oxford University Press, New York.

Takagi, H. 1987a. Queueing Analysis of Vacation Models, Part I: M/G/1 and Part II M/G/1 with Vacations. TRL Report TR87-0032. IBM Tokyo Research Laboratory, Tokyo, Japan.

Takagi, H. 1987b. Queueing Analysis of Vacation Models, Part III: M/G/1 with Priorities. TRL Report TR87-0038. IBM Tokyo Research Laboratory, Tokyo, Japan.

Takagi, H. 1990. Queueing Analysis of Polling Models, an Update. *Stochastic Analysis of Computer and Communication Systems* (H. Takagi, ed.). North-Holland, pp. 267–318.

Tanenbaum, A. S. 1988. *Computer Networks, 2nd Ed.* Prentice-Hall, Englewood Cliffs, N. J.

Tijms, H. C. 1986. *Stochastic Modeling and Analysis: A Computational Approach.* John Wiley, New York.

Trivedi, K. 1982. *Probability and Statistics with Reliability, Queueing, and Computer Science Applications.* Prentice-Hall, N. J.

van Arem, B. 1990. "Queueing Models for Slotted Transmission Systems". Ph. D. Dissertation, Twente University, The Netherlands.

Walrand, J. 1988. *An Introduction to Queueing Networks.* Prentice-Hall, Englewood Cliffs, N. J.

Weast, R. C., S. M. Selby, and C. D. Hodgman, eds. 1964. *Mathematical Tables from Handbook of Chemistry and Physics Twelfth Edition.* The Chemical Rubber Co., Cleveland, Ohio.

Welch, P. D. 1964. On a Generalized M/G/1 Queueing Process in which the First Customer Receives Exceptional Service. *Ops. Res.* **12**, 736–762.

Wolff, R. W. 1970. Work Conserving Priorities. *J. App. Prob.* **7:2**, 327–337.

Wolff, R. W. 1982. Poisson Arrivals See Time Averages. *Ops. Res.* **30:2**,

223–231.

Wolff, R. W. 1989. *Stochastic Modeling and the Theory of Queues.* Prentice-Hall, Englewood Cliffs, N. J.

Wolff, R. W. 1990. A Note on PASTA and Anti-PASTA for Continuous-Time Markov Chains. *Ops. Res.* **38:1**, 176–177.

Woodside, C. M., and E. D. S. Ho. 1987. Engineering Calculation of the Overflow Probabilities in Buffers with Markov-Interrupted Service. *IEEE Trans on Commun.* COM–35:12, 1272–1277.

Wortman, M. A., and R. L. Disney. 1990. Vacation Queues with Markov Schedules. *Adv. Appl. Prob.* **22**, 730–748.

Zhang, J., and E. J. Coyle. 1989. Transient Analysis of Quasi-Birth–Death Processes. *Commun. Statist., Stochastic Models.* **5:3**, 459–496.

I N D E X

$(a)^+$, 24
λ-matrix, 129
   null value, 129
   null vector, 129
   order, 129
AAL (*see* ATM adaption layer)
Abate, J. and Whitt, W., 51
Access lines, 5, 7, 249
Ackroyd, M.H., 27
Alternating renewal process, 196
   busy period, 197
   definition, 197
   expected cycle length, 198
   useful theorem, 197
Application layer, 10
Architecture, 3, 9, 14
ARPA, 5
Asynchronous transfer mode, 17, 19
ATM adaption layer, 19–20
ATM, 17, 19–20
Batch Markovian arrival process, 249, 265
Bertsekas, D. and Gallager, R., 6, 65
Beuerman, S. and Coyle, E.J., 98, 147
Bhargava, A. and Hluchyj, M.G., 17
BMAP (*see* Batch Markovian arrival process)
Bottlenecks, 8
Bruneel, H. (*see* Slotted time queueing systems)

Burke, P.J., 63, 66
Busy period, 29, 70–78, 124, 153, 155, 160, 162, 171–172, 188, 190, 201, 204–206, 212, 220–221, 227, 238
   exceptional first service, 172
   moments, 171
   sub-busy periods, 206
Carrier sense multiple access, 15
Caudal characteristic curve, 141
Chandramouli, Y., Neuts, M.F., and Ramaswami, V., 265
Chandy, K.M. and Sauer, C.H., 97
Characteristic function, 173–174
Chipalkatti, R., Kurose, J.F., and Towsley, D., 265
Churchill, R.V., 103, 176
Churchill, R.V. and Brown, J.W., 174
Circuit switching, 7
Closed queueing networks, 101–114
   application, 108
   moments of occupancy distribution, 109
   normalizing constants in closed form, 103–109
   throughput, 113
Coefficient of variation, 166, 195
Cohen, J.W., 44, 117
Common distribution, 26
Completion time, 219–220
   Laplace–Stieltjes transform, 232

Computer communication, 1–3
Conditional probability
    definition, 31
Connection oriented, 20
Connection-mode, 12
Connectionless-mode, 12
Conservation Law, 229
Continuous-Time Markov Chain
    definition, 43
Contraction map, 139
Cooper, R.B., 2, 60, 63, 95, 180, 212
Cooper, R.B. and Niu, S.C., 161, 201
Counting process, 30, 37
    independent increments, 38
    properties, 37
    stationary increments, 38
Coyle, E. and Liu, B., 141
CSMA (see Carrier sense multiple access)
Daigle, J.N., 161, 180, 273
Daigle, J.N. and Langford, J.D., 141
Daigle, J.N. and Lucantoni, D.M., 142, 144, 244
Daigle, J.N. and Magalhães, M.N., 51
Daigle, J.N. and Tang, S., 266
Daigle, J.N. and Whitehead, S.D., 160
Daigle, J.N., Lee, Y., and Magalhães, M.N., 259, 265
Data-link layer, 10
Datagram networks, 8
Datagram service, 7
Decomposition principle
    alternating renewal theory, 208
    type 1 customer, 206
    type 2 customer, 206
Discrete Fourier transform, 175
    aliasing, 176
    round-off error, 176
Disney, R.L. and Kiessler, P.C., 65, 67, 69, 97
Disney, R.L., McNickle, D.C., and Simon, B., 69
Distributed queue dual bus, 17
Distribution
    common, 26
    phase type, 21, 150
Distributions of the phase type, 150

absorption, 150
    example, 151
    infinitesimal generator, 150
Doshi, B.T., 213
DQDB (see Distributed queue dual bus)
Eigenvalue, 81–84
Eigenvector, 81–84, 124, 128
Erlang-k, 180
Erlang loss system, 92–95
Evans, R.V., 140
Exceptional first service, 22, 161, 171–172, 213, 272
Exponential distribution, 21, 23, 30, 32–33
    memoryless property, 30
    memoryless property is unique, 32
Exponential queues
    networks of, 45
Exponential random variables
    properties, 35
Exponential, 31, 37, 42, 45, 124, 126, 150–151, 183, 221, 232, 238, 241
Fast Fourier transform, 178
Fast packet, 18
    adaption sublayer, 17
    networks, 17
FCFS (see First-come-first-serve)
First-come-first-serve, 18, 21, 27, 152, 234, 244
FDDI (see Fiber distributed data interface)
Feedback, 96
Feller, W., 26, 31, 173–174
Fiber distributed data interface, 16–17
Formal parameters, 12
Forward recurrence time, 193
Fourier series
    basis function, 174
    coefficients, 174
Fourier–Stieltjes integral, 174
FPN (see Fast packet, networks)
Fuhrmann, W.S. and Cooper, R.B., 161, 205, 210
Fuhrmann–Cooper decomposition, 22, 161–162, 215, 272
Fundamental matrix, 259

G/G/s/K, 29
G/G/c
   tail probabilities geometrically decreasing, 180
G/M/1 paradigm
   matrix-geometric solution, 243
   rate matrix, 244
G/M/1
   embedded Markov chain, 239
   limiting solution, 241
   one-step transition probability, 240
   one-step transition probability matrix, 241
   waiting time, 241
Gavish, B. and Altinkemer, K., 99
Gavish, B. and Neuman, I., 99
Gelenbe, E. and Pujolle, G., 97, 114
Generating function, 105, 245, 247
GI/M/1/K, 29
Giffin, W.C., 80
Gordon, J.J., 21, 48, 96, 102–103, 107–108, 111–112
Gordon, W.L. and Newell, G.F., 101
Grassmann, W.K., 79–80, 88
Green, L. and Melamed, B., 60
Hahne, E.L., Choudhury, A.K., and Maxemchuk, N.F., 17
Hammond, J.L. and O'Reilly, P.J.P., 16
Harrison, M., 102, 107
Head of the line discipline
   average sojourn time, 223
   average waiting time, 223
   class 2 completion time, 219
   class 2 occupancy, 219
   Fuhrmann–Cooper decomposition, 215
   sojourn time, 229
   sub-busy periods, 216
   tagged type 1 customer, 217
   type 2 sub-busy periods, 221
Hewitt, E. and Stromberg, K., 139, 174
Hogg, R.V. and Craig, A.T., 182
HOL discipline (see Head of the line discipline)
Hunter, J.J., 105–106, 114, 122, 260
iid (see Independent and identically distributed)

Iliadis, I. and Denzel, W.E., 20
Independence, 26
Independent and identically distributed, 42
Independent increments, 38
Induced queueing process, 26
Infinitesimal generator, 44, 117, 127, 148
Inspection paradox, 190
Interarrival distribution, 28
Interarrival time, 25, 29, 42, 159, 240, 264
   sequence of, 41
Internet, 15–16
Internet service, 14
ISO 8348, 14
ISO 8473, 14
ISO-IP, 14
ISO/OSI, 3, 9–10, 14, 19
Jackson, J.R., 101
Jackson's theorem, 101
Jensen, A., 79, 84, 88
Jewell, W.S, 63
Jiang, I. and Meditch, J.S., 20
Keilson, J., 81
Keilson, J. and Servi, L., 161, 180, 184–185
Keilson, J. and Wishart, D.M.G., 88
Kelly, F.P., 97, 161, 201
Kendall, D.G., 29
Kim, H.S. and Leon-Garcia, A., 20
Kleinrock, L., 97, 99, 229
Kobayashi, H., 97, 101–102, 112
LAN (see Local area network)
Lancaster, P., 129
Langford, J.D., 185
Laplace–Stieltjes transform, 33, 160, 162–163, 165, 168, 170, 181, 186, 201, 219–220, 233
Last-come-first-serve, 97, 190
Last-come-first-serve–presumptive resume, 200–201, 204
   occupancy distribution, 201, 203
   remaining service time, 204
   unfinished work, 204
   waiting time, 204
Laurent series, 176

Lazowska, D.E., Zahorjan, J., Graham, G.S., and Sevcik, K.C., 97
LCFS (*see* Last-come-first-serve)
LCFS-PR (*see* Last-come-first-serve–presumptive resume)
Lea, C.-T., 20
Leon-Garcia, A., 114
Levy, H. and Kleinrock, L., 209
Levy, H. and Sidi, M., 213
Li, S.-Q., 265
Little, J.D.C., 61
Little's result, 98, 113, 130, 173, 199, 206, 228
Local area network, 3, 14–17
LU decomposition, 133
Lucantoni, D.M., 245, 249, 263
Lucantoni, D.M., Meier-Hellstern, K.S., and Neuts, M.F., 259, 264
$M/G/\infty$, 233
$M/G/1$, 21, 149, 160–161
    balance equations, 160
    busy period, 161, 170, 172, 196, 199
    curves, 183
    decomposition principle, 205
    departing customer leaves no customers, 165
    ergodic occupancy distribution, 173, 205
    exceptional first service, 204, 208–212, 238
    expected waiting time, 172
    future evolution, 160
    HOL, 214
    HOL-PR, 214
    LCFS-PR, 201
    Little's result, 166, 169–170
    number of customers left in the system, 160
    occupancy distribution, 180, 186
    one-step transition probability, 237
    order of service, 170
    server utilization, 165
    server vacations, 212
    set-up times, 209
    sojourn time, 168
    sub-busy period, 170
    waiting time, 196

$M/G/1$ paradigm
    batch Markovian arrival process, 249
    initial conditions, 255
    iterative algorithm, 255
    multiple servers, 265
    one-step transition probability matrix, 246
    simplification in computational technique, 260
$M/M/1$, 21, 96, 121, 155, 189–190, 203
$M/M/2$, 155
    busy period, 155
    Little's result, 156
    sojourn time, 156
Maclaurin series, 114
Markov chain, 100, 117, 127, 140, 152, 157–158, 160, 198, 246–247, 249, 251, 260, 264
    continuous time, 21, 43, 117, 152, 157
    customer departure, 160
    discrete time, 249, 260
    embed, 160, 235
    embedding, 22
    $G/M/1$ type, 242
    irreducible, 157
    $M/G/1$ type, 242
    stationary probabilities, 266
    stationary vector, 238
Matrix geometric solution, 138, 244
    Beuerman, S.L. and Coyle, E.J., 147
    moments, 146
    rate matrix, 138
    sufficient condition, 139
    survivor function, 146
    Zhang, J. and Coyle, E.J., 147
Matrix geometric, 138
    m-server queueing system, 158
    modifications in the solution procedure, 158
Mean-value analysis, 113–114
Melamed, B. and Whitt, W., 60
Memoryless, 30
Meteor-burst communications, 265
Moler, C. and van Loan, C.F., 80
Network layer, 10

Network of queues
    closed, 96, 101–114
    exponential servers, 96
    feedforward, 96
    joint occupancy probabilities, 101
    marginal occupancy
        density, 98, 100
    random routing, 99
    service times, 96
Networks of exponential queues, 96–114
Neuts, M.F, 21, 118, 137, 139–140, 148–151, 158, 235, 242–245, 263, 265
Nui, S.-C. and Cooper, R.B., 185
Noble, B. and Daniel, J.W., 81, 127
Normalizing constant, 102
    closed form, 107–109
    Gordon's approach, 102–104
    Harrison, 102
Null value, 129
Null vector, 129
Nussbaumer, H.J., 175, 178
$o(h)$, 40
Occupancy distribution
    example, 180, 183
One-step transition probability, 58, 236
Packets, 7–8, 37, 124, 126, 265
Paradigm
    G/M/1, 22, 235–236, 272
    M/G/1, 22, 235–236, 265, 272
    Markov chain, 235
Partial fraction expansions, 131
PASTA (see Poisson arrival sees time averages)
PDU (see Protocol data units)
Phase process, 118, 249
    minimum dimension, 251
Phase type distribution
    infinitesimal generator, 150–152, 157
Physical layer, 10
Platzman, L.K., Ammons, J.C., and Bartholdi, J.J., 170
Poisson arrival process
    cautions on using, 258
Poisson arrival sees time average, 60
Poisson process, 21, 23, 30, 41, 96, 163, 202, 212, 214, 240

superposition and decomposition, 96
counting process, 37
definition, 37, 39–40, 42–43
events not recorded, 44
events recorded, 44
exponential interarrival times, 42
interarrival times, 45
properties, 44
Pollaczek–Khintchine transform, 160
Presentation layer, 10
Press, W.H., Flannery, B.P., Teukolsky, S.A., and Vetterling, W.T., 133, 284, 293
Primitive, 12
Priority, 214, 223, 227, 229, 273
Probability generating function, 114, 246, 252
    bounded, 122
    definition, 114
    marginal, 121
    number of events from a Poisson process, 163
    remark, 247
Protocol data units, 12–13, 17
QBD (see Quasi-birth–death)
Quasi-birth–death, 118, 140
    boundary conditions, 120
    numerical example, 124
    state diagram, 118
Queueing delays, 8, 56, 60, 62, 64–65, 167–170
Queueing networks, 21, 96–114
Queueing system
    classification, 28
Ramaswami, V., 245, 248, 263
Ramaswami, V. and Lucantoni, D.M., 142, 244
Remaining service time, 189
Renewal interval, 193, 195
Renewal process, 191
    age, 193
    backward recurrence time, 193
    defective, 195, 200
    forward recurrence time, 193
    number of renewals, 192
    observed intervals, 191

residual life, 193
Renewal theory, 189
Residual life
    coefficient of variation, 195
    Laplace–Stieltjes transform, 194
Ross, S.M., 25, 43–44, 58, 65–67, 75,
    88, 195, 200
Saha, A. and Wagh, M.D., 20
Schwartz, M., 3, 97, 108–109, 113
Semi-Markov process, 160
Service discipline, 28
Service time, 24, 27–29, 124, 148, 150,
    161, 164, 170, 177, 190, 192, 201–202,
    204
Session layer, 10
Set-up times, 210
Sinha, R., 19
Slotted time queueing system
    number of arrivals, 252, 256–257
    occupancy, 249–263
Sojourn time, 24, 160, 162, 168, 188
Spectral radius, 141
Spragins, J.D., 3
Squared coefficient of variation, 166
Sriram, K. and Lucantoni, D.M., 272
Stallings, W., 3, 11, 16
Stationary increments, 38
Stationary probability vector, 250
Statistical multiplexer, 156, 249
Statistical multiplexing, 8, 152
    dial-up line, 156
    finite population, 152
    occupancy, 248–263
Stavrakakis, I., 265
Stern, T.E., 51, 117
Stewart, W.J., 266
Stidham, S., Jr., 63
Stochastic process, 25
    continuous-time, 43
    discrete-parameter, 25
    types, 160

Sumita, U. and Shanthikumar, J.G., 88
Tagged customer, 205
Takàcs, L., 208
Takagi, H., 213
Tanenbaum, A.S., 3
Taylor series, 114, 177
Terminals, 5, 7
Tijms, H.C., 180
Time-Homogeneous CTMC, 43
Token bus, 15
Token ring, 15–16
Traffic engineering
    Erlang loss system, 92–95, 154
    finite population, 154
Transition Probability Matrix for CTMC,
    44
Transport layer, 10
Trivedi, K., 97
Truncated Geometric Distribution, 183
Trunk, 5–8, 152, 249
Unfinished work, 27, 161, 201
User information, 13, 19–20
Vacation model, 212
Van Arem, B., 265
Virtual waiting time, 27
Waiting time, 1–2, 22, 24, 27, 29, 98,
    142, 160, 162, 189, 192, 201, 219–220,
    224, 229–230, 234, 244
Walrand, J., 97
WAN (see Wide area networks)
Weast, R.C., Selby, S.M., and Hodg-
    man, C.D., 75
Welch, P.D. (see Exceptional fast ser-
    vice)
Wide area networks, 3, 15–16
Window flow control, 108
Wolff, R.W., 53, 59–60, 201
Woodside, C.M. and Ho, E.D.S., 177
Wortman, M.A. and Disney, R.L., 213
Zhang, J. and Coyle, E.J., 147